Lecture Notes in Computer Science 15595

The series Lecture Notes in Computer Science (LNCS), including its subseries Lecture Notes in Artificial Intelligence (LNAI) and Lecture Notes in Bioinformatics (LNBI), has established itself as a medium for the publication of new developments in computer science and information technology research, teaching, and education.

LNCS enjoys close cooperation with the computer science R & D community, the series counts many renowned academics among its volume editors and paper authors, and collaborates with prestigious societies. Its mission is to serve this international community by providing an invaluable service, mainly focused on the publication of conference and workshop proceedings and postproceedings. LNCS commenced publication in 1973.

Luciana Morogan · Peter Roenne · Ion Bica
Editors

Innovative Security Solutions for Information Technology and Communications

17th International Conference, SecITC 2024
Bucharest, Romania, November 21–22, 2024
Revised Selected Papers

Springer

Editors
Luciana Morogan
Military Technical Academy "Ferdinand I"
Bucharest, Romania

Peter Roenne
University of Luxembourg
Esch-sur-Alzette, Luxembourg

Ion Bica
Military Technical Academy "Ferdinand I"
Bucharest, Romania

ISSN 0302-9743 ISSN 1611-3349 (electronic)
Lecture Notes in Computer Science
ISBN 978-3-031-87759-9 ISBN 978-3-031-87760-5 (eBook)
https://doi.org/10.1007/978-3-031-87760-5

This Springer imprint is published by the registered company Springer Nature Switzerland AG
The registered company address is: Gewerbestrasse 11, 6330 Cham, Switzerland

Preface

SecITC (International Conference on Security for Information Technology and Communications) is an annual international conference held in Romania focusing on all theoretical and practical aspects related to information technology and communications security. Its primary goal is connecting security and privacy researchers as well as professionals from different communities and providing a forum that allows informal exchanges necessary for the emergence of new scientific and industrial collaborations. Since 2015 the post-proceedings of the conference have been published in Springer LNCS.

The 17th edition of the conference, SecITC 2024, took place (both in person and online) from 21st to 22nd November, 2024, in Bucharest. It was organised jointly by the Bucharest University of Economic Studies, Advanced Technologies Institute and the Military Technical Academy "Ferdinand I", the latter being the main organizer of this edition, hosting the onsite event around the newly restored Aula Magna.

SecITC 2024 received 49 submissions. Each Program Committee (PC) member was assigned an average of three submissions for review. Each paper was assigned to at least three reviewers. The PC was helped by the reports and opinions of 11 external reviewers. As in previous years, the reviewing process used double-blind reviews. Reviewers and authors were asked to declare conflicts of interests for the submission, while Easychair was also set up to automatically add possible conflicts of interest. The system was also configured to ensure that PC members (including PC chairs) could not see reviewer assignments nor reviews of papers for which they had a conflict of interest. Based on the reviews, a total of 16 submissions were carefully selected for presentation at the conference, while the full papers are published in these proceedings. The papers cover a wide spectrum of the topics of the conference in all aspects of information security and privacy.

The SecITC 2024 programme featured two invited talks given by Peter Y. A. Ryan from University of Luxembourg and Carsten Schürmann, IT University of Copenhagen. We are grateful that both invited speakers accepted an invitation to publish extended abstracts of their talks in the present proceedings.

SecITC 2024 PC was co-chaired by Peter B. Rønne (University of Luxembourg) and Luciana Morogan (Military Technical Academy "Ferdinand I"), who selected the PC members and led their efforts in selecting the papers that appear in this volume.

We would like to thank everyone who contributed to the success of SecITC 2024. We are grateful to all PC members and external reviewers for their commitment and enthusiasm, which ensured that each submitted paper went through a thorough and fair review process. We thank all members of the Organizing Committee of SecITC 2024 for their professional work and support, with special appreciation to the local chair Ion Bica for his important contribution to the organization of the conference. We also wish to thank all authors who submitted to SecITC 2024 and all conference participants for making the conference an enjoyable experience. Finally, we are very grateful to our sponsors NextGen Software, Intervenţii Active în Atmosferă, Marctel S.I.T. S.R.L., Celesta Comexim S.R.L. and Asociaţia Ingenerilor Militari. Their kind contributions were instrumental in making the conference a highly successful event.

January 2025

Peter Roenne
Luciana Morogan

Organization

Program Committee

Iulian Aciobanitei	Military Technical Academy "Ferdinand I", Romania
Raja Naeem Akram	University of Aberdeen, UK
Claudio Agostino Ardagna	Università degli Studi di Milano, Italy
Afonso Arriaga	University of Luxembourg, Luxembourg
Lasse Berntzen	University of South-Eastern Norway, Norway
Ion Bica	Military Technical Academy, Romania
Guillaume Bouffard	National Cybersecurity Agency of France (ANSSI), France
Michele Carminati	Politecnico di Milano, Italy
Paolo D'Arco	University di Salerno, Italy
Roberto De Prisco	Universita' di Salerno, Italy
Eric Diehl	Sony Pictures, USA
Mihai Doinea	Bucharest University of Economic Studies, Romania
Constantin Catalin Dragan	University of Surrey, UK
Petr Dzurenda	Brno University of Technology, Czechia
Éric Freyssinet	LORIA, France
Dieter Gollmann	Hamburg University of Technology, Germany
Johann Groszschaedl	University of Luxembourg, Luxembourg
Rémi Géraud-Stewart	Ecole normale supérieure, France
Helena Handschuh	Rambus Inc., USA
Shoichi Hirose	University of Fukui, Japan
Vincenzo Iovino	Aragon ZK Research, Switzerland
Nesrine Kaaniche	Télécom SudParis, France
Mehmet Sabir Kiraz	De Montfort University, UK
Diana Maimut	Advanced Technologies Institute, Romania
Mark Manulis	Universität der Bundeswehr München, Germany
Luciana Morogan	Military Technical Academy, Romania
David Naccache	ENS, France
Ruxandra F. Olimid	University of Bucharest, Romania
Andrei George Oprina	Advanced Technologies Institute, Romania
Olivier Pereira	UCLouvain, Belgium
Marius Popa	Bucharest University of Economic Studies, Romania

Sara Ricci	Brno University of Technology, Czechia
Peter Roenne	University of Luxembourg, Luxembourg
P. Y. A. Ryan	University of Luxembourg, Luxembourg
Damien Sauveron	University of Limoges/CNRS/XLIM, France
Emil Simion	University POLITEHNICA of Bucharest, Romania
Agusti Solanas	Rovira i Virgili University, Spain
El Mamoun Souidi	Mohammed V University in Rabat, Morocco
Riccardo Spolaor	Shandong University, China
Pantelimon Stanica	Naval Postgraduate School, USA
Rainer Steinwandt	University of Alabama in Huntsville, USA
George Teseleanu	IMAR, Romania
Norbert Tihanyi	Eötvös Loránd University, Hungary
Ferucio Laurentiu Tiplea	Alexandru Ioan Cuza University of Iaşi, Romania
Mihai Togan	Military Technical Academy, Romania
Cristian Toma	Bucharest University of Economic Studies, Romania
Denis Trcek	University of Ljubljana, Slovenia
Valérie Viet Triem Tong	CentraleSupélec, France
Vlad-Florin Drăgoi	Aurel Vlaicu University of Arad, Romania
Qianhong Wu	Beihang University, China
Sule Yildirim-Yayilgan	Norwegian University of Science and Technology, Norway
Lei Zhang	East China Normal University, China

Additional Reviewers

Bena, Nicola
Buzatoiu, Alexandra
Ding, Zhengyang
Hristea, Cristian
Kilian, Sébastien
Li, Yin
Maimut, Diana
Teseleanu, George
Xu, Lin
Zhai, Mingzhe
Zurini, Madalina

Contents

Designing Human-centric security protocols

Peter Y. A. Ryan(✉)

University of Luxembourg, Esch-sur-Alzette, Luxembourg
peter.ryan@uni.lu

Abstract. Security protocols and mechanisms are, or at least should be, designed by technical people, ideally cryptographers. This is natural enough but it does have the consequence that the resulting protocols are suited for techie people but all too often badly suited to "real" people. The resulting mismatch of incentives and mindsets is a major source of security failures.

We discuss this issue along with possible remedies, illustrating it mainly with examples from the design of secure, verifiable voting systems, where it is thrown into sharp focus. In particular, we discuss the extent to which security mechanisms can be made transparent to users while minimizing trust assumptions.

1 Introduction

Security protocols, mechanisms and ceremonies are typically designed by cryptographers and information security experts. As a result, most deployed security mechanisms lack usability and understandability in the eyes of average users. This in turn may result in lack of uptake, failure to follow the steps of the protocol and often to security failures. In the latter case it is all too easy to blame the users[1] but this is unfair and misguided. Misguided because it almost certainly misses the real cause of the failure: poor design.

Such issues have a long history in cryptography and information security. The German Enigma cipher system provides some prime examples. Technically the Enigma system was a tour de force and with the right operating procedures would have been effectively unbreakable with the technology of the time. However, poor procedures opened up chinks in the armour. For example, to set up the machine to send a dispatch the cipher clerks were expected to choose a fresh, random three letter prefix to determine the initial rotor setting. However, humans are a notoriously poor source of entropy and clerks would often slip into reusing settings, using their girlfriends initials etc.

Voting systems are large-scale, highly socio-technical systems with plenty of interaction between users (voter, election officials, observers etc.). By definition the voters will be highly diverse in their capabilities, they might use the system

[1] Or "lusers" are they are sometimes pejoratively labelled.

L. Morogan et al. (Eds.): SecITC 2024, LNCS 15595, pp. 1–11, 2025.
https://doi.org/10.1007/978-3-031-87760-5_1

once every few years, and so the procedures have to be extremely easy to execute and understand. Verifiable voting systems seek to allow voters and observers to monitor the system's execution and detect any errors or manipulation of votes. This is a laudable goal, but it inevitably increases the number of and complexity of the human interactions with the system.

For voting systems we typically consider a particularly hostile threat environment: attackers can range from a coercive spouse or boss to hostile nation state. Furthermore the security community seeks solutions requiring minimal trust assumptions. All of these considerations make voting systems particularly challenging and human-centric design especially relevant.

The assurance argument for most end-to-end verifiable voting systems (essentially all aside from those that use trackers discussed later) can be broken down into three parts:

- Cast as intended.
- Recorded as cast.
- tallied as recorded.

If for each vote these three assertions are demonstrated then we can conclude that every vote will be counted as cast. From a human perspective the first of these is the most interesting as it involves assuring voters that their vote is accurately captured. But this must be achieved in a way that does not provide any way for the voter to convince a third party. Put differently, the voter should be assured that their vote is correctly encrypted in the ballot and that the ballot is subsequently correctly decrypted during the anonymising tally.

Many schemes have been proposed to achieve voter verifiability following this approach. Many ingenious approaches to achieving cast as intended assurance have been devised, some arguably too ingenious for their own good.

We see that already this three-stage verification approach may feel quite alien to most voters, or stakeholders for that matter. It typically involves furnishing the voter with some form of "receipt" or *protected ballot*[2]: an encryption of their vote. A digital copy of each cast ballot is posted to a bulletin board BB, or public ledger if you prefer. Voters should visit the BB and check that their receipt appears correctly. The collection of encrypted ballots on the BB must then be processed in a manner that guarantees to produce the correct outcome while preserving vote secrecy. This typically involves highly sophisticated cryptographic notions: verifiable shuffles, homomorphic encryption, zero-knowledge proofs etc.

It is perhaps unsurprising that such schemes have seen very little uptake in the real world, at best some isolated trials. The assurance argument is rather complex and hard for voters or even election officials to understand.

A further observation is that a voting system should should not only deliver the correct outcome but also demonstrate that the outcome is correct. The motivation for the design decisions and the security measures and counter-measures should be fully documented. The threat that a particular mechanism is intended to thwart should clearly stated. This will help ensure that the design fulfills

[2] To use Rivest's terminology.

its security goals but also help ensure that it remains secure as technology and threats evolve. All too often the final design is simply presented without providing the rationale for the chosen design (similar to an exam question, the designer should be required to show his workings). The upshot is that the reasons for design decisions are lost in the mists of time and so the mistakes of the past are repeated.

2 Can Security Mechanisms be Transparent to Users?

A natural way to simplify the user experience is to avoid users having to interact with security mechanisms at all. In some contexts, this may be a satisfactory approach, but it typically means that higher levels of trust in the system are required. For example, traditional voting, where the voter drops the ballot in a ballot box and leaves, involves the bare minimum voter involvement. However it also needs a high level in trust in the system, the election officials, counting staff etc.-voters have no way to confirm that their vote is correctly counted, or detect if it isn't. Some of this trust can be offset by allowing independent observers of various steps of the process.

DRE (Direct Recorded Electronic) machines require far higher levels of trust, essentially blind trust in the correctness of the code running in the machines, the tabulation servers etc. A small tweak to a line of code could alter the outcome in a way that is effectively undetectable.

We can return to the Enigma for another example: suppose that the machines were designed with an automatic, random initialization on power up. in this case there would be no need for the cipher clerk to provide an initialization and high-grade randomness could be guaranteed, but the initialization mechanism would have to be trusted. In the context, such trust might be reasonable: the Germans would have had full control of the design, construction, supply chain, maintenance, etc. of the machines. In more contemporary contexts such trust would be highly questionable, and we will see an example in the next section.

We should note that the word "transparency" in the title of this section is used in a fairly standard but rather special sense: invisible or, if you will, hidden from the users. This contrasts with another common meaning of the word: that the inner workings are exposed and open to scrutiny. In fact, we would like to achieve transparency in both senses: users do not need to concern themselves with the security mechanisms and yet these are open to scrutiny by interested parties.

3 Cast as Intended Assurance

As remarked earlier, from a human perspective the most interesting aspect of an end-to-end verifiable voting system is how the cast as intended requirement is achieved. In this section we sketch three proposals that seek, in very different ways, to make the protocol understandable and accessible.

3.1 Chaum's Visual Crypto Approach

An early attempt to design a procedure to provide voters with cast as intended assurance in a way that would be understandable and engender trust is due to Chaum, [2]. This makes ingenious use of visual crypto, [4] the voter inputs their choice to a device that generates two layers of pixel patterns which when overlaid with correct alignment display the choice. Each layer viewed separately is simply a random pattern of pixels. Each layer also carries an encryption under the EA public key of the pixel pattern displayed on the layer.

The device is linked to a printer that can print off the two layers onto two transparent sheets with the correct alignment, along with the encryptions of the pixel patterns. What emerges from the printer is two sheets overlaid, displaying the voter's choice. The voter should confirm the choice shown and separate the sheets and choose one at random to be cast-the other will be audited. Here, audited means opening up the encryption and checking that the pattern defined inside the encryption matches the pattern printed on the layer (Fig. 1).

(a) Original image

(b) First share. (c) Second share. (d) Overlay.

Fig. 1. Visual cryptography.

At the heart of this procedure we see a cut-and-choose style protocol at work: the voter chooses randomly between the two layers; one is audited and the other cast. The chance of the device cheating undetected, i.e. altering the voter's choice by creating a mismatch between the pixel pattern and contents of the encryption on one layer, are about 1/2. We leave it to the reader to decide just how convincing this is to the average voter or election official, but one assumes that seeing their choice in the clear in the printout from the printer will provide some assurance.

Despite the investment of a lot of time, effort and money in developing prototypes and trying to market the scheme it was eventually abandoned. This was presumably due in part to the complexity of the required equipment, in particular a printer capable of printing accurately in alignment on two sides of transparent sheets.

3.2 Markpledge

Another, highly ingenious approach due to Neff, [5], requires the voter to take part in an interactive zero-knowledge proof with a device in the booth. The receipt or protected ballot that the voter will emerge from the booth will have a list of the candidates down the left hand side. In the booth the voter inputs their selection, say the least ith candidate, to a device which commits in print to encryption of the identity 1 under the public key of the Election Authority, $\{1\}_{PK_{EA}}$, against the chosen candidate. There follows a ZK proof between the device and the voter in which the voter provides a random challenge value of say four digits. Suppose that the voter chooses 5497. The device prints the transcript of the proof, which we denote $\Pi_i(5497)$, next to the $\{1\}_{PK_{EA}}$. The voter should check that the transcript indeed shows the challenge value they provided (Fig. 2).

Candidates	Your vote	ZK Proof
Obelix		
Panoramix	$\{1\}_{PK_{EA}}$	$\Pi_2(5497)$
Asterix		
Idefix		

Fig. 2. MarkPledge ballot after the interactive ZK proof with the voter.

To mask the vote choice, the device prints against all the other options encryptions of 0, $\{0\}_{PK_{EA}}$, and fake transcripts of ZK proofs purporting to show that these are also encryptions of 1, $\{1\}_{PK_{EA}}$. To do this, the device generates a "challenge" value before making the commitment to the encryption, and simply crafts a commitment that will fit and produce a valid seeming transcript. Any third party seeing the receipt will be unable to distinguish between the transcripts of the real interactive proof and the fake transcripts. Only the voter knows which is the transcript of the real proof, i.e. the one for which they provided the challenge after the commitment was made by the device. On the other hand, anyone can verify the proof transcripts, i.e. audit the ballot (Fig. 3).

This scheme is of particular interest as it allows the casting of an audited ballot. All prior schemes forbid the casting of a ballot that has been audited as auditing typically undermines the secrecy of the encryption. It also provides a rather high level of assurance: the chances of a device cheating without being detected are about $1/10^4$, assuming that the challenge is random, that the voter checks

Candidates	Your vote	ZK Proof
Obelix	$\{0\}_{PK_{EA}}$	$\Pi_1(2638)$
Panoramix	$\{1\}_{PK_{EA}}$	$\Pi_2(5497)$
Asterix	$\{0\}_{PK_{EA}}$	$\Pi_3(6389)$
Idefix	$\{0\}_{PK_{EA}}$	$\Pi_4(1627)$

Fig. 3. MarkPledge ballot with the masking, fake ZK proof transcripts.

that the correct challenge appears in the "real" transcript etc. This contrasts with the odds of around 1/2 for other cut-and-choose style based approaches.

It is instructive to note a particular attack that was identified against an early version of the scheme. A coercer requires the voter to choose a challenge based on the commitment to the encryption against the chosen vote, for example simply the first four digits. Now the vote can be identified from the receipt. The countermeasure that was adopted is to ensure that the commitment is not visible to the voter, i.e. covered by an opaque shield, until after the challenge has been entered. The voter can tell the a commitment has been printed and committed but cannot read the actual value.

A company, VoteHere, was established to develop and market the approach but without success. Presumably the complexity of the voter interaction was simply too high for stakeholders to accept.

Note that here, as with Enigma, we might consider ways to simplify the voter's role, in particular the generation of the random challenge. This is analogous to the random three letter initialization of Enigma. We might consider the idea of the device generating the challenge, but clearly this would immediately obviate the whole purpose: a corrupt device could exploit this capability to construct a fake proof transcript for the interactive proof with the voter. An alternative, that was I believe considered, is to have a physical source of randomness in the booth, e.g. ten-sided dice. This removes the threat mentioned above but adds a further complication of the voter interface.

3.3 Prêt à Voter

Finally we sketch the approach to cast as intended of the Prêt à Voter scheme, [3]. This is interesting in that voters do not input their choice to a device to have this encrypted on-the-fly, Instead, voters are provided with pre-prepared paper ballots on which the various options are presented in plaintext in a randomised permutation ρ. What is encrypted is the term defining the candidate permutation ρ on the ballot (Fig. 4).

The voter indicates their choice by making a mark in the right-hand column, e.g. an X, against their choice and then detaches and discards the plaintext list, resulting in a receipt of the form shown in Fig. 5.

This creates, in an indirect fashion, an encryption of the vote. Cast-as-intended assurance follows from the well-formedness of the ballot, i.e. that the permutation buried in the encryption matches the candidate permutation shown

Candidates	Your vote
Obelix	
Panoramix	
Asterix	
Idefix	
	$\{\rho\}_{PK_{EA}}$
Destroy	Retain

Fig. 4. Prêt à Voter ballot form.

Your vote
X
$\{\rho\}_{PK_{EA}}$
Retain

Fig. 5. Prêt à Voter ballot receipt (encoding in this case a vote for "Asterix").

in the plaintext list of candidates. A pleasing feature of this approach is that such well-formedness audits can be performed by anyone, not just the voter. This means that need for voters to perform or initiate such audits is removed, so improving usability. Audits can be performed by independent entities before, during and after the voting period.

Note also that auditing a Prêt à Voter ballot does not undermine vote privacy- no vote information is encoded in a blank Prêt à Voter ballot. The fact that the voter does not communicate their choice to a device reduces the possibility of side-channel leakage that might occur when a device directly encrypts the voter's choice. Dispute resolution is also rather clean: a Prêt à Voter ballot is either well-formed or not. This contrasts with dispute resolution for Benaloh challenges, as discussed in the next section.

Again it is instructive to note a particular style of attack against Prêt à Voter: the *randomisation* attack. Here the coercer tells the voter that he must show him a receipt with a X in say the first place. In a simple implementation this will deny the voter the ability to cast their vote of choice, but rather force them to cast a random vote, dictated by the order on the ballot. This is an interesting style of attack as it does not violate any privacy property, the vote remains secret, so any analysis of the scheme against a privacy property would not uncover it. Counter-measures can be incorporated, for example providing voters with a choice of ballot forms, but this may not be practical for complex ballots with many candidates.

A variant of Prêt à Voter was developed and trialed for elections to the Lower House in Victoria State Australia in 2014. The trial was seemingly successful but the Victoria Electoral Commission decided not to continue with further trials, for reasons that were never made clear.

3.4 Benaloh Challenges

Cut-and-choose style ballot audits can also be performed in a sequential manner, as proposed by Benaloh, [1]. The device commits to an encryption, in print for example, and the voter decides either to audit or to cast this. If the voter opts to audit, and it passes audit, a fresh encryption is produced and committed and again the voter can again choose audit or cast, and so on until the voter is content and casts the last, non-audited encryption. This approach works for any scheme involving on-the-fly encryption of the vote. The idea is that the device should not know when it commits to the encryption if the voter will audit and so it runs a chance of being caught if it tried to in this round.

Again, this is theoretically very appealing but is problematic in practice. It complicates the voting ceremony, although it seems that most voters tend to ignore the audit option. And the fact that most voters skip auditing is an issue for assurance: the chance of a cheating device being detected is actually quite low. It is also tricky from a privacy point of view: ideally a voter intending to audit should input a random vote, but this again is rather hard for voters to understand (and might even give the device a hint that the ballot is about to be audited). Furthermore, dispute resolution is tricky: if a voter does dispute an audit it is hard to determine if the device actually cheated or the voter is lying or just mistaken about what vote they input to the device.

4 Tallied as Cast Verification

The examples given above all involve the three-stage E2E verification: cast as intended, recorded as cast and tallied as recorded. If all three assertions are verified then we are assured that all cast votes are tallied as cast. Note that this is necessary but not sufficient to guarantee a correct outcome, for this we need extra assurances, e.g. absence of ballot stuffing, votes are only cast by legitimate voters, one man one vote etc. Nonetheless it does get a long way toward trustworthy elections.

Such schemes have seen little uptake and this is probably attributable in large part to the challenges of understanding the assurance argument. This prompts the investigation of alternative approaches to trustworthy voting systems. A possible approach, which gives much more direct and intuitive verification, is to use private voter trackers: each voter is assigned a unique, secret tracker. Once the ballots have been anonymised and decrypted the votes are posted on the *BB* along with their corresponding tracker number. Voters can now check the presence of their vote in plaintext in the tally (Fig. 6).

This seems much more understandable and presumably more convincing to voters and stakeholders. But, of course, this simplicity comes at a cost: implemented naively such a scheme would invite coercion and vote-buying: the coercer

Candidate	Tracker
Asterix	90g4D2
Obelix	6Y89D
Panoramix	67TY32
Asterix	k034hJ
Idefix	M045f3
Asterix	7Jsb56
Panoramix	wp483N
Panoramix	3093vC
Asterix	Dfg56X

Fig. 6. Selene tally on the BB.

simply demands that the voter hand over their tracker. But such threats can be mitigated by, for example, notifying voters of their tracker only after the votes/trackers have been posted, allowing a coerced voter to equivocate to an alternative tracker that will satisfy the coercer. The Selene scheme, [6], does just this: a coerced voter can choose a tracker from the BB that points to the required vote and claim this as their own. Some fairly simple crypto under the bonnet allows the voter to fake the tracker using a secret trapdoor. On the other hand, an attacker lacking the trapdoor cannot mislead the voter as to their real tracker, so providing assurance that the voter gets her real, unique tracer.

It is hoped that such a scheme will prove more appealing to voters and stakeholders than the more traditional, three-stage verification approach. That said, there are downsides: while voting and verification is now quite simple, the coercion evasion procedure is little harder to understand and execute. Presumably though very few voters would actually have to invoke this procedure. There are also potential problems regarding possible collisions of faked trackers. So, once again, we have subtle trade-offs to evaluate and balance.

5 Conclusions

Security-critical systems typically have a major human involvement that can either bolster or undermine the security properties. Thoughtful design of security mechanisms and interfaces, with careful consideration of human capabilities and limitations, will lead to highly trustworthy systems. Poor design, with little consideration of the human aspects, will inevitably lead to insecure or undeployable systems.

The design of human/system interfaces for security-critical systems is immensely subtle and error-prone, as I hope that attacks mentioned above serve to illustrate. We do not yet have a systematic framework for analysing such interactions, so this remains more art than science.

It appears that there is an inevitable trade-off to be struck between on the one hand making security mechanisms transparent to users and on the other seeking to minimize trust assumptions. Where such a balance should be struck is not a purely technical question, and will depend on the context, the assumed threat environment etc. and is one that must be decided in consultation with the stakeholders.

All of this is fine but does beg the question: how in practice does one execute a good, human-centric design? I am not aware of any recipe for this but I think the following guidelines may be useful:

- Aim for simplicity, especially regarding the human interactions. Complexity harms usability and understandability and leads to error-prone, hard to analyse systems. This is of course the old KISS (Keep It Simple Stupid) principle, but is especially relevant here.
- Keep human characteristics, limitations, foibles etc. in mind-seek to minimise cognitive load, make the ceremony as linear as possible.
- Consult closely and early with the stake-holders to establish the requirements, constraints, trade-offs, assumed threat environment etc.
- Conduct user trials, surveys, focus groups etc. This is costly and time consuming but ultimately will be essential.

Acknowledgements. The author would like to acknowledge the support of the Fonds National de la Recherche (FNR) CORE project Real-World Implementation and Human-Centered Design of PAKE Technologies - ImPAKT (C21/IS/16221219/ImPAKT). I should also like to thanks Peter Roenne and Carsten Schurman for helpful comments.

References

1. Benaloh, J.: Simple verifiable elections. In: Proceeding of the 1st USENIXAccurate Electronic Voting Technology Workshop (2006)
2. Chaum, D.: Secret-ballot receipts: true voter-verifiable elections. IEEE Secur. Privacy **2**(1), 38–47 Jan-Feb (2004)
3. Chaum, D., Ryan, P., Schneider, S.: A practical voter-verifiable election scheme. In: di Vimercati, S.C., Syverson, P., Gollmann, D. (eds.) Computer Security – ESORICS 2005: 10th European Symposium on Research in Computer Security, Milan, Italy, September 12-14, 2005. Proceedings, pp. 118–139. Springer Berlin Heidelberg, Berlin, Heidelberg (2005). https://doi.org/10.1007/11555827_8
4. Naor, M., Shamir, A.: Visual cryptography. In: Alfredo de Santis, editor, Advances in Cryptology - EUROCRYPT 1994 - Workshop on the Theory and Application of Cryptographic Techniques, Proceedings, volume 950 of Lecture Notes in Computer Science (including subseries Lecture Notes in Artificial Intelligence and Lecture Notes in Bioinformatics), pp. 1–12, Germany, 1995. Springer Verlag. Workshop on the Theory and Application of Cryptographic Techniques, EUROCRYPT 1994 ; Conference date: 09-05-1994 Through 12-05-1994

5. Neff, A.: Practical high certainty intent verification for encrypted votes (2004). http://www.votehere.net/documentation/vhti
6. Ryan, P.Y.A., Rønne, P.B., Iovino, V.: Selene: voting with transparent verifiability and coercion-mitigation. In: Clark, J., Meiklejohn, S., Ryan, P.Y.A., Wallach, D., Brenner, M., Rohloff, K. (eds.) Financial Cryptography and Data Security, pp. 176–192. Springer Berlin Heidelberg, Berlin, Heidelberg (2016). https://doi.org/10.1007/978-3-662-53357-4_12

Election Security-by-Design

Carsten Schürmann(✉)

IT University of Copenhagen, Copenhagen, Denmark
carsten@itu.dk

Abstract. Security engineering is about improving the security of an existing software system by adding security controls to the implementation. In this paper we argue, that for election technologies, simply adding security controls is not enough. The only way to design an election system is ensure that it is fundamentally secure by carefully crafting a cryptographic voting protocol, a technique that is also called *security-by-design*. The more secure a system the more we can trust the result and the more easily we can defend against defamation and disinformation campaigns. Both properties, defense against cyber attacks and defense against disinformation are critical as past elections have demonstrated.

1 Introduction

Security engineering is about improving the security of an existing software system by adding security controls to the implementation. The idea behind security engineering is that functional, in the laboratory designed, and most likely insecure applications can be made secure by adding security controls: for example, a communication channel can be secured by using TLS, or a database could be encrypted at rest. These techniques are usually not enough for securing an otherwise insecure election systems. Consider, as an example, the implementation of a simple vote counting protocol where a group of people wants to decide which movie to watch tonight. This system most likely is not programmed with security in mind. Authentication of the users might be as simple as recording names. Votes most likely are not cryptographically secured. Integrity measures are most likely not installed, and in general, the group of participants, will not be terrible interested in security policies, such as vote privacy, verifiability, or dispute resolution, which would be difficult to design and implement. Everyone will, in all likelihood, accept the result and go to see the movie they wanted to see.

In this short paper, we argue, that the traditional understanding of security engineering is not enough for rendering an insecure implementation of a voting system secure. There are several reasons for this.

C. Schürmann—This work was supported in part by the Innovation Fund Denmark for the project DIREC (9142-00001B) grant P37B: Trust through Software Independence and Program Verification.

L. Morogan et al. (Eds.): SecITC 2024, LNCS 15595, pp. 12–17, 2025.
https://doi.org/10.1007/978-3-031-87760-5_2

First, any election technology should be truly software-independent [8,10]. This means that an undetected change or error in its software cannot cause an undetectable change or error in an election outcome. We argue that by adding security controls, an implementation may become more secure, however, it will not be possible to achieve true software-independence this way. Returning to the group of fiends who would like to pick a movie, if the functions that tallies votes has a bug, this will not become detectable by adding security controls.

Second, election systems are arguably socio-technical systems, which are designed, developed, deployed, and used by potentially untrustworthy people. The only way to understand the security of an election system is in the context of trust assumptions and security policies. Security controls do not consider security in a holistic way, they help to improve the security of a system locally, but they lack, in general, the power to do it globally. We discuss trust assumptions and security policies briefly in Sect. 2.

Lastly, there is the verifiability property that an election system must have should it be deemed trustworthy by voters: the ability to defend itself against attacks – cyber attacks and disinformation attacks – such as that the count was incorrect, or that not all voters were able to cast their votes, or that some voters cast more than one vote. The mechanisms provided by voting systems to provide verifiability are meant to establish trustworthiness of the election system. Verifiability mechanisms should produce *evidence* that can be independently verified, ideally also by the layman who otherwise would doubt the election outcome. This means that it is not the verifiability mechanism that should be trusted, it is evidence produced by this mechanism that must be designed in such a way that it can convince voters. We discuss different forms of evidence briefly in Sect. 3.

Evidence-based election systems provide mechanisms for evidence production. A possible security control to provide evidence is logging mechanisms—the challenge of designing them is that they may contain confidential information that must be appropriately protected. Security engineering of election technologies can only bring the implementor so far but to design properly a state-of-the-art election system with minimal trust assumptions and maximal security policies requires that all design decisions are taken at design state using a technique that we call security-by-design and present in Sect. 4.

2 Trust Assumptions and Security Policies

The security of a software system is specified by *trust assumptions* and *security policies. Trust assumptions* define which components of the system and which role need to be trusted and for what behaviors for it to operate according to specification—even if deployed in environments that are controlled by an adversary. In this sense, trust assumptions subsume what is commonly referred to as the *adversary model.* Paradoxically, the fewer trust assumptions there are, the more secure a software system becomes. In security, trust is a liability. We want to trust as little as possible and be sure about as much as possible. The *security policy* defines the security requirements that the software system should satisfy.

Common security policies in elections include vote privacy, receipt-freeness, and coercion resistance, among others. Vote privacy requires that the identity of the voter and the plaintext vote are severed during computation. In contrast to traditional paper elections election where anonymization is done by shuffling the paper ballots, electronic systems often use cryptographic algorithms, such as mix-nets [2] or ring signature schemes [9], and those introduce additional trust assumptions. Receipt-freeness requires that a voting system does not provide any receipts that may be sold by the voter (by demonstrating to others how they voted). Coercion-resistance is a stronger form of vote privacy that requires that a voter should be able to cast a vote independently, even when cast in an adversarial environment where a coercer may exercise undue influence, forcing the voter to vote in a particular way. There are also other security policies, such as dispute-resolution, that may be required for election systems. Clearly, the more security requirements are satisfied, the more secure a software system becomes.

3 Evidence

A necessary, albeit often forgotten, requirement for election software systems is the production of immutable evidence that witnesses the successful execution of each electoral operation and that can later be checked to establish the correct execution of said operations. This evidence includes digital signatures, message authentication codes and even cryptographic proofs of knowledge [7]. These proofs are complicated by their mathematical nature but they are also very practical as demonstrated by their use in other security architectures, for example blockchain applications such as Zcash[1] [3] and Monero.[2] In order to become trustworthy, an election technology should not only determine the election result but also provide the evidence necessary to back up the result. This evidence can establish the authenticity of artifacts, the correct decryption of ballots, the correct shuffling of the digital ballot box, or whichever other operation is executed as part of the election. Once immutable evidence is properly understood and adequately integrated in the voting protocol *by design*, one can argue for verifiability and dispute resolution.

4 Security-by-Design

In the hierarchy of secure software systems, election technologies rank pretty close to the top alongside any other software system used in critical infrastructure sectors. No matter which technology we consider, Internet voting systems, voter registration and identification systems, results transmission systems, or systems that handle electoral disputes, these systems do not run in isolation but process inputs for and by thousands if not millions of voters. Election technologies are

[1] See https://z.cash.
[2] See https://getmonero.org.

complex computer programs that consist of millions of lines of code and rely on long supply chains of libraries of unknown authorship and possibly proprietary and unreviewed software produced by vendors. Election officials are often newly recruited without much prior practical experience in elections but just training. Any trust assumptions that the software stack is error-free or that people behave in rational and predictable ways should be avoided.

In the same spirit, any trust assumption that introduces single points of failures, for example, by making the success of the entire election dependent on one single component or one single person, should also be avoided. The security policy could, for example, include that election officials do not have access to information that may be misused to cast fraudulent votes, or that cryptographic keys are managed using secret sharing schemes, which provides a thresholds schemes, where at least k out of n shareholders have to come to together to decrypt a result partially or to reconstruct the election secret key. These concepts cannot be added retroactively as security controls to an existing system: TLS encryption alone cannot replace a threshold encryption scheme.

It is often said that open-source software is necessary to increase the trustworthiness of election software. But this seems too simple-minded. There are many by now well-known vulnerabilities and cyber attacks against open-source projects in the supply chain of modern election systems, including log4j [4] and xz [5] attacks. Therefore, in addition to the transparency of the software development process for election systems, the requirement for immutable evidence is not only a good-to-have, it is a must-have. And again this means that standard security controls are not good enough as they currently do not support the creation of immutable evidence: A secure TLS connection, for example, that transfers sensitive vote data or an encrypted database that stores data securely at rest do not produce the kind of immutable evidence necessary to satisfy verifiability and dispute resolution requirements. Conversely, it is possible to integrate mechanisms for the generation of immutable evidence into the voting protocol in an well-orchestrated way by applying the security-by-design methodology, for example by passing security parameters throughout the entire application and enabling calls to cryptographic functions for encryption, signing, and commitments, or by defining entirely new cryptographic voting schemes for voter registration, voting, tallying, and auditing. A good example is the design of the Swiss Internet voting system.[3] For a review on the auditability of the Estonian voting system, consult [11].

For Internet voting systems, the security policy can comprise even more advanced security requirements, such as coercion resistance which generalizes vote privacy. For vote privacy, the link between vote and voter should be severed before counting in such a way that no adversary can learn how a voter voted. For coercion resistance, the voting system should offer mechanisms to the voter to protect against adversaries that force the voter to vote in a particular way. Techniques to thwart coercers exist, for example, flexible vote updating [6] or deniable re-voting [1], but again, neither case can be achieved by simply adding

[3] See https://www.bk.admin.ch/bk/en/home/politische-rechte/e-voting.html.

security controls to an existing protocol, as both techniques require profound changes in the way the voting protocol is constructed and structured. This is election security-by-design.

Which trust assumptions and which security policies are suitable for a particular election depends on many factors: National elections are substantially different from boardroom elections in the way voting can is conducted and results verification is performed. Different countries come with different trust profiles. There is high levels of public confidence in government and administration in several Western countries and in many post-conflict countries elections take place in an environment of deeply rooted distrust. The challenge is to determine suitable trust assumptions and security requirements for the respective context the election system is deployed in and then design software that is election-secure by design.

5 Conclusion

For some software systems, security engineering is sufficient to bring the security of the system to an acceptable level. In election security, the requirements are often so stringent and codependent, that adding security controls to an existing system renders the design and implementation complex without achieving the necessary security. The preferred solution is therefore to design a cryptographic voting protocol from scratch, with all of the security features necessary to satisfy the security policies under a given set of trust-assumptions, and guaranteeing thus election security-by-design.

References

1. Achenbach, D., Kempka, C., Löwe, B., Müller-Quade, J.: Improved coercion-resistant electronic elections through deniable re-voting. USENIX J. Election Technol. Syst. (JETS) (2015). https://www.usenix.org/conference/jets15/workshop-program/presentation/achenbach
2. Bayer, S., Groth, J.: Efficient zero-knowledge argument for correctness of a shuffle. In: Pointcheval, D., Johansson, T. (eds.) EUROCRYPT 2012. LNCS, vol. 7237, pp. 263–280. Springer, Heidelberg (2012). https://doi.org/10.1007/978-3-642-29011-4_17
3. Ben Sasson, E., et al.: Zerocash: decentralized anonymous payments from bitcoin. In: 2014 IEEE Symposium on Security and Privacy, pp. 459–474 (2014). https://doi.org/10.1109/SP.2014.36
4. Bloomberg.com: Inside the race to fix a potentially disastrous software flaw, 13 December 2021. https://www.bloomberg.com/news/articles/2021-12-13/how-apache-raced-to-fix-a-potentially-disastrous-software-flaw
5. Corbet, J.: A backdoor in xz (2024). https://lwn.net/Articles/967180/
6. Giustolisi, R., Garjan, M.S., Schuermann, C.: Thwarting last-minute voter coercion. In: 2024 IEEE Symposium on Security and Privacy (SP), May 2024, pp. 3423–3439. IEEE Computer Society, Los Alamitos (2024). https://doi.org/10.1109/SP54263.2024.00112. https://doi.ieeecomputersociety.org/10.1109/SP54263.2024.00112

7. Goldwasser, S., Micali, S., Rackoff, C.: The knowledge complexity of interactive proof systems. SIAM J. Comput. **18**(1), 186–208 (1989). https://doi.org/10.1137/0218012
8. Jamroga, W., Ryan, P.Y.A., Schneider, S., Schurmann, C., Stark, P.B.: A declaration of software independence (2023). https://arxiv.org/abs/2311.03372
9. Patachi, Ş, Schürmann, C.: Eos a universal verifiable and coercion resistant voting protocol. In: Krimmer, R., Volkamer, M., Braun Binder, N., Kersting, N., Pereira, O., Schürmann, C. (eds.) E-Vote-ID 2017. LNCS, vol. 10615, pp. 210–227. Springer, Cham (2017). https://doi.org/10.1007/978-3-319-68687-5_13
10. Rivest, R.L.: On the notion of 'software independence' in voting systems. Philos. Trans. R. Soc. A Math. Phys. Eng. Sci. **366**, 3759 – 3767 (2008). https://api.semanticscholar.org/CorpusID:15751386
11. Sutopo, A., Haines, T., Roenne, P.: On the auditability of the Estonian IVXV system. In: Essex, A., et al. (eds.) Financial Cryptography and Data Security, FC 2023 International Workshops, pp. 19–33. Springer, Cham (2024). https://doi.org/10.1007/978-3-031-48806-1_2

A Conceptual Framework to Leverage Heuristics for Effective Human-Machine Collaboration in Incident Handling

Mehdi Akbari Gurabi[1,2(✉)], Muhammad Usman Mansoor[2], Roman Matzutt[1], Avikarsha Mandal[1], and Stefan Decker[1,2]

[1] Fraunhofer FIT, Sankt Augustin, Germany
{mehdi.akbari.gurabi,roman.matzutt,avikarsha.mandal,
stefan.decker}@fit.fraunhofer.de
[2] RWTH Aachen University, Aachen, Germany
{mehdi.akbari.gurabi,usman.mansoor}@rwth-aachen.de

Abstract. Managing cybersecurity incidents increasingly depends on advanced levels of automation. However, human involvement remains essential due to the need for high accuracy and the risk of severe damage. Therefore, incident response requires a high degree of human-machine teaming to both simplify the complexity of modern incident handling tasks and ensure a reliable decision-making process. We introduce a conceptual framework designed to augment machine learning-based incident handling by integrating heuristic-based methods for improved efficiency. Integrating heuristic-based methods to compare the results of machine learning classifiers can potentially enhance human comprehension of the output of the machine learning model, thus facilitating human reasoning. We validate the practicality of the framework by applying it to the specific use case of email phishing detection, demonstrating that our approach supports operators for a more accurate phishing classification. The results demonstrate that our framework improves detection accuracy and also potentially enhances the interpretability of the incident handling process, leading to more effective human-machine collaboration in cybersecurity.

Keywords: Incident Handling · Human-machine Teaming · Incident Response

1 Introduction

The advancements in artificial intelligence (AI) and in particular, machine learning (ML), have the potential to enhance the level of automation in established methods of security incident detection [26]. However, such models lack the essential component of transparency. This lack of transparency makes it difficult for security professionals to understand how these models make their decisions [25]. This can lead to mistrust because of missed threats or a large number of false

L. Morogan et al. (Eds.): SecITC 2024, LNCS 15595, pp. 18–35, 2025.
https://doi.org/10.1007/978-3-031-87760-5_3

alarms. Relying solely on these methods also complicates the ability to detect and address biases in the models. This can lead to serious consequences, such as the misclassification of benign activities as threats, resulting in unnecessary resource allocation, or the overlooking of genuine threats due to incorrect confidence in model outputs. Given these limitations, there is a growing need for security solutions that not only accurately identify incidents but also offer human insight into the conclusions. This aspect is important for ensuring an efficient and reliable response [29].

This research contributes to the application of human-machine teaming in the domain of cybersecurity. The conceptual framework of this study has the potential to advise the development of future security systems that prioritize transparency and human-understandable results. We emphasize the critical role of human judgment in decision-making and introduce a pivotal step in AI-supported incident handling. This step allows humans to gain insight and evaluate the results generated by machine learning models, ensuring a more reliable and nuanced response. Eventually, it improves incident handling performance by facilitating automation of detection and further response steps. To achieve this goal, research demonstrates the potential to employ heuristics in simple and understandable detection systems [32]. By incorporating heuristic-based methods, we seek to support human reasoning and decision-making processes.

The primary research contributions of this work are twofold:

- Development of a conceptual framework that combines heuristic methods with machine learning techniques, enhancing the transparency and reliability of incident detection systems.
- Demonstration and validation of our framework for a practical use case of email phishing detection and response, which illustrates how the framework can be applied to real-world scenarios.

By addressing the challenges associated with the lack of transparency in AI-driven incident handling systems, this research provides a simple approach to improving the synergy between human operators and automated tools.

2 Related Work

Artificial intelligence is widely used in the domain of cybersecurity, particularly in incident detection. However, the nature of models has raised concerns about their understandability and trustworthiness among human operators [6]. This lack of transparency can hinder effective decision-making, especially when it comes to critical security incidents [13].

To address these challenges, recent research has explored various eXplainable Artificial Intelligence (XAI) methods to improve the interpretability of AI systems, ensuring that human operators can better understand and trust the results generated by these models [7]. Traditional AI models often function as black boxes, producing results without providing insight into the decision-making process. This has led to a growing interest in frameworks that prioritize human interpretability. For instance, XAI frameworks such as LIME [27] and SHAP [24] have been applied in this domain [35]. Despite all the attention, current research on the application of XAI in incident detection is still relatively limited, and further exploration is required to address the challenges and requirements of this domain [6]. The use of heuristic-based methods has been proposed as a means to provide intuition into ML results [20]. These methods rely on simple, rule-based approaches that align more closely with human cognitive processes [32], thereby enhancing the usability and reliability of AI and ML systems in cybersecurity.

In this context, human support systems are particularly crucial in scenarios where high precision and rapid response are essential. For example, phishing attacks still pose a significant security challenge for organizations worldwide, where adversaries try to deceive users into revealing information or performing actions [11]. Previous studies have demonstrated the effectiveness of combining ML with heuristic-based approaches to improve human decision-making in real-time for phishing attacks [17]. Further, Zhang *et al.* [35] introduced an explainable framework for detecting spam images using convolutional neural networks (CNNs). More recently, Ibrahim *et al.* combined random forest and long short-term memory (LSTM) models to detect spam emails and employed LIME to provide explanations [19]. Later, Calzarossa *et al.* proposed an explainable machine learning approach to detect phishing websites [5]. These approaches allow human operators to gain deeper insights into the factors influencing the AI's decisions.

Despite these advancements, there remains a key research gap regarding the integration of such human-supportive solutions for AI-driven incident handling throughout the entire incident handling lifecycle. Most existing approaches focus on specific aspects of incident detection, without fully addressing the challenges of integrating these solutions into comprehensive response systems. Our work addresses this gap by focusing on the integration of human-understandable insights from ML models into the incident response process, without relying on XAI. We propose a straightforward framework that leverages heuristics to facilitate effective human-machine teaming in incident handling.

3 Framework

To address the challenges associated with the transparency and trustworthiness of AI-driven cybersecurity systems, we introduce a conceptual framework named the Synergistic Incident Handling Framework (SIHF). This framework is designed to augment human insight into incident handling decisions effectively, by integrating heuristic methods to support ML results.

3.1 System Requirements

Research starts with a requirement analysis to identify the key features necessary for effective human-machine teaming in incident handling. We group the requirements into four categories: G1: Performance, G2: Human-Machine Interaction,

G3: Deployment, and G4: Functionality. The following system requirements were established based on a literature review [2,3,9,21]:

- **R1 (G1): High Accuracy with Minimal False Positives:** The incident detection models must achieve high accuracy while minimizing false positives, ensuring that human operators can trust the ML outputs.
- **R2 (G1): Efficiency in operation:** The framework should operate efficiently within typical computing constraints, allowing rapid incident detection and response.
- **R3 (G2): Human Escalation for Critical Decisions:** To limit the risks associated with full automation, critical decisions must be escalated to human operators for review and final approval.
- **R4 (G2): Flexible Integration with Existing Technologies:** The framework must integrate flexibly with existing diverse technological environments.
- **R5 (G2): Standard Interfaces and APIs:** The framework should utilize standard interfaces and APIs to facilitate communication and integration. This compatibility is important for the adoption of the solution across various security operations centers (SOCs).
- **R6 (G3): Infrastructure Independence:** The system should allow for infrastructure-independent deployment, possibly via containerization.
- **R7 (G4): Incident Type Identification:** The framework must be able to identify which response actions to carry out automatically, depending on the incident type.
- **R8 (G4): Importance of the Affected Asset:** Asset risk management should be considered to minimize damage from an incident or incorrect response actions. Automatic response actions might be appropriate for incidents that affect low-cost assets.
- **R9 (G4): Severity Assessment:** The framework should assess the severity of incidents, with less severe incidents being more suitable for automated response actions.
- **R10 (G4): Risk of Response Action:** The framework needs a mechanism to quantify the risk of implementing an action in the event of a false positive.

3.2 Framework Design

After identifying the system requirements, we design SIHF for incident detection and response, considering human-machine teaming in the workflow by incorporating heuristic methods. Figure 1 shows the SIHF components for human-machine teaming in incident handling. The framework operates as follows.

Incident Detection: The process begins with the detection of a security event, where an automated detection system, including several ML-based tools, is triggered. These tools generate initial ML results, such as classification scores or alerts.

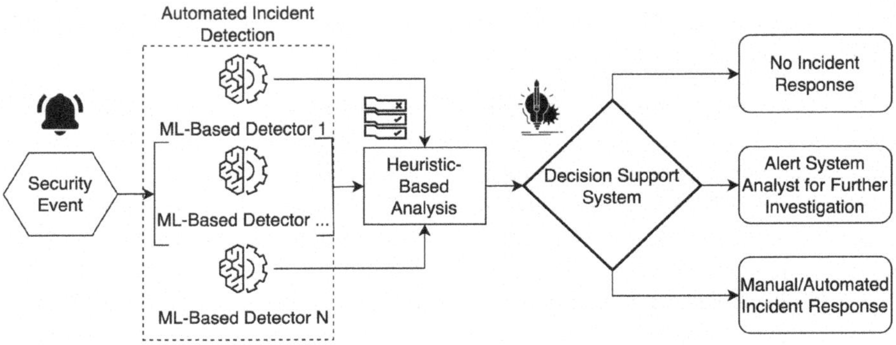

Fig. 1. SIHF conceptual framework where incident detection results come from multiple ML sources, and the heuristic-based result supports human operator in the decision step for an effective and reliable response or supervision of an automated decision.

Heuristic-Based Analysis: To improve the interpretability of AI results, SIHF applies a heuristic-based analysis. This analysis involves simple rule-based methods that closely align with human reasoning. For example, in phishing detection, heuristics might include rules based on URL characteristics, email formatting, or the presence of certain keywords. These heuristics help to provide context and insight, thereby facilitating decision-making for human operators based on the ML output. Moreover, post hoc explanations provided by XAI methods can be potentially leveraged at this step to map the ML results and enhance the understanding and evaluation process.

Decision Support System (DSS): Heuristic-based analysis feeds into a Decision Support System (DSS) designed to assist human operators in making informed decisions. The DSS presents the ML results along with heuristics, allowing the operator to understand the reasoning behind the models' conclusions. In cases where the AI results are ambiguous or critical decisions are required, the system escalates the decision to a human operator for final approval. Additionally, it can be used as a critical monitoring and documentation step in an automated or semi-automated incident response workflow.

Response Execution: Based on the decisions made by the human operator or the automated system, response actions are initiated. These actions can be manual or automated, depending on predefined thresholds and the nature of the incident.

The SIHF is designed to be simple, flexible, and scalable, capable of integrating with various security technologies and environments. It can be deployed across different SOCs without the need for significant infrastructure modifications. This flexibility ensures that SIHF can be widely adopted, enhancing incident handling processes across various organizations, and can be integrated with Security Information and Event Management (SIEM).

3.3 Integration with SIEM Systems

SIHF seamlessly integrates with SIEM systems to improve detection, analysis, and response to cybersecurity incidents. As depicted in Fig. 2, the SIEM system plays a central role by serving as the repository and knowledge base for incident data, detection results, and correlated alerts.

When an unseen incident is detected by the detection system or the ML engine, the results are stored in the SIEM database. The SIEM system aggregates these detection results, which may include primary data and alert severity, and correlates individual events into more complex incidents. This aggregated information, in addition to heuristic-based analysis, is then provided to the decision support system. It helps the human analyst in evaluating the accuracy of the alerts. The human analyst decides on the appropriate response actions. These actions can either be manual or automated, depending on the severity and type of incident detected. If an alert is identified as a false positive, no further action is taken, but the incident is still logged in the SIEM system for future reference. Human analysts' judgments are used to label suspicious incidents within the SIEM system's stored data. Suspicious cases occur when the confidence score of the combined results is insufficient to automatically classify an incident as true or false. All updated labels are then used to update and refine the ML models and the detection system. This iterative process ensures that the detection models evolve continuously, improving their accuracy and reliability over time. Through this integration, SIHF enhances the capabilities of the SIEM system by adding an additional layer of human oversight, ensuring that incident responses are accurate and informed by the most up-to-date threat intelligence.

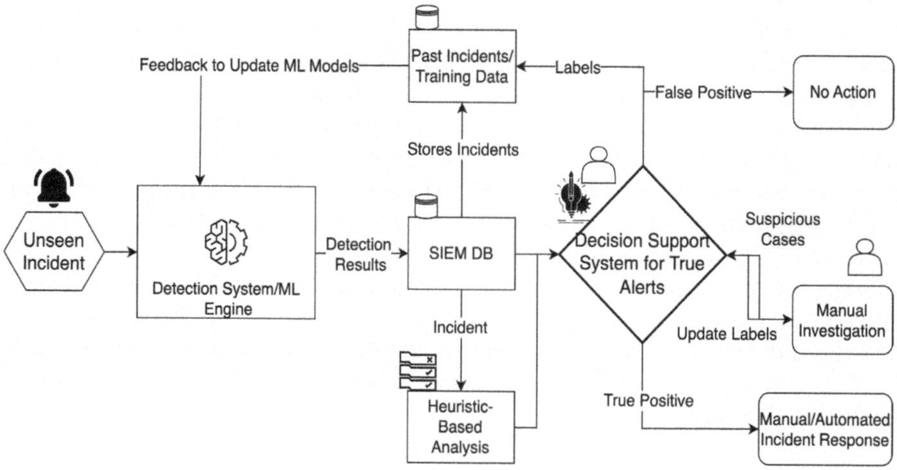

Fig. 2. Process of Semi-Automated Response and Recovery with the help of SIHF integrated with SIEM.

4 Realization

To demonstrate the practical application of our framework, we implemented it in the context of email phishing detection as a critical cybersecurity threat. This section details the process of developing and realizing the framework, from training classifiers to integrating heuristic-based analysis, and showcases how the framework enhances human decision-making in real-world scenarios. For this reason, we train text- and URL-based classifiers, followed by a Heuristic-based analysis to make the results understandable by human operators as the input for a simple decision support system.

4.1 Implementation of Phishing Detection Classifiers

As a foundational step, we developed and trained two primary classifiers: a text-based classifier and a URL-based classifier. These classifiers were chosen based on their relevance to phishing detection, where emails typically contain suspicious text and URLs that need to be analyzed for potential threats.

Text-Based Classification: The text classification employs various Natural Language Processing (NLP) techniques, such as Term Frequency- Inverse Document Frequency (TF-IDF) [34], Word2Vec [28], and Bidirectional Encoder Representations from Transformers (BERT) [12]. These methods were used to extract contextual embeddings from email text, capturing both semantic and syntactic relationships. These input features provide a rich representation that can be utilized by ML algorithms. The text classification methodology in the work involves the implementation of ten popular ML algorithms for classifying phishing emails. These algorithms were selected based on their proven success in binary classification tasks [4,31]. We further apply an ensemble classifier based on the results, which was mentioned as an approach in similar works [18,30]. The four best-resulted algorithms in our test for detecting phishing emails are utilized to train an ensemble classifier based on soft voting. The selected models consist of Support Vector Machine(SVM), Logistic Regression (LR), Random Forest (RF), and Gradient Boosting (GB). We utilized two email datasets, the Enron email dataset[1] for benign emails, and Nazario's phishing corpus[2] containing email phishing data. From the Enron dataset, we selected 4,280 benign emails to merge with the 3,833 verified phishing messages from Nazario to balance the dataset. We randomly selected 1,618 emails consisting of 856 benign and 762 phishing cases for the test set and compiled 6,495 emails to train the text-based classifier.

[1] https://www.kaggle.com/datasets/wanderfj/enron-spam,.

[2] https://monkey.org/~jose/phishing/.

URL-Based Classifier: In addition to the text classifier, a URL-based classifier is implemented based on a two-stacked one-dimensional Convolutional Neural Network (1D-CNN) [33], as it has been proven that such classifiers can separate benign from malicious domains with high accuracy [14]. This approach ensures a proof-of-concept for the purpose of combining the results of multiple ML detection systems (i.e., text-based and URL-based classifiers) to cover a wider range of potential incidents. The URL-based classifier is trained on phishing URLs from PhishTank[3] and benign URLs from Cisco Umbrella Top 1 Million Domains[4], implemented using TensorFlow. We generate a balanced dataset of phishing and benign URLs by randomly selecting URLs from the mentioned databases in the ratio of 40% phishing and 60% benign to compile a dataset of 200,000 samples for training the model. This classifier returns a confidence value between 0 and 1, where 1 means that it is unlikely to be a phishing URL and 0 is the highest likelihood.

4.2 Heuristic-Based Analysis

The next step in the realization of SIHF involved the integration of heuristic-based analysis to enhance the interpretability of the ML classifiers' outputs. In the context of phishing email detection, heuristics are simple rules that help identify patterns or characteristics commonly associated with phishing emails. Heuristics are relatively easy to understand and implement, making them useful for quickly identifying suspicious emails. They can be customized to fit the specific needs and characteristics of an organization, enhancing the effectiveness of ML classifiers with human insight. The heuristics are also effective in capturing characteristics that may not have been fully captured by the machine learning models due to biases in the training data. The heuristics used in this study are designed based on a review of the existing literature (e.g., [15,22]) to provide a rule-based classifier.

This heuristic-based analysis focuses on identifying specific patterns and characteristics commonly associated with phishing emails. This helps operators find information on emails and judge ML-based classifiers to achieve a more accurate decision. They are categorized into URL-based and visual heuristics to align with ML models' output.

URL-Based Heuristics: We implemented heuristics focused on the structure and content of URLs, such as the length of the URL, the presence of special characters, the number of subdomains, and the presence of IP addresses. These heuristics were derived from a review of the existing literature on phishing detection and mainly selected based on [22].

[3] https://phishtank.org.
[4] https://github.com/PeterDaveHello/top-1m-domains.

Visual and Content-Based Heuristics: Additionally, we applied heuristics to analyze the visual and content-related features of emails based on the defined heuristics in [15]. This included the presence of URLs, attachments, forms, scripts, HTML, buttons, image tags, and pop-up code or status changes.

4.3 Decision Support System

The outputs from the text- and URL-based classifiers, along with the heuristic-based analysis, were fed into the Decision Support System (DSS). The DSS plays an important role in the SIHF by presenting results in a format that is accessible and actionable for human operators. The DSS synthesizes the outputs from the ML classifiers and the heuristic analyses, providing a clear and concise summary of why an email was classified as phishing or benign. In situations where the MLs' classification is uncertain or critical decisions need to be made, the DSS escalates these decisions to human operators, who can review the outputs before taking action.

4.4 Incident Response

We further implement a proof-of-concept automated response flow using Apache Airflow[5]. We showcase the creation of an incident handling workflow based on SIHF. This workflow begins with the classification of incoming emails, followed by the application of heuristics and the generation of insights in the DSS. Based on predefined thresholds and calculated scores, the system can trigger automated responses, such as displaying warnings, flagging suspicious emails, blacklisting URLs, or escalating the incident to a human operator for further investigation. The workflow ensures that every action is documented, providing a clear audit trail for all decisions made. We define response actions based on the NIST incident handling guideline [8] and to address their cybersecurity framework [10]. The prototype workflow is shown in Fig. 3.

SIHF integrates with different technologies, for instance, the playbook management tool [1]. To achieve this, we developed a utility to translate the CACAO playbook specification, which standardizes the creation and sharing of cybersecurity playbooks [23], into directed acyclic graphs (DAGs) for the Apache Airflow workflow management platform. This two-way translator bridges the CACAO playbooks with Airflow, enabling seamless automation of cybersecurity response actions. It processes each workflow step in CACAO playbooks, creates an equivalent task in the DAG format, and generates a callable function for each step where relevant code can later be inserted. Moreover, the translator handles the connections between steps, automatically establishing the flow within the DAG and selecting the appropriate operator type for each task (e.g., *Dummy Operators* for steps without instructions or *Branch Operators* for conditional steps). It provides a template for migrating the playbook details if required. Since DAGs

[5] https://github.com/apache/airflow.

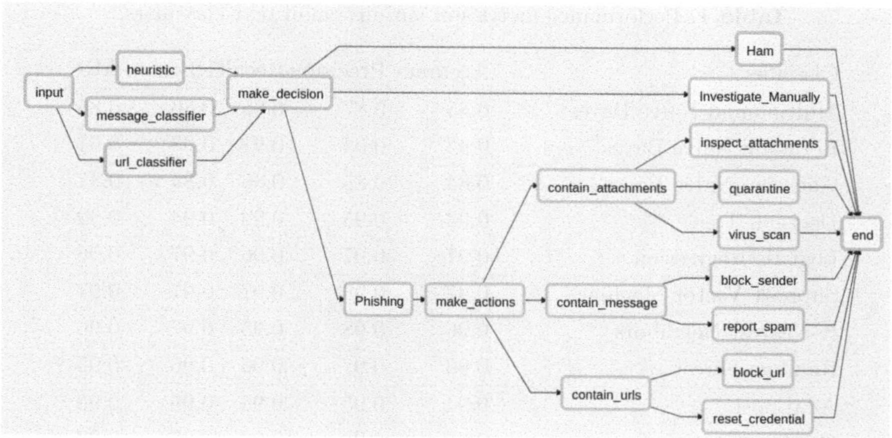

Fig. 3. The incident response workflow developed as a proof-of-concept for email phishing via Apache Airflow.

cannot contain cycles, the translator also detects and aborts the use of while-steps and cycles. Response automation can also facilitate the reporting process to Computer Emergency Response Teams (CERTs) and national authorities in the event of incidents [2]. Furthermore, automating the sharing of incident response knowledge can enhance organizations' capacities to respond effectively to incidents [16].

5 Evaluation

The evaluation of SIHF is conducted through a series of experiments focused on email phishing detection. This section presents the performance metrics of the ML classifiers, the impact of integrating heuristic-based analysis, and the overall effectiveness of the framework in improving human interpretability and decision-making.

5.1 Performance of ML Classifiers and Heuristic-Based Analysis

We begin by evaluating the performance of the text-based and URL-based classifiers developed as part of the SIHF. Classifiers are evaluated using standard metrics, including accuracy, precision, recall, F1 score, and Area Under the Curve (AUC), to determine their effectiveness in detecting phishing emails.

The results of the text-based phishing classifiers are shown in Table 1. We selected four models with the best performance (SVM, LR, RF, and GB) to shape an ensemble model based on soft voting. However, focusing on the accuracy of the ML models was not the main focus of the work; the metrics show promising results of the ensemble text classifier.

Table 1. Performance metrics of various email text classifiers.

Classifier	Accuracy	Precision	Recall	F1-score	AUC
Multinomial Naive Bayes	0.85	0.87	0.85	0.86	0.85
Bernoulli Naive Bayes	0.93	0.94	0.91	0.93	0.91
Gaussian Naive Bayes	0.84	0.85	0.86	0.84	0.87
Decision Tree	0.93	0.95	0.92	0.94	0.92
Logistic Regression	0.97	0.97	0.96	0.97	0.96
Support Vector Machine	0.97	0.98	0.97	0.97	0.97
K-Nearest Neighbors	0.96	0.98	0.95	0.97	0.96
Random Forest	0.96	0.97	0.96	0.96	0.95
AdaBoost	0.94	0.95	0.94	0.95	0.93
Gradient Boosting	0.97	0.98	0.96	0.97	0.97
Ensemble (SVM+LR+RF+GB)	0.98	0.98	0.97	0.98	0.97

Moreover, we introduce a basic model to combine multiple ML detection systems to enhance detection reliability. For demonstration purposes, we combine the scores of two classifiers (URL and text) by averaging the results with equal weights. The results indicate that the combined detection slightly improves the classification results and it potentially helps to reduce the effects of overfitting the models and biases in the training data.

Additionally, we combine heuristic-based analysis with the ML results to gain insight in addition to accurate output. The testing dataset contains 920 emails, split into 460 phishing and 460 benign emails. Performance metrics are shown in Table 2. The results show that adding heuristic-based analysis and the basic decision support system (represented as "Final decision" in Table 2) slightly enhances the classification outcomes. This approach increases the accuracy to 94%, with precision at 96%, recall at 94%, F1-score at 95%, and AUC at 94%., in addition to providing valuable insights for human operators.

Table 2. Performance metrics of a) ensemble text-based classifier, b) URL-based classifier, c) combined ML-based detection (i.e., average score of text- and URL-based classifiers), and d) final decision via the combination of heuristics with ML classifiers.

Classifier	Accuracy	Precision	Recall	F1-score	AUC
Text classifier (ensemble)	0.93	0.95	0.91	0.95	0.93
URL classifier (1D-CNN)	0.86	0.94	0.77	0.90	0.86
Combined ML detection	0.93	0.96	0.92	0.95	0.93
Final decision	0.94	0.96	0.94	0.95	0.94

5.2 Heuristic-Based Decision Support

One of the primary goals of the SIHF is to improve human understanding to judge the results of ML. This is evaluated by analyzing the decisions made by the framework and their impact on human decision-making. The DSS presented the ML results along with heuristic-based results, which security analysts should review. The heuristic rules, such as URL length and the presence of special characters, allow analysts to understand and trust the results more easily. The integration of heuristics into the DSS enabled security analysts to make more informed decisions, particularly in ambiguous cases where the MLs' confidence is low. The heuristics provide valuable context that enhances analysts' ability to judge the severity and credibility of potential threats. The decision support system also provides information for humans by representing the key features and thresholds used for classification. For example, the top splits in the tree often involved URL-based features, such as the presence of IP addresses or the number of subdomains, indicating their importance in identifying phishing emails. Security analysts can interpret the result of the ML models by following the

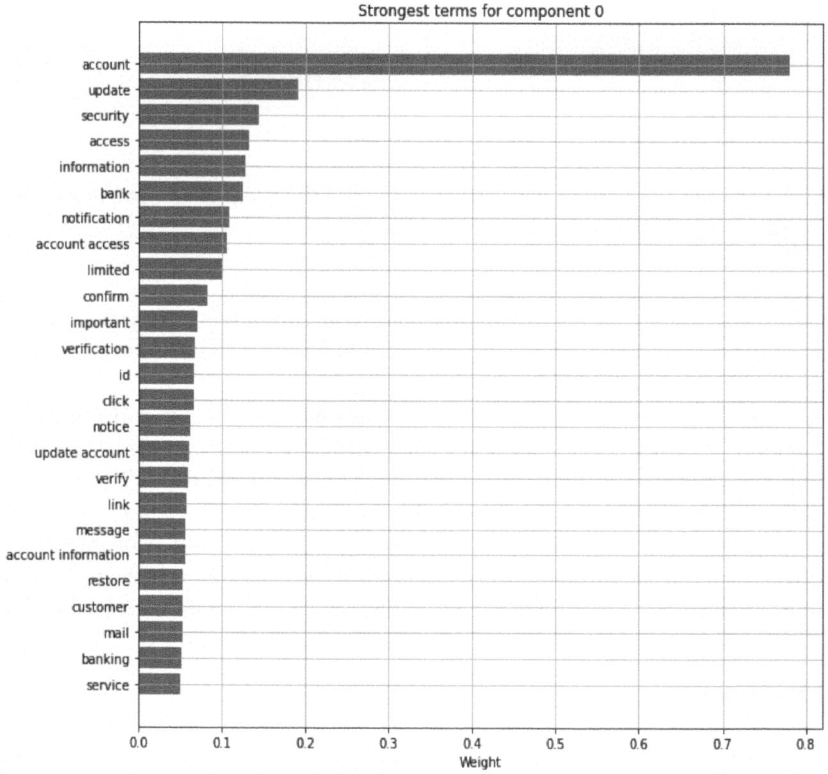

Fig. 4. An example of visualization support of the SIHF: feature representation of the text classifier: top 25 features for phishing class.

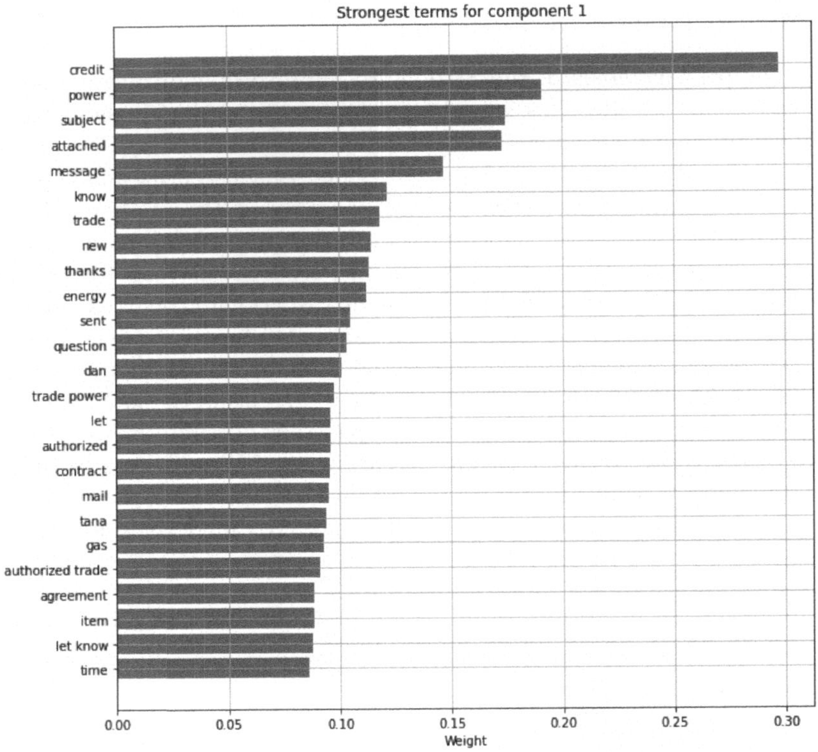

Fig. 5. An example of visualization support of the SIHF: feature representation of the text classifier: top 25 features for benign class.

branching logic. Integration of this analysis into the detection system improves clarity, which is important to build reliability in ML models to facilitate effective responses to security threats.

The decision support system provides human insight by representing the key features and thresholds used for classification. Visualization of heuristics can help the operator to make informed decisions. For example, SIHF provides statistics on the relative contribution of each feature to the final classification, allowing users to understand the reasoning behind the classification models. Figures 4 and 5 represent human support examples by visualizing the top 25 general characteristics of text classifiers for phishing and benign cases, respectively.

6 Discussion

The evaluation of SIHF highlights its potential to significantly enhance the interpretability of ML-driven cybersecurity systems and improve human decision-making during incident handling. This section discusses the implications of the findings, potential limitations, and directions for future research.

6.1 Framework Integration and Overall Effectiveness

The SIHF was designed with flexibility in mind. To evaluate this, we tested the framework's integration into various technological environments. The SIHF was deployed using Apache Airflow to manage the incident handling workflow. This setup allowed the system to scale, handling increasing volumes of email data without significant performance degradation. The use of containerized components also ensures that the framework can be adapted to different organizational infrastructures, demonstrating its flexibility.

The evaluation of SIHF demonstrates its effectiveness in enhancing the interpretability of ML-driven cybersecurity systems and improving the reliability of human decision-making. By combining ML classifiers with heuristic-based analysis, the framework provides security analysts with actionable insights that are both accurate and understandable. This leads to more profitable human-machine-teaming, resulting in a more effective and coordinated incident-handling procedure. Security analysts can also gain a deeper insight into incidents, enabling them to refine their own threat detection and response strategies and proactively address emerging risks.

To validate the effectiveness of SIHF, we applied it to a case study of email phishing detection. The results demonstrate the effectiveness of our approach in accurately identifying phishing emails while providing insight for operators. We recognize that the framework should be extended and adapted for various incidents and anomaly detection use cases in the future. This approach is applicable to other automated incident detection scenarios based on machine learning classification.

6.2 Limitations and Challenges

While the SIHF is demonstrated for the email phishing use case, it is important to acknowledge the potential limitations and challenges that may arise as the system is scaled and deployed. To assess the system's scalability and adaptability, we should conduct experiments with larger datasets and simulate the phishing attacks and suitable responses based on the organization's system architecture. As the volume of email traffic and the complexity of phishing attacks continue to evolve, the system will need to maintain its high accuracy and interpretability while adapting to the changes. Despite its strengths, one potential challenge is the reliance on heuristic rules, which may not cover all possible tactics or adapt quickly to new threat vectors. Moreover, we acknowledge the importance of testing the SIHF with real human operators and security analysts, as it aims to improve human-machine collaboration. We plan to conduct user studies to evaluate the effectiveness and usability of SIHF in real-world scenarios.

6.3 Future Work

Here we list the main future research and development directions for this framework:

Extending to Other Cybersecurity Domains: To validate the scalability and robustness of the SIHF, future studies should evaluate the framework using larger datasets and a wider variety of cyber threats. Although SIHF is validated in the context of email phishing detection, future work should explore its application to other cybersecurity domains, such as network intrusion detection and malware analysis. Extending the framework to these areas would demonstrate its versatility and broader applicability to improve human-machine collaboration across the cybersecurity landscape. This would provide a more comprehensive assessment of its performance and identify areas for further refinement and optimization. Our next step will be to explore such response scenarios for domain generation algorithms (DGAs) using the framework.

Incorporating Adaptive Heuristics: Future research should explore the development of adaptive heuristics that can evolve based on new data and emerging threats. This can address the limitation of static heuristic rules by involving the use of ML techniques to refine and update heuristic rules dynamically, ensuring that the framework remains effective against evolving tactics and new cyber threats.

User Feedback: A key area for future research is the incorporation of user feedback into the SIHF. By collecting and analyzing feedback from security analysts, the framework could be continuously improved to better meet the needs of human operators. This could also involve developing mechanisms for the framework to learn from user interactions, adapting its behavior to provide more relevant and tailored insights.

Integration with Advanced Security Tools: We plan to integrate the framework with advanced security tools, such as SIEM systems, Security Orchestration, Automation and Response (SOAR) platforms, and email gateways. This would allow the framework to be seamlessly incorporated into existing security operations, enhancing its utility in real-world scenarios.

Enhancing Machine-Readability of Incident Descriptions: We plan to explore the use of machine learning techniques to process textual descriptions of incidents into a machine-readable form, organizing them as a case base. This approach aims to improve incident response by improving simplicity, machine readability, flexibility, and scalability. Therefore, it allows for a faster and more accurate incident response.

7 Conclusion

The proposed framework represents a significant advancement in addressing the research gap for reliable automated incident handling systems. By combining machine learning models and heuristic-based analysis, the system demonstrates the ability to accurately identify malicious incidents while providing human-understandable reasons for decisions. Evaluation of the system validates its effectiveness, with heuristic-based analysis that provides intuitive insights into the classification results. The ability to comprehend the system's reasoning and identify potential biases is an important aspect. This approach offers several key benefits that address the pressing challenges security analysts face against incidents. SIHF demonstrates a valuable asset to support human operators toward automated response. It contributes to a more secure and resilient digital ecosystem.

Acknowledgments. This work has received funding from the European Union's Horizon 2020 research and innovation programme under grant agreement No. 101020560 (CyberSEAS) and grant agreement No. 101070052 (TANGO).

The authors have no competing interests to declare that are relevant to the content of this article.

References

1. Akbari Gurabi, M., Mandal, A., Popanda, J., Rapp, R., Decker, S.: Sasp: a semantic web-based approach for management of sharable cybersecurity playbooks. In: Proceedings of the 17th International Conference on Availability, Reliability and Securit,y pp. 1–8 (2022)
2. Akbari Gurabi, M., et al.: Requirements for playbook-assisted cyber incident response, reporting and automation. Digital Threats **5**(3) (Oct 2024). https://doi.org/10.1145/3688810
3. Anwar, S., et al.: From intrusion detection to an intrusion response system: fundamentals, requirements, and future directions. algorithms **10**(2), 39 (2017)
4. Bahel, V., Pillai, S., Malhotra, M.: A comparative study on various binary classification algorithms and their improved variant for optimal performance. In: 2020 IEEE Region 10 Symposium (TENSYMP), pp. 495–498. IEEE (2020)
5. Calzarossa, M.C., Giudici, P., Zieni, R.: Explainable machine learning for phishing feature detection. Qual. Reliab. Eng. Int. **40**(1), 362–373 (2024)
6. Capuano, N., Fenza, G., Loia, V., Stanzione, C.: Explainable artificial intelligence in cybersecurity: a survey. IEEE Access **10**, 93575–93600 (2022)
7. Charmet, F., et al.: Explainable artificial intelligence for cybersecurity: a literature survey. Ann. Telecommun. **77**(11), 789–812 (2022)
8. Cichonski, P., Millar, T., Grance, T., Scarfone, K.: Computer Security Incident Handling Guide, vol. 800. NIST Special Publication, Gaithersburg, MD, USA (2012)
9. Cichonski, P., Millar, T., Grance, T., Scarfone, K., et al.: Computer security incident handling guide. NIST Spec. Publ. **800**(61), 1–147 (2012)

10. Cybersecurity, C.I.: Framework for improving critical infrastructure cybersecurity. URL: https://nvlpubs. nist. gov/nistpubs/CSWP/NIST. CSWP **4162018**, 7 (2018)
11. Das, A., Baki, S., El Aassal, A., Verma, R., Dunbar, A.: Sok: a comprehensive reexamination of phishing research from the security perspective. IEEE Commun. Surv. Tutorials **22**(1), 671–708 (2019)
12. Devlin, J., Chang, M.W., Lee, K., Toutanova, K.: Bert: pre-training of deep bidirectional transformers for language understanding. arXiv preprint arXiv:1810.04805 (2018)
13. Drichel, A., Faerber, N., Meyer, U.: First step towards explainable dga multiclass classification. In: Proceedings of the 16th International Conference on Availability, Reliability and Security. ARES '21, Association for Computing Machinery, New York, NY, USA (2021). https://doi.org/10.1145/3465481.3465749
14. Drichel, A., Gurabi, M.A., Amelung, T., Meyer, U.: Towards privacy-preserving classification-as-a-service for dga detection. In: 2021 18th International Conference on Privacy, Security and Trust (PST), pp. 1–10. IEEE (2021)
15. Gangavarapu, T., Jaidhar, C.D., Chanduka, B.: Applicability of machine learning in spam and phishing email filtering: review and approaches. Artif. Intell. Rev. **53**(7), 5019–5081 (2020). https://doi.org/10.1007/s10462-020-09814-9
16. Gurabi, M.A., Nitz, L., Joglekar, C.M., Mandal, A.: Strengthening cyber defence through cooperative development and shared expertise in incident response playbooks. ERCIM NEWS **139**, 44–46 (2024)
17. Hernandes, P.R.G., Floret, C.P., De Almeida, K.F.C., Da Silva, V.C., Papa, J.P., Da Costa, K.A.P.: Phishing detection using url-based xai techniques. In: 2021 IEEE Symposium Series on Computational Intelligence (SSCI), pp. 01–06. IEEE (2021)
18. Hossain, F., Uddin, M.N., Halder, R.K.: Analysis of optimized machine learning and deep learning techniques for spam detection. In: 2021 IEEE International IOT, Electronics and Mechatronics Conference (IEMTRONICS), pp. 1–7. IEEE (2021)
19. Ibrahim, A., Mejri, M., Jaafar, F.: An explainable artificial intelligence approach for a trustworthy spam detection. In: 2023 IEEE International Conference on Cyber Security and Resilience (CSR), pp. 160–167. IEEE (2023)
20. Ignatiev, A.: Towards trustable explainable AI. In: Bessiere, C. (ed.) Proceedings of the Twenty-Ninth International Joint Conference on Artificial Intelligence, pp. 5154–5158. Association for the Advancement of Artificial Intelligence (AAAI), United States of America (2020). https://doi.org/10.24963/ijcai.2020/726, https://www.ijcai.org/Proceedings/2020/, https://ijcai20.org, international Joint Conference on Artificial Intelligence-Pacific Rim International Conference on Artificial Intelligence 2020, IJCAI-PRICAI 2020 ; Conference date: 07-01-2021 Through 15-01-2021
21. ISO/IEC: Iso/iec 27001 information security standard; information technology - security techniques - information security - information security management systems - requirements (2017). https://www.iso.org/standard/27001
22. Jeeva, S.C., Rajsingh, E.B.: Intelligent phishing URL detection using association rule mining. HCIS **6**(1), 1–19 (2016). https://doi.org/10.1186/s13673-016-0064-3
23. Ed. by Jordan, B., Thomson, A.: Cacao security playbooks version 2.0. oasis committee specification draft 05. Latest version: https://docs.oasisopen.org/cacao/security-playbooks/v2.0/security-playbooks-v2.0.html (October 2023)
24. Lundberg, S.M., Lee, S.I.: A unified approach to interpreting model predictions. In: Advances in Neural Information Processing Systems, vol.30 (2017)

25. Okada, S., et al.: Xai-driven adversarial attacks on network intrusion detectors. In: Proceedings of the 2024 European Interdisciplinary Cybersecurity Conference. p. 65-73. EICC '24, Association for Computing Machinery, New York, NY, USA (2024). https://doi.org/10.1145/3655693.3655714
26. Oreyomi, M., Jahankhani, H.: Challenges and opportunities of autonomous cyber defence (acyd) against cyber attacks. Blockchain and other emerging technologies for digital business strategies, pp. 239–269 (2022)
27. Ribeiro, M.T., Singh, S., Guestrin, C.: " why should i trust you?" explaining the predictions of any classifier. In: Proceedings of the 22nd ACM SIGKDD International Conference on Knowledge Discovery and Data Mining, pp. 1135–1144 (2016)
28. Rong, X.: word2vec parameter learning explained. arXiv preprint arXiv:1411.2738 (2014)
29. Spring, J.M., Illari, P.: Review of human decision-making during computer security incident analysis. Digital Threats: Res. Pract. **2**(2), 1–47 (2021)
30. Trivedi, S.K., Dey, S.: A study of ensemble based evolutionary classifiers for detecting unsolicited emails. In: Proceedings of the 2014 Conference on Research on Adaptive and Convergent Systems, pp. 46–51 (2014)
31. Veena, K., Manjula Shenoy, K., Ajitha Shenoy, K.: Performance comparison of machine learning classification algorithms. In: Advances in Computing and Data Sciences: Second International Conference, ICACDS 2018, Dehradun, India, April 20-21, 2018, Revised Selected Papers, Part II 2, pp. 489–497. Springer (2018)
32. Wolsing, K., Thiemt, L., Sloun, C.v., Wagner, E., Wehrle, K., Henze, M.: Can industrial intrusion detection be simple? In: European Symposium on Research in Computer Security, pp. 574–594. Springer (2022)
33. Yu, B., Pan, J., Hu, J., Nascimento, A., De Cock, M.: Character level based detection of DGA domain names. In: 2018 International Joint Conference on Neural Networks (IJCNN), pp. 1–8. IEEE (2018)
34. Yun-tao, Z., Ling, G., Yong-cheng, W.: An improved TF-IDF approach for text classification. J. Zhejiang Univ.-Sci. A **6**(1), 49–55 (2005)
35. Zhang, Z., Al Hamadi, H., Damiani, E., Yeun, C.Y., Taher, F.: Explainable artificial intelligence applications in cyber security: state-of-the-art in research. IEEE Access **10**, 93104–93139 (2022)

Locally Verifiable Signature Schemes: A Study of Aggregate and Multi-signatures

Ahmet Ramazan Ağırtaş[1,2], Neslihan Yaman Gökce[2(✉)], and Oğuz Yayla[2]

[1] Nethermind Research, London, UK
ahmet@nethermind.io
[2] Institute of Applied Mathematics, Middle East Technical University, Ankara, Turkey
{neslihan.yaman,oguz}@metu.edu.tr

Abstract. An aggregate signature scheme is a digital signature protocol that enables the aggregation of multiple signatures. Given n signatures on n distinct messages from n different users, it is possible to combine all these signatures into a single, concise signature. This single signature, along with the n original messages, convinces the verifier that the n users indeed signed their respective n original messages. However, the verifier must have access to all the original messages to perform the verification, highlighting a potential limitation in terms of accessibility and efficiency. Goyal and Vaikuntanathan introduced the concept of local verification, allowing the verifier to determine if a specific message m is part of the aggregated signature by only accessing the message m. In this paper, we extend the single-signer locally verifiable aggregate signature scheme initially proposed by Goyal and Vaikuntanathan, adapting it to a multi-signer context. Our generalization allows the verifier to validate multiple signatures simultaneously using an auxiliary value generated by the LocalOpen algorithm, thereby enhancing verification efficiency. By this generalization, we reduced the number of pairing operations in local verification by a factor of 1/3. Furthermore, we integrate this approach into the multi-signature scheme proposed by Boneh, Drijvers, and Neven, demonstrating its broader applicability and potential benefits in complex cryptographic systems. This integration results in a novel locally verifiable multi-signature scheme.

Keywords: aggregate signatures · locally verifiable signatures · multi-signatures

1 Introduction

A digital signature is a cryptographic technique crucial for ensuring the integrity and authenticity of electronic data, making it indispensable for secure transactions over open networks.

L. Morogan et al. (Eds.): SecITC 2024, LNCS 15595, pp. 36–56, 2025.
https://doi.org/10.1007/978-3-031-87760-5_4

A multi-signature scheme [2,3,10] is a protocol that allows multiple signers to collaboratively produce a compact signature σ for a message m, ensuring that a verifier can be convinced that all participating parties have signed the same m. In particular, the verification process involves the input of the n public keys, the message m, and the resulting multi-signature σ. At the end of the verification, σ can be rejected or accepted. This collaborative approach significantly supports security by distributing trust across several parties, thus mitigating the risks associated with key compromise or unauthorized access [6]. Multi-signature protocols play a crucial role in numerous applications, such as blockchain transactions, joint bank accounts, and distributed ledger technologies, where collective approval is paramount [15].

The concept of aggregate signatures was introduced by Boneh et al. [11] and has since been extensively studied [1,5,7,12,17,18]. It enables multiple individual signatures to be combined into a single compact signature, regardless of whether the signatures are on the same or different messages and created by different signers. Aggregate signatures provide significant efficiency benefits in systems where multiple signatures need to be verified, such as in blockchain networks, Internet of Things (IoT) applications, and other distributed systems, since computational power, bandwidth, and storage are limited in these environments. Besides that, aggregate signatures not only streamline the verification process but also maintain the same security guarantees as traditional digital signatures, making them an essential tool in modern cryptographic protocols [6]. Recent research on aggregate signatures has focused on enhancing privacy, reducing computational overhead, and adapting to specific application needs such as blockchain and group authentication. These innovations underscore aggregate signatures' flexibility and increasing relevance in advanced cryptographic systems [3,13,22].

The verification process for aggregate signatures requires access to all n messages. Therefore, the cost of the verification process increases linearly with the number of messages. To address this issue, Goyal, Rishab, and Vaikuntanathan [16] proposed the concept of locally verifiable aggregate signatures, which enables efficient verification for only one message instead of the whole message set. They present two constructions for single-signer locally verifiable aggregate signatures: one relying on the RSA assumption [4,19,23] and the other on the bilinear Diffie-Hellman inversion assumption [8,9,20] within the random oracle model.

Locally verifiable signature schemes have not been studied extensively yet since the proposed idea is already new. However, this concept has swiftly inspired considerable research effort. In literature, two notable works based on the local verification concept based on [16] are the works of Duan et al. [14] and Zue et al. [25]. Both works adapt the foundational concepts to address specific challenges in health data verification and sharing.

Locally verifiable signatures allow efficient verification by enabling a verifier to check the presence of a particular message in an aggregate signature without accessing the entire set of messages. There are several important uses for this concept. Certificate transparency logs can store compressed certificates as aggregate signatures. Users can verify the existence of a certificate by downloading a short hint instead of the entire log, reducing storage and computational costs while maintaining security. In blockchain applications, locally verifiable aggregate signatures can aggregate signatures of all transactions from a single payer. This allows users to efficiently prove the existence of a specific transaction with minimal communication. Additionally, it offers privacy benefits by enabling proof of a single transaction without revealing other transactions. On the other hand, in cryptocurrencies, multi-signature schemes allow multiple parties to jointly authorize a transaction. Locally verifiable multi-signatures can make the verification process more efficient by enabling the verification of individual signatures without accessing the entire transaction set.

In this paper, we first generalize the locally verifiable aggregate signature scheme proposed in [16]. It means that first, a hint is generated for any k out of ℓ messages using the local opening function. Then, a verifier can use the generated hint to verify selected k messages at once. Moreover, the multi-message local verification algorithm operates independently of the number of messages ℓ, which is a natural expectation from such an improvement. Secondly, we present a locally verifiable version of the multi-signature scheme proposed in [10]. This time, the localization is performed in the signers domain, instead of the messages domain. Similarly to that of multi-message local verification algorithm, locally verifiable multi-signature algorithm also operates independently of the total number of signers n.

The structure of the paper is as follows. In Sect. 2, we provide a concise overview, including definitions of bilinear pairings, computational problems such as Diffie-Hellman Inversion, Bilinear Diffie-Hellman Inversion, co-CDH problems, the generalized forking lemma, and locally verifiable aggregate signatures. In Sect. 3, we give the formal definition of our first contribution, namely Multi-Message Locally Verifiable Aggregate Signatures (MM-LVAS), and then give the details about the scheme. We also prove its security in the random oracle model. In Sect. 4, we first provide the formal definition of Locally Verifiable Multi-Signatures (LVMS) and then mention the details of the scheme. In the same section, we demonstrate its security in the random oracle model by employing the generalized forking lemma. Finally, the conclusion of our paper is given in Sect. 5.

Note that, throughout this paper, we consider three types of entities: signers, who execute key generation and signing operations; storage servers (or aggregators), who perform aggregation of the signatures and generate the hint; and verifiers, who carry out the verification processes.

2 Preliminaries

In this section, we define the concepts that we utilize in this paper. More precisely, we define bilinear pairings, underlying hard problems, generalized forking lemma, and locally verifiable aggregate signature schemes. In general, we denote the set of all positive integers up to n as $[n] := \{1, \ldots, n\}$. Additionally, the set of all non-negative integers up to n, i.e., $[0, n] := 0 \cup [n]$ is denoted as $[0, n]$.

2.1 Bilinear Pairings

Let $\mathbb{G}_1$ and $\mathbb{G}_2$ be two cyclic additive groups of prime order q and $\mathbb{G}_T$ be a cyclic multiplicative group with the same order. A pairing is a map $e : \mathbb{G}_1 \times \mathbb{G}_2 \to \mathbb{G}_T$ which satisfies the bilinearity and non-degeneracy properties:

- Bilinearity: $e(A^\alpha, B^\beta) = e(A, B)^{\alpha\beta}$ for all $\alpha, \beta \in \mathbb{Z}_q$, $A \in \mathbb{G}_1$ and $B \in \mathbb{G}_2$.
- Non-degeneracy: $e(A, B) \neq 1$ for all $A \in \mathbb{G}_1$ and $B \in \mathbb{G}_2$.

Note that, in general, we can classify pairings into two classes, i.e., symmetric and asymmetric pairings. The above definition belongs to the latter. In this paper, we use both symmetric and asymmetric ones in our constructions. For the symmetric ones, we will not give another definition, yet one can simply consider $\mathbb{G}_1 = \mathbb{G}_2$.

2.2 Computational Problems

Definition 1 (Diffie-Hellman Inversion Problem [8]). *For groups $\mathbb{G} = \langle g \rangle$ and $\mathbb{G}_T$ of order p, let $e : \mathbb{G} \times \mathbb{G} \to \mathbb{G}_T$ be an efficient and non-degenerate bilinear mapping. Let $x \in \mathbb{Z}_p^*$ be a randomly chosen secret and $q \in \mathbb{Z}$ be the hardness parameter of the problem, which is the length of the powers-in-exponent sequence given to the adversary. Given $g, g^x, g^{x^2}, \ldots, g^{x^q} \in \mathbb{G}$, the Diffie-Hellman Inversion (DHI) problem is to compute $g^{1/x} \in \mathbb{G}$.*

Definition 2 (Bilinear Diffie-Hellman Inversion Problem [8]). *For groups $\mathbb{G} = \langle g \rangle$ and $\mathbb{G}_T$ of order p, let $e : \mathbb{G} \times \mathbb{G} \to \mathbb{G}_T$ be an efficient and non-degenerate bilinear mapping. Let $x \in \mathbb{Z}_p^*$ be a randomly chosen secret and $q \in \mathbb{Z}$ be the hardness parameter of the problem, which is the length of the powers-in-exponent sequence given to the adversary. Given $g, g^x, g^{x^2}, \ldots, g^{x^q} \in \mathbb{G}$, the Bilinear Diffie-Hellman Inversion (q-BDHI) problem is to compute $e(g, g)^{1/x} \in \mathbb{G}_T$.*

Definition 3 (Computational co-Diffie-Hellman Problem [10]). *For groups $\mathbb{G}_1 = \langle g_1 \rangle, \mathbb{G}_2 = \langle g_2 \rangle$ of prime order q, define $Adv^{co\text{-}CDH}_{\mathbb{G}_1,\mathbb{G}_2}$ of an adversary $\mathcal{A}$ as*

$$\Pr\left[y = g_1^{\alpha\beta} : (\alpha, \beta) \xleftarrow{\$} \mathbb{Z}_q^2, y \leftarrow \mathcal{A}\left(g_1^\alpha, g_1^\beta, g_2^\beta\right)\right],$$

where the probability is taken over the random choices of $\mathcal{A}$ and the random selection of (α, β). $\mathcal{A}(\tau, \epsilon)$-breaks the co-CDH problem if it runs in time at most τ and has $Adv^{co\text{-}CDH}_{\mathbb{G}_1,\mathbb{G}_2} \geq \epsilon$. co-CDH is (τ, ϵ)-hard if no such adversary exists.

2.3 Generalized Forking Lemma

Pointcheval and Stern initially defined the forking lemma in [21], which has been widely used to establish the security of schemes based on Schnorr signatures within the random-oracle model [24]. Bellare and Neven later generalized this lemma in [6]. Boneh et al. used a further generalization of the forking lemma by Bagherzandi et al. [2] in their security proofs in [10]. In our work, we also utilize this latter generalized forking lemma in the security proofs of our second construction given in Sect. 4.

Let $\mathcal{A}$ be an algorithm interacting with a random oracle $H : \{0,1\}^* \to \mathbb{Z}_q$ and takes in as input. Let $f = (\rho, h_1, \ldots, h_{q_H})$ represent the randomness used during an execution of $\mathcal{A}$. Here, ρ denotes $\mathcal{A}$'s random tape, h_i is the response to $\mathcal{A}$'s i-th query to H, and q_H is the maximum number of random-oracle queries made by $\mathcal{A}$. Let Ω be the space of all randomness vectors like f and let $f|_i = (\rho, h_1, \ldots, h_{i-1})$ for any $i \leq q_H$. We consider an execution of $\mathcal{A}$ taking input in and randomness f, denoted $\mathcal{A}(in, f)$, as successful if it outputs a pair $\left(J, \{out_j\}_{j\in J}\right)$, where J is a multi-set that is a non-empty subset of $\{1, \ldots, q_H\}$ with $|J| = n$, and $(\{out_j\}_{j\in J})$ is a multi-set of side outputs. We say that $\mathcal{A}$ failed if it outputs $J = \emptyset$. Let ϵ be the probability that $\mathcal{A}(in, f)$ is successful for fresh randomness $f \xleftarrow{\$} \Omega$ and for input $in \xleftarrow{\$}$ IG generated by an input generator IG.

Lemma 1 (Generalized Forking Lemma [2]). *Let* IG *be a randomized algorithm generating in. Let $\mathcal{A}$ be a random algorithm running in time τ, making at most q_H random oracle queries that succeeds with probability ϵ. If $q > 8nq_H/\epsilon$, then $\mathcal{GF}_{\mathcal{A}}(in)$ runs in time at most $\tau \cdot 8n^2 q_H/\epsilon \cdot \ln(8n/\epsilon)$ and succeeds with probability at least $\epsilon/8$, where the probability is over the choice of $in \xleftarrow{\$}$* IG *and over the coins of $\mathcal{GF}_{\mathcal{A}}(in)$.*

In the following section, we formally define our first contribution, multi-message locally verifiable aggregate signature schemes, and then dive into the details of our scheme. We also provide its security analysis.

3 Multi-message Locally Verifiable Aggregate Signature Schemes

In [16], the authors proposed a pairing-based locally verifiable aggregate signature scheme which generates an auxiliary value aux for only one message using LocalOpen algorithm. Consequently, the local verification algorithm verifies whether the aggregated signature $\hat{\sigma}$ contains a signature for that single message m corresponding to aux. In this section, we extend this scheme to a multi-message setting. Next, we give a formal definition and the security definitions of our proposed scheme.

A locally verifiable aggregate signature scheme with multi-message setting is a tuple of seven algorithms, i.e., Setup, Sign, Verify, Aggregate, AggVerify, LocalOpen, LocalAggVerify, which are defined as follows:

Setup$(1^\lambda, 1^B) \to (vk^{local}, vk, sk)$. The setup algorithm takes the security parameter λ as input and outputs vk^{local} and a pair of signing and verification keys (vk, sk).

Sign$(sk, m) \to \sigma$. The signing algorithm takes a signing key sk and a message m as input and outputs a signature σ.

$\textsc{Verify}(vk, m, \sigma) \rightarrow 0/1$. The verification algorithm takes a verification key vk , a message m, and a signature σ as input. It outputs 1 if the signature is valid or 0 otherwise.

$\textsc{Aggregate}(vk, \{m_i, \sigma_i\}_i) \rightarrow \hat{\sigma}/\perp$. The signature aggregation algorithm takes a verification key vk, a sequence of tuples, each containing a message m_i and signature σ_i, and it outputs either an aggregated signature $\hat{\sigma}$ or $\perp$.

$\textsc{AggVerify}(vk, \{m_i\}_i, \hat{\sigma}) \rightarrow 0/1$. The aggregate verify algorithm takes a verification key vk, a sequence of messages m_i, and an aggregated signature $\hat{\sigma}$ as input, and outputs 1 if it is valid or 0 otherwise.

$\textsc{LocalOpen}(vk, \{m_i\}_{i\in[\ell]}, \{j_1, j_2, \ldots, j_k\} \subset [\ell]) \rightarrow aux$. The local opening algorithm takes a verification key vk, a sequence of messages m_i for $i \in [\ell]$, and indexes $\{j_1, j_2, \ldots, j_k\}$ as input. It outputs auxiliary information aux corresponding to the set of messages $\{m_{j_1}, m_{j_2}, \ldots, m_{j_k}\}$.

$\textsc{LocalAggVerify}(\hat{\sigma}, vk^{local}, m_{j_1}, m_{j_2}, \ldots, m_{j_k}, aux) \rightarrow 0/1$. The local aggregate verification algorithm takes an aggregated signature $\hat{\sigma}$, a local verification key vk^{local}, a set of messages $m_{j_1}, m_{j_2}, \ldots, m_{j_k}$, and auxiliary information aux as input. It outputs 1 if the aggregated signature $\hat{\sigma}$ contains the signatures for messages $\{m_{j_1}, m_{j_2}, \ldots, m_{j_k}\}$ under verification key vk, or not.

Now, we define the idea of security for the setup of multi-message locally verifiable aggregate signature scheme.

Definition 4 (Aggregated Unforgeability with Adversarial Opening). *A multi-message locally verifiable aggregate signature scheme MM-LVAS =* (Setup, Sign, Verify, Aggregate, AggVerify, LocalOpen, LocalAggVerify) *is considered a secure aggregate signature scheme against adversarial openings if for every admissible PPT attacker $\mathcal{A}$, there exists a negligible function $negl(\cdot)$ such that for all $\lambda \in \mathbb{N}$, the following holds*

$$\Pr\left[\textsc{LocalAggVerify}\left(\hat{\sigma}^*, vk^{local}, \{m_i^*\}_{i\in[k]}, aux^*\right) = 1 : \begin{array}{l}(vk, sk) \leftarrow \textsc{Setup}\left(1^\lambda\right)\\ \left(\hat{\sigma}^*, aux^*, \{m_i^*\}_{i\in[k]}\right) \leftarrow \mathcal{A}^{\textsc{Sign}(sk,\cdot)}\left(1^\lambda, vk\right)\end{array}\right] \leq negl(\lambda)$$

where $\mathcal{A}$ is admissible if at least one of the challenge messages $\{m_i^*\}_{i\in[k]}$ was not queried by $\mathcal{A}$ to the Sign$(sk, \cdot)$ *oracle.*

Definition 5 (Static Agg. Unforgeability with Adversarial Opening). *Before an adversary $\mathcal{A}$ receives the verification key vk, if it is restricted to provide both the message queries $\{m_i\}_{i\in[q]}$ and the challenge messages $\{m_i^*\}_{i\in[k]}$ at the beginning of the game in Definition 4, then we say that MM-LVAS is statically secure against adversarial openings.*

3.1 Description of Our Scheme

This section presents a generalized version of the single-signer locally verifiable aggregate signatures proposed by Goyal et al. [16]. In this construction, which is based on [9], a verifier can verify k out of ℓ messages at once using a generated common hint. Our construction inherits the following definitions and algorithms from [16].

Injective Message Hashing and Its Variants. An injective mapping from the message space $\mathcal{M}_\lambda = \{0,1\}^\lambda$ to the prime field $\mathbb{Z}_p$ for $p > 2^\lambda$ is used. To achieve static and fully adaptive security, we consider two straightforward mappings, $(HGen, H)$, namely identity mapping and random oracle mapping. The identity mapping employs a hash setup $HGen^{\mathcal{I}}$, which is a trivial algorithm that outputs hk. The corresponding hash function $H^{\mathcal{I}}(hk, m)$ simply returns m, interpreting the output m as a field element of $\mathbb{Z}_p$. For the random oracle mapping, let $\mathcal{H} = \{\mathcal{H}_\lambda\}_\lambda$ denote a family of hash functions where each $h \in \mathcal{H}_\lambda$ processes λ bits of input and produces λ bits of output. The hash setup $HGen^{\mathcal{H}}$ randomly selects a hash function $h \in \mathcal{H}_\lambda$ and outputs $hk = h$. The hash function $H^{\mathcal{H}}(hk = h, m) = h(m)$ maps m to $h(m)$, with the output interpreted as a field element of $\mathbb{Z}_p$.

Aggregation Algorithm. In LVAS [16], an efficient method based on Lagrange's inverse polynomial technique is suggested to aggregate all individual signatures. Similarly, we employed this technique for aggregation in our scheme. For a more detailed understanding of the aggregation technique, readers are encouraged to refer to [16].

Gen Algorithm. *Gen* is a probabilistic polynomial-time (PPT) algorithm that, given a security parameter λ (in unary), generates a λ-bit prime p, an efficient description of groups $\mathbb{G}, \mathbb{G}_T$ of order p, and a generator $g \in \mathbb{G}$. Additionally, it outputs an efficient non-degenerate bilinear map $e : \mathbb{G} \times \mathbb{G} \to \mathbb{G}_T$ such that $e(g,g) \neq 1_{\mathbb{G}_T}$ and for all $a, b \in \mathbb{Z}_p$, $e(g^a, g^b) = e(g,g)^{ab}$.

Next, we give the description of our proposed scheme in detail.

SETUP$(1^\lambda,\ 1^B) \to (vk^{local}, vk, sk)$. The setup process requires input parameters: the security parameter λ and the maximum allowed number of aggregations, denoted as B. It then generates vk^{local}, vk, and sk. It samples the bilinear group elements $\Pi = (p, \mathbb{G}, \mathbb{G}_T, g, e(\cdot,\cdot)) \leftarrow Gen(1^\lambda)$. It also samples a random element $\alpha \leftarrow \mathbb{Z}_p{}^*$. It additionally generates public parameters for message hashing through the process: hk $\leftarrow HGen(1^\lambda)$. The key pair is defined as $vk = (\Pi, hk, g^{\alpha^i}{}_{i\in[B]})$ and $sk = (\Pi, hk, \alpha)$. Furthermore, it establishes the local verification key as $vk^{local} = (\Pi, hk, g^\alpha)$.

SIGN$(sk, m) \to \sigma$. It parses sk as (Π, hk, α) and computes the hash of the message as $x = H(hk, m)$. The signature is then computed as $g^{(\alpha+x)^{-1}}$. Notice that this computation is doable since α is known.

VERIFY$(vk, m, \sigma) \to 0/1$. It parses vk as $(\Pi, hk, g^{\alpha^i}{}_{i\in[B]})$, and computes the hash of the message as $x = H(hk, m)$. It verifies whether $e(\sigma, g^\alpha g^x) = e(g,g)$, where g^α is obtained from the verification key vk^{local}. It outputs 1 if the verification is valid or 0 otherwise.

AGGREGATE$(vk, \{(m_i, \sigma_i)\}_{i\in[\ell]}) \to \hat{\sigma}/\bot$. The aggregation algorithm verifies each input signature σ_i,and returns $\bot$ if any fail. If all verifications pass, the aggregated signature is calculated as $\hat{\sigma} \leftarrow g^{\prod_i (\alpha+x_i)^{-1}}$, where $x_i = H(hk, m_i)$.

AGGVERIFY(vk, $\{m_i\}_{i\in[\ell]}, \hat{\sigma}) \rightarrow 0/1$. The aggregated signature verification algorithm parses the verification key vk as $(\Pi, \text{hk}, g^{\alpha^i}{}_{i\in[B]})$, and calculates the hash sequence as $x_i = H(hk, m_i)$ for all $i \in [\ell]$ where ℓ represents the number of aggregated messages. It symbolically computes the following polynomial P to determine the coefficients $\{\beta_i \in \mathbb{Z}_p\}_{i\in[\ell]\cup\{0\}}$,

$$P_{\{x_i\}_{i\in[\ell]}}(y) = \prod_{i\in[\ell]}(y + x_i) = \sum_{i=0}^{\ell} \beta_i y^i \pmod{p}. \tag{1}$$

Finally, it checks that $\ell \leq B$ and verifies $e\left(\hat{\sigma}, \prod_{i=0}^{\ell}(g^{\alpha^i})^{\beta_i}\right) = e(g, g)$, where g^{α^i} are taken from the verification key vk. If this equation holds, it outputs 1; otherwise, it outputs 0.

LOCALOPEN(vk, $\{m_i\}_{i\in[\ell]}, \{j_1, j_2, \ldots, j_k\} \subset [\ell]) \rightarrow aux$. The local opening algorithm parses vk as $(\Pi, \text{hk}, g^{\alpha^i}{}_{i\in[B]})$ and computes the sequence of hash messages as $x_i = H(hk, m_i)$ for all $i \in [\ell] \setminus \{j_1, j_2, \ldots, j_k\}$. It symbolically computes the following polynomial P to determine the coefficients $\{\tilde{\beta}_i \in \mathbb{Z}_p\}_{i\in[\ell-k]\cup\{0\}}$,

$$P_{\{x_i\}_{i\in[\ell]\setminus\{j_1,j_2,\ldots,j_k\}}}(y) = \prod_{i\in[\ell]\setminus\{j_1,j_2,\ldots,j_k\}}(y + x_i) = \sum_{i=0}^{\ell-k} \tilde{\beta}_i y^i \pmod{p}. \tag{2}$$

It then calculates the auxiliary opening information $aux = (aux_0, aux_1, \ldots, aux_k)$ are computed as

$$aux_0 = \prod_{i=0}^{\ell-k}(g^{\alpha^i})^{\tilde{\beta}_i}, \quad aux_1 = \prod_{i=0}^{\ell-k}(g^{\alpha^{i+1}})^{\tilde{\beta}_i}, \ldots, aux_k = \prod_{i=0}^{\ell-k}(g^{\alpha^{i+k}})^{\tilde{\beta}_i},$$

where g^{α^i} is obtained from the verification key vk. In general, aux_t for $t \in [k] \cup \{0\}$ is computed as

$$aux_t = \prod_{i=0}^{\ell-k}(g^{\alpha^{i+t}})^{\tilde{\beta}_i}.$$

LOCALAGGVERIFY($\hat{\sigma}$, vk^{local}, $m_{j_1}, m_{j_2}, \ldots, m_{j_k}, aux) \rightarrow 0/1$. The local verification algorithm parses the local verification key vk^{local} as $(\Pi, \text{hk}, g^{\alpha})$, as well as the auxiliary opening $aux = (aux_0, aux_1, \ldots, aux_k)$. It computes the message hashes as $x_i = H(hk, m_i)$ for $i \in \{j_1, j_2, \ldots, j_k\}$. It symbolically computes the following polynomial Q to determine the coefficients $\{A_i \in \mathbb{Z}_p\}_{i\in[k]\cup\{0\}}$,

$$Q_{\{x_{j_i}\}_{i\in[k]}}(y) = \prod_{i\in[k]}(y + x_{j_i}) = \sum_{i=0}^{k} A_i y^i \pmod{p}. \tag{3}$$

Finally, it verifies the following $k+1$ conditions:

$$\begin{aligned}
&e(\hat{\sigma}, {aux_0}^{A_0} \cdot {aux_1}^{A_1} \cdots {aux_k}^{A_k}) = e(g, g) \\
&e(g^\alpha, aux_0) = e(g, aux_1) \\
&e(g^\alpha, aux_1) = e(g, aux_2) \\
&\vdots \\
&e(g^\alpha, aux_{k-1}) = e(g, aux_k)
\end{aligned} \tag{4}$$

where g^α is taken from the local verification key vk^{local}. It outputs 1 if it is valid or 0 otherwise.

Remark 1. Note that the verification process only needs g^α while checking the equation, meaning the local verification key vk^{local} would be sufficient.

3.2 Security Analysis

Theorem 1 (Static Unforgeability). *Static unforgeability and static aggregated unforgeability are satisfied by MM-LVAS if the DHI assumption holds and $(HGen, H)$ is an identity hash.*

In addition, static aggregated unforgeability with adversarial openings is satisfied by MM-LVAS if the BDHI assumption holds and $(HGen, H)$ is an identity hash.

Theorem 2 (Full Unforgeability). *MM-LVAS meets full unforgeability and aggregated unforgeability if the DHI assumption holds and $(HGen, H)$ is instantiated in the ROM.*

Also, MM-LVAS meets full aggregated unforgeability with adversarial openings if the BDHI assumption holds and $(HGen, H)$ is instantiated in the ROM.

The proofs of Theorem 1 and Theorem 2 are given in the Appendices A and B, respectively.

In the next section, we first provide the formal definition of locally verifiable multi-signatures. Subsequently, we provide detailed information about the scheme and its security analysis.

4 Locally Verifiable Multi-signatures

In this section, we integrate the notion of local verification into multi-signature schemes. The multi-signature scheme that we choose to modify is the one given in [10]. Given a locally verifiable multi-signature scheme with n signers, the verifier can verify that the signatures of k out of n signers are included in the multi-signature using an auxiliary value aux.

A locally verifiable multi-signature scheme LVMS is a tuple of seven algorithms, i.e., Setup, Sign, Verify, Aggregate, AggVerify, LocalOpen, LocalAggVerify, which are defined as follows:

$\textsc{Setup}(1^\lambda) \to (vk, sk)$. The setup algorithm takes the security parameter λ and generates the bilinear group elements $\Pi = (q, \mathbb{G}_1, \mathbb{G}_2, \mathbb{G}_T, g_1, g_2, e)$. It outputs (sk, vk) for every signer $i \in [n]$.

$\textsc{Sign}(sk, m, VK) \to \sigma$. The signing algorithm takes a secret key sk, a message m, and the set of verification keys $VK = \{vk_1, vk_2, \ldots, vk_n\}$ as input, and it computes the signature σ.

$\textsc{Verify}(\sigma, m, VK) \to 0/1$. The verification algorithm takes a signature σ, a message m, and the set of verification keys VK and outputs 1 if the signature is valid or 0 otherwise.

$\textsc{Aggregate}(\{\sigma_i\}_{i=1}^n, m, VK) \to \hat{\sigma}/\bot$. The aggregation algorithm takes the individual signatures $\{\sigma_i\}_{i=1}^n$, the message m and the set of verification keys VK as input. It outputs either a multi-signature $\hat{\sigma}$ or $\bot$.

$\textsc{AggVerify}(\hat{\sigma}, m, VK) \to 0/1$. The aggregation verification algorithm takes the multi-signature $\hat{\sigma}$, the message m and the set of verification keys VK as input. It outputs 1 if it is valid or 0 otherwise.

$\textsc{LocalOpen}(j_1, j_2, \cdots, j_k, m, VK) \to aux$. The local opening algorithm takes indices $j_1, j_2, \ldots, j_k$, the message m and the set of verification keys VK as input. It outputs an auxiliary value aux corresponding to the signers.

$\textsc{LocalAggVerify}(aux, \{vk_{j_i}\}_{i=1}^k, m, \hat{\sigma}, VK) \to 0/1$. The local verification algorithm takes an auxiliary information aux, verification keys $\{vk_{j_i}\}_{i=1}^k$, the message m, a multi-signature $\hat{\sigma}$ and the entire set of verification keys VK as input. It outputs 1 if it is valid or 0 otherwise.

Definition 6 (Unforgeability of Multisignature with Adversarial Opening). *An adversary $\mathcal{A}$ is called a $(\tau, q_S, q_H, \epsilon)$-forger for locally verifiable multi-signature scheme LVMS = (*$\textsc{Setup}$, $\textsc{Sign}$, $\textsc{Verify}$, $\textsc{Aggregate}$, $\textsc{AggVerify}$, $\textsc{LocalOpen}$, $\textsc{LocalAggVerify}$*) if it runs in time τ, makes q_S signing queries, makes q_H random oracle queries and satisfies*

$$\Pr\left[\textsc{LocalAggVerify}(aux^*, \{vk_i\}_{i\in[k]}, m^*, \hat{\sigma}^*, VK^*) = 1 : \begin{array}{l}(vk, sk) \leftarrow \textsc{Setup}(1^\lambda)\\ (\hat{\sigma}^*, \{vk_i\}_{i\in[k]}, m^*, VK^*, aux^*) \leftarrow \mathcal{A}^{\textsc{Sign}(sk,\cdot)}(1^\lambda, vk)\end{array}\right] \geq \epsilon$$

where $vk \in \{vk_i\}_{i=1}^k \subset VK^*$. If there exist no such an adversary, we say that LVMS is $(\tau, q_S, q_H, \epsilon)$-unforgeable. Note that $\mathcal{A}$ is admissible if m^* was not queried by $\mathcal{A}$ to the $\textsc{Sign}(sk, \cdot)$ *oracle.*

4.1 Description of Our Scheme

In this section, we propose a multi-signature scheme with local verification property, which we refer to as LVMS. Our proposed scheme is derived from the MSP scheme proposed by Boneh, Drijvers, and Neven in [10]. Note that since this scheme is a multi-signature scheme, the number of signed messages is only one. We provide the following scheme for the local verification of k out of n signatures. Assume the hash functions $H_0 : \{0,1\}^* \to \mathbb{G}_1$ and $H_1 : \{0,1\}^* \to \mathbb{Z}_q$. Remember that we refer the set of all verification keys $\{vk_1, vk_2, \ldots, vk_n\}$ as VK.

SETUP(1^λ) $\rightarrow$ (vk_i, sk_i). The setup algorithm samples the bilinear group elements $\Pi = (q, \mathbb{G}_1, \mathbb{G}_2, \mathbb{G}_T, g_1, g_2, e)$. It also generates secret keys randomly such that $sk_i \xleftarrow{\$} \mathbb{Z}_q$, computes $vk_i \leftarrow {g_2}^{sk_i}$ and outputs (sk_i, vk_i) for each signer i.

SIGN$(sk_i, m, VK) \rightarrow \sigma_i$. The signing algorithm computes $\sigma_i \leftarrow H_0(m)^{a_i \cdot sk_i}$, where $a_i \leftarrow H_1(vk_i, VK)$.

VERIFY$(\sigma_i, m, vk_i, VK) \rightarrow 0/1$. The verification algorithm verifies whether the following equation holds or not and outputs 1 if it is valid or 0 otherwise.

$$e(\sigma_i, g_2) \stackrel{?}{=} e(H_0(m), {vk_i}^{a_i})$$

AGGREGATE$(\{\sigma_i\}_{i=1}^n, m, VK) \rightarrow \hat{\sigma}/\bot$. The aggregation algorithm firstly verifies all the input signatures σ_i, and it returns $\bot$ if any fail. Otherwise, it computes the multi-signature as follows:

$$\hat{\sigma} \leftarrow \prod_{i=1}^{n} \sigma_i$$

AGGVERIFY$(\hat{\sigma}, m, VK) \rightarrow 0/1$. The aggregate verification algorithm checks the following equality and outputs 1 if it is valid or 0 otherwise.

$$e(\hat{\sigma}, g_2) \stackrel{?}{=} e\Big(H_0(m), \prod_{i=1}^{n} vk_i^{a_i}\Big)$$

LOCALOPEN$(j_1, j_2, \cdots, j_k, m, VK) \rightarrow aux$. The local opening algorithm takes indices $\{j_i\}_{i=1}^k \subset [n]$, the message m and all verification keys. It outputs an auxiliary value aux corresponding to the signers in the set $\{j_i\}_{i=1}^k$.

$$aux = e\Big(H_0(m), \prod_{\substack{i=1,\\ i \neq j_1, j_2, \ldots, j_k}}^{n} vk_i^{a_i}\Big)$$

LOCALAGGVERIFY$(aux, \{vk_{j_i}\}_{i=1}^k, m, \hat{\sigma}, VK) \rightarrow 0/1$. The local verification function takes an auxiliary information aux, verification keys $\{vk_{j_i}\}_{i=1}^k$, the message m and a multi-signature $\hat{\sigma}$ as input. It then checks the following equation and outputs 1 if it is valid or 0 otherwise.

$$e(\hat{\sigma}, g_2) \stackrel{?}{=} aux \cdot e\Big(H_0(m), \prod_{i=1}^{k} vk_{j_i}^{a_{j_i}}\Big)$$

4.2 Security Analysis

Theorem 3. *LVMS is an unforgeable multi-signature scheme under the computational co-Diffie-Hellman problem in the random-oracle model. More precisely, LVMS is $(\tau, q_S, q_H, \epsilon)$-unforgeable in the random-oracle model if $q > 8q_H/\epsilon$ and if co-CDH is $((\tau + q_H \cdot \tau_{\exp_1} + q_S \cdot \tau_{exp_1}) \cdot 8q_H^2/\epsilon \cdot \ln(8q_H/\epsilon), \epsilon/(8q_H))$-hard, where*

l is the maximum number of signers involved in a single multi-signature, $\tau_{\exp_1}$ and $\tau_{\exp_2}$ denote the time required to compute exponentiations in $\mathbb{G}_1$ and $\mathbb{G}_2$, respectively, and $\tau_{\exp_1^i}$ and $\tau_{\exp_2^i}$ denote the time required to compute i-multi-exponentiations in $\mathbb{G}_1$ and $\mathbb{G}_2$, respectively.

The proof of Theorem 3 is given in Appendix C.

4.3 Cost Analysis

In this section, we present a comparative analysis of our proposed algorithms against the locally verifiable aggregate signature scheme [16] and the multi-signature scheme with key aggregation [10], which are shown in Tables 1 and 2, respectively. Our analysis includes the number of operations required in each phase of the algorithms. Note that the numbers in these tables do not include field element operations, as these operations are dominated by group operations.

Table 1. Comparative Cost Analysis: LVAS vs MM-LVAS

Phases	LVAS [16]	MM-LVAS
Setup	ℓ $\text{Exp}_\mathbb{G}$	ℓ $\text{Exp}_\mathbb{G}$
Sign	1 Hash 1 $\text{Exp}_\mathbb{G}$	1 Hash 1 $\text{Exp}_\mathbb{G}$
Verify	1 Hash 1 $\text{Mul}_\mathbb{G}$ 1 $\text{Exp}_\mathbb{G}$ 1 pairing	1 Hash 1 $\text{Mul}_\mathbb{G}$ 1 $\text{Exp}_\mathbb{G}$ 1 pairing
Aggregate	2ℓ Hashes 1 $\text{Inv}_\mathbb{G}$ 2ℓ $\text{Exp}_\mathbb{G}$ $(2\ell-1)$ $\text{Mul}_\mathbb{G}$ ℓ pairings	2ℓ Hashes 1 $\text{Inv}_\mathbb{G}$ 2ℓ $\text{Exp}_\mathbb{G}$ $(2\ell-1)$ $\text{Mul}_\mathbb{G}$ ℓ pairings
Agg. Signature Verification	ℓ Hashes $(\ell+1)$ $\text{Exp}_\mathbb{G}$ 1 pairing	ℓ Hashes $(\ell+1)$ $\text{Exp}_\mathbb{G}$ 1 pairing
Local Opening	$(\ell-1)$ Hashes 2ℓ $\text{Exp}_\mathbb{G}$ $2(\ell-1)$ $\text{Mul}_\mathbb{G}$	$(\ell-k)$ Hashes $(k+1)(\ell-k+1)$ $\text{Exp}_\mathbb{G}$ $(k+1)(\ell-k)$ $\text{Mul}_\mathbb{G}$
Local Verification	1 Hash 1 $\text{Mul}_\mathbb{G}$ 1 $\text{Exp}_\mathbb{G}$ 3 pairings	k Hashes $(k+1)$ $\text{Exp}_\mathbb{G}$ k $\text{Mul}_\mathbb{G}$ $(2k+1)$ pairings

$\text{Mul}_\mathbb{G}$, $\text{Exp}_\mathbb{G}$ denote multiplication and exponentiation in group $\mathbb{G}$, respectively.
ℓ, k denote number of all messages and number of messages to be verified, respectively.

Table 2. Comparative Cost Analysis: MSP vs LVMS

Phases	MSP [10]	LVMS
Key Generation	1 $\mathrm{Exp}_{\mathbb{G}_2}$	1 $\mathrm{Exp}_{\mathbb{G}_2}$
Key Aggregation	n Hashes (H_1) n $\mathrm{Exp}_{\mathbb{G}_2}$ $(n-1)$ $\mathrm{Mul}_{\mathbb{G}_2}$	none
Sign (Comp. of individual signatures)	1 Hash (H_0) 1 Hash (H_1) 1 $\mathrm{Exp}_{\mathbb{G}_1}$	1 Hash (H_0) 1 Hash (H_1) 1 $\mathrm{Exp}_{\mathbb{G}_1}$
Sign (Comp. of multi-signature)	$(n-1)$ $\mathrm{Mul}_{\mathbb{G}_1}$	$(n-1)$ $\mathrm{Mul}_{\mathbb{G}_1}$
Verify	none	1 $\mathrm{Exp}_{\mathbb{G}_2}$ 1 Hash (H_0) 1 Hash (H_1) 2 pairings
Multisignature/Aggregate Signature Verification	1 Hash (H_0) 2 pairings	n $\mathrm{Exp}_{\mathbb{G}_2}$ $(n-1)$ $\mathrm{Mul}_{\mathbb{G}_2}$ 1 Hash (H_1) 1 Hash (H_0) 2 pairings
Local Opening	none	$(n-k)$ $\mathrm{Exp}_{\mathbb{G}_2}$ $(n-k-1)$ $\mathrm{Mul}_{\mathbb{G}_2}$ 1 Hash (H_1) 1 Hash (H_0) 1 pairing
Local Verification	none	k $\mathrm{Exp}_{\mathbb{G}_2}$ $(k-1)$ $\mathrm{Mul}_{\mathbb{G}_2}$ 1 $\mathrm{Mul}_{\mathbb{G}_T}$ 1 Hash (H_1) 1 Hash (H_0) 2 pairings

$\mathrm{Exp}_{\mathbb{G}_i}$ Exponentiation in group $\mathbb{G}_i$ for $i \in \{1, 2\}$.
$\mathrm{Mul}_{\mathbb{G}_i}$ Multiplication in group $\mathbb{G}_i$ for $i \in \{1, 2, T\}$.
H_0, H_1 Hash functions are as in the schemes.

As can be seen from Table 1, the cost difference between the two algorithms primarily arises in the local opening and local verification phases. This difference is due to MM-LVAS's ability, unlike LVAS, to perform local verification for k distinct messages at once. When local verification is carried out for k messages using the LVAS algorithm, $3k$ pairing operations are required in the local verification phase. In contrast, the same verification can be completed using MM-LVAS with $2k+1$ pairing operations.

As evidenced by the "none" entries in certain cells of Table 2, LVMS and MSP [10] do not incorporate the same set of algorithms. Notably, we did not designate an entity responsible for the key aggregation process in LVMS. If key aggregation were assigned to a specific party or one of the signers, a reduction in the total computational cost could be expected. As a result, adding local verification property to MSP scheme required additional algorithms, which, naturally, introduced extra cost to the overall scheme.

5 Conclusion

In this work, we first propose a multi-message locally verifiable aggregate signature scheme, which builds upon and generalizes the scheme proposed in [16]. With the locality property, the local opening function generates an auxiliary value corresponding to a subset of messages. This allows a verifier to determine if the final aggregated signature includes the signatures of these messages using a single auxiliary value. This eliminates the need for the verifier to access to all messages during the verification phase, thereby significantly enhancing the efficiency of the verification process by introducing only the auxiliary value. With this generalization, we reduced the number of pairing operations required for local verification by one-third. Additionally, we present a locally verifiable multi-signature scheme, which is based on the work in [10]. In this context, the local opening function produces an auxiliary value for specific signers. This allows a verifier to efficiently verify which signer's/signers' signatures are included in the multi-signature. Note that as the number of signatures to be verified increases, the verification phase operates more efficiently in both schemes.

Future research could extend the concept of local verification to various other signature schemes, potentially discovering new methods to further improve the efficiency of the verification process.

Acknowledgments. The second author is partially supported by the Scientific and Technological Research Council of Turkey (TÜBİTAK) 2211-A graduate scholarship programs.

Disclosure of Funding. The authors have no competing interests to declare that are relevant to the content of this article.

A Proof of Theorem 1

Proof. Note that aggregated unforgeability is more general than regular unforgeability, so here we consider the proof of aggregated unforgeability for our scheme. However, the aggregation technique of our signature scheme is the same as the original scheme in [16]. Since the entire proof is the same, we recommend readers look at that paper to get more detailed information about the proof of this part.

Here, we will show that our signature scheme, which relies on the hardness of BDHI, satisfies aggregated unforgeability with adversarial openings. Assume that there is a PPT adversary $\mathcal{A}$ that breaks aggregated unforgeability with adversarial openings with non-negligible probability ϵ. Based on this, we will construct a PPT adversary $\mathcal{B}$ that breaks the q-BDHI assumption in $\mathbb{G}_T$ with $\epsilon - negl$ probability for some negligible function $negl$.

Since we demonstrate only static security, the adversary $\mathcal{A}$ submits all of its signature queries $Q := \{m_i\}_{i\in[q_s]}$ together with the challenge messages $C := \{m_i^*\}_{i\in[k]}$ at the start of reduction algorithm $\mathcal{B}$. Since $\mathcal{A}$ is admissible, there exists an index $j^* \in [k]$ such that $m_{j^*}^* \in C \setminus Q$. We set $S := Q \cup C \setminus \{m_{j^*}^*\}$. Let B be the aggregation bound. The reduction algorithm $\mathcal{B}$ breaks the q-BDHI assumption in $\mathbb{G}_T$, where the hardness parameter q is such that $q \geq |S| + B$.

The BDHI challenger generates the bilinear group parameter set $\Pi = (p, \mathbb{G}, \mathbb{G}_T, h, e(\cdot,\cdot))$, and a sequence of group elements $\{h_i = h^{a^i}\}_{i=0}^q$ for a randomly selected element $a \leftarrow \mathbb{Z}_p{}^*$ and sends $(\Pi, h_1, \ldots, h_q)$ to $\mathcal{B}$.

Now, $\mathcal{B}$ will compute the signatures of the messages in Q and verification key $vk = \{g_i = g^{\alpha^i}\}_{i=1}^B$ in order to send back to adversary $\mathcal{A}$.

We will first focus on how the verification key is computed by $\mathcal{B}$. The reduction $\mathcal{B}$ sets the signing key $\alpha = a - m_{j^*}^*$ and the base group element $g = h_0^{\delta \prod_{m\in S}(\alpha+m)} = h_0^{\delta \prod_{m\in S}(a-m_{j^*}^*+m)}$ after sampling a random exponent $\delta \in \mathbb{Z}_p^*$. Then, for each $i \in [q]$, we have $g_i = h_0^{\delta(a-m_{j^*}^*)^i \prod_{m\in S}(a-m_{j^*}^*+m)}$. For ease of notation, we will use g, h as g_0, h_0, respectively. In order to compute each $g_j, j \in [B]$, $\mathcal{B}$ needs to define the following set of polynomials.

$$\forall j \in [0, B], \quad P_j(X) = (X - m_{j^*}^*)^j \prod_{m\in S}(X - m_{j^*}^* + m) = \sum_{i=0}^{|S|+j} \beta_j^{(i)} X^i \pmod p$$

Then, $\mathcal{B}$ computes each g_j as shown below:

$$g_j = h^{\delta P_j(a)} = h^{\delta \sum_{i=0}^{|S|+j} \beta_j^{(i)} a^i} = \prod_{i=0}^{|S|+j} h^{\delta \beta_j^{(i)} a^i} = \prod_{i=0}^{|S|+j} h_i^{\delta \beta_j^{(i)}} \pmod p$$

It sets the verification key vk and vk^{local} as $vk = (p, \mathbb{G}, \mathbb{G}_T, g_0, e(\cdot,\cdot), hk = \epsilon, \{g_i\}_{i=1}^B)$ and $\mathrm{vk}^{local} = (p, \mathbb{G}, \mathbb{G}_T, g_0, e(\cdot,\cdot), hk = \epsilon, g_1)$. Note that g_0 is a generator, computed as previously mentioned, different from the one supplied by the BDHI challenger.

Now, $\mathcal{B}$ needs to calculate the signatures of all query messages $m_1, \ldots, m_{q_s}$ as

$$\forall i \in [q_s], \quad \sigma_i = g^{(a-m_{j^*}^*+m_i)^{-1}} = h^{\delta \frac{P_0(a)}{a-m_{j^*}^*+m_i}} = h^{\delta \prod_{m\in S\setminus\{m_i\}}(a-m_{j^*}^*+m)}.$$

Let Q_{-i} be the following polynomial with coefficients $\{\gamma_i^{(j)} \in \mathbb{Z}_p{}^*\}_{j=0}^{|S|-1}$

$$\forall i \in [q_s], \quad Q_{-i}(X) = \prod_{m\in S\setminus\{m_i\}} (X - m_{j^*}^* + m) = \sum_{j=0}^{|S|-1} \gamma_i^{(j)} X^j \pmod p.$$

Then,

$$\sigma_i = h^{\delta Q_{-i}(a)} = h^{\delta \sum_{j=0}^{|S|-1} \gamma_i^{(j)} a^j} = \prod_{j=0}^{|S|-1} h_j^{\delta \gamma_i^{(j)}}.$$

Now, the reduction algorithm $\mathcal{B}$ sends vk and $\{\sigma_i\}_{i\in[q_s]}$ to adversary $\mathcal{A}$. $\mathcal{A}$ then sends its forged signature $\hat{\sigma}^*$ and $aux^* = (aux_0, aux_1, \ldots, aux_k)$. $\mathcal{B}$ then checks if $\hat{\sigma}^*$ is a valid signature by executing the local verification algorithm. It aborts if it is an invalid signature. Otherwise, the next step for $\mathcal{B}$ is to compute $e(h,h)^{\frac{1}{a}}$.

Note that for all $i \in [k], aux_i = aux_0^{\alpha^i}$ from the equation (4). Then, also using the equation (3), we get

$$\prod_{i=0}^{k} aux_i^{A_i} = \prod_{i=0}^{k} aux_0^{A_i \alpha^i} = aux_0^{\sum_{i=0}^{k} A_i \alpha^i} = aux_0^{\prod_{i\in[k]}(\alpha + m_i^*)}.$$

Using the equation above and the first equation of (4), we get

$$e(g,g) = e\left(\widehat{\sigma}^*, aux_0^{\prod_{i\in[k]}(a - m_{j^*}^* + m_i^*)}\right) = e\left(\widehat{\sigma}^*, aux_0^{\prod_{m\in C}(a - m_{j^*}^* + m)}\right).$$

Moreover, we have

$$e(g,g) = e\left(h^{\delta P_0(a)}, h^{\delta P_0(a)}\right) = e\left(h,h\right)^{\delta^2 P_0(a))^2}.$$

Therefore, by merging the previous two equations, we get

$$e(\widehat{\sigma}^*, aux_0) = e(h,h)^{\delta^2 \frac{P_0(a)^2}{\prod_{m\in C}(a - m_{j^*}^* + m)}}.$$

Then, $\mathcal{B}$ computes the polynomial

$$P^*(X) = \frac{P_0(X).P_0(X)}{\prod_{m\in C}(X - m_{j^*}^* + m)} = \frac{\beta_{-1}^*}{X} + \sum_{i=0}^{|S\backslash C|+|S|-1} \beta_i^* X^i \pmod{p}$$

so that $e(\widehat{\sigma}^*, aux_0) = e(h,h)^{\delta^2 P^*(a)}$. As we continue from the previous equation,

$$\begin{aligned}
e(\widehat{\sigma}^*, aux_0) &= e(h,h)^{\delta^2\left(\frac{\beta_{-1}^*}{a} + \sum_{i=0}^{|S\backslash C|+|S|-1} \beta_i^* a^i\right)} \\
&= e(h,h)^{\delta^2 \frac{(\beta_{-1}^*)}{a}} \cdot e(h,h)^{\delta^2 \sum_{i=0}^{|S\backslash C|+|S|-1} \beta_i^* a^i} \\
&= e(h,h)^{\delta^2(\frac{\beta_{-1}^*}{a})} \cdot \prod_{i=0}^{|S\backslash C|+|S|-1} e(h,h)^{\delta^2 \beta_i^* a_i} \\
&= e(h,h)^{\delta^2(\frac{\beta_{-1}^*}{a})} \cdot \prod_{i=0}^{|S\backslash C|+|S|-1} e(h^{a^{\lceil i/2\rceil}}, h^{a^{\lfloor i/2\rfloor}})^{\delta^2 \beta_i^*} \\
&= e(h,h)^{\delta^2(\frac{\beta_{-1}^*}{a})} \cdot \prod_{i=0}^{|S\backslash C|+|S|-1} e(h_{\lceil i/2\rceil}, h_{\lfloor i/2\rfloor})^{\delta^2 \beta_i^*}.
\end{aligned}$$

Thus, the reduction algorithm $\mathcal{B}$ outputs BDHI solution as

$$e(h,h)^{1/a} = \left(e(\widehat{\sigma}^*, aux_0)^{1/\delta^2} \cdot \prod_{i=0}^{|S\setminus C|+|S|-1} e\left(h_{\lceil i/2 \rceil}, h_{\lfloor i/2 \rfloor}\right)^{-\beta_i^*} \right)^{1/\beta_{-1}^*}.$$

As a result, whenever there exists an admissible adversary $\mathcal{A}$, the algorithm $\mathcal{B}$ can break BDHI assumption with $\epsilon - negl$ probability for some negligible function $negl$ for $q \geq |S| + B$. □

B Proof of Theorem 2

As in the previous proof, it will be sufficient to prove the part for adversarial openings.

Proof. We can reduce full aggregated unforgeability with adversarial openings to BDHI in the ROM with some modifications as in the previous proof.

Assume that there is a PPT adversary $\mathcal{A}$ that breaks full unforgeability with adversarial openings with non-negligible probability ϵ. Then, we will construct a PPT adversary $\mathcal{B}$ that breaks q-BDHI assumption in $\mathbb{G}_T$ with $\epsilon/Q^{RO} - negl$ probability for some negligible function $negl$. Here, Q^{RO} denotes the number of queries $\mathcal{A}$ makes to the random oracle. The reduction algorithm $\mathcal{B}$ is explained below. It is constructed similar to that in the proof of Theorem 1, except that it now exploits programmability.

Remember from the previous proof that the set of signature queries and challenge messages are $Q := \{m_i\}_{i \in [q_s]}$ and $C := \{m_i^*\}_{i \in [k]}$, respectively. At the beginning of the game, the adversary $\mathcal{A}$ queries the random oracle for all of the messages in the set $U := Q \cup C$. At the same time, the reduction algorithm $\mathcal{B}$ programs the random oracle, meaning samples the hash values associated with the messages. Now, $\mathcal{B}$ chooses an element $m_{j^*}^*$ such that $j^* \in [k]$ expecting that $m_{j^*}^* \notin Q$ and sets $\alpha = a - h_{m_{j^*}^*}$ implicitly.

The q-BDHI challenger samples the bilinear parameters $\Pi = (p, \mathbb{G}, \mathbb{G}_T, h, e(\cdot,\cdot))$, and a sequence of group elements $\{h_i = h^{a^i}\}_{i=0}^q$ for a randomly selected element $a \leftarrow \mathbb{Z}_p{}^*$ and sends $(\Pi, h_1, \ldots, h_q)$ to $\mathcal{B}$. The reduction algorithm $\mathcal{B}$ computes the verification key vk, computed in the same way as in the previous proof, and then sends it to the adversary $\mathcal{A}$. After that, $\mathcal{A}$ sends the hash values of the signature query set Q, which is named H_Q, to the reduction algorithm $\mathcal{B}$. The reduction algorithm aborts if $h_{m_{j^*}^*} \in H_Q$. Otherwise, $\mathcal{B}$ sends the signatures of queried messages to the adversary $\mathcal{A}$. Similar to the case of vk, $\mathcal{B}$ computes the signatures in an analogous way to the previous proof. The remaining operations are the same as the proof of the Theorem 1. As a result, the probability that $\mathcal{B}$ breaks q-BDHI assumption turns out to be $\epsilon/Q^{RO} - negl$ for some negligible function $negl$. Note that we have $1/Q^{RO}$ factor emerges from the probability of $\mathcal{B}$ guessing $m_{j^*}^*$ correctly. □

C Proof of Theorem 3

Proof. Suppose we have a $(\tau, q_S, q_H, \epsilon)$-forger $\mathcal{F}$ against the LVMS scheme. Consider an input generator IG that generates random tuples $(A, B_1, B_2) = (g_1^\alpha, g_1^\beta, g_2^\beta)$, where $\alpha, \beta \in \mathbb{Z}_q$ are chosen uniformly at random. Finally, consider an algorithm $\mathcal{A}$ that, given the input (A, B_1, B_2) and randomness $f = (\rho, h_1, \ldots, h_{q_S})$, proceeds as follows.

Algorithm $\mathcal{A}$ selects an index $k \in \{1, \ldots, q_H\}$ randomly and executes the forger $\mathcal{F}$ using the input $vk^* \leftarrow B_2$ with random tape ρ. It addresses the i-th H_0 query from $\mathcal{F}$ by randomly sampling $r_i \in \mathbb{Z}_q$ and returning $g_1^{r_i}$ if $i \neq k$. The k-th H_0 query is answered by returning A. Without loss of generality, it is assumed that $\mathcal{F}$ does not repeat any H_0 queries. $\mathcal{A}$ responds to $\mathcal{F}$'s H_1 queries by discriminating them as follows:

1. If this is a query on (vk, VK) with $vk \in VK$ and $vk^* \in VK$, and this is the first such query with VK,
   (a) $\mathcal{A}$ selects a random value for $H_1(vk_j, VK)$ for each $vk_j \neq vk^*$
   (b) $\mathcal{A}$ sets $H_1(vk^*, VK)$ to h_i, where the query is the i-th query of this type
   (c) $\mathcal{A}$ returns $H_1(vk, VK)$.
2. If this is a query on (vk, VK) with $vk \in VK$ and $vk^* \in VK$, and a query with VK has already been made before, $\mathcal{A}$ returns the previously assigned value.
3. For any other kind of queries, $\mathcal{A}$ simply returns a random value in $\mathbb{Z}_q$.

When $\mathcal{F}$ makes a signing query on a message m with signers VK, $\mathcal{A}$ looks up $H_0(m)$. If this is A, then $\mathcal{A}$ aborts with output $(0, \perp)$. Otherwise, it must be of form g_1^r and $\mathcal{A}$ can simulate the honest signer by computing $\sigma \leftarrow B_1^r$.

When $\mathcal{F}$ fails to output a successful forgery, then $\mathcal{A}$ outputs $(0, \perp)$. If $\mathcal{F}$ successfully outputs a forgery for a message m so that $H_0(m) \neq A$, then $\mathcal{A}$ again outputs $(0, \perp)$. Otherwise, $\mathcal{F}$ has output a forgery $(aux, \{vk_i\}_{i=1}^k, m, \hat{\sigma}, VK)$ such that

$$e(\hat{\sigma}, g_2) = aux \cdot e\left(A, \prod_{i=1}^{k} vk_i^{a_i}\right)$$

where $vk^* \in \{vk_i\}_{i=1}^k \subset VK$ and $a_i = H_1(vk_i, VK)$.

Let j_f be the index such that $H_1(vk^*, VK) = h_{j_f}$. Then, $\mathcal{A}$ outputs $(J = \{j_f\}, \{(\hat{\sigma}, VK, aux, h_{j_f})\})$.

The running time of algorithm $\mathcal{A}$ is the running time of algorithm $\mathcal{F}$ plus the additional computations made by $\mathcal{A}$. Let q_H denote the total number of hash queries made by $\mathcal{F}$, including queries to both H_0 and H_1. $\mathcal{A}$ requires a single exponentiation in $\mathbb{G}_1$ to respond to H_0 queries; hence, it requires a maximum of $q_H \cdot \tau_{\text{exp}_1}$ to answer the hash queries. For signing queries with a VK of size at most l, $\mathcal{A}$ computes one exponentiation in $\mathbb{G}_1$, which costs τ_{exp_1}. Therefore, the total signing queries cost is $q_S \cdot \tau_{exp_1}$. As a result, the total runtime of $\mathcal{A}$ is $\tau + q_H \cdot \tau_{\text{exp}_1} + q_S \cdot \tau_{exp_1}$. $\mathcal{A}$'s overall success probability is $\epsilon_{\mathcal{A}} = \epsilon / q_H$, which is the probability that $\mathcal{F}$ succeeds and that $\mathcal{A}$ correctly guessed the hash index of $\mathcal{F}$'s forgery, which occurs with probability at least $1/q_H$.

We prove the theorem by constructing an algorithm $\mathcal{B}$ that solves the co-CDH problem in ($\mathbb{G}_1$,$\mathbb{G}_2$) given an input of a co-CDH instance $(A, B_1, B_2) \in \mathbb{G}_1 \times \mathbb{G}_1 \times \mathbb{G}_2$ and a forger $\mathcal{F}$. Specifically, $\mathcal{B}$ uses the previously mentioned algorithm $\mathcal{A}$ to execute the generalized forking algorithm $\mathcal{GF}_{\mathcal{A}}$ from Lemma 1 on input (A, B_1, B_2). Observe that the co-CDH-instance is distributed identically to the output of IG. If $\mathcal{GF}_{\mathcal{A}}$ outputs $(0, \perp)$, then $\mathcal{B}$ aborts. If $\mathcal{GF}_{\mathcal{A}}$ outputs $(\{j_f\}, \{out\}, \{out'\})$, then $\mathcal{B}$ proceeds as follows. $\mathcal{B}$ parses out as $(\hat{\sigma}, VK, aux, h_{j_f})$ and out' as $(\hat{\sigma}', VK', aux', h'_{j_f})$. Note that out and out' were obtained from two executions of $\mathcal{A}$ with randomness f and f' such that $f|_{j_f} = f'|_{j_f}$ for some integer $j_f \leq q_S$. This means that these executions are identical up to the j_f-th H_1-query of the type (1) that has not been queried before, but they differ at j_f. To be more specific, this indicates that $VK = VK'$ since VK is an argument to this query. Moreover, $aux = aux'$ because all of the values used to compute aux are calculated before the forking point. As a consequence, we get $e(\hat{\sigma}, g_2) = aux \cdot e(A, \prod_{i=1}^{k} vk_i^{a_i})$ and $e(\hat{\sigma}', g_2) = aux \cdot e(A, \prod_{i=1}^{k} vk_i^{a'_i})$. Without loss of generality, we assume that $vk^* = vk_1$. Then, the previous two equations can be written as $e(\hat{\sigma}, g_2) = aux \cdot e(A, (vk^*)^{h_{j_f}} \prod_{i=2}^{k} vk_i^{a_i})$ and $e(\hat{\sigma}', g_2) = aux \cdot e(A, (vk^*)^{h'_{j_f}} \prod_{i=2}^{k} vk_i^{a_i})$, respectively. By getting the ratio of these equations, we obtain $e(\hat{\sigma}/\hat{\sigma}', g_2) = e(A, {B_2}^{h_{j_f} - h'_{j_f}})$. From this, we get $\hat{\sigma}/\hat{\sigma}' = A^{\beta \cdot (h_{j_f} - h'_{j_f})}$. As a result, $\mathcal{B}$ can compute a solution to the co-CDH instance as $(\hat{\sigma}/\hat{\sigma}')^{1/(h_{j_f} - h'_{j_f})} = g_1^{\alpha\beta}$.

Using Lemma 1, we know that if $q > 8q_H/\epsilon$, then $\mathcal{B}$ runs in time at most $(\tau + q_H \cdot \tau_{\exp_1} + q_S \cdot \tau_{exp_1}) \cdot 8q_H^2/\epsilon \cdot \ln(8q_H/\epsilon)$ and succeeds with probability $\epsilon' \geq \epsilon/(8q_H)$. □

References

1. Ahn, J.H., Green, M., Hohenberger, S.: Synchronized aggregate signatures: new definitions, constructions and applications. In: Proceedings of the 17th ACM Conference on Computer and Communications Security, pp. 473–484 (2010)
2. Bagherzandi, A., Cheon, J.-H., Jarecki, S.: Multisignatures secure under the discrete logarithm assumption and a generalized forking lemma. In: Proceedings of the 15th ACM Conference on Computer and Communications Security, pp. 449–458 (2008)
3. Baldimtsi, F., et al.: Subset-optimized bls multi-signature with key aggregation. Cryptology ePrint Archive (2023)
4. Barić, N., Pfitzmann, B.: Collision-free accumulators and fail-stop signature schemes without trees. In: International Conference on the Theory and Applications of Cryptographic Techniques, pp. 480–494. Springer (1997)
5. Bellare, M., Namprempre, C., Neven, G.: Unrestricted aggregate signatures. In: Automata, Languages and Programming: 34th International Colloquium, ICALP 2007, Wrocław, Poland, July 9-13, 2007. Proceedings 34, pp. 411–422. Springer (2007)

6. Bellare, M., Neven, G.: Multi-signatures in the plain public-key model and a general forking lemma. In: Proceedings of the 13th ACM Conference on Computer and Communications Security, pp. 390–399 (2006)
7. Boldyreva, A., Gentry, C., O'Neill, A., Yum, D.-H.: Ordered multisignatures and identity-based sequential aggregate signatures, with applications to secure routing. In: Proceedings of the 14th ACM Conference on Computer and Communications Security, pp. 276–285 (2007)
8. Boneh, D., Boyen, X.: Secure identity based encryption without random oracles. In: Annual International Cryptology Conference, pp. 443–459. Springer (2004)
9. Boneh, D., Boyen, X.: Short signatures without random oracles. In: International Conference on the Theory and Applications of Cryptographic Techniques, pp. 56–73. Springer (2004)
10. Boneh, D., Drijvers, M., Neven, G.: Compact multi-signatures for smaller blockchains. In: International Conference on the Theory and Application of Cryptology and Information Security, pp. 435–464. Springer (2018)
11. Boneh, D., Gentry, C., Lynn, B., Shacham, H.: Aggregate and verifiably encrypted signatures from bilinear maps. In: Annual International Conference on the Theory and Applications of Cryptographic Techniques, pp. 416–432. Springer (2003)
12. Boneh, D., Gentry, C., Lynn, B., Shacham, H.: A survey of two signature aggregation techniques (2003)
13. Brodsky, M.F., Choudhuri, A.R., Jain, A., Paneth, O.: Monotone-policy aggregate signatures. In: Annual International Conference on the Theory and Applications of Cryptographic Techniques, pp. 168–195. Springer (2024)
14. Duan, R., Song, Y., Gan, X.: Locally verifiable aggregate signature scheme for health monitoring systems. In: International Conference on Computer Engineering and Networks, pp. 1–10. Springer (2023)
15. Gennaro, R., Goldfeder, S., Narayanan, A.: Threshold-optimal DSA/ECDSA signatures and an application to bitcoin wallet security. In: Applied Cryptography and Network Security: 14th International Conference, ACNS 2016, Guildford, UK, June 19-22, 2016. Proceedings 14, pp. 156–174. Springer (2016)
16. Goyal, R., Vaikuntanathan, V.: Locally verifiable signature and key aggregation. In: Annual International Cryptology Conference, pp. 761–791. Springer (2022)
17. Lu, S., Ostrovsky, R., Sahai, A., Shacham, H., Waters, B.: Sequential aggregate signatures and multisignatures without random oracles. In: Advances in Cryptology-EUROCRYPT 2006: 24th Annual International Conference on the Theory and Applications of Cryptographic Techniques, St. Petersburg, Russia, May 28-June 1, 2006. Proceedings 25, pp. 465–485. Springer (2006)
18. Ma, D., Tsudik, G.: Forward-secure sequential aggregate authentication. In: 2007 IEEE Symposium on Security and Privacy (SP'07), pp. 86–91. IEEE (2007)
19. Micali, S., Rabin, M., Vadhan, S.: Verifiable random functions. In: 40th Annual Symposium on Foundations of Computer Science (cat. No. 99CB37039), pp. 120–130. IEEE (1999)
20. Mitsunari, S., Sakai, R., Kasahara, M.: A new traitor tracing. IEICE Trans. Fundam. Electron. Commun. Comput. Sci. **85**(2), 481–484 (2002)
21. Pointcheval, D., Stern, J.: Security arguments for digital signatures and blind signatures. J. Cryptol. **13**, 361–396 (2000)
22. Qiu, T., Tang, Q.: Predicate aggregate signatures and applications. Cryptology ePrint Archive, Paper 2023/1694 (2023). https://eprint.iacr.org/2023/1694

23. Rivest, R.L., Shamir, A., Adleman, L.: A method for obtaining digital signatures and public-key cryptosystems. Commun. ACM **21**(2), 120–126 (1978)
24. Schnorr, C.-P.: Efficient signature generation by smart cards. J. Cryptol. **4**, 161–174 (1991)
25. Zhu, L., Xie, Y., Zhou, Y., Fan, Q., Zhang, C., Liu, X.: Enabling efficient and secure health data sharing for healthcare IoT systems. Futur. Gener. Comput. Syst. **149**, 304–316 (2023)

Towards Intelligent User Enumeration Based Profiling

Mario Bischof(✉) and Edy Portmann

Human-IST Institute, University of Fribourg, Fribourg, Switzerland
{mario.bischof,edy.portmann}@unifr.ch

Abstract. In contrast to the rising supremacy of hyperscaler artificial intelligence, it becomes a particularly interesting question what attackers with limited computational resources are capable of by utilizing machine learning on a smaller scale. A very inconspicuous but yet powerful vulnerability to leverage for profiling is user enumeration, i.e., knowing if a user is registered on an application. Its risk is often intentionally accepted in favor of usability. It can typically be exploited via public components such as login forms, which are accessible without special restrictions. In this paper, we present a novel approach for profiling not documented in literature. By training models on a small dataset based on user enumeration data from 396 test subjects and 111 web applications we are able to predict individual attributes about an unknown person behind an arbitrary e-mail address. For this, we developed AccountGrabber, a dedicated user enumeration tool and a mean-based prediction algorithm, which can generate fuzzy output values reflecting possible nuances of human perception. To support the feasibility of our idea, we compare its performance to 9 classical classification algorithms and conclude with suggestions for future improvements to more complex profiling.

Keywords: profiling · user enumeration · open source intelligence · offensive security · machine learning

1 Introduction

Continuously researching new attacks criminals may use to their advantage is a critical skill to anticipate developments in the security industry. It allows to forecast future threats and it serves as a mechanism to push the innovation of defenses. Security improving activities which are conducted in the role of an active attacker are called offensive security [1].

A particular sub-field of the offensive side of cyber security is open source intelligence (OSINT) [2,3]. It means gaining relevant information from publicly available data, a technique heavily used by all kinds of threat actors. Common sources for OSINT are social media platforms or online communities in general, where lots of personal information is shared. But OSINT can also be gained from metadata, which is more subtle, such as usage time of day of an application.

L. Morogan et al. (Eds.): SecITC 2024, LNCS 15595, pp. 57–69, 2025.
https://doi.org/10.1007/978-3-031-87760-5_5

One vulnerability which provides specifically interesting metadata is user enumeration. User enumeration means to find out, if a user (username, e-mail or phone number) is registered on an application. It is an old and well known flaw, which usually receives moderate security ratings during audits. Old vulnerabilities tend to become neglected over time and thus become understudied. At the same time, they may hold fresh potential to be exploited in new ways, because technological capabilities have evolved in the meantime. One such recent evolution is artificial intelligence, which experts have anticipated to have a heavy impact on changing the threat landscape [3–5].

In this paper, we present a novel approach for profiling by exploring machine learning on user enumeration data. To our knowledge, no similar method is currently known in literature. We are able to predict a specific personal attribute of an unknown individual behind an arbitrary e-mail address. We introduce our method on the example of gender identification, which was studied in the past using large corpuses of human language [6,7], but has never been done on user enumeration data, which is far more sparse by nature.

Methodology. For this project, we followed the design science research methodology [8] which creates new knowledge through the design of novel/innovative artifacts (tooling, dataset and algorithm) and the analysis of the artifact's use and/or performance with reflection and abstraction (testing and evaluation).

Contributions. The contributions of this paper are summarized as follows:

- We implemented and introduce the *user enumeration tool AccountGrabber*. Based on it we built a user enumeration *dataset*. We provide *analyses* of vulnerability types encountered during data acquisition and the dataset.
- We propose, implement and evaluate a *mean membership prediction algorithm* to predict specific attributes of a person behind an unknown e-mail address. We further provide an *optimized version* using weights with improved performance. The algorithm also has the ability to produce fuzzy output values reflecting more human-like perceptions.
- We give a *comparison* of our approach by implementing and evaluating the same problem with 9 classical machine learning algorithms.

Paper Outline. Section 2 provides a conceptual overview of the project. The user enumeration, our tooling, the choice of web applications and the observed vulnerability types are explained in Sect. 3. Data sources used for our study are elaborated in Sect. 4. The dataset for training/testing is discussed in Sect. 5. Our prediction algorithm and the evaluation and comparison to classical machine learning is documented in Sect. 6. The paper closes in Sect. 7 with final conclusions and thoughts on how to improve and expand the idea in the future.

2 High-Level Concept

The overview of the concept of our solution is illustrated in Fig. 1. From a high level perspective, the process is divided in a data acquisition and learning part and a classification part. The data acquisition and learning part is responsible for the collection, selection and reduction of the data as well as the training and optimization of the models. The classification part takes care of testing, evaluating and executing the actual use case of the prediction. In this paper, we focus on a single binary classification problem to predict one attribute of a specific person behind a user enumeration pattern (gender identification), but we expect this idea can be expanded arbitrarily to perform more complex predictions, depending on the amount, richness and quality of the data available.

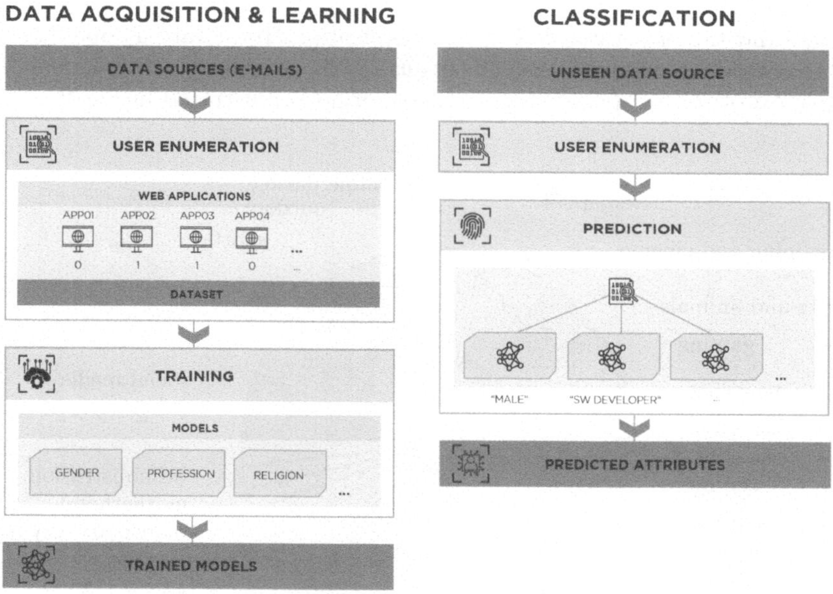

Fig. 1. Conceptual overview.

3 User Enumeration

3.1 The AccountGrabber Tool

To perform user enumeration we used a self-developed python-based tool called *AccountGrabber*. It sends HTTP requests using the requests library [9]. In some more complex cases, the Selenium web-driver was used [10]. The development was done incrementally, adding a web application using the following steps:

1. Identify all functions of an application that take an e-mail address as input
2. Ensure that these functions have deterministic and different responses if an existing or an unknown e-mail is supplied
3. Choose the function easiest to abuse (e.g., single request-response)
4. Implement and test the user enumeration based on a registered and an unknown e-mail address

We kept the amount of HTTP requests and its sizes as minimal as possible to save lines of code. Content like body parameters, cookies, headers, etc. which is not explicitly necessary was omitted by trimming each request just as much so that the server backend will still accept it. To detect if an e-mail is registered on a platform, the corresponding response is parsed via regular expressions for the occurrence of a specific pattern, header or return code, indicating the existence of the account.

3.2 Targeted Platforms

Our tool did target a total of 111 web applications from various domains. We tried to cover as many different fields of interest as possible to achieve a balanced picture. An overview of the category distribution is illustrated in Fig. 2.

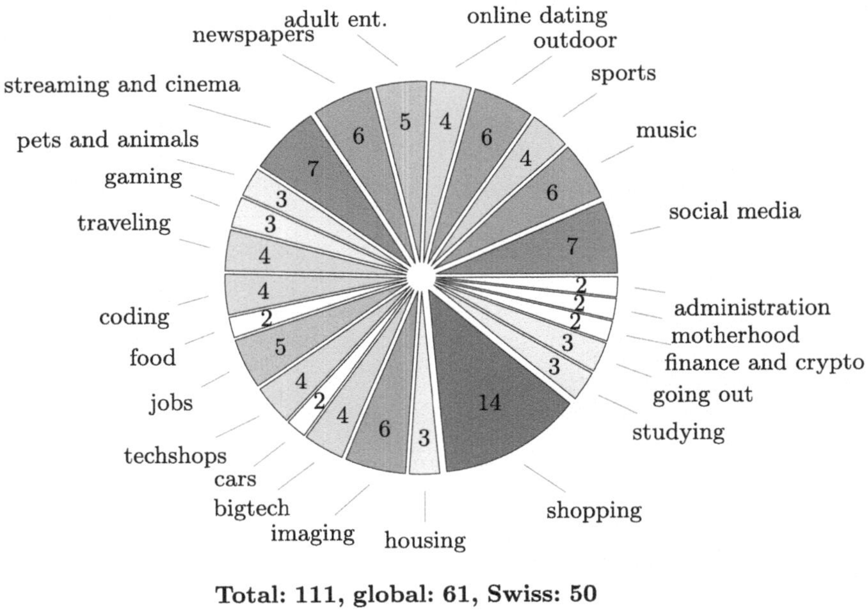

Fig. 2. Categorization of targeted web applications.

One of the main criteria in choosing the platforms was whether the applications were essentially vulnerable to user enumeration. E.g., web services for health insurance or online gambling did show a high level of security and thus were not vulnerable, so none of them could be used. Since we did specifically aim at the Swiss audience, 50 of the evaluated web applications are Swiss based services and 61 are global applications. Although the tool works for arbitrary e-mails, it will provide most meaningful results if used on a Swiss person's e-mail.

3.3 Types of User Enumeration Vulnerabilities

There are multiple ways user enumeration can be done. In essence, some functionality on the targeted platform has to be found, which does leak if a provided e-mail address is already known. It was a crucial requirement for our tooling, that the owner of an e-mail address is not accidentally informed, e.g., by receiving mail-notifications for unsuccessful logins or forgotten password requests. In the worst case, a new user account for a not yet registered e-mail is accidentally created by wrongfully handling registration forms. This would also falsify future results, because the attack itself would create accounts that have not existed before. All procedures developed for this tooling ensure that no accidental notifications, account creations or lockouts do occur.

The following provides an overview of vulnerability types we observed with its number of occurrences. It also includes the number of applications, which required the dedicated handling of cryptographic tokens (CSRF or authentication) or CAPTCHA anti-bot mechanisms. Further, if no plain HTTP implementation was possible due to the complexity of cookie-handling and anti-fraud measures, we reverted to using Selenium in some cases.

API GET (18). This is the simplest method. A single HTTP GET request, which includes the e-mail address as a URL-parameter and returns a response with the information if an account exists or not, e.g., the string 'True'. Often these are single "one-shot" calls to API-endpoints dedicated to verification such as: /ajax-validation/email-address?value=<email>
or: /admin-ajax.php?/action=login_check_email&email='<email>.

API POST (38). The POST variant is similar to GET but requires a specific HTTP POST body content, e.g.,: &check_what=email&email=<email>. This body can often be long and in JSON format, requiring a multitude of attributes.

Login-Form (24). This method abuses the login form. Unlike the prior two one-shot methods, this usually requires more than one request, since a specific sequence of header values and cookies is expected. Typically, a session to the website is necessary and multiple calls need to be sent to gather everything to craft the final login request. HTTP bodies come in classical POST, JSON or also WebKitForm format.

Signup-Form (31). Registration forms can be abused to leak information without actually creating a new user account. This is done by breaking the validation of the input fields, e.g., a form returns all validation errors at once: if an empty password is submitted, the form submission may fail, but it also responds whether a user exists for the provided e-mail address. Many similar situations like this can be observed with varying complexity but the basic principle remains the same. This method typically requires specific cookies/tokens/headers to be present, which are extracted from the initial response loading the form. Similar to the login, this process may require multiple requests to craft the final call.

Tokens (23). Tokens usually authenticate a visitor in the sense that succeeding requests prove they come from the same browser context. E.g., a CSRF token is a random value provided by the server to the client when a site is initially loaded. This value is resubmitted on subsequent calls, enabling the server to verify it is indeed coming from the same browser. Depending on the framework, these tokens have many different names and forms. They can be extracted via regular expressions and included in headers, cookies or GET/POST parameters to create HTTP calls that the backend will accept.

CAPTCHAs (15). Some web applications issue CAPTCHAs to prevent mass submission of online forms. In some cases it was not possible to find a captcha-free function to exploit. However, our tool is able to automatically bypass, i.e., solve simple alpha-numeric CAPTCHAs by using image recognition services [11] such as Amazon Rekognition [12].

Selenium (22). Some web applications require a large amount of cookies to be present in specific chronological order to identify legitimacy. Fraud detection methods often measure the time between requests to identify bots. These situations drastically increase the amount of work required to implement a plain HTTP protocol based method. In such cases, it is easier to use a webdriver like Selenium, which directly instruments the browser to fill in fields, handle cookies and send requests. Since bot preventions may detect the use of standard Selenium, using a modified web-driver to prevent detection [13] is helpful.

Mitigation. Standard mitigation techniques against user enumeration attacks are well known and fairly easy to apply. The main idea is to ensure that all functions/forms, which take an email address, phone number or user name as input must behave exactly identical regardless of the fact that an account exists or not. This must be ensured for any kinds of feedbacks, either directly visible to the enduser in the browser or invisible, e.g., in HTTP headers. Further, even response timing can be used for user enumeration attacks [14], implementing a constant runtime for highly critical functions may provide additional protection.

4 Data Sources

We compiled a list of Swiss e-mail addresses from various public sources, including information dumps and public web scraping. At minimum, the following properties are known: first name, last name, age/date of birth and gender. This list was expanded with additional volunteer entries. The selection of entries to be included was done randomly, independent from specific attribute values. The overall age distribution is illustrated as a dotted gray line in Fig. 3. The highest concentration is somewhere around the age of 40, which seems to be a reasonable peak for a random selection of people able to use the internet.

Since our data sources contained more male than female entries, the selection process ended up with an imbalance of 171 female and 225 male subjects. We can see that the age distributions of both genders are similar, illustrated in Fig. 3 as red and blue lines, again confirming the randomness of the selection. Although the whole dataset consists of only 396 entries, it reflects the average internet users on a small scale.

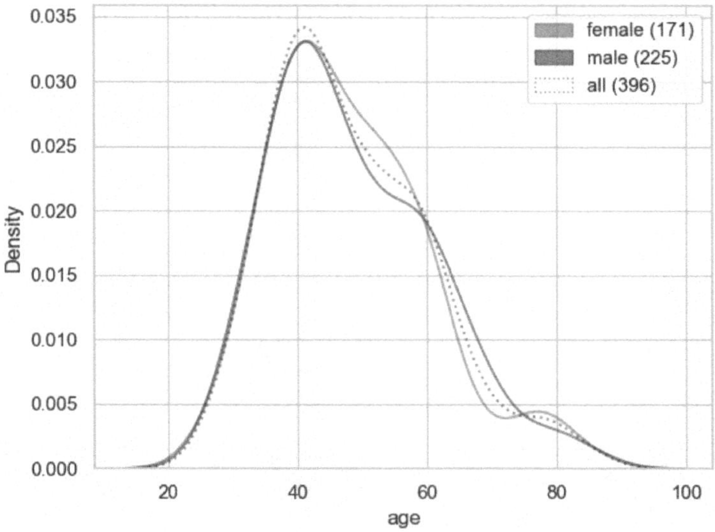

Fig. 3. Age distribution (Color figure online).

5 Dataset

Using the data sources explained in the last section, we created our dataset by running the AccountGrabber tool from Sect. 3. For each test subject, user enumeration on 111 web applications was done. This generated $396 \cdot 111 = 43'956$ result values. The final dataset is structured as illustrated in Fig. 4. Each test subject's results is a separate row spl_i. A column pl_i are the results of a specific platform. The value 1 means that the e-mail address was registered and 0 means it was not. By using this matrix-like representation it is very easy to do calculations over single rows, as our prediction algorithm in Sect. 6 will show. We also include the gender ($gndr$) with 0 representing male and 1 female.

	gndr	pf_1	pf_2	pf_3	pf_4	pf_5	pf_6	pf_7	pf_8	...	pf_{111}
spl_1	0	1	1	0	0	0	1	0	1	...	1
⋮	1	1	0	1	1	0	0	1	0	...	0
⋮	⋮	⋮	⋮	⋮	⋮	⋮	⋮	⋮	⋮	⋮	⋮
spl_{396}	0	0	0	0	1	1	0	0	1	...	0

Fig. 4. Dataset layout.

Trend Observations. Based on the collected data, we can make some interesting observations. Figure 5 shows the user count by gender of some selected platforms.

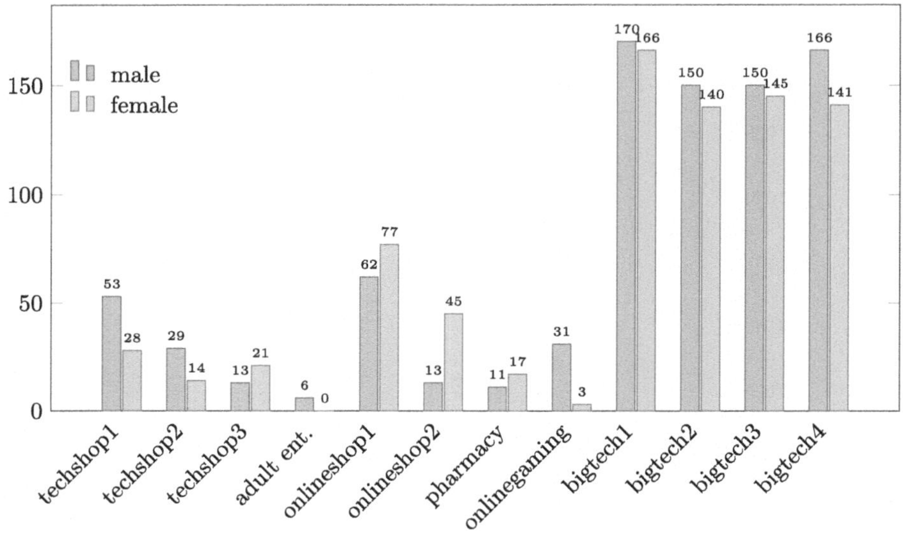

Fig. 5. Gender distribution.

For example, the online gaming or adult entertainment platforms seem to be heavily dominated by users leaning towards the male side. On the contrary, the online pharmacy seems to lean more towards the female side. Similar observations can be done by looking at the average platform ages. E.g., whilst applications for baby accessories, software development, travel tracking or online gaming show a low average age, conservative news platforms or cinema websites show higher average ages. Also, we can discover more by looking at metadata, e.g., the total number of registrants per platform. Services of Big Tech companies such as Google or Apple are widely used by almost everyone, which is clearly reflected in the last four bars of Fig. 5. On the other hand, services such as online gaming have a smaller share of the whole dataset. Thus, it is possible to get a feeling for the magnitude of user bases from these numbers.

Platform Significance. An important additional observation is that there are only 17 web applications out of 111 with more female than male registrants. This suggests that predicting the female side could possibly be harder, since there are less web applications (i.e., features), which are distinctive to identify a user as belonging to this side of the spectrum. This assumption turned out to be true, as discussed in the following section.

6 Profiling

6.1 Attribute Prediction

Since our dataset is quite small, we decided to start by investigating a simple binary classification to prove the feasibility of the idea. The most obvious property we can try to predict would be gender, since it is available for all samples and the set of possible classes is small. However, we plan to further expand on this idea in the future by predicting more complex examples and thus explore more advanced profiling, as concluded in Sect. 7.

6.2 Mean Based Membership Algorithm

Algorithm. To get an intuition if classification will work on our data, we have developed our own algorithm (see Algorithm 1) that uses mean values to make predictions. For the sake of simplicity, we cut down the set of male values to the same size as the female set (171), so that the dataset is balanced. The algorithm iterates through all male and female values in row_m and row_f lines 2 and 3 consecutively. The values being predicted in the current iteration are first removed from the datasets with *drop*() at lines 4 and 5 and inserted back again with *insert*() at lines 15 and 16 after the prediction. This ensures that no information about the instance to be predicted is leaked into the mean values. Mean values for all web platforms for male and female entries are then calculated in line 6. These are between 0 and 1 per platform representing the total proportion percentage of male or female registrants, e.g., a high male value means many male users are on this platform. We subtract the female from the male means in line 6. This way we can identify the tendency of each platform to gravitate to a specific side. The current rows, i.e., prediction candidates, are then multiplied with the means in lines 7 and 8, resulting in a vector containing only the mean values of the platforms the current person is effectively registered on. Since the difference from line 6 is not balanced at 0, we introduce a shift factor for the classification decision in lines 9 and 12, which is subtracted from the sum of all remaining mean values. The shift factor was found using exhaustive search, maximizing the balance of correct predictions for both classes. Algorithm 1 counts male true positives (tp) and false positives (fp), but it will work in the same way for female values.

Optimization. Algorithm 1 can be further optimized by assigning more weight to certain platforms during the classification. We compiled lists of the most impactful platforms for each class by identifying the ones that are heavily used by a certain side, similar to the first eight platforms in Fig. 5. This resulted in 11 female and 49 male weighting platforms. We determined optimal weight factors by exhaustive search, leading to improved classification results. These weights need to be applied prior to running Algorithm 1 as shown in Algorithm 2, once for each class.

Performance. The performance of our algorithm is shown in Table 1. It achieves fairly acceptable success with an f1-score of 0.67 for the standard and 0.70 for the optimized variant. In regard to our dataset being extremely sparse with only 396 samples, it does work surprisingly well and it shows that simple classifications just based on user enumeration is possible. We believe that the precision can be increased if the algorithm is improved, better algorithms are applied or especially if more/richer data is available. However, we suspect Algorithm 1 to not scale specifically well on very large datasets, since it recalculates mean values on a per prediction candidate basis. This could be subject for future optimizations.

Algorithm 1. Mean membership algorithm

```
Require: mvals, fvals
    tp ← 0, fp ← 0, sfactor ← 0.45
for i = 0 to len(mvals) do
    row_m ← mvals.get(i)
    row_f ← fvals.get(i)
    mvals.drop(i)
    fvals.drop(i)
    means ← mvals.means() − fvals.means()
    weights_f ← means ∗ row_f
    weights_m ← means ∗ row_m
    if weights_m.sum() − sfactor ≥ 0 then
        tp ← tp + 1
    end if
    if weights_f.sum() − sfactor ≥ 0 then
        fp ← fp + 1
    end if
    mvals.insert(i + 0.5, row_m)
    fvals.insrt(i + 0.5, row_f)
end for
```

Algorithm 2. Optimization

```
for pf in platforms do
    if pf.name in list then
        pf ← pf ∗ wfactor¹
    end if
end for
```

[1] *male* : 1.12, *female* : 1.2

Table 1. "Algorithm performance"

	normal	optimized
tp	114	119
fp	54	48
precision	0.6786	0.7125
recall	0.6666	0.6959
f1	0.6726	0.7041

Fuzziness. An interesting property of Algorithm 1 is that it is not only able to output the class membership, but it is also able to produce a fuzzy value resembling a membership degree. Its output is a real number between:

$$\{x \mid -1 \geq x \leq 1\} \tag{1}$$

For example, if we would want to predict if someone behind an e-mail address is a sporty person, instead of just grouping the results into sporty or not-sporty, the algorithm can provide a degree of sportiness. This can be leveraged to emulate a non-digital, more analogue human centered perception, allowing to interpret a value in degrees of intensity. Fuzziness becomes even more interesting if the goal is to build more advanced profiles, which combine attributes to predict higher level interests or personality traits such as, e.g., extro- or introversion.

6.3 Classical Machine Learning Algorithms

To compare the performance of Algorithm 1 and assess the mainstream feasibility of the idea, we implemented the given binary classification problem using 9 different machine learning algorithms suitable for the task using the scikit-learn library [15]. The results are listed in Table 2. It lists the performance of two classes with 0 representing male and 1 female. Optimal hyperparameters were determined by either using gridsearch or a manual exhaustive search. Our complete dataset as described in Sect. 5 was randomly split into $\frac{1}{3}$ test set and $\frac{2}{3}$ training set using a fixed seed to compare the performances on the same test/-training data selection. Table 2 also states if the training data was scaled[s] or not, whichever yielded better performance. For algorithms not producing a constant output, i.e., slight variations each run, results are averaged over 20 executions.

Table 2. Overview of evaluated algorithms.

algorithm	class	prec.	recall	f1	hyperparameters
random forest[s]	0	0.75	0.70	0.73	`n_estimators=1400`
	1	0.52	0.58	0.54	`min_samples_split=5`
					`min_samples_leaf=1`
					`max_features='sqrt'`
					`max_depth=80, bootstrap=False`
ANN[s]	0	0.72	0.65	0.68	`batch_size=5`
	1	0.46	0.54	0.49	`epochs=100`
SGD[s]	0	0.80	0.59	0.67	`alpha=1.0, loss='log_loss'`
	1	0.50	0.72	0.58	`n_jobs=-1`
logistic regression[s]	0	0.78	0.68	0.72	`solver='lbfgs', penalty='l2'`
	1	0.52	0.64	0.57	`max_iter=1000`
SVC	0	0.83	0.51	0.63	`C=10, degree=1, gamma=0.001`
	1	0.47	0.81	0.60	`kernel='rbf', probability=True`
gaussian	0	0.82	0.43	0.56	`var_smoothing=0.0811...`
	1	0.44	0.83	0.58	
decision tree[s]	0	0.73	0.67	0.70	`max_depth=7`
	1	0.48	0.56	0.51	
perceptron[s]	0	0.74	0.77	0.75	`max_iter=16`
	1	0.54	0.50	0.52	
KNN	0	0.75	0.55	0.63	`n_neighbors=4`
	1	0.44	0.67	0.53	
mean normal	0	0.68	0.67	0.67	
mean optimized	0	0.71	0.70	0.70	

[s] = scaled

6.4 Evaluation

Depending on the algorithm the performance varies significantly. Perceptron, random forest and logistic regression produced the best results with f1-scores ranging from 0.72 to 0.75 for male classification (class 0), resembling a notable improvement over our optimized mean based approach. The performances of Decision tree, artificial neural network (ANN) and stochastic gradient descent (SGD) are almost on par with our algorithm. The support vector classifier (SVC), k-nearest neighbors (KNN) and Gaussian Naive Bayes algorithms did yield worse results despite hyperparameter optimization. Looking at female (class 1), the performance of all algorithms drops. Firstly, this can be attributed to the fact that our dataset contains about one third less female samples than male. Secondly, the number of distinctive features (i.e., web platforms) representing a female user (11) is significantly lower than male (49), as pointed out in Sect. 6.2.

Therefore, this penalty was expected. This could possibly be overcome by enriching the dataset with more distinguishing web applications and more female samples in general. Also, since the total number of samples is 396, we believe the overall performance to greatly improve if more data was used for training. Nonetheless, the evaluation shows that conventional algorithms can offer an additional improvement in terms of precision over Algorithm 1.

7 Conclusions and Future Work

This work showed that predicting attributes of an unknown e-mail owner solely based on user enumeration data can be done and it already works surprisingly well on a small dataset. Therefore, user enumeration poses an increased risk to online privacy in the age of artificial intelligence. If implemented on a larger scale, extensive databases containing detailed information about seemingly anonymous e-mail owners could be created. There are many possible scenarios emerging from this posing different degrees of risk such as deanonymization, targeted phishing campaigns, blackmailing or persecutions based on personal attributes.

Our mean based membership prediction algorithm can compete with conventional machine learning algorithms and its performance is ranked in the upper middle field, with some classical approaches still performing better. An additional strength lies within its ability to provide fuzzy results, emulating the human capability to perceive nuances. This could be particularly promising to create more versatile profiles consisting of combinations of attributes, enabling to resemble higher level profile properties. Since it probably does not scale particularly well on large datasets, its computational performance should be optimized. Alternatively, fuzzyfied classical machine learning algorithms could be studied.

In future developments, we believe it will be possible to predict more complex attributes like political orientation, religion, sportiness, intellect or other, more specific personal interests. A critical bottleneck to overcome is the gathering of enough user enumeration data. One possibility is to develop a free public web service to scale data collection. Further, profiling must also not be limited to the specific use case presented in this paper. Data from many other and possibly more easily accessible sources could be used to craft more comprehensive profiles and improve predictions as part of a bigger framework [16].

Acknowledgments. This work was supported by InfoGuard AG. We thank the whole RedTeam for the continuous support and feedback. We also thank Katrin Schobersteiner, Tobias Oberdoerfer, Nicolas Forster, and Berke Kara for their valuable help.

References

1. Happe, A., Cito, J: Understanding hackers' work: an empirical study of offensive security practitioners. In: Proceedings of the 31st ACM Joint European Software Engineering Conference and Symposium on the Foundations of Software Engineering, pp. 1669–1680 (2023). https://doi.org/10.1145/3611643.3613900

2. Bradbury, D.: In plain view: open source intelligence. Comput. Fraud Secur. **2011**, 5–9 (2011). https://doi.org/10.1016/S1361-3723(11)70039-2
3. Yadav, A., Kumar, A., Singh, V.: Open-source intelligence: a comprehensive review of the current state, applications and future perspectives in cyber security. Artif. Intell. Rev. **56**, 12407–12438 (2023). https://doi.org/10.1007/s10462-023-10454-y
4. Lella, I., Tsekmezoglou, E., Svetozarov Naydenov, R., Ciobanu, C., Malatras, A., Theocharidou, M.: ENISA Threat Landscape 2022, European Union Agency for Cybersecurity (2022)
5. Admass, W., Munaye, Y., Diro, A.: Cyber security: state of the art, challenges and future directions. Cyber Secur. Appl. **2**, 100031 (2024). https://www.sciencedirect.com/science/article/pii/S2772918423000188
6. Basti, R., Jamoussi, S., Charfi, A., Hamadou, A.: Arabic Twitter user profiling: application to cyber-security. In: WEBIST, pp. 110–117 (2019)
7. Ikae, C., Savoy, J.: Gender identification on Twitter. J. Assoc. Inf. Sci. Technol. **73** (2021)
8. Vaishnavi, V.K., Vaishnavi, V.K., Kuechler, W.: Design Science Research Methods and Patterns: Innovating Information and Communication Technology, 2nd edn. CRC Press (2015). https://doi.org/10.1201/b18448
9. Reitz, K.: Requests: HTTP for Humans (2024). https://requests.readthedocs.io/en/latest/
10. ThoughtWorks: Selenium (2024). https://www.selenium.dev
11. Hassanat, A.: Bypassing captcha by machine a proof for passing the Turing test. CoRR. abs/1409.0925 (2014). http://arxiv.org/abs/1409.0925
12. Amazon: Amazon Rekognition Documentation (2024). https://docs.aws.amazon.com/rekognition/
13. ultrafunkamsterdam: undetected-chromedriver (2024). https://github.com/ultrafunkamsterdam/undetected-chromedriver
14. InfoSec Write-ups: Authentication Vulnerabilities- Lab 5 Username enumeration via response timing (2023). https://infosecwriteups.com/authentication-vulnerabilities-lab-5-username-enumeration-via-response-timing-16b07552275a
15. Pedregosa, F., et al.: Scikit-learn: machine learning in Python. J. Mach. Learn. Res. **12**, 2825–2830 (2011)
16. Bischof, M., Portmann, E.: FATPaSE: proposing a computationally intelligent framework for automated target profiling and social engineering. In: 2023 IEEE International Conference on Systems, Man, and Cybernetics (SMC), pp. 4022–4027 (2023). https://doi.org/10.1109/SMC53992.2023.10394207

CodeFlowGen: A Generator of Synthetic Source Code with Scalable Control Flow Paths for Evaluating Static Analysis Tools

Răzvan-Mihai Bolunduț(✉), Adrian-Viorel Coleșa, and Radu-Marian Portase

Department of Computer Science, Technical University of Cluj-Napoca, Cluj-Napoca, Romania
razvan.bolundut@yahoo.com

Abstract. We present CodeFlowGen, a tool for generating scalable synthetic test programs to evaluate the performance of program analysis techniques. CodeFlowGen creates test cases that scale across all three abstraction levels defined by the LLVM infrastructure: the call graph, control flow graph, and instruction chain. Users can fine-tune the number of functions, calls, and control flow paths within the generated test programs. Additionally, CodeFlowGen supports the generation of computational chains for variables, facilitating data-level analysis.

CodeFlowGen was employed to evaluate a static analysis method for mapping Linux kernel system calls to capability checks. Comprehensive execution time measurements for all mapping algorithms prove the tool's effectiveness in creating large, realistic test programs, highlighting the scalability of the tested algorithms. To ease the tool's usage, a general, language-independent benchmark is created and published.

CodeFlowGen provides a state-of-the-art systematic method for generating test cases that can be used for measuring the effectiveness of static analysis algorithms on scalable inputs.

Keywords: Static program analysis · Scalability · Synthetic program · Performance evaluation · Call Graph · Control Flow Graph · Linux Kernel · System Call

1 Introduction

Performance validation is crucial for ensuring that algorithms behave as expected when applied to scalable input. It often proves invaluable for determining expected performance and identifying areas for improvement. In program analysis, performance evaluation is essential due to the common challenge of *path explosion* vastly stated in related works such as [6,17] or [14].

Path explosion refers to the exponential growth in the number of possible execution paths that must be considered during analysis. This poses serious

L. Morogan et al. (Eds.): SecITC 2024, LNCS 15595, pp. 70–83, 2025.
https://doi.org/10.1007/978-3-031-87760-5_6

feasibility concerns for techniques like those in [3,10], and [16], especially when applied to large programs.

A prominent issue in performance validation is the need for more resources or appropriate test programs to evaluate algorithms. Works such as [16] and [8] propose promising analysis techniques but fail to adequately address performance concerns, hindering their credibility. To address this, we propose a synthetic program generation tool designed to create test programs scaling:

1. the number and depth of paths in the *call graph*
2. the number of *execution paths* within each function of the program
3. the number of *computational instructions*

To meet these objectives, CodeFlowGen[1] generates a compilable C source with a dummy functionality. This is achieved by leveraging contextualised templates to generate source code. A robust class hierarchy representing the main constructs of the C programming language (functions, call statements, conditional blocks, etc.) ensures consistency with language conventions. The source files are compiled into LLVM intermediate representation (IR) and executable format using the `clang` compiler.

Together with the synthetic test generation tool, this paper makes another important contribution. It introduces a benchmark for scalability evaluation of static analysis [4] composed of over 6K test programs containing up to 100 functions and 5K calls, each function being scaled up to 20K basic blocks each. Using this benchmark, analysis algorithms can be validated according to the methods presented in this paper.

The resulting tool was employed to validate an analysis pipeline developed for mapping the Linux system calls to capability checks made during their execution [5]. The Linux kernel analysis pipeline comprises five stages that operate across the three layers of abstraction in a program:

- *Function-level analysis* marks the call chains between a system call and a capability check made through calls to functions in the `capable` family.
- *Control-flow analysis* identifies relevant execution paths and marks the branch conditions that define them.
- *Instruction-level analysis* tracks the values of the expressions used in the identified branch conditions [10].

In contrast to LiCA [16], our proposed pipeline has undergone extensive performance testing with scalable input. This was important given the difficulty of compiling the Linux Kernel into LLVM IR (support for this is still in its early stages). Without the ability to test directly on the target executable, evaluating the scalability of the underlying algorithms is crucial. To achieve this, our generator creates test cases comparable in size to the execution sub-tree rooted at a generic system call's handler function in the Linux kernel.

The results demonstrate the feasibility of the mapping technique on scalable input and the effectiveness of the synthetic test generator in producing large programs comparable to the Linux Kernel.

---

[1] The tool is publicly available at: https://github.com/razvan171514/CodeGen.

Following this introduction, Sect. 2 analyses the layers of abstraction within a general executable program. Section 3 details the algorithms that scale these layers. Once the implementation details of the CodeFlowGen tool are covered, Sect. 4 discusses the tool's limitations and evaluates the scaling properties of the test program. Section 5 reviews related work that would greatly benefit from this evaluation methodology. Finally, Sect. 6 summarises the results, identifies limitations, and suggests directions for future improvement.

2 Background

To design a viable solution for generating scalable test programs, it is essential to closely examine the general structure of an executable. This section outlines the theoretical aspects considered, focusing on the abstraction layers defined by the LLVM compiler, as scaling will be applied to each of these layers.

Function-level abstraction organises instructions according to the functions they belong to. This enables an analysis of the program's call structure in terms of entire functions. The LLVM structure that represents this abstraction layer is the *call graph* (CG), an example of which can be observed in Fig. 1a. In this graph, nodes represent the functions, and edges represent the calls between them.

Moving closer to the instructions defined by the executable, the second layer of abstraction is the **control flow layer**. Here, instructions are grouped into *basic blocks*, which are containers of instructions which execute sequentially without interruption. In other words, when the execution of the program reaches a basic block, all instructions in that block will be executed on that execution path. Basic blocks end with either a return statement (`ret` instruction) or a branch instruction (`br`). The LLVM data structure that maintains this information is called a *control flow graph* (CFG). A CFG is generated by the compiler for each function in the analyzed module. The nodes in this graph represent the basic blocks, while the edges represent possible control flow transitions between them. Figure 1b illustrates a graphical representation of the CFG, where the structure of the code can be inferred from the graph.

In order to better understand the structure of a CFG, one may take as an example the code in Listing 1.1 which generates the structure presented in Fig. 1b. There, the yellow blocks represent the entry and exit of the function. The terminator of the entry block is a branch instruction corresponding to the if statement on line (2). If the then branch is taken, the blue blocks depict the basic structure of an if-then-else statement (lines (3) to (5)). Conversely, the red blocks represent the structure of the loop statement on lines (7) and (8). Here, the uppermost block contains the loop's stopping condition. If the condition evaluates to false, control flow is directed to the exit block; otherwise, it loops back to the block itself.

```
1 int syscall_handler(int arg1, char *arg2) {
2     if (arg1 % 2 == 0)
3         if (((int)arg2[3]) % 2 == 1) arg1 += 5;
4         else arg1 -= 6;
```

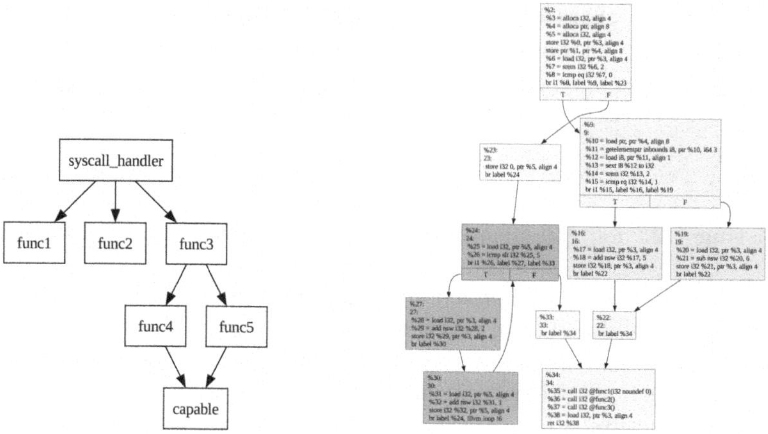

(a) Call Graph

(b) CFG grouping the LLVM IR instructions for the **syscall_handler** function

Fig. 1. Graphical representations of LLVM abstractions. (Color figure online)

```
    else  for (int i=0; i<5; ++i) arg1+=2;
    func1(0); func2(); func3();
    return arg1;
}
```

Listing 1.1. Listing showing the code that generated the CFG in Fig. 1b

The final layer of abstraction is the **IR instruction**, which can be seen in Fig. 1b as the text within the blocks.

3 CodeFlowGen Design and Implementation

To generate scalable programs in terms of the LLVM abstraction layers defined above, a well-defined entity diagram that identifies language constructs and their relationships must be devised. Figure 4 in Appendix A shows the main elements taken into consideration.

Before proceeding to the algorithms for generating scalable programs, it is essential to note that the framework generates the C syntax without the help of other abstract syntax tree (AST) generators. To lower its complexity, the generator heavily relies on templates. Listings 1.2 and 1.3 show two examples of templates used to generate to generate "for" and "while" loop statements, respectively. In both cases, `loop_init` represents a variable initialisation step, `loop_condition` the stopping condition for the loop, and `loop_post_instr` modifies the initialized variables. In order to simplify implementation, both follow a similar type of indexed loop in which the loop body is executed a fixed amount of times as stated by a loop counter. We used textual replacement in all our language constructs (functions, if-then-else statements, etc.). This allows the statement bodies (in this case `loop_body`) to take the shape of another statement template, thus being able to recursively enlarge them as needed.

```
for(${loop_init};
    ${loop_condition};
    ${loop_post_instr})
{
    ${loop_body}
}
```

Listing 1.2. "for" loop template

```
${loop_init};
while(${loop_condition})
{
    ${loop_body}
    ${loop_post_instr};
}
```

Listing 1.3. "while" loop template

In order to generate well formed program replicas against which analysis algorithms can be validated from a performance standpoint, CodeFlowGen must be able to generate scalable structures at all three layers of abstraction. Each of the following sections presents in detail the algorithms used for scaling the corresponding structure. First, a scalable call graph represents the skeleton of functions and calls that, from a top-level prsprvtive, constitutes the module. This stage results in a collection of "bare" calling functions (functions which call each other but do not perform any operation). Generating scalable CFGs solves this issue by giving each function a dummy purpose. This stage essentially creates the possible paths of execution that the program may take. By leaving the generation here, the variables checked in conditions can be considered constants, since their value does not change. This means that only one execution path may be taken. In order to generate a more realistic program replica, the last stage generates instructions that compute the variables and add dependencies between them, thus multiplying the possible execution scenarios.

3.1 Scalable CG Generation

A module corresponds to a collection of functions, i.e., the test program itself. Each function in the module is connected to another function via a call instruction, where each call referencing the caller and callee function instances. By using the caller's symbol table and the callee's header argument list, contextual arguments are generated, satisfying the type constraints of the callee's function signature. This allows the functions to call one another, constructing a replica of the first layer of abstraction presented in Sect. 2.

The process of generating a module can be viewed as generating its call graph. To simplify this, a "mock-up graph" is generated, which mirrors the structure of the call graph but contains no actual function information. For each node in the "mock-up graph", a function object is instantiated, and for each edge, a contextual call instruction is generated, constructing the module's call graph. The "mock-up graph" is a directed acyclic graph (DAG) and a connected graph, ensuring that all generated functions in the synthetic program influence the analysis process.

The CG generation algorithm starts with a list of function templates and a target number of edges, returning the call graph as an adjacency list. The algorithm first checks if the number of edges is valid given the number of functions, ensuring the graph is connected and acyclic. Then, for each node in the list, a

Algorithm 1. Pseudo-code for generating a random module

```
Input
    FuncL List of functions in the module
    E       Number of calls between functions in the module
Output
    G       Adjacency list of the call graph corresponding to the module
V ←Len(FuncL)
G ← ∅
if ¬(V − 1 ≤ E ≤ V∗(V−1)/2) then
    return error
end if
for I ⊨ 0 → (V − 1) do                                   ▷ Ensure connected call graph
    G[FuncL[I]] ← G[FuncL[I]] ∪ {FuncL[I + 1]}
end for
C ← V − 1
while C < E do
    Src ←RandomNode(FuncL)
    Dst ←RandomNode(FuncL)
    if Src ≠ Dst then
        G[Src] ← G[Src] ∪ {Dst}
        C ← C + 1
        if ¬ValidGraph(G) then
            G[Src] ← G[Src] \ {Dst}
            C ← C − 1
        end if
    end if
end while
```

function is connected to the next. Additional edges are added at random until the specified number is reached, ensuring that the graph remains acyclic. Each edge in the call graph corresponds to a call instruction in C code.

3.2 Scalable Control Flow Graph Generation

The control flow graph (CFG) differs from the call graph (CG) in that it is also determined by the compiler and depends on how the compiler generates the sequence of instructions. Using random statements to generate a CFG is unreliable, so a predictable block of code is used instead. Replicating an if-then-else control block scales the CFG while maintaining predictability.

The if-then-else statement generates four basic blocks: a *condition computation* block, the *then* and *else* blocks, and the *end of statement* block (see Fig. 2).

Algorithm 2 describes the generation of a scalable control flow graph. The CFG is scaled in two dimensions: depth (nested if-then-else) and length (chain of if statements). Using this method for scaling a CFG gives a fixed number of execution paths, relation which depends on the two dimensions as follows:

```
void function1()
{
    /* instr */
    if (cond1) {
        /* instr */
    } else {
        /* instr */
    }
    /* instr */
}
```

Listing 1.4. Example "if" statement

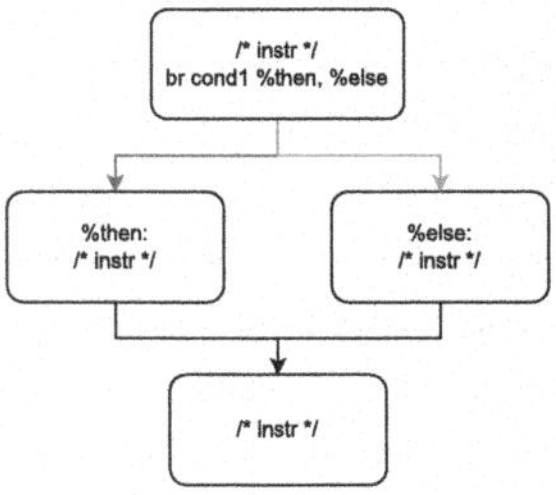

Fig. 2. CFG generated for the single if statement on the left.

Algorithm 2. Pseudo-code for generating a scalable control flow graph

```
1: Input
2:     WD    Depth of the innermost if statement
3:     LD    Length of the chain of depth-zero if statements
4: Output
5:     CFG   Template for a function's CFG
6: CFG ← {}
7: DepthTemp ←GenerateOnDepth(WD)
8: for I = 0 → LD do
9:     CFG ← CFG ∪ {DepthTemp}
10: end for
11: return CFG
12:
13: function GenerateOnDepth(WD)
14:     Template ← {NoOp()}
15:     if WD = 0 then
16:         return Template
17:     end if
18:     If ← IfThenElse()
19:     If.then ← GenerateOnDepth(WD − 1)
20:     If.else ← GenerateOnDepth(WD − 1)
21:     Template ← Template ∪ {If, NoOp()}
22:     return Template
23: end function
```

$LD * 2^{WD}$. For each template generated by `DepthTemp`, there are 2^{WD} possible execution paths. Replicating this LD times (line (8) of Algorithm 2) results in the said number of paths. This method ensures scalability while keeping execution time and memory usage within reasonable bounds.

The resulting CFG will present the property of being a perfectly balanced tree as evident from lines (19) and (20) of Algorithm 2. Another noteworthy aspect is the placement of calls in the generated template. There are multiple possibilities depending on user preference. By default, to provide the highest degree of difficulty to the analysis algorithms, the calls are placed at the end of the function, in the basic block containing the `ret` instruction. The advantage of this approach is that analysis must consider all paths reaching that block before analyzing the calls. Although an advantage from this perspective, this call placement hurts the realism of the generated functions. Often calls occur only on particular conditions. To accommodate this realistic behaviour CodeFlowGen offers the possibility of shuffling the calls and randomly place them in any of the function's basic blocks.

3.3 Scalable Computation Chain Generation

For both use-define chain methods [10] and symbolic execution [3], instructions represent the scope of analysis. To validate such analysis algorithms, the synthetic tests must provide a scalable set of instructions that serve as input for either approach. This feature focuses on the variables in the symbol table of a function (logical structure containing all variables defined in the function body), generating a computation chain for each one. Non-conditional instructions are used to avoid affecting the already generated CFG.

Algorithm 3 presents the method used for generating scalable instructions for computing each variable found in a function's symbol table. From an empty set, the operations list is appended with an operation as follows: a `BinaryOp` placeholder object is created and filled accordingly (lines (10) to (16)). The left hand side (`I.lhs`) is set to the variable itself while the right hand side (`I.rhs`)

Algorithm 3. Pseudo-code for generating a scalable sequence of operations computing a variable's value

```
Input
    CL      Length of the statement chain computing a variable
    SymbT   Symbol table of the function F
    Var     Variable definition subject to chain generation
Output
    OpS     Operation set computing variable Var
OpS ← {}
for counter C = 0 → CL do
    Op ← BinaryOp()
    Op.result ← Var
    Op.lhs ← Var
    Op.op ← RandomBinaryOp()
    Op.rhs ← RandomVariable(SymbT, Var.type)
    if Op.rhs = ∅ then                          ▷ No variable of compatible type
        Op.rhs ← RandomConstant(Var.type)
    end if
    OpS ← OpS ∪ {Op}
end for
```

gets a random variable, from the symbol table, of compatible type with the result (`Var`) or a constant in case no such variable is found. The operation itself is not of interest, so a random operation such as $+$, $-$, $*$ or $/$ is chosen at random.

```
int var1 = 21;
float var2 = 12.3f;
short var3 = 5;
char var4 = 'g';
```

Listing 1.5. Example declaration block of a function

```
var1 = var1 / var3;
var1 = var1 * (int)var4;
var1 = var1 + 19;
```

Listing 1.6. Example computation chain for `var1`

Listing 1.5 shows an example declaration block. Applying Algorithm 3 to `var1` produces the result in Listing 1.6. Just as in the case of the CFG (Sect. 3.2), the list of operations is placed by default in the entry block of the function. This behaviour can be modified so that the generated instructions are shuffled and placed in random blocks.

4 Evaluation

4.1 Feasibility of CodeFlowGen in Generating Program Replicas

During the development of the synthetic code generator the abstractions described in Sect. 2 were taken into consideration. Naturally, the dimensions of the underlying program structures, namely number of vertices and edges associated to the CG and CFG become a good metric to use in order to evaluate whether the generator is able to construct programs of comparable size to existing code bases. We acknowledge that the number of possible execution paths or their length may other valid metric, but such a measurements applied on a very large code-base becomes a computational challenge that does not make a reasonable impact for this validation purpose.

In order to compute the dimensions of both the CG and CFG, an analysis pass is implemented in the LLVM optimizer. The purpose of the pass is to count the number of vertices and edges of both graph structures. Since a CFG is generated for each function, and in real scenarios functions will inevitably be of different sizes and complexities, an average number of basic blocks and transitions (edge between two basic blocks) is computed in order to compliment the method used by CodeFlowGen to generate control flows (see Sect. 3.2 for more details).

Table 1. Table showing the dimension of the original code-base and the synthetic replica generated by CodeFlowGen

Program	Original Code-base			
	Call graph		Control flow graph (Avg.)	
	No. Functions	No. Calls	No. Basic Blocks	No. Transitions
git	226	527	32.58	50.25
nano	265	943	14.62	22.67
Linux Kernel File System	4861	11736	52.12	56.69
Linux Kernel Core	8621	19417	52.19	53.85
	Synthetic replica			
	Call graph		Control flow graph	
	No. Functions	No. Calls	No. Basic Blocks	No. Transitions
git	226	527	46 (wd = 4, ld = 1)	60
nano	265	943	22 (wd = 3, ld = 1)	28
Linux Kernel File System	4861[1]	11736[1]	94 (wd = 5, ld = 1)	124
Linux Kernel Core	8621[1]	19417[1]	94 (wd = 5, ld = 1)	124

[1]May produce recursion depth limit reached error depending on system settings

Table 1 presents the results from applying the metric described above on the programs presented in the first column, in contrast with the dimension measurements taken on the synthetically generated replicas. There are a few important observations to be made. First, the dimension of the call graph can always reach exactly the same measures as the original call graph. This is due to the fact that the CG is entirely a logic defined structure which can easily by replicated to a close degree of resemblance. This is not the case for the CFG. Due to the way in which the CFG is generated (Sect. 3.2) only an approximation can be reached by modifying the width and length depth parameters. From these parameters the number of basic blocks (N_{BB}) and transitions between them (N_{Tr}) can be computed as follows from Eq. 1.

$$N_{BB}(w_d, l_d) = l_d * 2^{w_d+1} \tag{1a}$$

$$N_{Tr}(w_d, l_d) = l_d * 2^{w_d} \tag{1b}$$

From this feasibility evaluation we can conclude that CodeFlowGen is capable of generating program replicas that are within reasonable bounds from original code. CodeFlowGen is designed to provide test cases which present some degree of difficulty (in terms of program structure) when analyzed, therefore the word "replica" is used only from the perspective of the metric described in this section and does not consider any details about path structure or other considerations such as these.

4.2 Algorithm Validation Using CodeFlowGen

The usage of CodeFlowGen follows a generic validation setup. First, a configuration is created to set the limits for testing the specified dimensions. Once a suitable configuration is prepared, a set of test programs is generated. The algorithms are then run on the generated test bench, and performance metrics are collected to measure their execution. The measured performance data must be saved, and visualisations are displayed. These steps are repeated for each dimension identified in the mathematical complexity of the tested algorithm.

This method is exemplified by applying it to the analysis pipeline we developed for mapping Linux Kernel syscalls to capabilities [5]. The first stage of this pipeline involves marking all the paths in the kernel starting from the syscall handler function and ending at a capability-checking function. This stage can be modelled as a graph search problem using the call graph (CG) structure presented in Sect. 2. The optimal complexity for this stage is $O(V + E)$, where V represents vertices (functions) and E represents edges (calls). This linearity in both vertex and edge dimensions is straightforward.

To experimentally validate these mathematical expectations, a comprehensive test bench was created containing 977 test programs generated according to the following rules:

1. A *constant* number of functions with an *increasing* number of calls.
2. An *increasing* number of functions with a *constant* number of calls.
3. An *increasing* number of functions with an *increasing* number of calls.

Figure 3 shows the results of running the first stage of the analysis against the input generated by CodeFlowGen. The results clearly demonstrate that the implemented algorithm follows the expected $O(V + E)$ complexity. First, by increasing the number of edges while keeping the number of vertices constant, the function approximating the complexity is linear (red curve). This behaviour holds true when increasing the number of vertices while keeping the number of edges constant (green curve), as well as when increasing both dimensions simultaneously (blue curve).

Using the same methodology, all pipeline stages were validated from a performance perspective. The usage of [5] to exemplify the validation process proves that CodeFlowGen is capable to generate valuable input, since each pipeline stage described in [5] works with a different level of abstraction.

5 Related Work

The need for validation is a primary concern for any developer or researcher posing a new solution for any problem. Thus, generating valid benchmarks naturally is ones primary goal while evaluating proposed algorithms. This is not

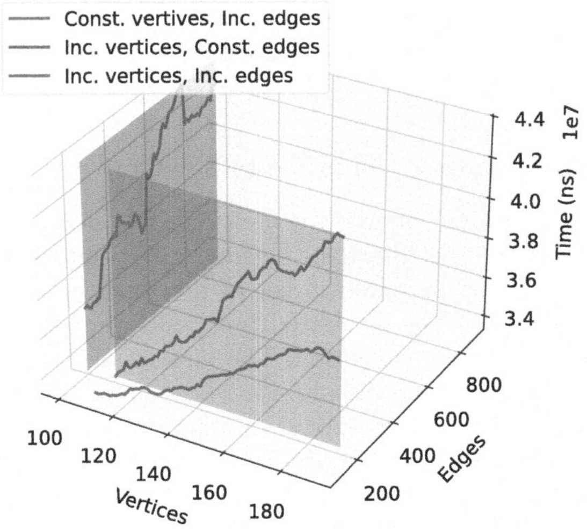

Fig. 3. Results of scalability testing for the CG analysis stage.

different in the case of program analysis techniques. Benchmarking static analysis algorithms can be broken down into two main categories: correctness and completeness benchmarks and execution time performance benchmarks.

The first category is addressed in works such as [2,7,11,12] or [1]. Their primary focus is the detection of vulnerabilities in software applications of various types (C/C++ programs, Java or Web applications). The evaluation of these tools is conducted based on their accuracy when tested against benchmark programs that contain the targeted vulnerabilities. Taking [2] as an example, it uses the Toyota ITC [15] to validate 12 open-source static analyzers for C/C++ code. Toyota ITC suite contains 638 programs containing 51 types of defects categorized in 9 main classes. Each of these tests comes with a counterpart, the same program, but with the particular defect fixed. This brings the total number of test cases to 1276 programs. More details about the variations of the tests in Toyota ITC can be found in Table 1 of [2]. By running each of the analyzers against this test suite, the authors of [2] were able to compute the *detection rate*, *false positive rate*, *productivity* and their newly introduced *robust detection rate*, thus being able to form a ranking based on the defect type and these evaluation metrics. In contrast to these works, the current paper focuses on the evaluation of static analysis algorithms from the perspective of their scalability, validating their merit on ever increasing program sizes.

Works such as [9] address the second category of benchmarking. By using a stochastic parse tree approach, the authors of [9] managed to scale systematically, according to probabilities assigned to language grammar production rules, test cases ranging from 300 to 5M lines of Java code. They used the generated test sets to evaluate several Java compilers and program analysis tools.

One tool that proved to generate similar output to the one of CodeFlowGenis ChatGPT [13]. Using the prompt: "Generate a mock-up C program containing 10 functions and a random number of calls between them, such that one of the function to be the starting one (main) and the call graph to not be disconnected. Each of the functions must contain a nested if-then-else statement with a depth of 2." ChatGPT was able to generate a very similar output to the one that CodeFlowGen would generate with the arguments set as follows: 10 functions, each having a CFG with $w_d = 2$ and $l_d = 1$. With promising results, there are still many concerns about the reliability of such tools when generating large programs. We also observed a strong negative feedback loop with respect to changes in the prompt. All of these concerns are addressed or not applicable to CodeFlowGen making it a more reliable and easier to use tool.

6 Conclusions

As performance testing is highly valuable for evaluating the scalability of program analysis techniques, CodeFlowGen offers a state-of-the-art, automated, and user-friendly way to generate the necessary test cases.

This tool can generate scalable programs across all three abstraction levels described in Sect. 2. Call graph scaling introduces complex interpretational call logic, which in turn allows the control flow graph of each function to be expanded. These two stages provide a robust foundation for testing analysis techniques. Additionally, to accommodate instruction-level analysis, CodeFlowGen includes instruction chain generation capabilities.

While these achievements are noteworthy, it is important to acknowledge the tool's limitations. Firstly, CodeFlowGen does not currently support pointer-type operations, which limits its applicability, as such operations are commonly used in practice. Secondly, the call graph generation stage, as described in Sect. 3.1, involves repeated calls to ensure no cycles are introduced into the graph. This validation process impacts the tool's overall performance. These limitations highlight key areas for future improvements.

Once the aspects mentioned earlier are dealt with, future work can be grouped into two main categories.

1. **Performance improvement measures** which include mostly parallelization of the stages, will drastically improve CodeFlowGen's performance while generating very large test cases.
2. **Functionality improvements** by adding pointer related operations together with control flow graph randomization and conditional instruction chains (computations guarded by conditions – e.g. in the then or else blocks of if statements) the complexity and realism of the test programs will follow more closely the originals.

A Appendix Domain Model for C Language Constructs

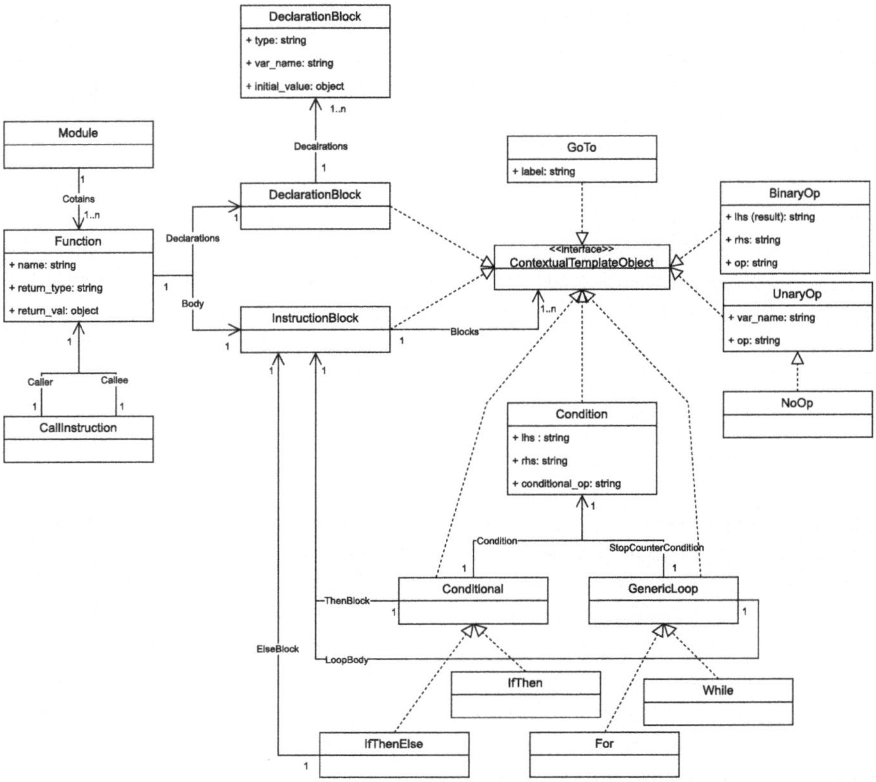

Fig. 4. Figure showing the domain model for the C constructs used by CodeFlowGen.

References

1. Alqaradaghi, M., Kozsik, T.: Comprehensive evaluation of static analysis tools for their performance in finding vulnerabilities in Java code. IEEE Access **12**, 55824–55842 (2024). https://doi.org/10.1109/ACCESS.2024.3389955
2. Arusoaie, A., Ciobâca, S., Craciun, V., Gavrilut, D., Lucanu, D.: A comparison of open-source static analysis tools for vulnerability detection in c/c++ code. In: 2017 19th International Symposium on Symbolic and Numeric Algorithms for Scientific Computing (SYNASC), pp. 161–168 (2017). https://doi.org/10.1109/SYNASC.2017.00035
3. Baldoni, R., Coppa, E., D'elia, D.C., Demetrescu, C., Finocchi, I.: A survey of symbolic execution techniques. ACM Comput. Surv. **51**(3) (2018). https://doi.org/10.1145/3182657
4. Bolunduț, R.M.: CFG-generator (2024). https://github.com/razvan171514/cfg-codegen. Accessed 29 Sept 2024
5. Bolunduț, R.M., Coleșa, A., Portase, R.M.: A path sensitive and scalable approach for mapping the capabilities required for Linux Kernel defined system calls using static analysis techniques. In: 2024 IEEE International Conference on Communication Problem-Solving (ICCP), October 2024

6. Boonstoppel, P., Cadar, C., Engler, D.: RWset: attacking path explosion in constraint-based test generation. In: Ramakrishnan, C.R., Rehof, J. (eds.) TACAS 2008. LNCS, vol. 4963, pp. 351–366. Springer, Heidelberg (2008). https://doi.org/10.1007/978-3-540-78800-3_27
7. Delaitre, A., Stivalet, B., Fong, E., Okun, V.: Evaluating bug finders – test and measurement of static code analyzers. In: 2015 IEEE/ACM 1st International Workshop on Complex Faults and Failures in Large Software Systems (COUFLESS), pp. 14–20 (2015). https://doi.org/10.1109/COUFLESS.2015.10
8. Hasan, M.M., Ghavamnia, S., Polychronakis, M.: Decap: deprivileging programs by reducing their capabilities. In: Proceedings of the 25th International Symposium on Research in Attacks, Intrusions and Defenses, RAID '22, pp. 395–408. Association for Computing Machinery, New York (2022). https://doi.org/10.1145/3545948.3545978
9. Hussain, I., et al.: RUGRAT: evaluating program analysis and testing tools and compilers with large generated random benchmark applications. Softw. Pract. Exp. **46**(3), 405–431 (2016). https://doi.org/10.1002/spe.2290
10. Kennedy, K.: Use-definition chains with applications. Comput. Lang. **3**(3), 163–179 (1978). https://doi.org/10.1016/0096-0551(78)90009-7
11. Lipp, S., Banescu, S., Pretschner, A.: An empirical study on the effectiveness of static c code analyzers for vulnerability detection. In: Proceedings of the 31st ACM SIGSOFT International Symposium on Software Testing and Analysis, ISSTA 2022, pp. 544–555. Association for Computing Machinery, New York (2022). https://doi.org/10.1145/3533767.3534380
12. Nunes, P., Medeiros, I., Fonseca, J.C., Neves, N., Correia, M., Vieira, M.: Benchmarking static analysis tools for web security. IEEE Trans. Reliab. **67**(3), 1159–1175 (2018). https://doi.org/10.1109/TR.2018.2839339
13. OpenAI: ChatGPT (GPT-4) (2023). https://chat.openai.com/. Accessed Sept 2024
14. Ryan, K., Sturton, C.: Countering the path explosion problem in the symbolic execution of hardware designs (2023). https://arxiv.org/abs/2304.05445
15. Shiraishi, S., Mohan, V., Marimuthu, H.: Test suites for benchmarks of static analysis tools. In: 2015 IEEE International Symposium on Software Reliability Engineering Workshops (ISSREW), pp. 12–15 (2015). https://doi.org/10.1109/ISSREW.2015.7392027
16. Sun, M., Song, Z., Ren, X., Wu, D., Zhang, K.: LiCA: a fine-grained and path-sensitive Linux capability analysis framework. In: Proceedings of the 25th International Symposium on Research in Attacks, Intrusions and Defenses, RAID 2022, pp. 364–379. Association for Computing Machinery, New York (2022). https://doi.org/10.1145/3545948.3545966
17. Xiao, X., Zhang, X.s., Li, X.d.: New approach to path explosion problem of symbolic execution. In: 2010 First International Conference on Pervasive Computing, Signal Processing and Applications, pp. 301–304 (2010). https://doi.org/10.1109/PCSPA.2010.80

Cyber Threats to Green Hydrogen Production Within a Solar Microgrid

Mehmet Bozdal[1,2](✉) and Zoya Pourmirza[1]

[1] University of Birmingham, Birmingham B15 2SQ, UK
m.bozdal@bham.ac.uk
[2] Abdullah Gül University, 38080 Kayseri, Turkey

Abstract. The transition towards sustainable energy systems depends heavily on the reliable operation of renewable energy infrastructure, which is increasingly interconnected and digitized. Therefore, ensuring cybersecurity resilience is essential for maintaining the reliability and safety of renewable energy systems in a rapidly evolving digital landscape. This paper investigates the economic implications of data integrity and system configuration attacks on a green hydrogen production system within a solar microgrid. Through a comprehensive analysis, the vulnerability of the system to cyber intrusions that manipulate relay settings, electricity prices, and hydrogen level, is examined. Drawing on a multidisciplinary framework encompassing energy economics, cybersecurity, and renewable energy technologies, a methodological approach is developed to quantify the direct economic impacts of attacks. Simulation results indicate that such attacks can decrease profits by up to 14%.

Keywords: Cybersecurity · Green Hydrogen · Solar Microgrid

1 Introduction

As countries worldwide strive to achieve net-zero carbon emissions, there has been a significant expansion in renewable energy capacities. Over the past decade, the global installed capacity of renewable energy has surged from 480 gigawatts (GW) in 2012 to 1945 GW in 2021. This dramatic increase indicates the widespread adoption of renewable technologies, including wind, hydro, and solar power. Notably, photovoltaic (PV) solar power has seen particularly rapid growth, with its installed capacity rising from 100 GW in 2012 to 942 GW in 2021 [1]. This significant growth in PV capacity reflects its crucial role in the overall expansion of renewable energy sources globally.

Although solar power offers significant potential, its intermittent nature and misalignment with peak energy demand periods present significant challenges. Addressing these operational issues requires energy systems capable of storing or reallocating surplus solar energy generated during off-peak hours. One effective solution is the conversion of excess electrical energy into hydrogen through electrolysis, a process that splits water molecules into hydrogen and oxygen using electricity [2]. Hydrogen produced using renewable resources, referred to as "green hydrogen," provides a sustainable method for

L. Morogan et al. (Eds.): SecITC 2024, LNCS 15595, pp. 84–95, 2025.
https://doi.org/10.1007/978-3-031-87760-5_7

storing energy and addressing these challenges. By converting surplus solar energy into green hydrogen, energy systems can enhance grid stability. Beyond its environmental advantages, green hydrogen production also demonstrates strong economic potential for small- and medium-scale ventures. Projections indicate that within the next decade, green hydrogen will become a competitive option in large-scale industrial markets [3].

The deployment of hybrid solar-hydrogen systems requires seamless interaction with dynamic market electricity prices. These systems must be equipped with communication links that enable real-time decision-making, where power relays divert electricity either to the grid or to electrolysers based on price fluctuations. This necessitates robust and automated communication networks to ensure system reliability and operational efficiency. However, the increasing reliance on digital technologies and interconnected systems in renewable energy infrastructure introduces significant vulnerabilities to cyber threats. In 2015, the Ukrainian power grid suffered major outages due to a cyber-attack that exploited remote control vulnerabilities in the Supervisory Control and Data Acquisition (SCADA) system. The grid remained offline for approximately three hours before being manually restored [4]. This attack highlights the potential severity of cyber-attacks on critical infrastructure. However, not all cyber-attacks result in immediate outages; some may lead to significant economic impacts or cause equipment overloading without immediate detection. False data injection attacks, which have been extensively examined in the literature [5, 6], are examples of such threats. These attacks can undermine the optimal power flow within a grid, leading to economic losses and the potential degradation or failure of generators and other critical equipment.

As hydrogen systems are integrated into renewable energy infrastructure, they become vulnerable to similar cyber threats. Han et al. [7] demonstrated that hydrogen-integrated energy systems are vulnerable to false data injection attacks, which can cause incorrect operational decisions and disrupt network stability. Additionally, a denial-of-service attack [8] was used to disable the electrolyser and fuel cell, highlighting how targeted cyberattacks can incapacitate key components of hydrogen systems.

This study evaluates the impact of cyber-attacks on the economic performance of green hydrogen production systems, with a particular focus on how altering relay settings can disrupt electricity flow, leading to inefficient energy management and financial losses. By manipulating relay configurations, attackers could interfere with critical operational decisions, resulting in suboptimal energy allocation. Additionally, the study explores how attackers may exploit fluctuations in electricity prices and solar radiation data to force the microgrid into making economically disadvantageous decisions, such as selling electricity at unprofitable rates or diverting resources unnecessarily toward hydrogen production.

The contributions of this paper are three-fold:

- First, an analysis of how solar-based green hydrogen production systems are susceptible to attacks.
- Second, a detailed investigation of attack methodologies and their impact on system performance.
- Third, an evaluation of the economic effects of cyber-attacks on operational decisions within these systems.

The structure of the paper is organized as follows: Sect. 2 provides background information on grid balancing and green hydrogen production. In Sect. 3, the attack vectors, dataset, and simulation environment are described. Section 4 presents the experimental results. Finally, Sect. 5 concludes the paper with a discussion of the key findings and their implications.

2 Background

The transition towards sustainable energy systems requires a thorough understanding of the network dynamics and technologies associated with renewable energy, particularly green hydrogen production systems integrated with solar energy. This section provides essential context for evaluating the economic and cybersecurity vulnerabilities of these systems.

2.1 Solar Power and Grid Balance: The Duck Curve Effect

The "duck curve" depicted in Fig. 1 illustrates the daily impact of renewable energy sources, including wind and PV solar power, on the net load of an electrical grid in California from 2015 to 2023 [9]. As shown in the figure, the net load undergoes a significant reduction around midday when solar output peaks. This reduction is followed by a sharp increase in netload during the late afternoon and evening, driven by rising consumer demand and decreasing solar radiation. The deepening of the curve over time reflects an increasing disparity between energy supply and demand, with 2023 data showing instances where the net load falls below zero.

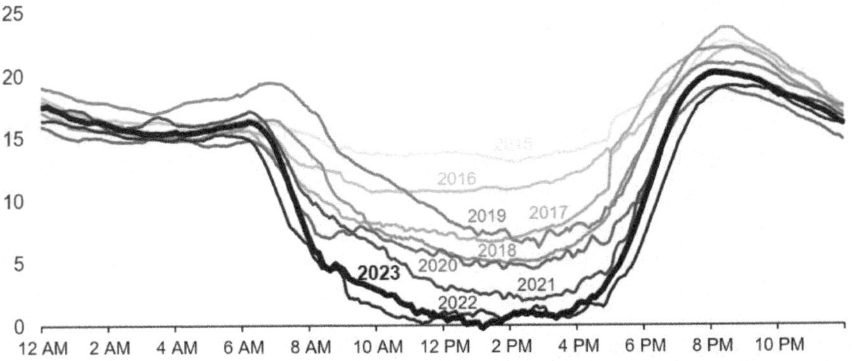

Fig. 1. Net electricity demand in California from March to May, 2015–2022 [10].

These dynamics underscore the challenges faced by electricity markets, which are heavily influenced by the balance between supply and demand, generation costs, and regulatory frameworks. Market mechanisms, including wholesale markets, power purchase agreements (PPAs), and energy auctions, are crucial in determining electricity pricing and trading activities. These prices are not static; they fluctuate in response to real-time grid conditions, such as the oversupply of solar power during midday, which can lead to negative pricing and the need for curtailment. Additionally, grid capacity constraints pose significant challenges due to the lack of sufficient grid infrastructure to utilize energy from production sites to consumption points. Addressing these challenges is essential for optimizing the economic performance of renewable energy systems.

Energy storage solutions have become essential tools for effectively managing fluctuations in supply and demand within energy systems. For instance, California has significantly expanded its battery storage capacity from 0.2 GW in 2018 to 4.9 GW in 2023 [10]. This expansion allows excess solar energy generated during peak hours to be stored and later used when demand rises and renewable supply decreases. Additionally, hydrogen storage presents a promising alternative, offering substantial advantages such as large-scale capacity, versatility across various applications—including fuel cells and industrial processes—and a potential reduction in carbon emissions. Nevertheless, several challenges persist, including high associated costs, energy losses during conversion, and the necessity for extensive infrastructure development.

The increasing divergence between supply and demand, as illustrated by the "duck curve," highlights the urgent need for advanced grid management strategies. These strategies must include not only energy storage but also a thorough understanding of market dynamics, as the financial outcomes of energy systems are directly impacted by the complex interplay of these factors. Adapting to these conditions is essential for maintaining grid stability and ensuring the economic viability of renewable energy initiatives.

2.2 Green Hydrogen Production Within the Solar Microgrid

In the integrated green hydrogen production system within the solar microgrid, as illustrated in Fig. 2, the decision-making process is dynamically influenced by real-time electricity prices, which are characterized by the balance between supply and demand, as well as curtailment rules and prevailing weather conditions. The system architecture comprises solar photovoltaic (PV) panels that generate electricity, which can either be sold to the grid or utilized for hydrogen production, depending on market conditions.

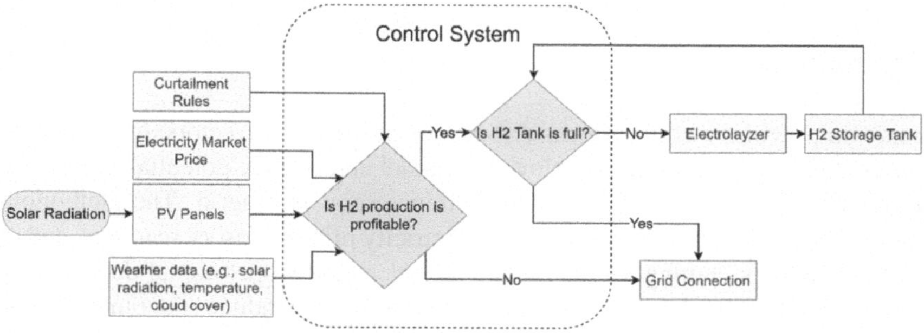

Fig. 2. Flowchart of the green hydrogen production within a solar microgrid.

The control system plays a crucial role in this decision-making process by analysing current electricity prices, network load, sensor readings (such as solar radiation levels and hydrogen storage levels), and weather forecasts. When the control system determines that selling electricity is economically advantageous, the generated electricity is directed to the grid. Conversely, if hydrogen production is more profitable, the solar electricity is routed to electrolysers for hydrogen generation. The system's economic efficiency depends on the ability to make accurate and timely decisions.

Several scenarios are considered in this decision-making process:

- **Scenario 0: Hydrogen Storage Capacity Reached:** When the hydrogen storage tank is at full capacity, all generated electricity is directed to the grid, irrespective of market pricing. In cases of negative pricing and suitable grounding conditions, the electricity may be grounded. Additionally, the stored hydrogen can be utilized to generate electricity if a gas-to-power system is available. Alternatively, the hydrogen can be transported using cryogenic liquid tanker trucks, facilitating its distribution for off-site applications or further processing.
- **Scenario 1: High Electricity Prices:** During periods of high electricity prices, the system prioritizes selling electricity to the grid to maximize profits.
- **Scenario 2: Low Electricity Prices:** During periods of low electricity prices, solar energy is diverted to produce hydrogen via electrolysis. The resulting hydrogen can then be stored for future use or sale.

The decision-making process is designed to optimize economic outcomes by continuously evaluating the profitability of selling electricity versus producing hydrogen. This evaluation involves not only immediate market conditions but also the long-term value of stored hydrogen, the costs associated with system transitions, and the potential for future price fluctuations.

Integration of hydrogen as an energy storage solution offers several advantages, including the ability to store excess energy over extended periods, enhancing grid stability, and enabling the use of solar energy even during periods of low sunlight. However, several challenges remain, such as the high initial costs of electrolysis systems, energy losses during conversion, and the need for substantial infrastructure development. Addressing these challenges is essential for maximizing the economic and environmental benefits of hydrogen storage within solar microgrids.

3 Methodology

This section provides a comprehensive overview of the attack vectors, implementation strategies, and simulation setup employed to model and analyse potential cyber-attacks on a green hydrogen production system within a solar microgrid. The methodology focuses on the exploitation of variations in electricity prices, sensory readings, and control system settings, aiming to manipulate the microgrid's operational decisions. The primary goal of the attackers, as modelled in this study, is to induce economically disadvantageous decisions that compromise both the financial performance and operational stability of the microgrid.

3.1 Attack Vectors

Attacks may be initiated through the compromise of devices (e.g., controllers, sensors) or networks (e.g., man-in-the-middle attacks). These compromises enable the insertion of false data, modification of original data, or alteration of control logic, thereby disrupting the microgrid's control systems. For instance, compromising the firmware of a PLC as shown in [11] or a sensor allows attackers to manipulate data inputs that guide operational decisions, potentially causing the microgrid to make suboptimal decisions, such as selling electricity at a loss or halting hydrogen production unnecessarily. Furthermore, vulnerabilities in existing communication protocols may facilitate man-in-the-middle (MitM) attacks [12]. Such attacks undermine the integrity of communication channels, allowing the insertion of inaccurate data or the alteration of transmitted information.

When a device or network is compromised, the following attack scenarios may potentially emerge:

a) **Denial of Service (DoS) Attacks**

DoS attacks aim to disrupt the availability of critical services within the microgrid by overwhelming or disabling control systems, communication networks, or other essential components. Such attacks as shown in [13] can incapacitate the system's ability to process legitimate data or execute critical operations, causing delays in decision-making, complete system shutdowns, or forced operation in a fail-safe mode, which is often less efficient and more costly. For example, a DoS attack on the communication network might prevent the control system from receiving real-time electricity price updates, resulting in outdated operational decisions.

b) **Configuration Modification Attacks**

Configuration modification attacks involve altering settings and configurations within the microgrid's control systems, such as programmable logic controllers (PLCs) [11] or relay settings. The result is the disruption of normal microgrid operations, leading to incorrect price signals and inefficient energy management.

c) **Data Injection and Modification Attacks**

Data injection and modification attacks target system integrity by inserting false data or altering existing information in system communications. In a hydrogen microgrid, such attacks could manipulate critical variables, including electricity prices or hydrogen storage levels, to destabilize operations and cause economic inefficiencies. For instance, artificially inflating electricity prices during periods of low demand might drive the microgrid to prioritize electricity sales over hydrogen production, resulting in suboptimal energy management. Conversely, reducing electricity prices could mislead the system into prioritizing hydrogen production when selling electricity would be more profitable. Additionally, falsifying hydrogen storage levels can disrupt the balance between electricity sales and hydrogen production, such as falsely reporting a full tank to halt hydrogen production when it is economically beneficial.

3.2 Data Sources

The simulation of the microgrid's operational decision-making processes relies on precise and reliable data sources. For this study, the California Independent System Operator (CAISO) Hourly Day-Ahead Locational Marginal Prices [14] for 2021 are employed. CAISO, responsible for managing the majority of California's electricity grid, facilitates energy trading in both the Day-Ahead Market (DAM) and the Real-Time Market (RTM). The fluctuating prices in these markets, driven by dynamic supply and demand conditions, are critical inputs for the simulation model.

To synchronize environmental conditions with market data, solar irradiance information for the corresponding period is obtained from the National Solar Radiation Database (NSRDB) [15], managed by the National Renewable Energy Laboratory (NREL). This dataset provides comprehensive meteorological and solar radiation metrics, including temperature, pressure, relative humidity, wind speed, and direction, in addition to solar radiation metrics such as Global Horizontal Irradiance (GHI), Direct Normal Irradiance (DNI), and Diffuse Horizontal Irradiance (DHI). For this research, GHI data is utilized.

Both datasets are structured with 24 samples per day, resulting in a total of 8760 samples over the entire year.

3.3 Simulation Environment

Hydrogen production within a solar microgrid was simulated using a MATLAB script integrated with a Simulink model. The simulation aimed to evaluate the annual impacts of cyber-attacks on hydrogen output and energy distribution. It utilized hourly solar irradiance data sourced from the NREL and hourly electricity prices obtained from CAISO day-ahead market.

The Simulink model represents the operational characteristics of a microgrid for green hydrogen production. Key components of the model include:

- **Solar Array**: The output current is determined by irradiance, which influences the solar-generated current.
- **Electrolyser Block**: This block models the electrochemical process of hydrogen production, calculating hydrogen output based on electrical energy supplied and the water temperature in the tank.
- **Control Relay**: Simulates the microgrid's decision-making process, switching between feeding electricity into the grid or using it for hydrogen production, based on real-time electricity market prices.

Key hourly metrics include hydrogen production (kg), solar energy output (kWh), grid electricity input (kWh), and electrolyser energy consumption (kWh).

4 Experimental Results

4.1 Relay Setting Modifications

This attack scenario involves the malicious alteration of relay settings, aimed at disrupting the normal operation of the system. Although the decision-making process of the system can be inherently complex, it is simplified in this study. Under default conditions, the system is configured to produce hydrogen when the electricity price falls below $50 per megawatt-hour. Conversely, electricity is sold to the grid when the price exceeds this threshold. In relay setting modification, the threshold is intentionally modified to observe the resulting impact on system performance. In this attack scenario, the threshold is modified in increments of $10, ranging from $0 to $100, including specific values of $45 and $55, to evaluate its impact on system profitability. The results obtained from these modifications are summarized in Table 1.

Table 1. Simulation results of hydrogen production and electricity sales on varying price thresholds in California for 2021.

Threshold (USD/MWh)	Electricity Sold (MWh)	Electricity to Electrolyser (MWh)	Electricity Revenue (Million USD)	H2 Production (Ton)	Hydrogen Revenue (Million USD)	Total Revenue (Million USD)
0	38917	80	2023	634	4	2027
10	38125	872	2019	6911	44	2063
20	36671	2326	1996	18435	117	2113
30	33338	5659	1910	44842	284	2193
40	25125	13872	1621	109925	696	2317
45	21256	17741	1457	140587	890	2347
50	17214	21783	1265	172618	1093	2358
55	13306	25692	1061	203588	1289	2349
60	10271	28726	886	227637	1441	2327
70	5969	33028	609	261721	1657	2265
80	3808	35189	448	278851	1765	2213
90	2353	36644	325	290381	1838	2163
100	1539	37458	248	296826	1879	2126

The simulation results, indicate that the system generates a total of 38,997 MWh. The system either sells this electricity to the grid or uses it to produce hydrogen, depending on the price threshold. At lower threshold values, the system prioritizes electricity sales, resulting in higher grid revenue but lower hydrogen production. For instance, with a threshold set at $0/MWh, the system produces 634 tons of hydrogen and achieves a total profit of $2.027 billion, primarily from electricity sales. As the threshold increases, the system's focus shifts towards hydrogen production, with total profit reaching a peak of $2.358 billion at the default threshold of $50/MWh. However, at higher thresholds, while hydrogen production increases, total profit declines due to a significant reduction in electricity sales revenue. The economic impact of this attack is visualized in Fig. 3.

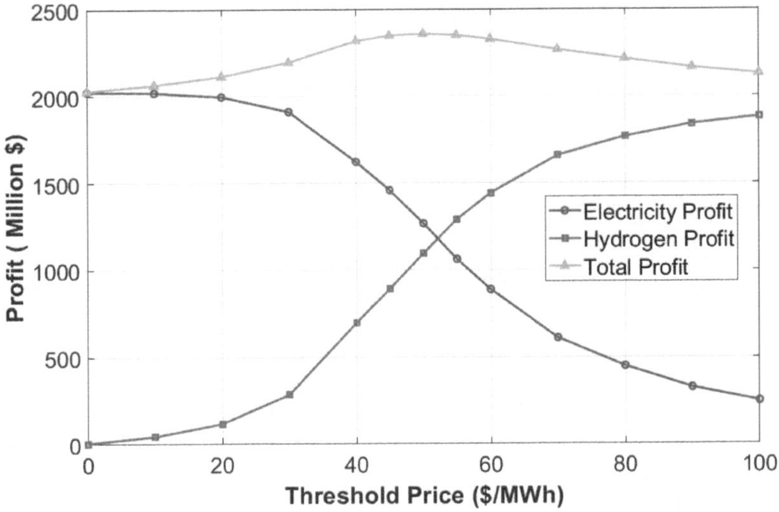

Fig. 3. Impact of threshold modifications on profitability in green hydrogen production.

4.2 Data Injection/Modification Attacks

Electricity Price Inflation/Deflation: This attack scenario simulates the injection / modification of false data into the system, targeting electricity price data during periods of high solar radiation (between 11:00 and 17:00). The goal of price inflation attack is to influence the system's operational decisions, shifting the focus from producing hydrogen to selling electricity, despite favourable market conditions for hydrogen production. Conversely, the price deflation attack reduces electricity prices to shift the system's operation towards hydrogen production. The system is normally set to produce hydrogen when the price is below $50 per MWh and sell electricity when it exceeds this threshold. During the attack, electricity prices are artificially inflated to $100 per MWh as shown in Fig. 4 or deflated to $25 per MWh as shown in Fig. 5, thereby disrupting the system's decision-making process.

Hydrogen Storage Tank Level Manipulation: In this attack scenario, the adversary manipulates the system by falsely signalling that the hydrogen storage tank has reached full capacity. This forces the microgrid to divert all surplus electricity to the grid, regardless of current market prices, even when selling conditions are economically unfavourable. The duration of the attack can range from a few hours to an entire day. When sustained throughout the day, the hydrogen-integrated solar microgrid is effectively reduced to operating as a traditional solar microgrid without energy storage capabilities. Figure 6 illustrates the attack's impact, highlighting the resulting profit disparity.

Both electricity price inflation and hydrogen storage level attacks impact the system's operation similarly, despite differing causes. In the hydrogen storage level attack, the system is manipulated to perceive the storage as full, which effectively halts hydrogen production due to the apparent lack of available storage capacity. On the other hand, in

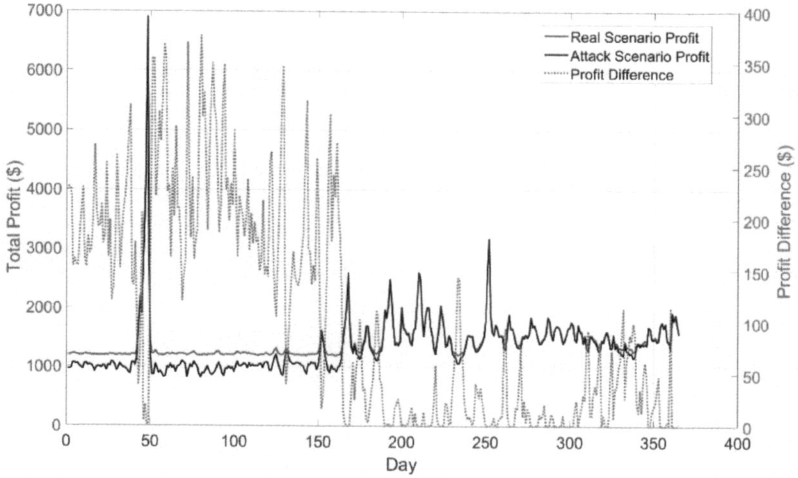

Fig. 4. The effect of electricity price inflation increased to $100 between 11:00 and 17:00, on the profitability of a solar microgrid.

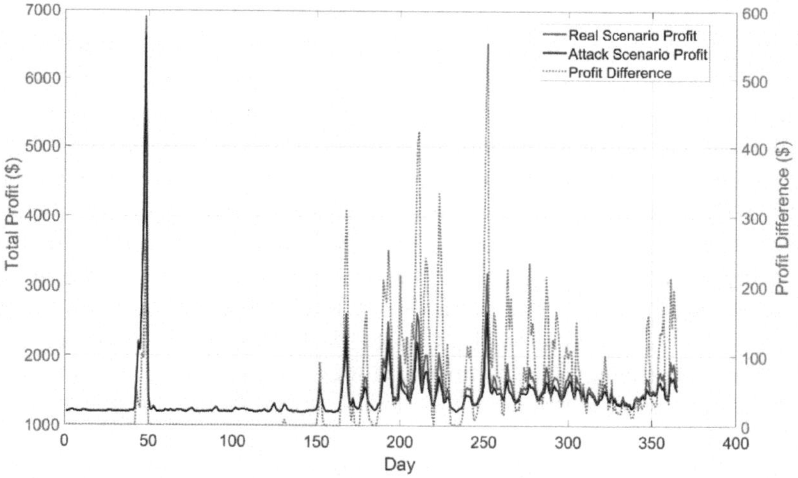

Fig. 5. The effect of electricity price deflation, decreased to $25 between 11:00 and 17:00, on the profitability of a solar microgrid.

the electricity price inflation attack, artificially risen electricity prices lead the system to incorrectly assume that selling electricity to the grid is more profitable than producing hydrogen. Conversely, in the price deflation attack, electricity prices are decreased, misleading the system into prioritizing hydrogen production and halting electricity sales, even when market conditions are more favourable for selling electricity.

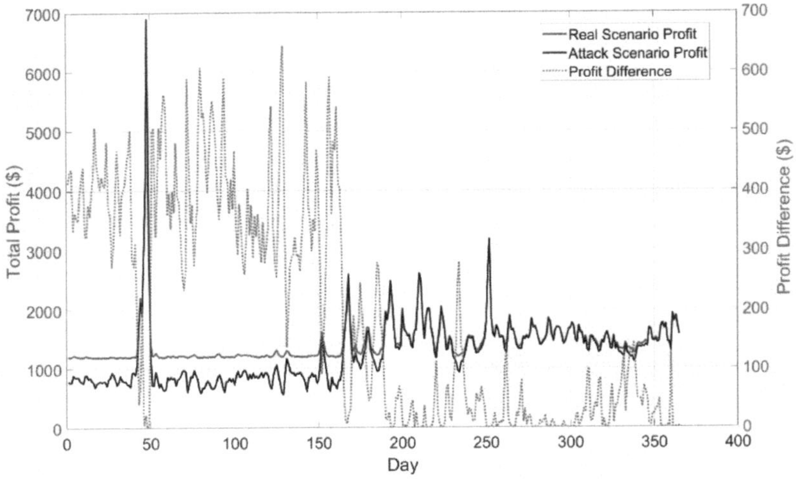

Fig. 6. The effect of hydrogen level manipulation on profitability in solar microgrid.

5 Conclusion

The results presented in this research highlight the significant vulnerabilities of a green hydrogen production system within a solar microgrid to various forms of cyber-attacks. By manipulating relay settings, data inputs, or hydrogen storage levels, adversaries can drastically alter the system's operational decisions, adversely affecting both hydrogen production and electricity sales. In one simulated scenario, profits were reduced from 2,358 to 2,027, representing a 14% decrease. These attacks may exploit existing vulnerabilities in legacy systems or target new points of weakness introduced by digitalization. Although the research primarily evaluates the economic impact of such cyber intrusions, further research is necessary to explore the low-level implementation of these attacks and how system behaviour is affected at a more granular level. Given that energy systems are critical infrastructure, robust security measures – such as encrypted authentication and advanced intrusion detection systems- should be also implemented.

Acknowledgment. This research is supported by the Hydrogen Integration for Accelerated Energy Transitions Hub (HI-ACT), funded by Engineering and Physical Sciences Research Council (EPSRC) under Programme Grant EP/X038823/1.

References

1. Yolcan, O.O.: World energy outlook and state of renewable energy: 10-Year evaluation. Innov. Green Dev. **2**(4), 100070 (2023). https://doi.org/10.1016/j.igd.2023.100070
2. Moriarty, P., Honnery, D.: Intermittent renewable energy: the only future source of hydrogen? Int. J. Hydrogen Energy **32**(12), 1616–1624 (2007). https://doi.org/10.1016/j.ijhydene.2006.12.008
3. Glenk, G., Reichelstein, S.: Economics of converting renewable power to hydrogen. Nat. Energy **4**(3), 216–222 (2019). https://doi.org/10.1038/s41560-019-0326-1

4. SANS Industrial Control Systems, Analysis of the Cyber Attack on the Ukrainian Power Grid Defense Use Case (2016)
5. Liu, Y., Ning, P., Reiter, M.K.: False data injection attacks against state estimation in electric power grids. ACM Trans. Inf. Syst. Secur. (2011). https://doi.org/10.1145/1952982.1952995
6. Tan, R., et al.: Modeling and mitigating impact of false data injection attacks on automatic generation control. IEEE Trans. Inf. Forensics Secur. **12**(7), 1609–1624 (2017). https://doi.org/10.1109/TIFS.2017.2676721
7. Han, H., Li, Q., Tang, W.: Intraday optimization control of IES with hydrogen injection under attack scenarios. In: Proceedings - 2021 IEEE Sustainable Power and Energy Conference: Energy Transition for Carbon Neutrality, iSPEC 2021, pp. 2518–2527 (2021). https://doi.org/10.1109/iSPEC53008.2021.9735596
8. Yıldız, S., Yildirim, B., Özdemir, M.T.: Enhancing load frequency control and cybersecurity in renewable energy microgrids: a fuel cell-based solution with non-integer control under cyber-attack. Int J Hydrogen Energy, February 2024. https://doi.org/10.1016/j.ijhydene.2024.02.145
9. Denholm, P., O'connell, M., Brinkman, G., Jorgenson, J.: Overgeneration from Solar Energy in California: A Field Guide to the Duck Chart (2013). www.nrel.gov/publications
10. U.S. Energy Information Administration (EIA), As solar capacity grows, duck curves are getting deeper in California. Accessed 08 Aug 2024. https://www.eia.gov/todayinenergy/detail.php?id=56880
11. Alsabbagh, W., Langendorfer, P.: A Control Injection Attack against S7 PLCs-Manipulating the Decompiled Code. In: IECON Proceedings (Industrial Electronics Conference). IEEE Computer Society (2021). https://doi.org/10.1109/IECON48115.2021.9589721
12. Fritz, J.J., Sagisi, J., James, J., St Leger, A., King, K., Duncan, K.J.: Simulation of Man in the Middle Attack On Smart Grid Testbed
13. Huseinovic, A., Mrdovic, S., Bicakci, K., Uludag, S.: A Survey of Denial-of-Service Attacks and Solutions in the Smart Grid. IEEE Access **8**, 177447–177470 (2020). https://doi.org/10.1109/ACCESS.2020.3026923
14. U.S. Energy Information Administration (EIA): Wholesale Electricity Market Data. Accessed 11 Aug 2024. https://www.eia.gov/electricity/wholesalemarkets/data.php?rto=caiso
15. National Renewable Energy Laboratory (NREL): NSRDB: National Solar Radiation Database. Accessed 12 Aug 2024. https://nsrdb.nrel.gov/data-viewer

Stateful Fuzzing of OPC UA

Cristian Daniele(✉), Mark Fijneman, and Erik Poll

Radboud University, Nijmegen, The Netherlands
{cristian.daniele,mark.fijneman,erik.poll}@ru.nl

Abstract. Fuzzing is a widely used and effective testing technique used to discover bugs in systems. Fuzzers like AFL++ (and its descendants) daily find plenty of bugs in open-source implementations. Unfortunately, the statefulness of some systems (such as protocol implementations) limits the effectiveness of stateless fuzzers since they cannot dig deep into the state model. For such stateful systems, it is necessary to take states into account to get the best results.

For example, in recent years, the research community has shown great interest in the security of the OPC UA, a protocol used in Industrial Control Systems. Although a few bugs were found during previous analyses of the protocol, they did not consider the statefulness of the protocol. In this paper, we fuzz three OPC UA implementations with three different fuzzers (AFLnwe, BooFuzz and AFLNet) and find three novel bugs overlooked in the previous analyses. Our results highlight the importance of considering the systems' stateful nature when choosing the fuzzer to use. Also, they emphasise the importance of having complete grammar when opting for grammar-based fuzzers, i.e., fuzzers that need the messages and state model specification in input.

Keywords: Protocol testing · Stateful fuzzing · OPC UA

1 Introduction

During the last few years, the fuzzing community highlighted the need for fuzzers specifically tailored to stateful systems [8]. This need is demonstrated by the plethora of stateful fuzzers the community developed to tackle stateful software of different natures (e.g., network [19], embedded [11,18], or IoT protocols [10]). Unfortunately, security analysts often know very little about the nature of the systems they are testing and about the state model they might implement. Also, the lack of documentation and the incomplete protocol specification can lead security analysts to make the wrong assumption about the statefulness of the system.

In this paper, we fuzz three OPC UA implementations by using the stateless fuzzer AFLnwe[1], the grammar-based fuzzer BooFuzz [14] and the stateful fuzzer AFLNet [15]. The contribution of this paper is twofold:

---

[1] https://github.com/thuanpv/aflnwe.

L. Morogan et al. (Eds.): SecITC 2024, LNCS 15595, pp. 96–107, 2025.
https://doi.org/10.1007/978-3-031-87760-5_8

1. we show that wrong assumptions about the stateful nature of a system can lead to misreading its robustness. In fact, the previous efforts [5,6,9] overlooked the stateful nature of OPC UA, thereby missing three novel bugs;
2. as a consequence, we prove that stateless fuzzers achieve poor results when testing the robustness of stateful systems. Moreover, we show how the effectiveness of a grammar-based fuzzer strongly depends on the quality of the grammar provided in input.

The paper is structured as follows: Sect. 2 introduces the background by presenting an overview of fuzzing and the OPC UA protocol. Section 3 presents the earlier efforts. In Sect. 4, we fuzz three OPC UA implementations with AFLnwe, BooFuzz and AFLNet. In Sect. 5, we discuss the results, in Sect. 6, we present the future work and in Sect. 7 we conclude by highlighting the contribution of the paper.

2 Background

2.1 Stateless and Stateful Fuzzing

Fuzzing is a testing technique widely used to find vulnerabilities in software. The idea behind fuzzing is straightforward: the fuzzer sends many malformed messages to the Software Under Test (SUT) waiting for crashes or unexpected system behaviours. Even though fuzzing is very effective in testing stateless systems, it does not always work well when dealing with the stateful ones. With the term *stateful systems*, we mean all those systems that need an internal state to work correctly. In those systems, the response to a certain message m_i is not exclusively influenced by m_i, but also by the former messages $\{m_{i-1}, m_{i-2}, \dots\}$. For this reason, while stateless fuzzers only have to mutate single messages (by mutating, for example, the message m_i into the message m_i^1); stateful fuzzers also need to mutate the message order (often called *trace*). For example, a valid—and perhaps interesting—mutation over the trace $t_0 = \{m_1, m_2, m_3\}$ is the trace $t_1 = \{m_1, m_3, m_2\}$.

Among the other techniques for stateful fuzzing [8], two stood out in the last years: grammar-based and coverage-guided fuzzing.

Grammar-Based Fuzzers require the definition of the structure of the messages and the structure of the state model. Also, it is possible to give the fuzzer information about the *most interesting* states – in terms of chances of triggering bugs – to fuzz. Despite this approach being originally devised to fuzz stateless systems, it works also with the stateful ones. Stateful systems usually rely on specific protocols and message specifications that can be expressed through grammar. In other words, the only difference between stateless and stateful grammar-based fuzzers relies on the grammar used. The former only use the grammar of the message, the latter also the grammar of the traces.

One of the limits of this approach is that the grammar provided has to be complete since it has to cover all the message fields and system states. An example of a stateful grammar-based fuzzer is Boofuzz [14], which we use to fuzz three OPC UA implementations (Sect. 4.2).

Coverage-Guided Fuzzers, also known as stateful grey-box fuzzers, do not require a grammar in input but, instead, use *seed traces* and *feedback* from the system to infer and explore the state model of the SUT and generate interesting traces. More in detail, they start their fuzzing campaign with a set of seed traces they will then mutate. To increase the probability of generating interesting traces, they use feedback from the system to steer the generation of new inputs. An example of a stateful coverage-guided fuzzer is AFLNet [15], which we used in our experiments (Sect. 4.3).

The majority of the (stateless and stateful) coverage-guided fuzzers inject instrumentation into the SUT to generate test cases that, with a high probability, will cover new parts of the code.

Nevertheless, conventional (stateless) coverage-guided fuzzers usually have a hard time fuzzing stateful systems as they do not have the knowledge to browse around the state model. An example of a stateless fuzzer able is AFLnwe, which we used to test three OPC UA implementations (Sect. 4.1).

2.2 OPC UA

OPC UA is a stateful protocol used for the communication between Industrial Control Systems (ICS). The protocol requires the client to open a secure channel (or an authenticated session) and discover *service sets*, i.e. a group of messages that are used to fulfil one purpose within an OPC UA connection. In order to evaluate the state coverage of the fuzzers, we inferred the OPC UA state model by hand by looking at the specification [2] and by observing OPC UA network traffic (for the three implementations) between client and server (Fig. 1).

In this paper, we focus on the commands (called *message types* in the specification) that are responsible for establishing connections with an OPC UA server. These commands are included within a service set. For example, the commands service sets *SecureChannel*, *Discovery*, and *Session* are required to establish a connection between a client and a server.

More in detail, we pay attention to nine commands (or message types), spread out in four service sets.

- *Basic message types*
  1. Hello
- *SecureChannel service set*
  2. OpenSecureChannel
  3. CloseSecureChannel
- *Discovery service set*
  4. FindServers
  5. FindServersOnNetwork
  6. RegisterServer
  7. GetEndpoints
- *Session service set*
  8. CreateSession
  9. ActivateSession

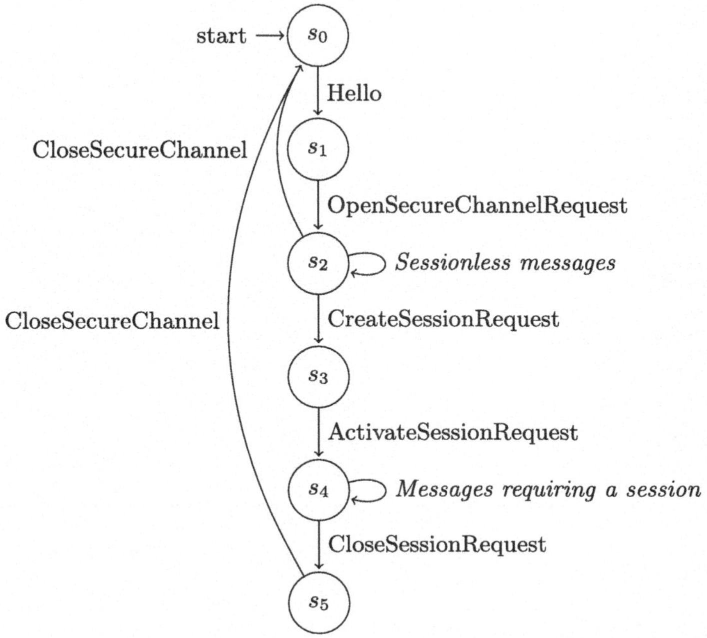

Fig. 1. Manual reconstruction of the OPC UA state model.

3 Previous Fuzzing Efforts

In the last years, different organizations have shown interest in testing the robustness of OPC UA both on the implementation [5,6,9] and protocol level [13,17]. Despite the considerable effort, all the attempts made to test the robustness of the protocol implementations overlooked the stateful nature of OPC UA. This wrong assumption precluded the possibility of finding bugs that rely deeply on the state model (Sect. 5.1),which we found with the stateful fuzzer AFLNet.

3.1 German Federal Office for Information Security (BSI)

In 2017 the German Federal Office for Information Security, also known as BSI, published an extensive security analysis of OPC UA where they analysed the ANSI C implementation [6]. They tested the implementation with the fuzzer *Peach* [3] but no crashes were found.

In 2022, they tested open62541 by using the black-box fuzzer BooFuzz[2] and the coverage-guided fuzzer[3] libFuzzer [9], both with ASan[4]. The latter fuzzing campaign found several crashes, including a heap buffer overflow in an old open62541 implementation.

[2] The code for the fuzzing campaigns is on GitHub at https://github.com/fkie-cad/blackbox-opcua-fuzzing.

[3] mistakenly called white-box fuzzing in the report.

[4] https://github.com/google/sanitizers/wiki/addresssanitizer.

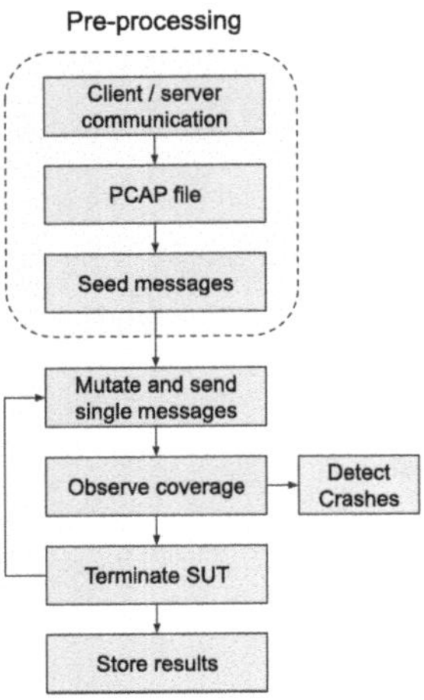

Fig. 2. AFLNwe.

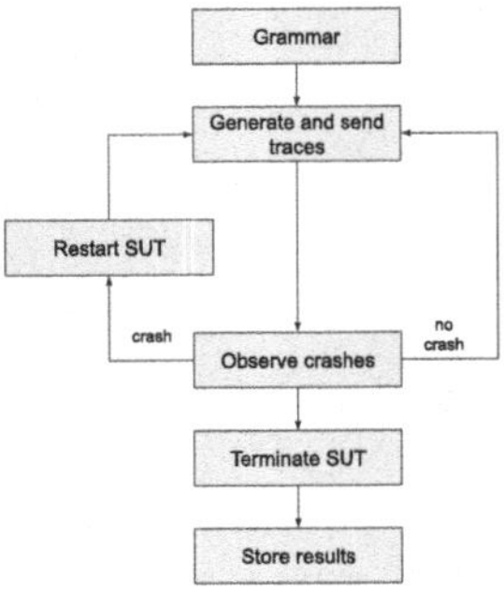

Fig. 3. BooFuzz.

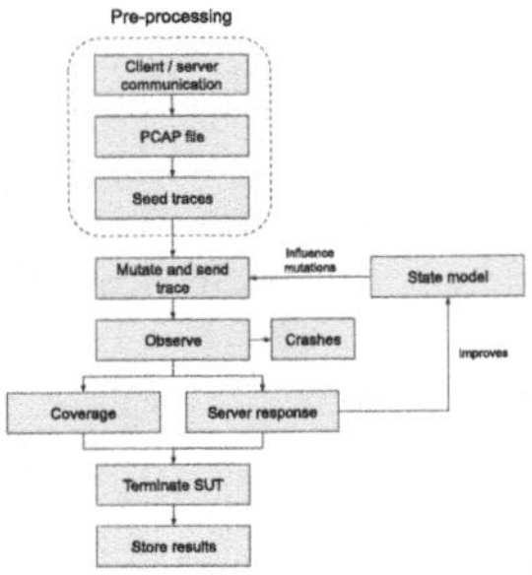

Fig. 4. AFLNet.

3.2 Kaspersky Lab ICS CERT

In 2018, researchers from Kaspersky Lab ICS CERT ran a modified version of AFL (able to deal with network system calls) on the C implementation OPC UA ANSI C implementation and found nine vulnerabilities [5]. However, the ANSI C implementation they tested is no longer maintained and it is not available for download.

4 Fuzzing OPC UA

We fuzzed three OPC UA open source implementations (i.e., open62541, ANSI-C implementation, and FreeOpcUa) with AFLnwe, BooFuzz and AFLNet for 10 h. We used the ASan in all our experiments. The code is available online.[5]

As summarized in Table 1, AFLnwe only found a bug in the initial state of the protocol, BooFuzz did not find any reproducible bug and AFLNet discovered the same bug found by AFLnwe and two new ones. The three fuzzing campaigns are discussed in more detail below.

4.1 AFLnwe Fuzzing Campaign

Experiments. We tested the OPC UA implementations with AFLnwe, a fork of AFL++ able to send messages over the sockets. AFLnwe—being stateless—does not use any notion of a state model but only takes in input seed messages. We collected such messages by sniffing the communications between a sample client and a server. The flowchart of the AFLNwe experiments is presented in Fig. 2.

[5] https://anonymous.4open.science/r/opcua-fuzzing-3743/README.md.

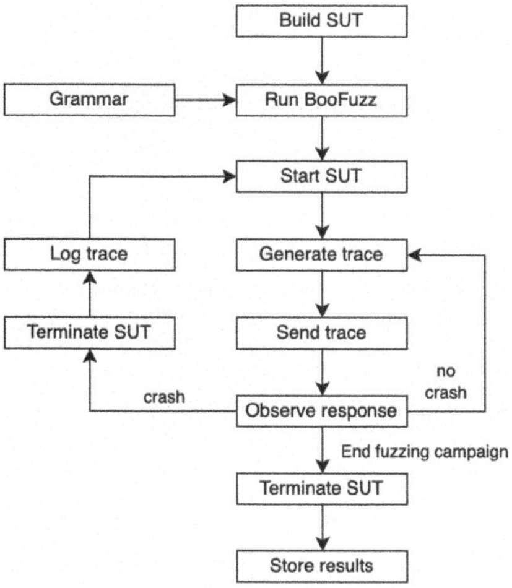

Fig. 5. Flowcharts of different fuzzers.

Findings. In less than 2 h, AFLnwe found a bug in the initial state of the FreeOpcUa implementation. The crash is triggered by the server binary terminating due to an uncaught error, stating that the buffer size given to *InputFromBuffer* is invalid. More in detail, error is triggered when the length of the buffer size is 0. In fact, for a coding error, the buffer size can have a value of 0 when both the message and the OPC UA header are 8 bytes long. Despite the project is not actively maintained anymore, we reported the bugs to the developers, who asked us to open a pull request to fix the bug (on which we are currently working).

4.2 BooFuzz Fuzzing Campaign

Experiments. The flowchart of the BooFuzz experiments is presented in Fig. 3. The grammar used to fuzz OPC UA covers the following sequence of messages[6]:

- Hello
- Hello → OpenSecureChannelRequest
- Hello → OpenSecureChannelRequest → CloseSecureChannel
- Hello → OpenSecureChannelRequest → FindEndpoints *(Sessionless message)*
- Hello → OpenSecureChannelRequest → GetEndpoints *(Sessionless message)*
- Hello → OpenSecureChannelRequest → FindServersOnNetwork *(Sessionless message)*

[6] We used the same grammar used by BSI.

- Hello → OpenSecureChannelRequest → RegisterServer2 *(Sessionless message)*
- Hello → OpenSecureChannelRequest → CreateSessionRequest
- Hello → OpenSecureChannelRequest → CreateSessionRequest → ActivateSessionRequest

Please note that such a grammar does not cover $S5$ and does not allow sending messages that require a prior session establishment.

The fuzzer takes the grammar in input and then generates a trace that then forwards to the SUT and monitors potential crashes. If no crash is detected, the fuzzer proceeds with the generation of a new trace. On the contrary, if a crash is triggered, the fuzzer restarts the SUT.

BooFuzz Findings. BooFuzz could not find any bug in any recent version of open62541, FreeOpcUA and ANSI-C implementation with the grammar presented in Sect. 4.2. The limited state coverage (four states out of five), together with the (stateless) mutation strategy of BooFuzz justifies the poor results. Also, Boofuzz—to keep the mutation under control—only mutates the last message of each sequence and not the single messages or their order. In other words, it only uses the grammar as a prefix to reach a certain state that then fuzzes. This approach limits the generation of traces where the order of the messages is changed. Unfortunately, enabling the mutation of the entire trace is not a solution, since—without any feedback from the system—it would produce thousands of malformed traces.

4.3 AFLNet Fuzzing Campaign

Experiments. The flowchart of the AFLNet experiments is presented in Fig. 4. As we did for AFLnwe (Sect. 4.1), we collected some seed traces by sniffing a communication between a client and a server via *tcp dump* (pre-processing).

The traffic sniffed allows the fuzzer to reach all the states presented in Fig. 1, as it includes the following traces:

- Hello → OpenSecureChannelRequest → FindServers *(Sessionless message)* → CloseSecureChannelRequest
- Hello → OpenSecureChannelRequest → GetEndpoints *(Sessionless message)* → CloseSecureChannelRequest
- Hello → OpenSecureChannelRequest → CreateSessionRequest → ActivateSessionRequest → ... *(Messages requiring a session)* → CloseSessionRequest → CloseSecureChannelRequest

It is worthwhile to notice that, unlike for BooFuzz, the last captured trace allows fuzzing $S5$ and $S4$ *after* having established a proper session.

Table 1. Bugs found by AFLnwe, BooFuzz and AFLNet

	AFLnwe		BooFuzz		AFLNet		Runtime
Implementation	Unique crashes	States covered	Unique crashes	States covered	Unique crashes	States covered	
open62541	0	1/5	0	4/5	0	5/5	∼10 h
ANSI-C implementation	0	1/5	0	4/5	**1**	5/5	∼10 h
FreeOpcUa	**1**	1/5	0	4/5	**2**	5/5	∼10 h

AFLNet takes the seed files in input, mutates and forwards them to the SUT. In addition to crashes, the fuzzer observes the feedback on two aspects: the *code coverage* and the *server response.* It uses the information about the coverage to steer the generation of new traces thanks to its grey-box nature. Moreover, it observes the response of the server to infer the state model of the system and use it during the mutation of new traces.

To properly infer the state model, AFLNet requires two *abstraction functions* (one for the requests and one for the responses) to map raw messages into meaningful strings. The *request* abstraction function we implemented takes in input the whole message, reads the *Payload size* and returns the *Payload.* The *response* abstraction function simply extracts the response codes from the server responses.

Findings. AFLNet found one crash in the ANSI-C implementation and two crashes in the FreeOPCUa one, as shown in Table 1.

ANSI-C Implementation Crash. AFLNet found a bug (a segmentation fault) in the ANSI-C implementation. The crash is triggered when sending a *find_servers* request with a *null* URL. The source of the bug is a string comparison when the first string is null and the second is *"Nano_Server".* Using *strncmp* with a null string on either side is considered undefined behaviour, and causes a segmentation fault in this case. However, the bug is present only in the example server provided with the ANSI-C implementation and not the main code of the stack itself. Since this stack is no longer directly supported or available, we did not report this bug.

FreeOpcUa Crashes. AFLNet found two unique crashes (Table 1), one of which is the same one discovered by AFLnwe (Sect. 4.1). The second crash is triggered when a memory limit of 50MB is set. However, new connections are still accepted until a connection limit is hit.

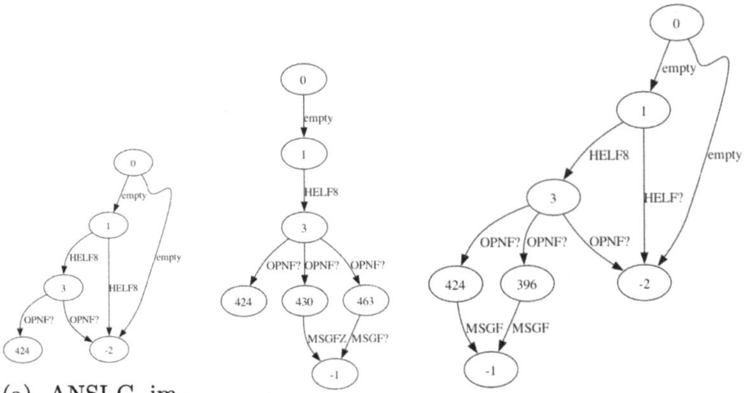

(a) ANSI-C implementation. (b) FreeOpcUA. (c) Open62541 state model.

Fig. 6. State models inferred by AFLNet. Edge labels represent the message to trigger the transaction; state labels represent the response code.

5 Discussions

5.1 Bugs Found

Two of the three bugs found are not shallow, i.e., they cannot be triggered from the first state but need to be triggered from the states $S2$ and $S4$.

This explains why AFLnwe—being stateless—could only find one bug (the shallow one), while AFLNet could also find the others. In fact, AFLNet (like other stateful fuzzers [8]) considers the statefulness of the system and infers—during the fuzzing campaign—the state model of the SUT (as shown in Fig. 4 and explained in Sect. 4.3). Also, its coverage-guided nature helps to prioritise interesting messages and states. In addition, AFLNet performs mutations over the traces and keeps a queue of interesting messages for every state, making the selection of interesting messages state-aware.

On the other hand, Boofuzz did not find any bugs. The poor performances can be attributed to its black-box nature, which does not allow the fuzzer to prioritise interesting messages, and to the inability to perform mutation on the trace level. Also, the grammar used by BooFuzz is not complete (as it does not cover $S5$) and does not allow sending messages that require a prior session establishment (as explained in Sect. 4.2).

5.2 Limits and Applications of Stateless Fuzzers

All the fuzzers based on AFL—being exclusively devised to tackle stateless systems—restart the SUT after every message. The resets bring the SUT back to the initial state, thereby allowing the fuzzer to send messages only to the shallow state. In other words, the restart stops the fuzzer from exploring deeper states whatsoever. This behaviour prevents AFLnwe from triggering any deep bug. Moreover, stateless fuzzers do not have any notion of state models and, thus, are not capable of focusing on specific states or performing stateful mutations (as explained in Sect. 2).

Nevertheless, stateless fuzzers might still be used to bypass the statefulness of the systems [7]. For example, fuzzers like libFuzzer [1] allow writing *fuzzing target* to specific functions to bypass the statefulness of some systems. Unfortunately, this solution allows fuzzing only small portions of code and makes bugs triggered by weird message compositions impossible to find. Also, this approach makes the crash not reproducible as the complete trace to trigger the bug is unknown. OSS-fuzz [16] used this approach to fuzz an older version of open62541 and found vulnerabilities, but, unfortunately, it is not possible to trigger those bugs from the outside as the fuzzer only found the last input, i.e. the very last message of the trace that triggered the bug.

Another solution to fuzz stateful systems with stateless fuzzers is cramming multiple messages into one. This would allow the encapsulation of entire traces in one message only, making the restart of the SUT not an issue.

5.3 Limits and Applications of Grammar-Based Fuzzers

Grammar-based fuzzers can be used to fuzz stateful systems. As already mentioned in Sect. 2, for a grammar-based fuzzer the statefulness of the system does not play an important role as the grammar can describe both the message fields and the state model.

Nevertheless, grammar-based fuzzers struggle in fuzzing stateful systems because of the need for an accurate description of the grammar for both the messages and the traces. Also, having precise grammar would not make black-box grammar-based fuzzers very effective. In fact, they would have to deal with such a large grammar that would make the traces generation random. To mitigate this problem some fuzzers (like BooFuzz, Sect. 4.2), only mutate the last message of the trace, missing—perhaps—interesting mutations on the trace level.

6 Future Work

As explained in Sect. 4, we used limited grammar for BooFuzz and non-comprehensive network traffic for AFLNet. Improving such information might improve the code coverage and find new vulnerabilities. Also, we limited our research to open-source OPC UA implementations, but many more exist as has been documented by Erba et al. [12].

We only used network-based fuzzers in both experiments. However, network communication introduces a high amount of latency. To improve fuzzing performance, the SUT could be rewritten to read and write messages through faster channels [4].

7 Conclusions

In this paper, we compare the effectiveness of stateless and stateful fuzzers in fuzzing a stateful system. Table 1 shows that stateless fuzzers achieve poor performance in fuzzing stateful systems because – as expected – they can only find bugs in the initial state. Indeed, AFLnwe only found one shallow bug in the FreeOpcUA implementation.

Grammar-based fuzzers can be used for stateful fuzzing, but only when the analysts provide good grammar. Also, the fuzzer needs to be able to both mutate individual messages and mutate the order of messages. In our experience, BooFuzz does not mutate the order of messages but uses the grammar only to reach specific states.

On the contrary, stateful fuzzers work fine with only seed traces (that are often easy to generate) and provide a fast yet effective assessment of the robustness of the SUT. Indeed, in addition to the bug found by AFLnwe, AFLNet found two other, deeper bugs in two different implementations.

Acknowledgement. We thank OMRON for introducing the OPC UA protocol to us. Research funded by NWO as part of the INTERSECT project (NWA.1160.18.301).

References

1. Libfuzzer. https://llvm.org/docs/LibFuzzer.html
2. open62541. OPC UA Foundation. https://reference.opcfoundation.org/Core/Part6/v105/docs/7.1.3
3. Peach fuzzer (2004). https://gitlab.com/peachtech/peach-fuzzer-community
4. Andarzian, S.B., Daniele, C., Poll, E.: On the (in) efficiency of fuzzing network protocols. Annals of Telecommunications (2024)
5. Cheremushkin, P., Temnikov, S.: OPC UA security analysis. Kaspersky Lab ICS CERT (2018). https://ics-cert.kaspersky.com/publications/reports/2018/05/10/opc-ua-security-analysis/
6. Gappmeier, D., Plöb, Z., Störtkuhl, F.: OPC UA security analysis. BSI (2017). https://www.bsi.bund.de/SharedDocs/Downloads/DE/BSI/Publikationen/Studien/OPCUA/OPCUA.pdf
7. Daniele, C.: Is stateful fuzzing really challenging? arXiv preprint arXiv:2406.07071 (2024)
8. Daniele, C., Andarzian, S.B., Poll, E.: Fuzzers for stateful systems: Survey and research directions. ACM Comput. Surv. **56**(9), 1–23 (2024)
9. vom Dorp, J., Merschjohann, S., Meier, D., Patzer, F., Karch, M., Haas, C.: OPC UA security analysis. BSI (2022). https://www.bsi.bund.de/SharedDocs/Downloads/DE/BSI/Publikationen/Studien/OPCUA/OPCUA_2022.html
10. Eceiza, M., Flores, J.L., Iturbe, M.: Fuzzing the internet of things: A review on the techniques and challenges for efficient vulnerability discovery in embedded systems. IEEE Internet of Things J. 10390–10411 (2021)
11. Eisele, M., Maugeri, M., Shriwas, R., Huth, C., Bella, G.: Embedded fuzzing: a review of challenges, tools, and solutions. Cybersecurity **5**(1), 18 (2022)

12. Erba, A., Müller, A., Tippenhauer, N.O.: Security analysis of vendor implementations of the OPC UA protocol for industrial control systems. In: Proceedings of the 4th Workshop on CPS & IoT Security and Privacy. ACM (2022)
13. Mühlbauer, N., Kirdan, E., Pahl, M.O., Carle, G.: Open-source OPC UA security and scalability. In: IEEE International Conference on Emerging Technologies and Factory Automation (ETFA) (2020)
14. Pereyda, J.: Boofuzz. https://github.com/jtpereyda/boofuzz
15. Pham, V.T., Böhme, M., Roychoudhury, A.: Aflnet: A greybox fuzzer for network protocols. In: Conference on Software Testing, Validation and Verification (ICST) (2020)
16. Serebryany, K.: OSS-Fuzz - Google's continuous fuzzing service for open source software. USENIX (2017)
17. Tran Van, A., Levillain, O., Debar, H.: Mealy verifier: an automated, exhaustive, and explainable methodology for analyzing state machines in protocol implementations. In: International Conference on Availability, Reliability and Security (2024)
18. Yun, J., Rustamov, F., Kim, J., Shin, Y.: Fuzzing of embedded systems: a survey. ACM Comput. Surv. **55**(7), 1–33 (2022)
19. Zhang, Z., Zhang, H., Zhao, J., Yin, Y.: A survey on the development of network protocol fuzzing techniques. Electronics **12**(13), 2904 (2023)

Efficiency Analysis of Lightweight Post-Quantum Cryptographic Algorithms

Andrei Istrate, Dan Avram, and Iulian Aciobăniţei(✉)

Military Technical Academy "Ferdinand I", Bucharest, Romania
iulian.aciobanitei@mta.ro

Abstract. The proliferation of Internet of Things (IoT) devices demands cryptographic algorithms that balance security with resource efficiency, especially as quantum computing development threatens classical cryptography. In this paper, we evaluate the energy consumption of post-quantum cryptographic (PQC) algorithms, with an emphasis on lightweight algorithms suitable for IoT environments. Given the critical nature of IoT systems, ensuring both security and minimal energy consumption is essential. We analyzed a selection of PQC algorithms standardized by NIST, comparing their energy performance with classical counterparts such as RSA and ECDH. Using a microcontroller, processes such as key generation, encryption, and decryption were measured. Special attention is paid to how different mathematical structures, such as lattice-based cryptography, influence energy usage. The results highlight the efficiency of lattice-based schemes, such as CRYSTALS-Kyber, in key encapsulation tasks, outperforming classical cryptographic methods in both speed and energy consumption. Our findings are useful for researchers working on the integration of PQC in energy-sensitive applications, such as IoT.

Keywords: Post Quantum Computing · Lightweight Cryptography · Internet of Things · IoT · PQC

1 Introduction

The Internet of Things is an emerging technology with significant potential, ranging from connected personal devices to extensive industrial drone networks. Security remains a critical concern for IoT technologies, as the computational cost of cryptographic algorithms for digital encryption and authentication can be prohibitive for resource-constrained IoT devices, which are often deployed in large numbers and sometimes in remote and inaccessible areas [1]. Production cost, size, and battery life are prioritized over security for these low-end, lightweight devices.

As IoT technologies integrate into various sectors such as agriculture, industrial production, medical services, military applications, and daily life, it is essential to enforce adequate digital encryption and authentication standards. A

L. Morogan et al. (Eds.): SecITC 2024, LNCS 15595, pp. 108–117, 2025.
https://doi.org/10.1007/978-3-031-87760-5_9

major challenge in applying cryptography to IoT is the high computational cost, which typically scales with the key size of the algorithm used. Moreover, recent improvements in quantum computing are expected to request and cause updates to cryptographic standards. Quantum computing could lead to the adoption of even more complex cryptographic algorithms, worsening the current challenges faced by IoT systems. Quantum computers capable of running Shor's algorithm [2] could efficiently solve Integer Factorization and Discrete Logarithm problems, which are fundamental to current public-key cryptosystems. Furthermore, Grover's algorithm [3] can speed up the search for symmetric keys by providing a quadratic improvement for unstructured search problems. As a result, while symmetric ciphers might need to increase their key sizes to maintain security, asymmetric cryptography will need a fundamental overhaul to address the threats posed by quantum computing.

Therefore, it is essential to seek post-quantum cryptography(PQC) solutions, with their selection based on the resources of the target platforms and the energetical behavior of the algorithms. As presented in Sect. 2, research literature contains analysis on the efficiency of post-quantum cryptographic algorithms. To our knowledge, there are no papers focused on lightweight-specific algorithms with a detailed analysis of what may cause the low or high energy consumption.

The main goal of this paper is to determine energy efficiency across different classes of PQC algorithms, with a particular focus on lightweight algorithms, which are critical for resource-constrained IoT environments.

The rest of the paper is organized as follows. Section 2 presents the current research and standardization landscape in the field. Next, we present the methodology used to obtain the energy measurements in Sect. 3. The results of our simulations are presented in Sect. 4 and their interpretation is detailed in Sect. 5. Section 6 is reserved for conclusions.

2 State of the Art

The current section is reserved for an overview of the current landscape regarding PQC algorithms for IoT. Firstly, NIST standards are presented and in the second subsection, research literature is analyzed.

2.1 Working Standards

The National Institute of Standards and Technology (NIST) plays a crucial role in improving the technological infrastructure by establishing accurate rules in fields such as cybersecurity and cryptography. Notably, NIST leads efforts in post-quantum cryptography to develop secure systems for the future of quantum computing.

On April 2–3, 2015, the Workshop on Cybersecurity in a Post-Quantum World took place, where NIST began the research era in quantum-resistant cryptographic algorithms for key agreement and digital signatures, with the aim of engaging academia, industry, and government to address the threat quantum computing poses to current public key cryptography [4]. Since then, five editions of the PQC Standardization Conference have been organized, the most recent held in April 2024, and the sixth edition scheduled for five months later.

Ou of the 69 post-quantum algorithms from the first round submission, three of them (CRYSTALS-Kyber, CRYSTALS-Dilithium, and SPHINCS+) where selected by NIST. These have been included in FIPS 203, 204, and 205 in August 2024 [5].

To provide a diverse range of options, NIST is inviting researchers to submit new algorithms which are able to strengthen the existing FIPS standards for public key agreement (e.g., BIKE, SIKE) and digital signatures (e.g. CROSS, MEDS, Raccoon, Biscuit, UOV). This is to ensure that the cryptographic ecosystem is resilient against potential attacks and to explore different mathematical problems (lattice, isogeny, code-based, multivariate etc.).

The recent NIST standardization of three post-quantum cryptographic algorithms marks a significant advancement in the field of quantum-resistant cryptography. These standards, codified as FIPS, contain detailed specifications and implementation guidelines for algorithms designed to withstand attacks from a cryptographically relevant quantum computer (CRQP). Given the rapid progress in quantum computing research, the emergence of such a CRQP within the next decade is increasingly probable [6].

- FIPS-203. This standard outlines a set of algorithms known as Module-Lattice-Key-Encapsulation Mechanism (ML-KEM). These algorithms are intended to be used alongside symmetric-key cryptographic methods for quantum-safe data encryption. They leverage the strength and computational complexity of the Module Learning with Errors problem. The standard specifies three parameters: ML-KEM-512, ML-KEM-768, and ML-KEM-1024, with the higher numbers providing increased security at the cost of reduced performance in terms of speed and key length
- FIPS-204. This standard specifies the Module-Lattice-Based Digital Signature Algorithm (ML-DSA), which can be used to generate and verify digital signatures. It ensures the authenticity of the signer, the integrity of the transaction, and non-repudiation
- FIPS-205. This standard outlines the Stateless Hash-Based Digital Signature Algorithm (SLH-DSA), which is based on SPHINCS+. Similar to FIPS 204, it is designed for digital signatures and ensures the authenticity of the signer, the integrity of the transmitted data, and provides non-repudiation

Post-quantum algorithms can be configured with various parameter sets to achieve different levels of security. Defined by NIST and shown in Table 1, these are equivalent to the computational effort required to break AES keys or find collisions in hash functions [7].

Table 1. Security Levels

Level	Equivalent effort to break
1	AES128
2	SHA256
3	AES192
4	SHA384
5	AES256

Currently, NIST is working tirelessly to accept more post-quantum cryptographic solutions, with plans to publish additional standards in the near future to ensure diversity in the field.

2.2 Relevant Research Literature

PQC algorithms generally require more computational power than traditional public-key encryption [8], having a strong impact on IoT devices, which often have limited energy, memory, and processing capabilities. Researchers have acknowledged this issue and are willing to study PQC performance for resource-constrained environments.

Many papers have explored the estimation of energy consumption for different sensor nodes. These works generally involve simulators [9] and utilize built-in protocols that are widely used in wireless sensor network implementations. In contrast, our study delves into post-quantum cryptographic algorithms, a recent development that has not yet been incorporated into IoT communication protocols. Simulators, however, lack the flexibility to make granular code changes or integrate external cryptographic libraries, limiting their effectiveness in evaluating these new algorithms for IoT applications.

According to another study [10], the combination of Kyber with either Falcon or Dilithium offers the best performance in TLS handshakes, considering the impact of key and signature lengths on communication, while Kyber and SPHINCS+ are the slowest option.

Similarly to our research, another study evaluated the energy consumption of two NIST round 3 candidate algorithms, CRYSTALS-Dilithium and FALCON [11], on different devices (Raspberry Pis and PCs). This study shows that RSA consumes slightly less power, confirming the more complex operations for post-quantum algorithms. However, processing time is an important factor that can tell us the energy required for an iteration.

Another paper [12] has a more detailed approach of power measurements for a wider variety of algorithms and versions, both reference and optimized. These measurements were performed directly on a PC processor, using a specialized programmable API and showed that different underlying problems may affect the level of power consumption.

Our work differs from these previous works by comparing the power consumption for a selection from the most recent PQCs (the current algorithms recently included in FIPS and a selection from the additional round as alternatives), employing a different target platform. By applying our methodology, we can analyze even more algorithms to determine their efficiency based on the underlying mathematical problem. This information can be useful in the selection process for standardization.

3 Methodology

We approached measuring the energy consumption of six algorithms, three of which have been standardized by FIPS. Each solution is implemented in C and its parameter set specifications are published on the NIST website. The implementation of standardized algorithms can be found at [13], and the remaining 3 solutions take part of Round 1 Additional Signatures of NIST's PQC Standardization Process and are published in [14] and [15].

We took measurements for key generation, signature, and signature verification for each algorithm. We averaged the results of 100 iterations for processing time and clock cycles observations and involved the execution of each operation in a loop for power measurement. The signatures were generated on pseudorandom messages with a length of 32 bytes. This study focused on 6 PQC algorithms and 2 classic cryptography algorithms (RSA and ECC based). We intend to expand our analysis in a future work. For the PQC algorithms, we simply call the 3 main functions from the reference implementation, while for RSA or ECDSA we use MbedTLS library [16].

The target device is a microcontroller [17] programmed using the Arduino development environment through an USB-A - MicroUSB cable, featuring an ARM Cortex M7 processor and 1 MB of RAM. Programmatic methods were sufficient for measuring execution times and processor cycles, but energy consumption required a more nuanced approach, involving the exploration of several measurement techniques.

Initially, we used an amperemeter with a precision of up to 20mA as a reference. Subsequently, we used an oscilloscope [18] to acquire data from a current sensor [19] connected in series with the microcontroller and an USB multimeter. Upon comparing the results obtained from all three methods, we observed that the USB multimeter provided the most accurate results when compared to the dedicated amperemeter. Consequently, we selected the USB multimeter due to its ease of use, as we could read the instant current intensity on its dedicated display, as shown in Fig. 1.

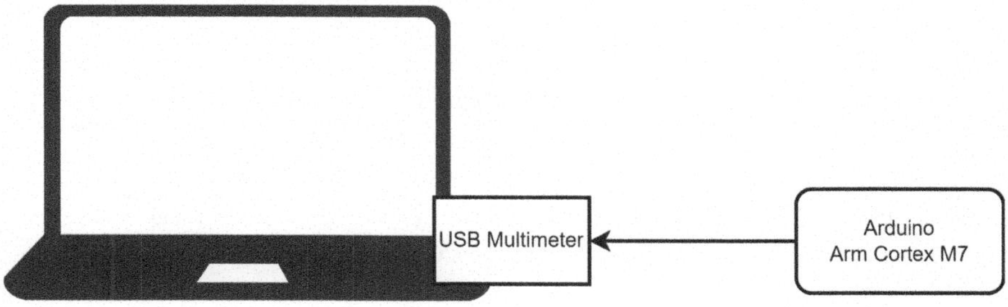

Fig. 1. Experimental setup.

The reference sources for the tested algorithms were used to avoid libraries implementation differences and to ensure the relevance of the measurements. All code was compiled with identical flags within the Arduino development environment. It is important to note that the experiment was conducted at a microprocessor frequency of 600 MHz, because frequency variations affect power consumption, which in turn affects algorithm energy usage. Reducing execution time can decrease energy consumption, but this depends on the optimization method [20].

To summarize our methodology, we performed the measurements taking into account the following key points:

- ARM Cortex M7 microprocessor
- USB multimeter for energy consumption measurement
- 100 iterations for each algorithm, then used the average
- For energy consumption, we excluded consumption measured in idle time

4 Results

The results obtained for post-quantum algorithms indicate that many of them are strong contenders against current ones, and the mathematical foundations behind them somehow explain the differences in processing times and resource consumption.

Table 2 shows the energy consumption in millijoules (mJ), processing time in milliseconds (ms), and power in milliwatts (mW) for the first post-quantum algorithm accepted for standardization in the KEM section, allowing comparison with the classic elliptic curve Diffie-Hellman key exchange algorithm. Round 4 algorithms were not included, either because their keys are too large for the device's capacity (McEliece) or because they require implementations from other libraries (HQC, BIKE).

Table 2. ML-Kem and classic ECDH consumption

Algorithm	Key generation			Encrypt			Decrypt			Security
	Power	Time	Energy	Power	Time	Energy	Power	Time	Energy	
Kyber 512	555	0.800	0.444	545	1.103	0.601	525	1.236	0.648	1
Kyber 768	555	1.339	0.743	550	1.767	0.971	525	1.930	1.013	3
Kyber 1024	555	2.096	1.163	550	2.621	1.441	535	2.816	1.506	5
ECDH(secp256r1)	495	1.382	0.684	500	1.930	0.965	-	-	-	1

Table 3 outlines the CPU cycles involved in each operation for key agreement algorithms, addressed in kilo clock cycles (kcc).

Table 3. ML-KEM and classic ECDH CPU cycles

Algorithm	Key generation	Encrypt	Decrypt	Security
Kyber 512	477	659	738	1
Kyber 768	799	1057	1153	3
Kyber 1024	1258	1574	1690	5
ECDH(secp256r1)	823	1107	-	1

Table 4 shows the energy consumption in millijoules (mJ), processing time in milliseconds (ms), and power in milliwatts (mW) for digital signature algorithms, allowing for comparison with the classic RSA and ECDSA.

Table 5 presents the CPU cycles involved in each operation for digital signature algorithms, addressed in kilo clock cycles (kcc).

Table 4. Digital signature consumption

Algorithm	Key generation			Sign			Verify			Security
	Power	Time	Energy	Power	Time	Energy	Power	Time	Energy	
Dilithium 2	580	2.428	1.408	550	4.048	2.223	560	2.623	1.468	1
Dilithium 3	585	4.137	2.420	550	7.688	4.228	575	4.200	2.415	3
Dilithium 5	575	6.990	4.019	565	9.687	5.473	560	7.223	4.044	5
SphincsSHA256-128 s	525	855.843	449.317	525	6575.020	3451.885	525	6.510	3.417	1
SphincsSHA256-128f	525	13.502	7.088	525	316.314	166.064	525	18.680	9.807	1
Falcon 512	515	138.421	71.286	445	7.554	3.361	465	0.610	0.283	1
Falcon 1024	515	326.513	168.154	435	16.105	7.005	460	1.300	0.598	5
HAWK 512	490	56.221	27.548	505	2.682	0.270	480	1.652	0.158	1
HAWK 1024	500	247.771	123.885	515	5.921	3.049	490	3.522	1.725	5
CROSS Level 1	555	0.814	0.451	530	53.246	28.220	540	24.854	14.415	1
RSA 2048	565	852.346	481.575	575	31.826	18.299	580	0.902	0.523	1
ECDSA (secp256r1)	495	23.477	11.621	500	9.780	4.890	500	9.753	4.876	1

Table 5. Digital signature CPU cycles

Algorithm	Key generation	Encrypt	Decrypt	Security
Dilithium 2	1472	2453	1590	1
Dilithium 3	2507	10691	2545	3
Dilithium 5	4236	18113	4377	5
SphincsSHA256-128 s	529205	4016912	3878	1
SphincsSHA256-128f	8316	194148	11468	1
Falcon 512	46860	4574	382	1
Falcon 1024	177513	9645	788	5
HAWK 512	28351	1625	1001	1
HAWK 1024	115345	3581	2132	5
CROSS Level 1	503	32390	15145	1
RSA 2048	593849	26891	742	1
ECDSA (secp256r1)	14170	5882	5758	1
ECDH(secp256r1)	823	1107	-	1

5 Discussion

The results are categorized by cryptographic method and proposed security level. We analyze the energy consumption of these algorithms to identify the most energy-efficient schemes. We observed that during idle time, the measured power consumption was around 460–465 mW, so the tested algorithms have an impact ranging from 7% to 20%. Our results claim that lattice-based schemes seem to be energy-efficient, having a fast processing time that compensates the increased power consumption, as shown in Table 3.

Table 2 shows that the first accepted Key Encapsulation Method algorithm does quite well in terms of energy usage compared to classical ECDH. As far as key generation is concerned, it is almost 43% faster at security level 1 and 3–4% faster at a higher security level (3). When secret computation is approached, Kyber is 41% faster for the first security level. This supports the results of other studies, even though the target platform is different, that Kyber can do better than existing ECDH in terms of power consumption [21].

As far as digital signature is concerned and in terms of efficiency, CROSS outperformed other algorithms in key generation, while HAWK excelled in message signing. FALCON proved to be the most efficient for signature verification. Although Dilithium is already included in FIPS-204, the findings shown in Table VI and VII highlight the potential of alternative solutions. An important fact is that HAWK is 23 times slower on key generation, but approximately 30% faster in signing and verification at the corresponding security levels (1 and 5). Despite the fact that HAWK and Dilithium are lattice-based, most of the Round 1 Additional Signatures candidates are lattice-based, so it could have a great chance to be standardized. However, NIST is searching for algorithms with different underlying problems to complete the area.

When we look to SPHINCS+, it seems to be the slowest and most inefficient from the selection, and this may be due to extensive computation on hash-based function calls. This gives a good chance as an additional solution to CROSS, which is code-based. CROSS may be the most efficient when looking for key generation, but 10–12 times slower than Dilithium at signing and verification for security level 1. Still, CROSS has an important disadvantage: it is a greater energy consumer than SPHINCS+ for verification.

From a different perspective, many of the examined PQC solutions seem to be great competitors for the well-known RSA, ECDSA, ECDH and a similar study confirms based on measurements in a hybrid TLS context [22], claiming that Kyber and Dilithium are a better duo than ECDSA and ECDH, and much better than RSA and ECDH, when it comes to power consumption.

To enhance the comprehensiveness of our study, it would be beneficial to include as many algorithms as possible for a more detailed comparison and selection. This would enable us to make more informed choices based on specific needs.

6 Conclusions

In this study, we evaluated the energy efficiency of various PQC algorithms, focusing on their use in lightweight IoT devices. Our results show that lattice-based algorithms, particularly CRYSTALS-Kyber for key encapsulation, outperform traditional methods like RSA and ECDH from a speed and energy consumption perspective. As for digital signatures, while Dilithium performed well, HAWK proved to be a strong alternative, especially in message signing. These results highlight the ability of PQC algorithms to address the security needs of post quantum-era, without heavily impacting energy use. Future research should examine a broader range of algorithms and explore further optimizations for specific hardware.

References

1. Liu, T., Ramachandran, G., Jurdak, R.: Post-quantum cryptography for internet of things: a survey on performance and optimization (2024)
2. Shor, P.W.: Algorithms for quantum computation: discrete logarithms and factoring
3. Grover, L.K.: A fast quantum mechanical algorithm for database search
4. Computer Security Resource Center. In: First PQC Standardization Conference. https://csrc.nist.rip/events/2018/first-pqc-standardization-conference
5. National Institute of Standards and Technology: Announcing approval of three federal information processing standards (FIPS) for post-quantum cryptography. https://csrc.nist.gov/news/2024/postquantum-cryptography-fips-approved
6. Greig, J. Store now, decrypt later

7. National Institute of Standards and Technology: Security (evaluation criteria). https://csrc.nist.gov/projects/post-quantum-cryptography/post-quantum-cryptography-standardization/evaluation-criteria/security-(evaluation-criteria)
8. Malina, L., et al.: Post-quantum era privacy protection for intelligent infrastructures
9. Sabovic, A., Delgado, C., Bauwens, J., De Poorter, E., Famaey, J.: Accurate online energy consumption estimation of IoT devices using Energest
10. Dong, B., Wang, Q.: Evaluating post-quantum cryptography on embedded systems: a performance analysis
11. Hines, K., et al.: Post-quantum cipher power analysis in lightweight devices
12. Roma, C.A., Tai, C.E.A, Hasan, M.A.: Energy efficiency analysis of post-quantum cryptographic algorithms
13. National Institute of Standards and Technology: Selected algorithms 2022. https://csrc.nist.gov/Projects/post-quantum-cryptography/selected-algorithms-2022
14. National Institute of Standards and Technology: Round 4 submissions. https://csrc.nist.gov/Projects/post-quantum-cryptography/round-4-submissions
15. National Institute of Standards and Technology: Round 1 additional signatures. https://csrc.nist.gov/Projects/pqc-dig-sig/round-1-additional-signatures
16. MbetTLS library. https://github.com/Mbed-TLS/mbedtls
17. Teensy 4.1 Development Board. https://www.pjrc.com/store/teensy41.html
18. Fully integrated, hall effect-based linear current sensor with 2.1 kVRMS voltage isolation and a low-resistance current conductor. https://www.sparkfun.com/datasheets/BreakoutBoards/0712.pdf
19. Analog Discovery 2: 100MS/s USB oscilloscope, logic analyzer and variable power supply. https://digilent.com/shop/analog-discovery-2-100ms-s-usb-oscilloscope-logic-analyzer-and-variable-power-supply/?srsltid=AfmBOopqUursfkItEVDl_1N0Dok-cWbyBTuPl86eOwsDNLU3r6SNmfeE
20. Pinto, G., Castor, F.: Energy efficiency. ACM
21. Post-quantum Kyber benchmarks (ARM-Cortex M4). https://www.wolfssl.com/post-quantum-kyber-benchmarks-arm-cortex-m4/
22. Tasopoulos, G., Dimopoulos, C., Fournaris, A.P., Zhao, R.K., Sakzad, A., Steinfeld, R.: Energy consumption evaluation of post-quantum TLS 1.3 for resource-constrained embedded devices

Card-Based Arithmetic Operations and Application to Statistical Data Aggregation

Shun Odaka and Yuichi Komano(✉)

Chiba Institute of Technology, Tsudanuma, Narashino 2–17–1, Japan
komano@net.it-chiba.ac.jp

Abstract. Card-based cryptography enables players to compute bitwise operations securely, such as bitwise AND and addition of integers. Several multiparty computation protocols and zero-knowledge proof protocols utilizing these secure computations have been developed as applications. However, the realization of an efficient protocol for integer multiplication and division remains an open problem. This paper proposes card-based protocols for multiplication and division based on integer commitment. Compared to general constructions for protocols for multiplication and division based on binary integer commitment, the proposed protocols exhibit superior simplicity and efficiency. Furthermore, these protocols introduce novel applications for card-based cryptography to secure statistical data aggregation.

Keywords: Card-based cryptography · Integer commitments · Multiplication · Division · Statistical data aggregation

1 Introduction

Card-based cryptography employs a physical deck of cards, such as $\clubsuit\clubsuit\cdots\heartsuit\heartsuit\cdots$, to implement cryptographic protocols, including secure multiparty computations [3,7] and zero-knowledge proofs [2,4,14], through manual swapping and the shuffling of cards. For instance, a protocol for secure bitwise AND operations can be developed using face-down cards (e.g., [1,8]).

Two integer representations exist in card-based cryptography. The first is *a binary integer commitment*, where an integer is regarded as a binary string, and each bit is represented by two cards $\clubsuit$ and $\heartsuit$ with the following encoding rule: $\clubsuit\heartsuit = 0$ and $\heartsuit\clubsuit = 1$. Based on this commitment, we can construct numerous fundamental protocols such as bitwise AND and OR operations, and by combining them, we can develop a protocol for arbitrary functionality [7]. The number of cards is logarithmic in the input size; however, several card operations are required to realize complex functionalities, such as the multiplication or division of integers.

L. Morogan et al. (Eds.): SecITC 2024, LNCS 15595, pp. 118–134, 2025.
https://doi.org/10.1007/978-3-031-87760-5_10

The second representation is *an integer commitment*, in which an integer is represented as a card sequence, comprising one ♡ and $k-1$ ♣'s. In this representation, position of ♡ is an integer. Although a protocol requires the same number of cards as the maximum integer appearing in the computation, the number of card operations can be reduced compared with protocols based on binary integer commitment. Based on integer commitment, protocols for modular addition [13], modular multiplication [12], and subtraction of integers [18] have been proposed. However, the protocol for modular multiplication is less efficient. In addition, a protocol for integer division based on integer commitment is yet to be developed.

From a practical perspective, card-based cryptography is a promising tool for addressing social problems without relying on untrustworthy black-box computers or for helping non-experts to understand various cryptographic concepts. However, owing to a lack of efficient protocols for integer multiplication or division, its applications remain limited. In this paper, we propose efficient protocols for multiplication and division based on integer commitment, thus opening up a new application for statistical data aggregation. This aggregation facilitates the development of a safe and reliable questionnaire without the risk of leaking answers from computers or handwritten forms.

1.1 Our Contribution

The contributions of this paper are as follows:

- We propose card-based protocols for the multiplication, exponentiation, and division of integers based on integer commitment. The proposed integer commitment-based protocols are easier to implement compared to those generally constructed based on binary integer commitment. Additionally, the proposed protocols are committed, meaning that outputs from the proposed protocol, such as a product and a quotient, can be used as inputs for subsequent protocols.
- As an application of the proposed protocols, we discuss secure statistical data aggregation; a grand total (average), a cross tabulation (contingency table), an association rule learning, and a weighted mean with non-response adjustment. We believe that a questionnaire using a secure data aggregation is also a promising application of card-based cryptography, because the card-based protocols use no black-box computer and a respondent can answer their opinion easily without fear of leaking it from a computer. To the best of our knowledge, this is the first paper to discuss statistical data aggregation as an application of card-based cryptography.

1.2 Related Work

Suga [16] proposed a card-based protocol to estimate the similarity between two opinions using a Likert scale. In this protocol, two users privately input their opinions using up-down cards, ↑↓. However, it is only used to estimate the similarity of opinions; it is impossible to use this protocol for other statistical data aggregations. In addition, because it is a non-committed protocol (that is, cards are turned face-up to obtain a result), aggregating three or more opinions recursively using this protocol is also impossible.

Table 1. Arithmetic operations based on the integer commitment

Operation	Input	Cards	Shuffles	Notes
smodadd2 [13]	(sec, sec)	$2k'$	1	modular-addition in $\mathbb{Z}/k'\mathbb{Z}$
ssub2 [18] (App.B)	(sec, sec)	$4k$	1	subtraction of $x, y \in [0, k-1]$ in $\mathbb{Z}$
smodmul2 [12]§3.3	(sec, sec)	${k'}^2 + k'$	$3k' - 7$	modular-multiplication in $\mathbb{Z}/k'\mathbb{Z}$
smul1 (§3.2)	(sec, const)	$n(k-1)+1$	0	multiply $i \in [0, k-1]$ by $n \in \mathbb{N}$
sdiv1 (§3.3)	(sec, const)	$k + d + n$	2	divide $i \in [0, k-1]$ by $n \in \mathbb{N}$, $d = k/n$
spow1 (§3.4)	(sec, const)	$(k-1)^n + 1$	0	base is in $[0, k-1]$, power is in $n \in \mathbb{N}$
smul2 (§3.5)	(sec, sec)	$2k^2 - 3k/2 + 10$	13	inputs are in $[0, k-1]$
sdiv2 (§3.6)	(sec, sec)	$6\lceil\frac{(k-1)}{2^{\ell-1}}\rceil(2^{\ell-1} - 1)$ $+8k+2$	$8\ell + 3$	inputs are in $[0, k-1]$, $\ell = \lfloor\log_2(k-1)\rfloor + 1$

In this paper, we propose card-based protocols for arithmetic operations. The proposed protocols require only black-red cards, which are commonly used in card-based cryptography. Moreover, because the proposed protocols are committed (i.e., a result is obtained with face-down cards in the same encoding rule as inputs), the output of each of the proposed protocols can be used as an input for a subsequent protocol. In other words, the proposed protocols can be used for the aggregation of three or more opinions and other types of data.

Table 1 summarizes the protocols for arithmetic operations based on the integer commitment. In this table, "Input" indicates whether each of two operands (inputs) of each protocol is a secret value (sec) or a public constant (const). For instance, both operands of smodadd2 are secret values and addition with modular reduction is performed without disclosing their values. "Cards" indicates the number of cards used in each protocol, including cards for input and output. "Shuffles" indicates the total number of shuffling operations used in each protocol. In "Note," we use a notation of $[a, b]$ for integers a, b with $a \leq b$, which represents a set of integers $\{a, a+1, \cdots, b\}$.

A naïve construction of secure multiplication by a constant $n \in \mathbb{N}$ is adding a secret value (to be multiplied) n times with smodadd2 [13]; however, this naïve construction requires n shuffles. In contrast, our smul1 provided in Sect. 3.2 requires no shuffling operation.

Ruangwises and Itoh [12] proposed a secure modular multiplication smodmul2 in $\mathbb{Z}/k'\mathbb{Z}$. In this paper, we propose secure multiplication smul2 in $\mathbb{Z}$. Our smul2 takes integers in $[0, k-1]$, each represented by k cards, and outputs a product represented by $(k-1)^2+1$ cards. To multiply the integers in $[0, k-1]$ by smodmul2 without a modular reduction, k' should be $(k-1)^2$. In this case, smodmul2 requires $O(k^4)$ cards, whereas smul2 only requires $O(k^2)$ cards. Moreover, the number of shuffles required for smodmul2 depends on k, whereas that required for smul2 is constant and independent of k.

2 Preliminaries

In this section, we first explain the notation used in this paper and thereafter describe how and what physical cards are utilized. Subsequently, we review the shuffling operations used in the proposed protocol; "a complete shuffle [10]" and "a pile-shifting shuffle [9,15]."

2.1 Physical Cards

In this paper, we use a set of physical cards ♣♡ with symbols ♣ or ♡ written on the face. This set of cards is referred to as the *black-red cards*. We assume that the same symbol ? is written on the back of the black-red cards, and that symbols on the faces cannot be distinguished from the backs.

2.2 Integer Commitment

Let us encode an integer $i \in [0, k-1]$ with k black-red cards as

where each number above the card represents an index. We call k face-down cards representing an integer i with the above encoding *an integer commitment with a base k*. Integer commitment is represented by ??···? or ?|||, and is denoted as $E_k(i)$. Such integer commitment has often been used in previous studies on card-based cryptography (e.g., [6,13,17]).

In this paper, we discuss the application of card-based cryptography and data aggregation using arithmetic operations such as integer addition, subtraction, multiplication, and division. Based on integer commitment, protocols for modular addition [11], subtraction [18], and modular multiplication [12] have been developed, as summarized in Table 1.

2.3 Shuffle Operations

In this paper, we use two types of shuffling operation.

The first is *a complete shuffle* [10], in which cards are rearranged in a uniformly random order. By shuffling the face-down cards with this operation and turning them over to face-up, the cards can be reused in subsequent steps.

The second is *a pile-shifting shuffle* [9,15] which is a shuffling operation in which several piles of cards of the same size are cyclically shifted at random.

A pile-shifting shuffle was applied to k piles, considering two cards in the same column as a single pile. The transition is:

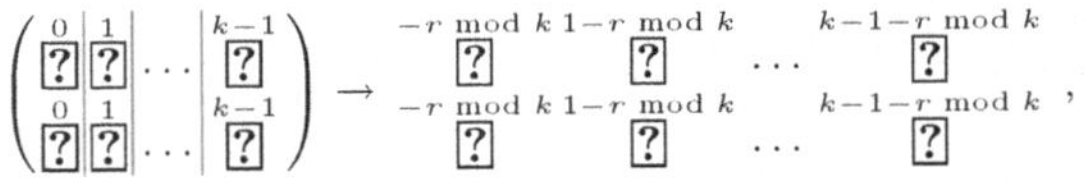

where $r \in [0, k-1]$ is a random number corresponding to the cyclic shift generated by the pile-shifting shuffle.

3 Arithmetic Operations with Physical Cards

In this section, we propose protocols for arithmetic operations based on the integer commitment. We first introduce a base extension protocol and then provide protocols for multiplication, division, and exponentiation. Although Ruangwises and Itoh [12] proposed a protocol for modular multiplication in $\mathbb{Z}/k'\mathbb{Z}$, we propose protocols for arithmetic operations in $\mathbb{Z}$.

3.1 Base Extension

A base extension protocol extends the base of the integer commitment from k to $k'(> k)$. For an integer commitment $E_k(x)$ to an integer $x \in [0, k-1]$ with a base k, the protocol extends the base by placing $k' - k$ ♣'s to the right of the commitment and turning them over to generate $E_{k'}(x)$:

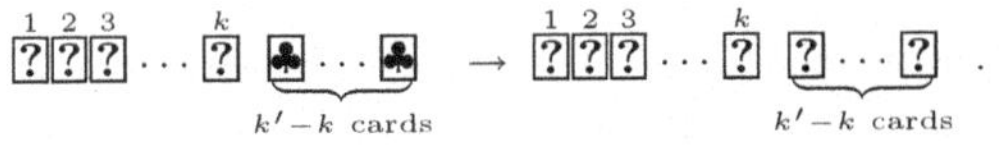

3.2 Secure Multiplication with Constant: smul1

This protocol, given an integer commitment to $i \in [0, k-1]$ with base k and integer $n \geq 1$, generates an integer commitment to ni with base $n(k-1)+1$ as follows:

Protocol 1. (Secure multiplication with a constant: smul1)

1. For $j = k, k-1, \cdots, 2$, repeat the following step.
   (a) Insert $n-1$ ♣'s between the j-th card and the $(j-1)$-th card from the left and turn them over:

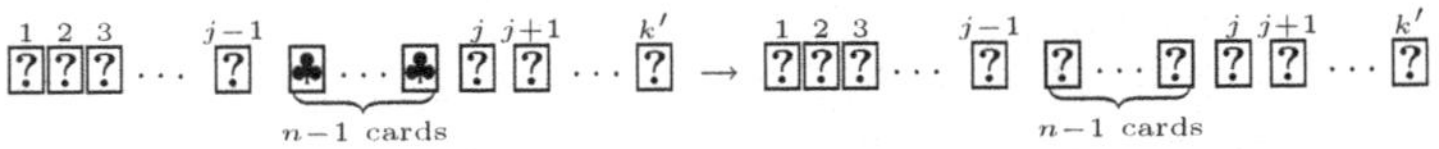

   where $k' = k + (k-j+1)(n-1)$.

This protocol requires $n(k-1)+1$ cards and no shuffling operations.

3.3 Secure Division with Constant: sdiv1

This protocol uses an integer commitment to $i \in [0, k-1]$ with base k and integer $n \geq 1$ as the inputs. Regarding k and n, we assume that $k = dn$ is true for $d \in \mathbb{Z}$. Otherwise, we apply the base extension of Sect. 3.1 such that $k = dn$ holds. With these inputs, the proposed protocol generates integer commitments to quotient $q = \lfloor i/n \rfloor$ and reminder $r = i \bmod n$ with bases d and n, respectively.

Protocol 2. (Secure division with a constant: sdiv1)

1. Arrange an integer commitment $E_k(i)$, given as an input, into a matrix. Then, for each row and column, rearrange cards in the reverse order:

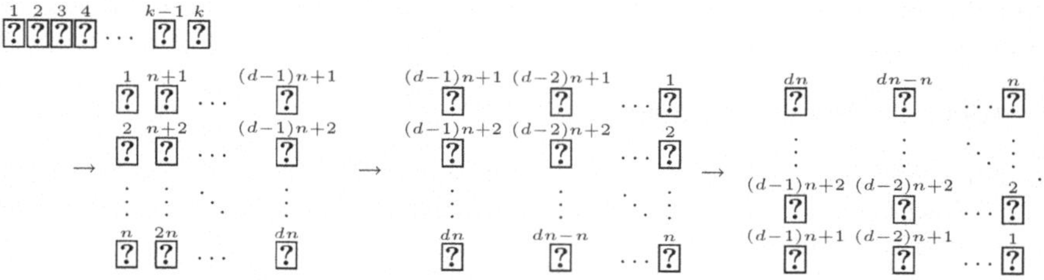

2. For the first row, place ♡ to the right of the last card. For other rows, place ♣ to the right of the last card. Then, turn the placed cards over and apply a pile-shifting shuffle:

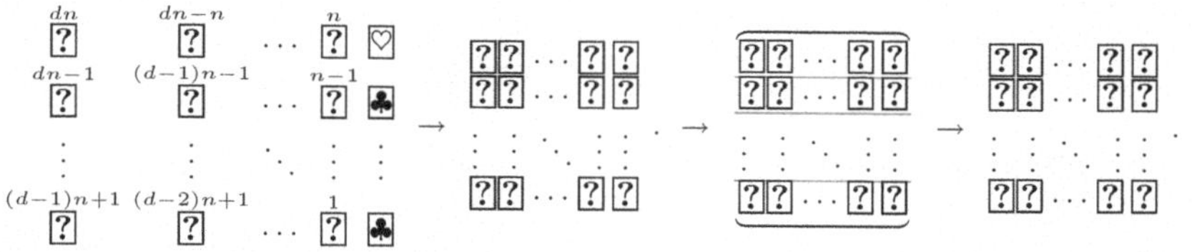

3. Place ♡ and $d-1$ ♣'s in the $(n+1)$-th row and turn them over. Then, apply a pile-shifting shuffle to the first d columns:

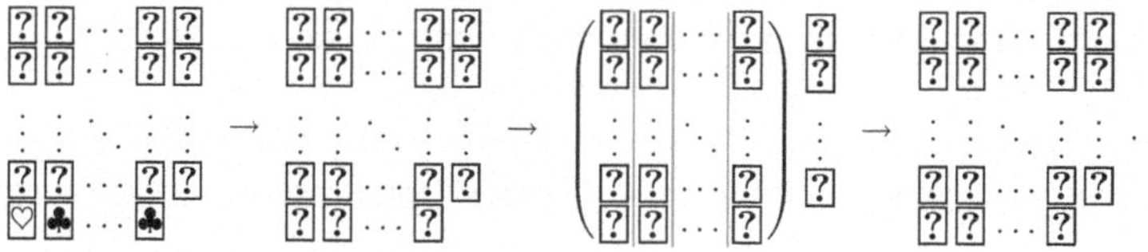

4. Turn the first d cards in the first n rows over to be face-up. Note that one of them is ♡, and the other $nd-1$ are ♣'s. Then, cyclically shift the first d columns so that ♡ moves to the d-th column. Consequently, d cards in the $(n+1)$-th row become an integer commitment $E_d(q)$ to a quotient q. After that, cyclically shift the first n rows so that ♡ moves to the n-th row. Consequently, n cards in the $(d+1)$-th column becomes an integer commitment $E_n(r)$ to a reminder r. An example of transition is:

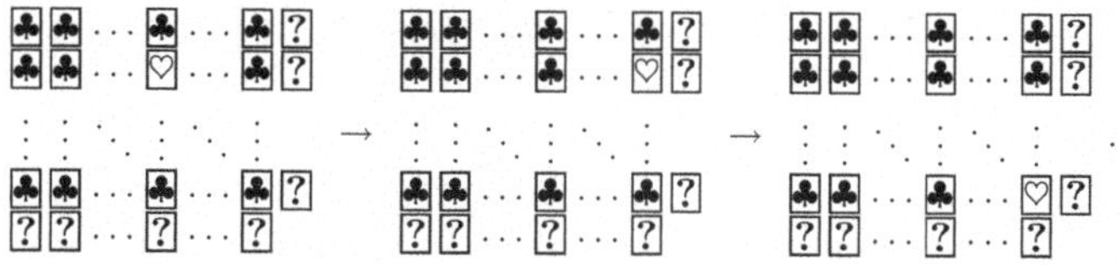

This protocol requires $k + d + n$ cards, and two shuffles.

3.4 Secure Squaring: ssq

In this section, we present a protocol that, for an integer commitment to $i \in [0, k-1]$ with a base k, generates an integer commitment to an integer $i^2 \in [0, (k-1)^2]$ with a base $(k-1)^2+1$. We can also construct a protocol for exponentiation with an arbitrary public exponent spow1 by changing the number of ♣'s inserted in ssq.

The proposed protocol inserts ♣'s between the cards of an integer commitment, such that the j-th card from the left moves to the $\{(j-1)^2+1\}$-th card. Note that an integer commitment to integer i contains ♡ as the $(i+1)$-th card from the left, and this ♡ is moved to the (i^2+1)th card from the left to become an integer commitment to i^2.

Protocol 3. **(Secure squaring:** ssq)

1. For $j = k, k-1, \cdots, 3$, repeat the following step.
   (a) Insert $2(j-2)$ ♣'s between the j-th card and $(j-1)$-th card from the left and turn them over:

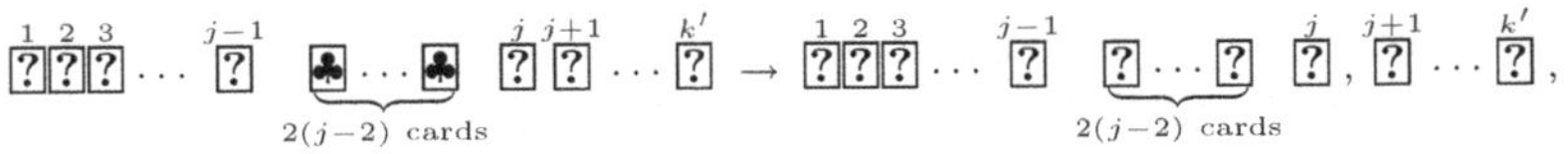

where $k' = k + \sum_{m=j}^{k} 2(m-2)$.

This protocol requires $(k-1)^2+1$ cards and no shuffling operations.

3.5 Secure Multiplication: smul2

In this section, we propose a protocol for integer commitments to $x, y \in [0, k-1]$ with base k to generate an integer commitment to the product $xy \in [0, (k-1)^2]$ with base $(k-1)^2+1$. When constructing smul2, we assume that k is even; if k is odd, we extend the base by one with the base extension of Sect. 3.1.

The proposed protocol generates a commitment to xy using an equation[1]:

$$\left(\frac{x}{2}+\frac{y}{2}\right)^2 - \left(\frac{x}{2}\right)^2 - \left(\frac{y}{2}\right)^2 = \frac{xy}{2}. \tag{1}$$

Let $q_x, q_y \in \mathbb{Z}$ and $r_x, r_y \in \{0,1\}$ be quotients and remainders appeared in division of x and y each by 2: Suppose $x = 2q_x + r_x$ and $y = 2q_y + r_y$. Substituting these equations into Eq. (1) and doubling both sides, we have:

$$xy = 2\left\{(q_x+q_y)^2 - q_x^2 - q_y^2 + a + b\right\} + c, \tag{2}$$

where $a = q_x r_y \in \{0, q_x\}, b = q_y r_x \in \{0, q_y\}$, and $c = r_x r_y \in \{0,1\}$.

[1] We can compute a commitment to xy with an equation $xy = \left\{(x+y)^2 - x^2 - y^2\right\}/2$ instead of Eq. (1); however, it requires more cards.

We use two sub-protocols to compute $E_{(k-1)^2+1}(xy)$ from Eq. (2). Sub-protocol 1 takes an integer commitment $E_k(x)$ as an input and outputs three copies of an integer commitment $E_{k/2}(q_x)$ and two copies of an integer commitment $E_2(r_x)$ using sdiv1 (where the public constant divisor is 2) and a copy protocol as subroutines. The second sub-protocol, Sub-protocol 2, takes integer commitments $E_{k/2}(q_x)$ and $E_2(r_y)$ as inputs, and outputs an integer commitment $E_{k/2}(a)$ to $a = q_x r_y \in \{0, q_x\}$, by selecting $E_{k/2}(0)$ or $E_{k/2}(q_x)$ depending on whether $E_2(r_y)$ is an integer commitment to 0 or 1, respectively. Owing to space limitations, we provide the details of the subprotocols in Appendix A. With these subprotocols, we have smul2 as follows:

Protocol 4. (Secure Multiplication: smul2**)**

1. Run Sub-protocol 1 with $E_k(x)$ as an input to generate three copies of $E_{k/2}(q_x)$ and two copies of $E_2(r_x)$. Similarly, run Sub-protocol 1 with $E_k(y)$ as an input to generate three copies of $E_{k/2}(q_y)$ and two copies of $E_2(r_y)$.
2. Run Sub-protocol 2, with $E_2(r_x)$ and $E_{k/2}(q_y)$ obtained in Step 1, to generate $E_{k/2}(b)$. Similarly, run Sub-protocol 2 with $E_2(r_y)$ and $E_{k/2}(q_x)$ to generate $E_{k/2}(a)$.
3. With $E_2(r_x)$ and $E_2(r_y)$ obtained in Step 1, generate a commitment to a bitwise AND $E_2(c) = E_2(r_x \wedge r_y)$ by using the six-card AND protocol [8].
4. Apply the base extension of Sect. 3.1 to two copies each of $E_{k/2}(q_x)$ and $E_{k/2}(q_y)$ obtained in Step 1, to change their bases from $k/2$ to k. Then, we have two copies each of $E_k(q_x)$ and $E_k(q_y)$.
5. Run smodadd2 [13] with integer commitments $E_k(q_x)$ and $E_k(q_y)$ obtained in Step 4. Then, we have an integer commitment $E_k(q_x + q_y)$.
6. Run ssq (Protocol 3), with $E_k(q_x + q_y)$ obtained in Step 5, to generate an integer commitment $E_{(k-1)^2+1}((q_x + q_y)^2)$. Similarly, run ssq, with $E_k(q_x)$ obtained in Step 4, to generate an integer commitment $E_{(k-1)^2+1}(q_x^2)$.
7. Rearrange cards of $E_{(k-1)^2+1}(q_x^2)$ except its leftmost card in the reverse order (this commitment becomes $E_{(k-1)^2+1}(-q_x^2 \bmod ((k-1)^2+1))$). Then, run smodadd2 [13], with the rearranged cards and $E_{(k-1)^2+1}((q_x+q_y)^2)$ obtained in Step 6 (*i.e.*, subtracting $E_{(k-1)^2+1}(q_x^2)$ from $E_{(k-1)^2+1}((q_x+q_y)^2)$), to generate an integer commitment $E_{(k-1)^2+1}(2q_xq_y + q_y^2)$.
8. Apply the base extension of Sect. 3.1 to the remaining copy of $E_{k/2}(q_y)$ obtained in Step 1, to change its base from $k/2$ to k. Then, we have an integer commitment $E_k(q_y)$. After that, run ssq, with $E_k(q_y)$ to generate $E_{(k-1)^2+1}(q_y^2)$.
9. Similar to Step 7, subtract $E_{(k-1)^2+1}(q_y^2)$ from $E_{(k-1)^2+1}(2q_xq_y + q_y^2)$ obtained in Steps 8 and 7, respectively, to generate an integer commitment $E_{(k-1)^2+1}(2q_xq_y)$.
10. Apply the base extension of Sect. 3.1 to $E_{k/2}(a)$ obtained in Step 2, to change its base from $k/2$ to $(k-1)^2+1$. Then, we have an integer commitment $E_{(k-1)^2+1}(a)$. After that, run smodadd2 [13], with $E_{(k-1)^2+1}(2q_xq_y)$ and $E_{(k-1)^2+1}(a)$, to generate an integer commitment $E_{(k-1)^2+1}(2q_xq_y + a)$.
11. Apply the base extension of Sect. 3.1 to $E_{k/2}(b)$ obtained in Step 2, to change its base from $k/2$ to $(k-1)^2+1$. Then, we have an integer commitment

$E_{(k-1)^2+1}(b)$. After that, run smodadd2 [13], with $E_{(k-1)^2+1}(2q_xq_y+a)$ and $E_{(k-1)^2+1}(b)$, to generate an integer commitment $E_{(k-1)^2+1}(2q_xq_y+a+b)$.
12. Run smul1 (Protocol 1) with $E_{(k-1)^2+1}(2q_xq_y+a+b)$ obtained in Step 11 to double it. Then, we have an integer commitment $E_{2(k-1)^2+1}(4q_xq_y+2a+2b)$. Note that the maximum value of $4q_xq_y+2a+2b$ does not exceed $(k-1)^2$, and the last $(k-1)^2$ cards do not contain ♡. Therefore, we can remove these cards (*i.e.*, reducing a base) and obtain an integer commitment $E_{(k-1)^2+1}(4q_xq_y+2a+2b)$.
13. Apply the base extension of Sect. 3.1 to $E_2(c)$ obtained in Step 3, to change its base from 2 to $(k-1)^2+1$. Then, we have an integer commitment $E_{(k-1)^2+1}(c)$. After that, run smodadd2 [13], with $E_{(k-1)^2+1}(4q_xq_y+2a+2b)$ and $E_{(k-1)^2+1}(c)$, to generate an integer commitment $E_{(k-1)^2+1}(4q_xq_y+2a+2b+c)$ which is $E_{(k-1)^2+1}(xy)$.

In Steps 5, 7, 9, 10, 11, and 13, the proposed protocol executes smodadd2. Note that q_x and q_y are less than or equal to $(k-1)/2$, $xy = 4q_xq_y+2a+2b+c$ and the sums appearing in these steps are less than $(k-1)^2+1$. Therefore, no reduction occurs with smodadd2 and the sums are correctly calculated as integers in $\mathbb{Z}$.

The protocol above seems to require additional cards for the base extension and smul1; however, we can reuse the face-up cards removed in the previous steps without a shuffle. Consequently, this protocol requires $2k^2-3k/2+10$ cards and 13 shuffles.

3.6 Secure Division: sdiv2

In this section, we propose a protocol for integer commitments to $x, y \in [0, k-1]$ with a base k to generate integer commitments to a quotient $q = \lfloor x/y \rfloor \in [0, k-1]$ and to a remainder $r = x \bmod y \in [0, y-1]$ with base k. It also outputs a flag called *a zero-flag*, which indicates that $y = 0$ and that the resulting commitments are meaningless.

Let us consider equation $x = qy+r$. By reconsidering q in the binary representation as $q = \Sigma_{i=0}^{\ell-1} 2^i q_i$ (where ℓ is the bit length of $k-1$, i.e., $\ell = \lfloor \log_2(k-1) \rfloor + 1$), the equation becomes

$$x = \left(\Sigma_{i=0}^{\ell-1} 2^i q_i\right) y + r = \Sigma_{i=0}^{\ell-1} \left(2^i q_i y\right) + r \ . \tag{3}$$

The proposed protocol determines q_j for $j = \ell-1, \ell-2, \cdots, 0$ by comparing $x - \Sigma_{i=j+1}^{\ell-1} \left(2^i q_i \text{ y}\right)$ to $2^j y$. If $x - \Sigma_{i=j+1}^{\ell-1} \left(2^i q_i \text{ y}\right)$ is less than $2^j y$, then q_j is 0. Otherwise, q_j equals one. Specifically, we prepare an integer commitment to a partial quotient denoted by $E_k(q')$ and initialize it using $E_k(0)$. Then, for $j = \ell-1, \ell-2, \cdots, 0$, if $x \geq 2^j y$ holds for commitments $E_k(x)$ and $E_k(2^j y)$, then $E_k(2^j)$ is added to $E_k(q')$, and $E_k(2^j y)$ is subtracted from $E_k(x)$. Consequently, $E_k(x)$ becomes an integer commitment to reminders r and $E_k(q')$ becomes an integer commitment to quotient q.

We also adopt another (second) idea to reduce the number of cards for comparing x with $2^j y$: The idea is not to calculate $2^j y$ with smul1 as it is, but to multiply a part of y, specifically, the first m_j cards of $E_k(y)$ where $m_j = \lceil (k-1)/2^j \rceil + 1$. Because $2^j m_j$ exceeds $k-1$, it is sufficient to multiply the first m_j cards of $E_k(y)$ by 2^j compared with $E_k(x)$. Using this concept, we can skip the insertion ♣'s among the last $k - m_j$ cards of $E_k(y)$.

Protocol 5. (Secure division: sdiv2)

1. Copy $E_k(y)$ into two by using the copy protocol [12].
2. Place $k-2$ ♣'s to the left of $E_k(y)$, and turn the face-up cards over. Then, arrange cards into two rows by moving the first $k-1$ cards to the first row, and the other cards to the second row. The transition is:

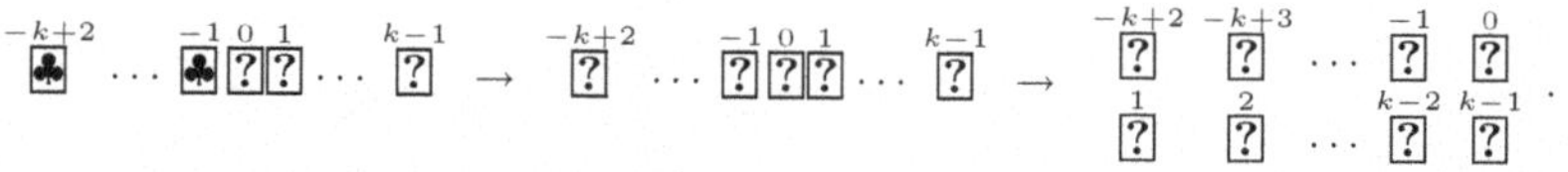

3. Place ♡ and ♣ to the right of the first and second rows, respectively, and over the face-up cards over:

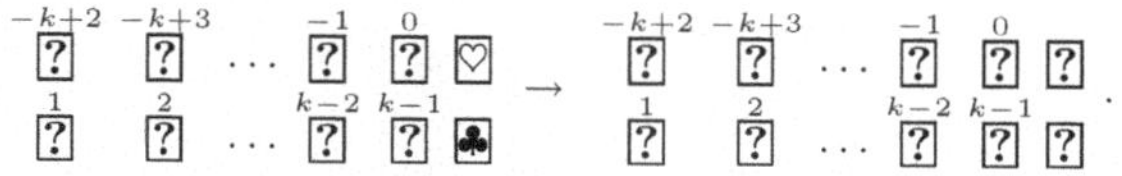

4. Apply a pile-shifting shuffle to two rows. Then, apply a pile-shifting shuffle to the first $k-1$ columns. The transition is:

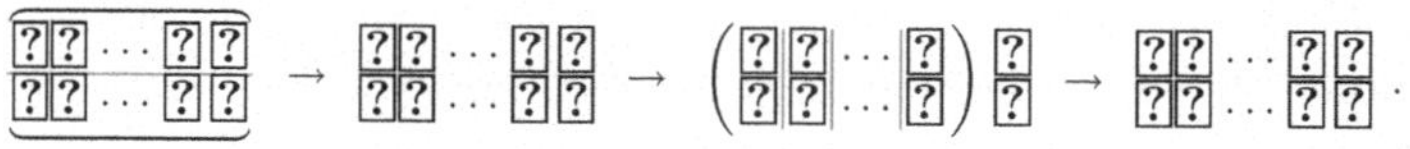

5. Turn the first $k-1$ cards in each row over. One of them is ♡ and the other $2k-3$ are ♣'s. Then, arrange the rightmost card of the row containing ♡ and the rightmost card of the other row in a sequence. These two cards become a zero-flag, which is $E_2(1)$ if $y = 0$ or $E_2(0)$ otherwise.
6. Initialize an integer commitment (write it as $E_k(q')$, and it finally becomes an integer commitment $E_k(q)$ to a quotient) with $E_k(0)$.
7. Repeat the following steps for $j = \ell - 1, \ell - 2, \cdots, 0$.
   (a) Apply the base extension of Sect. 3.1 to $E_k(x)$ to change its base from k to n_j, where $n_j = (m_j - 1)(2^j - 1) + k$ for $m_j = \lceil (k-1)/2^j \rceil + 1$. Then, we have an integer commitment $E_{n_j}(x)$.
   (b) Copy $E_{n_j}(x)$ and $E_k(y)$ into two and three, respectively, by using the copy protocol [12].
   (c) For two of three $E_k(y)$'s, insert $2^j - 1$ ♣'s into the i-th card and the $(i+1)$-th card for $i \in [1, m_j - 1]$ (that is, the last $m_j - k$ cards of $E_k(y)$ are unchanged from our second idea). Consequently, we have two $E_{n_j}(y')$'s, where $y' = 2^j y$ if $y < m_j$, or $y' = n_j - (k - y)$ otherwise. The transition is:

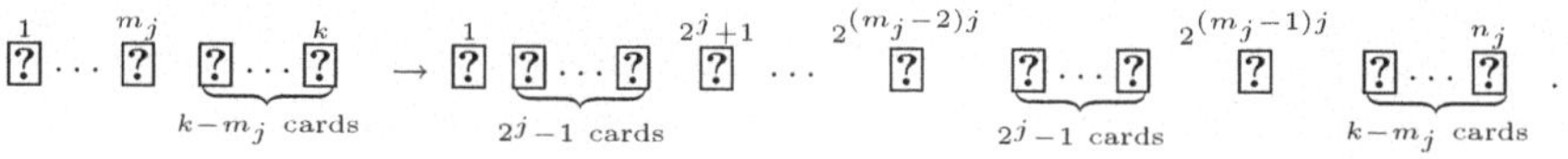

(d) Run ssub2 [18] (Appendix B) with $E_{n_j}(x)$ and $E_{n_j}(y')$ obtained in Steps 7(b) and 7(c), respectively. Place ♣ to the left of $E_{n_j}(x-y')$ and turn it over. Then, arrange a sequence of cards into two rows, by moving the first and last n_j cards to the first and second rows, respectively. The transition is:

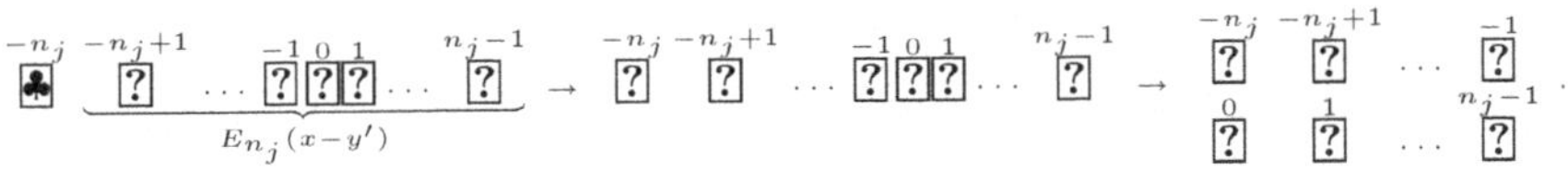

(e) Place $E_k(0)$ and $E_{n_j}(0)$ to the right of the first row. Place $E_k(2^j)$ and the remaining $E_{n_j}(y')$ obtained in Step 7(c) to the right of the second row. Then, turn the face-up cards over. The transition is:

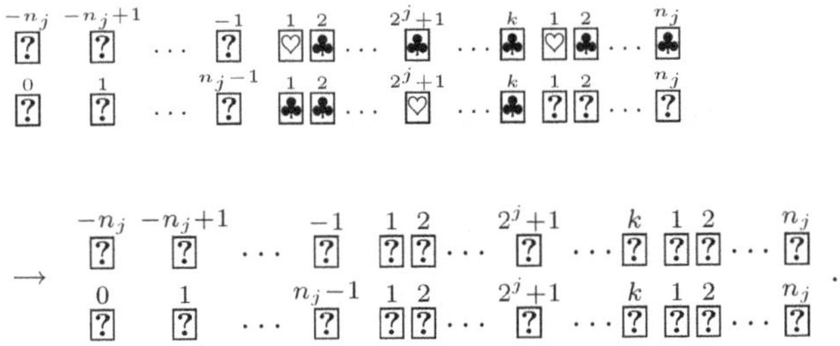

Later, one of the sequences of k cards in the middle of each row is added as $E_k(2^j q_j)$ to $E_k(q')$, depending on the j-th bit q_j of the quotient q. Similarly, one of the sequences with n_j cards in the right are subtracted from $E_{n_j}(x)$ to replace it with $E_{n_j}(x-2^j q_j y)$.

(f) Apply a pile-shifting shuffle:

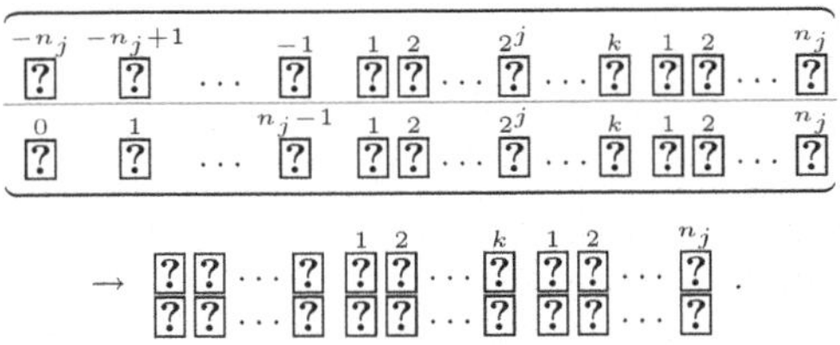

(g) Apply a pile-shifting shuffle to the first n_j columns:

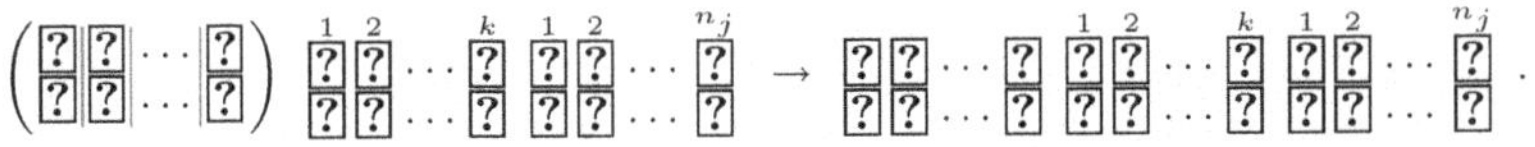

(h) Turn the first n_j cards in each row over. One of them is ♡ and the other $2n_j-1$ are ♣'s. Then, run sadd2 with the middle k cards of the row containing ♡, $E_k(2^j q_j)$, to $E_k(q')$. Moreover, rearrange the right n_j cards of the same row in the reverse order except for the leftmost one, to generate $E_{n_j}(-2^j q_j y \bmod n_j)$. Then, run sadd2 with the rearranged cards and $E_{n_j}(x)$ obtained in Step 7(b). The result is either $E_{n_j}(x)$ (when $q_j=0$) or $E_{n_j}(x-2^j y)$ (when $q_j=1$).

(i) Apply a complete shuffle[2] to the middle k and the right n_j cards of the other row, to reuse these cards in the following steps.
(j) Among the right n_j cards, $E_{n_j}(x)$, obtained in Step 7(h), there is no ♡ in the last $n_j - k$ cards. Therefore, remove these $n_j - k$ cards to reduce the base from n_j to k. Then, go to the next iteration with this $E_k(x)$ and the remaining $E_k(y)$ obtained in Step 7(b).

8. Output the consequent $E_k(q')$ and $E_k(x)$ as $E_k(q)$ and $E_k(r)$, respectively.

The above protocol requires $\max_j\{6n_j\} + 2k + 2$ cards, which are $6(\lceil (k-1)/2^{\ell-1}\rceil)(2^{\ell-1} - 1) + 8k + 2$ because the maximum value of n_j is obtained at $j = \ell - 1$ and $8\ell + 3$ shuffles.

4 Application to Secure Statistical Data Aggregation

The proposed protocols for arithmetic operations enable secure data aggregation, such as grand total (average), cross-tabulation (contingency table), association rule learning, and a weighted mean with nonresponse adjustment, where inputs are given as integer commitments in secret. Table 2 summarizes the operations required for statistical data aggregation.

Table 2. Statistical data aggregations and required operations

Statistical processing	Required operations
Grand total	sadd2, sdiv1
Cross tabulation	sadd2, sdiv2
Association rule learning	sadd2, sdiv1, sdiv2
Weighted mean with non-response adjustment	sadd2, smul2, sdiv1

The grand total calculates a sum of input data or their average with "(sum of data)/(total number of data)." In general, the "total number of data" is a public value, and sdiv1 makes the aggregation possible.

Cross-tabulation is a method for discovering the relationship between data and attributes, such as age and gender. It calculates "(total value of data for some attribute)/(total number of data for the attribute)." Because the denominator depends on the secret attribute of the answer, sdiv2 is required.

Association rule learning is a method for discovering the relationship between attributes in transactions using three indices: support, confidence, and lift. The support is calculated as "(number of transaction containing attributes A and

[2] we can replace the complete shuffle to the middle k cards and the right n_j cards in the other row, with a pile-shifting shuffle only to the right n_j cards. In this case, we modify Step 7(h) so that $E_k(2^j q_j)$ is added also to the middle k cards in the other row when it is added to $E_k(q')$. Regardless of q_j, the result becomes $E_k(2^j)$ which can be reused without leaking any information.

B) / (total number of transactions)." A confidence is calculated as "(number of transactions containing attributes A and B)/(number of transaction containing A)," etc. A lift is calculated as "(number of transactions containing attributes A and B)/((number of transaction containing A)×(number of transaction containing B))," etc. These calculations require sdiv1 or sdiv2.

The weighted mean with non-response adjustment is used to draw valid conclusions about population features from sample data [5]. It calculates "(Σ(value of each data) $\times$ (estimation weight))/(total number of data)." The estimation weight is a coefficient used to achieve an unbiased estimation when considering non-respondents, which is calculated using the amount of data and its original population for each attribute. The estimation weight is a secret value if the data are aggregated for hidden attributes; in this case, smul2 is required to calculate the numerator.

Cross-tabulation and association rule learning use sdiv2, but if the denominator is zero, a zero-flag in Protocol 5 may leak the information that there are no data for the corresponding attribute. We can hide information about the attributes by calculating statistical values with sdiv2 for all attributes and summing zero-flags with a protocol for the bitwise-OR operation. In this case, only the information in which there are no data for some attribute(s), that is, some statistical values may be meaningless, is leaked.

5 Conclusion

In this paper, we propose protocols for arithmetic operations such as multiplication and division based on integer commitment. The security of the proposed protocols is ensured by shuffling operations. In addition, we discuss the application of card-based cryptography to statistical data aggregation. The development of efficient card-based protocols that are useful for statistical data aggregation will be the subject of future research.

Acknowledgments. This work was supported by Grant-in-Aid for Scientific Research (JP24K14951).

A Proposed Sub-Protocols for smul2

In Sect. 3.5, we used two sub-protocols in smul2. In this section, we provide details of these sub-protocols. As in Sect. 3.5, we assume that a base k is even.

First, we explain the details of Sub-protocol 1. It takes $E_k(x)$ as an input and outputs three copies of $E_{k/2}(q_x)$ and two copies of $E_2(r_x)$ as follows:

Sub-protocol 1.

1. Rearrange cards of $E_k(x)$ into two rows, by moving an i-th card from the left to the first row if i is odd or to the second row otherwise. Then, rearrange cards of each row in the reverse order. The transition is:

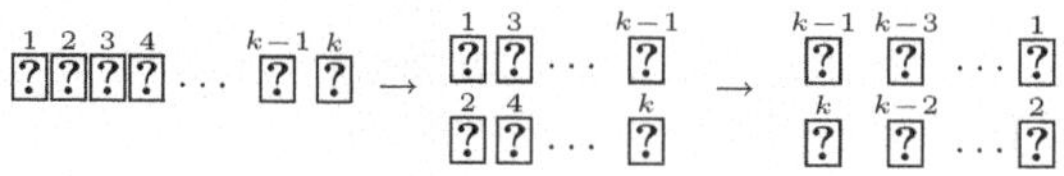

2. Place ♡♣ and ♣♡ to the right of the first and second rows, respectively. Then, turn the face-up cards over:

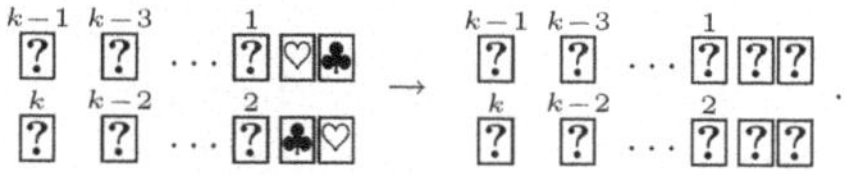

3. Apply a pile-shifting shuffle:

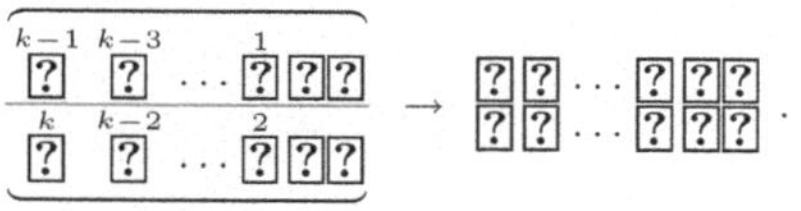

4. Place ♡ and $(k/2-1)$ ♣'s in each from the third to the fifth rows. Then, turn the face-up cards over. The transition is:

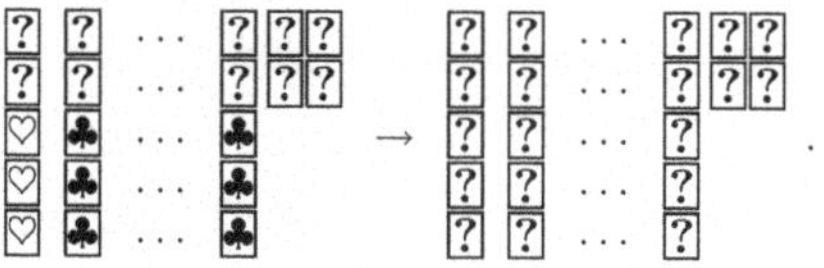

5. Apply a pile-shifting shuffle to the first $k/2$ columns:

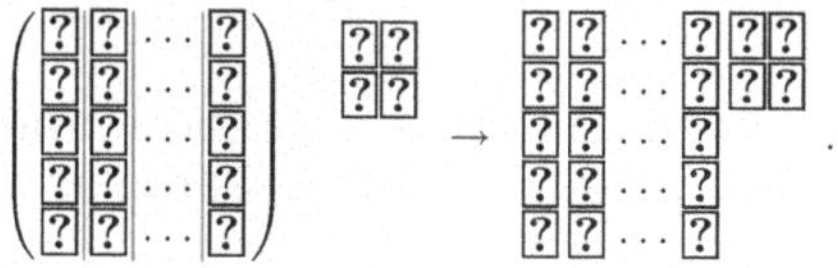

6. Turn the first $k/2$ cards in the first and the second rows to be face-up. One of them is ♡ and the other $k-1$ are ♣'s. Then, shift the first $k/2$ columns cyclically so that ♡ moves to the $(k/2)$-th column. After that, the third to fifth rows become three copies of $E_{k/2}(q_x)$. An example of transition is:

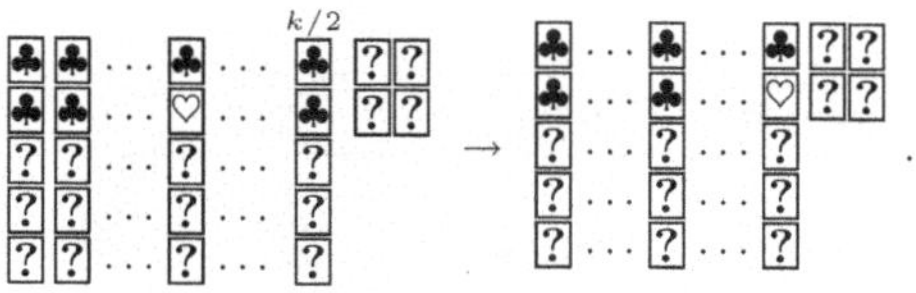

7. The last two cards in the row containing ♡ appeared in Step 6 are $E_2(r_x)$, whereas the last two cards in the other row among the first and second rows are $E_2(1 - r_x)$. Rearrange the cards of $E_2(1 - r_x)$ in the reverse order, to change it to $E_2(r_x)$. Finally, we have two copies of $E_2(r_x)$.

Next, we provide details of Sub-protocol 2. As inputs, $E_2(r_x)$ obtained by Sub-protocol 1 (with input $E_k(x)$) and $E_{k/2}(q_y)$ obtained by Sub-protocol 1 (with input $E_k(y)$) and outputs $E_{k/2}(b)$.

Sub-protocol 2.

1. Arrange two cards of $E_2(r_x)$ so that the first card from the left is placed at the first row, and the second one is placed at the second row. Then, place one ♡ and $k/2 - 1$ ♣'s to the right of the card in the first row. Next, place cards of $E_{k/2}(q_y)$ to the right of the card in the second row. After that, turn the face-up cards in the first row over. The transition is:

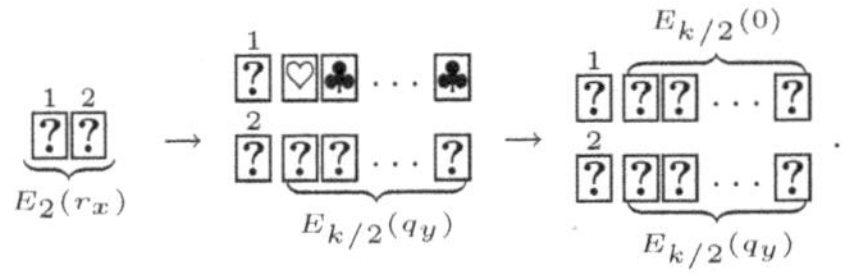

2. Apply a pile-shifting shuffle:

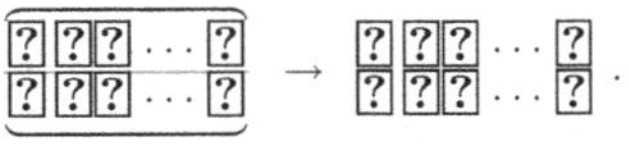

3. Turn the leftmost card in each row over. Then, output the $k/2$ face-down cards of the row where ♡ appears in the first column, as $E_{k/2}(b)$.

B Secure Subtraction of Kuzuma et al. [18]

In this section, we review the subtraction protocol proposed by Kuzuma et al. [18]. For integer commitments $E_k(x)$ and $E_k(y)$ to integers $x, y \in [0, k-1]$, this protocol outputs a commitment (but *not* an integer commitment) to $x - y \in [-(k-1), k-1]$ with $2k - 1$ black-red cards.

Protocol 6. (**Secure subtraction**, ssub2, **of** [18])

1. Place cards of $E_k(x)$ in the first row and put $k - 1$ ♣'s to the left. In addition, place cards of $E_k(y)$ in the second row and put $k - 1$ ♣'s to the right. Then, turn the face-up cards over. The transition is:

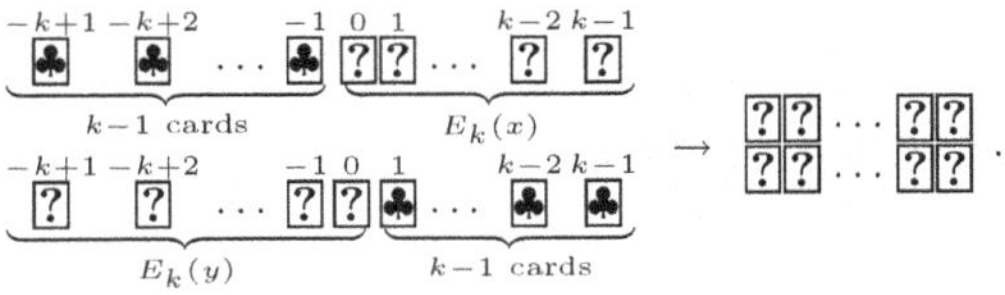

2. Apply a pile-shifting shuffle:

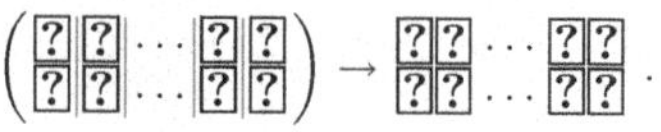

3. Turn cards in the second row over. Then, shift columns cyclically so that ♡ in the second row moves to the right. An example of the transition is:

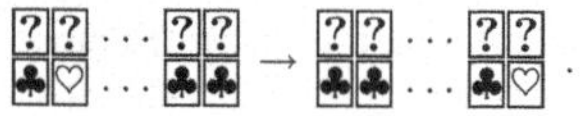

4. Output cards in the first row as a commitment to $x - y$. In this commitment, a card with an index $x - y$ in the following card sequence is ♡ and the other $2k - 2$ cards are ♣'s:

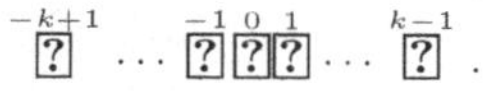

References

1. Den Boer, B.: More efficient match-making and satisfiability the five card trick. In: Quisquater, J.J., Vandewalle, J. (eds.) Advances in Cryptology—EUROCRYPT '89. LNCS, vol. 434, pp. 208–217. Springer, Berlin, Heidelberg (1990). https://doi.org/10.1007/3-540-46885-4_23
2. Gradwohl, R., Naor, M., Pinkas, B., Rothblum, G.N.: Cryptographic and physical zero-knowledge proof systems for solutions of Sudoku puzzles. Theor. Comput. Syst. **44**(2), 245–268 (2009). https://doi.org/10.1007/s00224-008-9119-9
3. Koch, A.: The landscape of security from physical assumptions. In: 2021 IEEE Information Theory Workshop (ITW), pp. 1–6. IEEE, Los Alamitos, CA, USA (2021). https://doi.org/10.1109/ITW48936.2021.9611501
4. Komano, Y., Mizuki, T.: Card-based zero-knowledge proof protocol for pancake sorting. In: Bella, G., Doinea, M., Janicke, H. (eds.) Innovative Security Solutions for Information Technology and Communications - 15th International Conference, SecITC 2022. LNCS, vol. 13809, pp. 222–239. Springer, Cham (2023). https://doi.org/10.1007/978-3-031-32636-3_13
5. Meinck, S.: Computing sampling weights in large-scale assessments in education. Survey Insights: methods from the field, weighting: practical issues and 'how to' approach. Retrieved (2015). https://surveyinsights.org/?p=5353
6. Miyahara, D., Hayashi, Y., Mizuki, T., Sone, H.: Practical card-based implementations of Yao's millionaire protocol. Theor. Comput. Sci. **803**, 207–221 (2020). https://doi.org/10.1016/j.tcs.2019.11.005
7. Mizuki, T., Shizuya, H.: Computational model of card-based cryptographic protocols and its applications. IEICE Trans. Fundam. Electron. Commun. Comput. Sci. **E100.A**(1), 3–11 (2017). https://doi.org/10.1587/transfun.E100.A.3

8. Mizuki, T., Sone, H.: Six-card secure AND and four-card secure XOR. In: Deng, X., Hopcroft, J.E., Xue, J. (eds.) Frontiers in Algorithmics. LNCS, vol. 5598, pp. 358–369. Springer, Berlin, Heidelberg (2009). https://doi.org/10.1007/978-3-642-02270-8_36
9. Nishimura, A., Hayashi, Y., Mizuki, T., Sone, H.: Pile-shifting scramble for card-based protocols. IEICE Trans. Fundam. Electron. Commun. Comput. Sci. **101**(9), 1494–1502 (2018). https://doi.org/10.1587/transfun.E101.A.1494
10. Nuida, K.: Efficient card-based millionaires' protocols via non-binary input encoding. In: Shikata, J., Kuzuno, H. (eds.) Advances in Information and Computer Security - 18th International Workshop on Security, IWSEC 2023. Lecture Notes in Computer Science, vol. 14128, pp. 237–254. Springer (2023)
11. Ruangwises, S.: Two standard decks of playing cards are sufficient for a ZKP for Sudoku (2021). https://arxiv.org/abs/2106.13646
12. Ruangwises, S.: Using five cards to encode each integer in Z/6Z. In: Ryan, P.Y.A., Toma, C. (eds.) Innovative Security Solutions for Information Technology and Communications - 14th International Conference, SecITC 2021. Lecture Notes in Computer Science, vol. 13195, pp. 165–177. Springer (2021)
13. Ruangwises, S., Itoh, T.: Securely computing the n-variable equality function with $2n$ cards. Theor. Comput. Sci. **887**, 99–110 (2021). https://doi.org/10.1016/j.tcs.2021.07.007
14. Sasaki, T., Miyahara, D., Mizuki, T., Sone, H.: Efficient card-based zero-knowledge proof for Sudoku. Theor. Comput. Sci. **839**, 135–142 (2020). https://doi.org/10.1016/j.tcs.2020.05.036
15. Shinagawa, K., et al.: Card-based protocols using regular polygon cards. IEICE Trans. Fundam. Electron. Commun. Comput. Sci. **E100.A**(9), 1900–1909 (2017). https://doi.org/10.1587/transfun.E100.A.1900
16. Suga, Y.: A card-based protocol that lets you know how close two parties are in their opinions (agree/disagree) by using a four-point likert scale. In: Applied Cryptography and Network Security Workshops - ACNS 2023, vol. 13907, pp. 716–721. Springer (2023)
17. Takashima, K., et al.: Card-based protocols for secure ranking computations. Theor. Comput. Sci. **845**, 122–135 (2020). https://doi.org/10.1016/j.tcs.2020.09.008
18. Tomoki Kuzuma et al.: SIG technical report. IPSJ, 2024-CSEC-104(40), pp. 1–8 (2024). (in Japanese)

Privacy-Preserving Multi-party Search via Homomorphic Encryption with Constant Multiplicative Depth

Mihail-Iulian Pleşa[1,2,3](✉) and Ruxandra F. Olimid[1,2]

[1] Department of Computer Science, University of Bucharest, Bucharest, Romania
ruxandra.olimid@fmi.unibuc.ro
[2] Research Institute of the University of Bucharest (ICUB), Bucharest, Romania
[3] Orange Services, Bucharest, Romania
mihail.plesa@orange.com

Abstract. We propose a privacy-preserving multiparty search protocol using threshold-level homomorphic encryption, which we prove correct and secure to honest but curious adversaries. Unlike existing approaches, our protocol maintains a constant circuit depth. This feature enhances its suitability for practical applications involving dynamic underlying databases.

Keywords: Leveled Homomorphic Encryption (LHE) · Multi-Party Computation (MPC) · Privacy-preserving searching

1 Introduction

In today's data-driven world, vast amounts of information are generated and stored across numerous distributed databases. These data sets, often scattered across different organizations and geographical locations, hold immense potential for valuable insights and analyses. However, the decentralized nature of this data poses significant challenges for comprehensive analysis, as traditional methods require data aggregation, which can be impractical because of privacy concerns and regulatory constraints. Although last years' advances made cryptographic primitives such as Multi-Party Computation (MPC) and Homomorphic Encryption (HE) feasible and usable in many real-case scenarios, there is still room for improvement.

Some industry-oriented applications include securely searching for an IP address across multiple blocklists, sharing threat intelligence data to mitigate cyber threats, conducting collaborative vulnerability assessments, and coordinating incident response efforts. Central to these applications is privacy-preserving searching in a multi-party environment.

Contribution. We propose a protocol that allows one party to perform a search over multiple independent databases. The security of our construction is based

L. Morogan et al. (Eds.): SecITC 2024, LNCS 15595, pp. 135–148, 2025.
https://doi.org/10.1007/978-3-031-87760-5_11

on the threshold version of a Leveled Homomorphic Encryption (LHE) scheme [5,8,9,11,13]. The primary distinction of our proposal, compared to other similar solutions, is that our protocol employs a constant number of consecutive multiplications, maintaining a constant multiplicative depth regardless of the database size. This feature makes the protocol particularly well-suited for searches in dynamic data sets, where the number of entries is continually changing. Our contribution can be summarized as follows:

1. We introduce an algorithm with constant multiplicative depth for searching the 0 element into a linear array;
2. We use the proposed algorithm as a building block to construct a multi-party privacy-preserving searching protocol (based on LHE), which we prove secure in the honest-but-curious model;
3. We compare our protocol with other solutions in terms of the complexity of the searching algorithm, communication rounds, and multiplicative depth.

Outline. Section 2 presents the related works. Section 3 gives the necessary background, including the description of an LHE scheme. Section 4 defines the searching problem and discusses some general approaches to solving it. Section 5 introduces our protocol and gives the correctness and security proofs. Section 6 compares our proposal with existing protocols. The last section concludes and points out further directions of research.

2 Related Works

Searching over encrypted data has, at its core, efficient algorithms for secure equality testing. Traditionally, these algorithms were based either on Homomorphic Encryption (HE) or on secure Multi-Party Computation (MPC) protocols [12,24]. Regarding searchable encryption based on HE, in [25], the authors proposed a decentralized system for searching through genomic data using Fully Homomorphic Encryption (FHE). In [23], the authors describe a system for performing cloud-based computations of arbitrary depth over data under an FHE scheme. To address the challenge of noise growth in encrypted data, the authors utilized a specialized third-party equipped with hardware acceleration for FV encryption and decryption [13]. In [2], the authors proposed a method for searching over FHE-encrypted data realized by approximating the searching algorithm with a polynomial of degree logarithmic in the size of the database. Their method is based on the evaluation of the searching circuit over encrypted data within multiple distinct finite fields of small characteristics.

There are also other solutions to the problem of privacy-preserving collaborative analytics, based on garbled circuits and secret sharing [6,14,20,22]. The main difference between these approaches and the HE approach lies in their handling of data and communication requirements. HE allows computations to be performed directly on encrypted data, maintaining continuous data confidentiality with typically fewer communication rounds. In contrast, garbled circuits and secret sharing require splitting the data into parts and distributing these parts among multiple parties, which necessitates multiple rounds of communication and interaction to perform computations and reconstruct the results.

Over the years, several surveys on searchable encryption have been published [3,4,7,15].

3 Preliminaries

3.1 Notations

Let $\mathbb{Z}^+$ be the set of positive integers, including 0. We represent uni-dimensional arrays by bold values, e.g., $\mathbf{v}$. We denote by $x \leftarrow^R X$ a uniformly random sampling of x from the set X. Let λ be the security parameter. For (pk, sk) a public-private key pair, let $[m]$ be the encryption of m (we ignore to index by pk for encryption and sk for decryption whenever this is clear from the context). Similarly, $[\mathbf{v}]$ represents a uni-dimensional array of ciphertexts.

Let $\mathcal{P} = \{P_1, \ldots, P_p\}$ be the set of p, $p \geq 2$, parties that take part in the searching protocol. Without losing generality (after a possible reordering), let P_1 be the querying party. Each party owns a private database $\mathbf{D}_i, i = 1, \ldots, p$, which we assume to be in the form of a vector of elements.

3.2 Homomorphic Encryption

Overview. Homomorphic Encryption (HE) is an encryption scheme that supports homomorphic operations on encrypted data without performing decryption. The *multiplicative depth* of a circuit is the maximum number of multiplications along any path of the circuit and usually represents a bottleneck: a large multiplicative depth normally conducts to large parameters and ciphertexts, thus a high evaluation time.

A Fully HE (FHE) scheme allows any number of computations and the evaluation of arbitrary circuits of unbounded depth, while a Leveled HE (LHE) allows a predetermined number of operations and, thus, the evaluation of circuits of bounded depth. LHE schemes have a larger ciphertext expansion, but each operation is cheaper than in normal HE schemes [1].

Description. Let $\Pi = (\mathsf{KeyGen}, \mathsf{Enc}, \mathsf{Dec})$ be an LHE scheme. Figure 1 defines the main homomorphic operations supported by an LHE scheme.

Besides the public encryption key pk and the private decryption key sk, these schemes employ a public evaluation key to facilitate homomorphic operations on encrypted data. Specifically, there is a public evaluation key evk for homomorphic multiplication [8,9,11,13]. Also, note that EvalSign is not a native homomorphic operation, but we include it in Fig. 1 because of its significance in our protocol. This functionality can be implemented using EvalAdd and EvalMul through polynomial representation [16,17].

In this paper, we explore the use of BGV, BFV, and CKKS schemes, any of which can instantiate the proposed protocol [8,9,11,13,18], with CKKS being distinct in its design to handle approximate data. The security of such schemes

Let $\Pi = (\mathsf{KeyGen}, \mathsf{Enc}, \mathsf{Dec})$ be an LHE scheme, where:

- $\mathsf{KeyGen}(1^\lambda)$: on input the security parameter λ, it returns a pair (pk, sk) of public-private keys and an evaluation key evk;
- $\mathsf{Enc}_{\mathsf{pk}}(m) \rightarrow [m]$: on input the public key pk and a plaintext m, it returns a ciphertext $[m]$;
- $\mathsf{Dec}_{\mathsf{sk}}([m]) \rightarrow m'$: on input the private key sk and a ciphertext $[m]$, it returns a plaintext m' ($m' = m + e$ for some small enough, acceptable error e).

Then Π supports the evaluations (in the following, we ignore the errors and use the public key pk whenever no other key is explicitly mentioned):

1. $\mathsf{EvalAdd}([m_1], [m_2]) \rightarrow [m_1 + m_2]$: on input the ciphertexts $[m_1]$ and $[m_2]$ (the encryption of two plaintexts m_1 and m_2 respectively), it returns $[m_1 + m_2]$ a valid encryption of $m_1 + m_2$;
2. $\mathsf{EvalMul}_{\mathsf{evk}}([m_1], [m_2]) \rightarrow [m_1 m_2]$: on input the ciphertexts $[m_1]$ and $[m_2]$ (the encryption of two plaintexts m_1 and m_2, respectively), it returns a ciphertext $[m_1 m_2]$ that encrypts $m_1 m_2$;
3. $\mathsf{EvalAddScalar}([m], \alpha) \rightarrow [m + \alpha]$: on input the ciphertext $[m]$ (the encryption of a plaintext m) and the scalar α, it returns a ciphertext $[m+\alpha]$ that encrypts $m + \alpha$;
4. $\mathsf{EvalMulScalar}([m], \alpha) \rightarrow [\alpha m]$: on input the ciphertexts $[m]$ and the scalar α, it returns a ciphertext $[\alpha m]$ that encrypts αm;
5. $\mathsf{EvalSign}([m]) \rightarrow [b]$: on input a ciphertext $[m]$ (the encryption of a plaintext m), it returns [b], the encryption of a bit b indicating the sign of m: $b = 0$, for $m \leq 0$ and $b = 1$, otherwise.

Fig. 1. Leveled HE - Simplified description.

is based on the Ring Learning With Errors problem (RLWE) [21]. Both BGV and BFV are proven to be IND-CPA secure [8,9,13]. CKKS [11], with the modifications in [18], has been proven to be IND-CPA-D secure, an IND-CPA variant specific for approximate encryption [19][1].

Threshold LHE. Our protocol makes use of the Threshold FHE (TFHE) introduced in [5]. In this context, the parties $\{P_1, \ldots, P_p\}$ in $\mathcal{P}$ collaborate to create a unique public encryption key pk, with each party receiving a distinct share sk_i of the corresponding private key sk. Thus, the key generation algorithm $\mathsf{TFHE.KeyGen}(setup)$ becomes a multi-party protocol in which every party $P_i, i = 1, \ldots, p$ outputs the public key pk, the public evaluation key evk, and a secret private-key share sk_i. The encryption and evaluation algorithms remain

[1] IND-CPA-D extends IND-CPA to capture resistance against passive attacks for approximate HE schemes by allowing access to a decryption oracle (in approximate schemes the adversary does not have, by construction, the ability to decrypt even if he/she knows the public key and the homomorphic computation being performed). IND-CPA-D is equivalent to IND-CPA for exact HE schemes.

the same as for the underlying FHE. The decryption algorithm also becomes a multi-party protocol $\mathsf{TFHE.Dec}_{sk_1,\ldots,sk_p}([m])$. Hence, $\mathsf{TFHE.Dec}$ enables the decryption of a ciphertext $[m]$ only when the parties in $\mathcal{P}$ allow decryption[2]. Note that $\mathsf{TFHE.Dec}$ is asymmetric in the sense that at the end of the protocol, only one party - the party that initiated the protocol - finds the plaintext (the plaintext remains hidden for the other parties). TFHE is proven secure in the Universal Composability (UC) framework [5].

4 The Problem

4.1 Problem Definition

Overview. A set of $p \geq 3$ parties $\mathcal{P} = \{P_1, \ldots, P_p\}$ posses each a local database $\mathbf{D}_1, \ldots, \mathbf{D}_p$. One of these parties, called the *querying party* (let this party be P_1, without loss of generality after a possible reordering), wishes to search for a particular element within the collection of all the other parties' databases. The problem asks for the search to be *privacy-preserving*, in the sense that the queried element and the query result should remain hidden to all except the querying party, and no other information (e.g., wrt the content of the databases) must be disclosed. In particular, in case of a positive search result, the querying party should not be able to identify the party (parties) that possess the queried element.

We assume an *honest-but-curious model*, where each party follows the protocol correctly but is interested in learning as much as possible. In this model, parties do not deviate from the protocol's prescribed description; however, they may attempt to infer additional information from the data they observe during the execution of the protocol.

Privacy Requirements. The privacy requirements are as follows, and they should hold, at least up to a negligible probability:

1. The querying party P_1 should learn nothing about the individual databases $\mathbf{D}_2, \ldots, \mathbf{D}_p$ apart from the fact that the searched element exists or not in at least one database (except its own $\mathbf{D}_1$).
2. Any database owner except the querying party P_1 should learn nothing about the searched element, the result of the protocol, or the individual databases.
3. Any coalition of parties that excludes the querying party P_1 should learn nothing about the searched element, the result of the protocol, or the individual databases.

The third privacy requirement generalizes the second requirement, extending it from single parties to coalitions of parties, which only strengthens the protocol's security.

---

[2] In fact, this is an all-or-nothing (i.e., the threshold equals the total number of parties) decryption because all p parties need to cooperate.

Operational Requirements. We assume a dynamic setup in which participants can join or leave the group at any time. Additionally, the local databases are not static; they can undergo changes such as updates, deletions, and additions of elements. Considering the dynamic nature of the group of participants, we assume an appropriate key management system, which is beyond the scope of this paper. For instance, when the group of parties is altered, the keys are re-generated to ensure continued security and privacy.

4.2 Generic Approaches to Solve the Problem

We discuss different approaches to solve the problem. We do not instantiate these solutions but keep them in terms of generic cryptographic building blocks.

Multi-Party Computation (MPC). The problem reduces to a secure MPC protocol where each party inputs its array, and the querying party inputs the value to be searched for. The output is 1 if there exists at least one party other than the querying party that has the value of interest and 0 otherwise. A similar approach can use the appurtenance of a set: all parties, except the querying party, compute a joined (encrypted) database using MPC, and the querying party further checks the appurtenance of the queried element to this set.

Private Set Intersection (PSI). The querying party inputs to a PSI protocol a set containing the searched element only. To maintain the privacy of the searching party, one might consider masking it within a vector populated with randomly chosen elements that are guaranteed not to belong to the database, such as by selecting elements outside a predefined range for the database entries. By construction, the PSI protocol reveals only the intersection of the sets and nothing else. This approach requires multi-party *unbalanced* PSI, a primitive that still raises many open questions.

Simplified Select Query. More complex solutions based on garbled circuits and secret sharing can also be employed for privacy-preserving general queries [6,14, 20,22]. Within this context, our problem can be formulated as a straightforward membership query.

Our Method. Our approach is modeled as a privacy-preserving searching problem based on leveled HE that requires a constant number of communication rounds regardless of the number of parties or the dimension of their databases. A comparison (e.g., in terms of performance evaluation) of our protocol with the approaches mentioned above (e.g., a PSI-based solution) is left for future work.

5 Our Protocol

5.1 0-Searching Algorithm

We introduce Algorithm 1 - $\mathsf{0SA}$ for searching the 0 element within an arbitrary array of length n with non-negative entries, $\mathbf{v} = (v_1, v_2, \ldots, v_n)$, $v_i \geq 0$. The search algorithm receives as input the array $\mathbf{v}$ and outputs s, which is negative or zero if the $\mathbf{v}$ contains at least one 0 and is strictly positive otherwise. We define a function $H : \mathbb{Z}^+ \rightarrow \{0, 1\}$ as follows:

$$H(x) = \begin{cases} 1, \text{if } x > 0, \\ 0, \text{otherwise.} \end{cases} \tag{1}$$

Correctness (0SA). We consider the two possible cases: (a) $\mathbf{v}$ contains no 0 element, and (b) $\mathbf{v}$ contains at least one 0 element. (a) Suppose that the array $\mathbf{v}$ contains no 0 elements (i.e., $\forall v_i \in \mathbf{v}, v_i \neq 0$). Then, $s = n(1 - r)$. Since $r < 1$, it follows that $s > 0$. (b) Suppose that the array $\mathbf{v}$ contains k elements equal to 0, $1 \leq k \leq n$. Then, $s = (n - k) - nr$. Since $r \geq \frac{n-1}{n} \geq \frac{n-k}{n}$, it follows that $s \leq 0$.

The main advantage of the 0SA is that its circuit representation has a constant multiplicative depth, given by the number of consecutive multiplications used by the circuit that computes the function H. Since the number of consecutive multiplication is constant, the algorithm can be adapted to run over encrypted data using an LHE scheme. Algorithm 2 - 0EncSA delineates the procedure for searching over encrypted data by simply replacing the operations with the corresponding operations over ciphertexts (i.e., replaces sum with EvalAddScalar and H with EvalSign) The algorithm takes as input an array of ciphertexts and produces an encrypted result corresponding to the output of Algorithm 1 - 0SA if it had been executed directly on the corresponding plaintext.

Algorithm 1. 0-Searching algorithm (0SA)

Input: $\mathbf{v}$
Output: s
$r \leftarrow^{R} \left[\frac{n-1}{n}, 1\right)$
$s = \sum_{i=1}^{n} (H(v_i) - r)$.
return s

Algorithm 2. 0-Searching algorithm over encrypted data (0EncSA)

Input: $[\mathbf{v}]$
Output: $[s]$
$r \leftarrow^{R} \left[\frac{n-1}{n}, 1\right)$
$[s] = \mathsf{EvalSign}([v_1])$
$[s] = \mathsf{EvalAddScalar}([s], -r)$
for $i = 2$ **to** n **do**
    $[aux] = \mathsf{EvalSign}([v_i])$
    $[aux] = \mathsf{EvalAddScalar}([aux], -r)$
    $[s] = \mathsf{EvalAdd}([s], [aux])$
end for
return $[s]$

Algorithm 3. Squared Euclidean distance over encrypted data (EuclDist)

Input: $[m_1], m_2$
Output: $\left[(m_1 - m_2)^2\right]$
$m_2 \leftarrow -m_2$
$[c] \leftarrow \mathsf{EvalAddScalar}([m_1], m_2)$
$[d] \leftarrow \mathsf{EvalMul}(c, c)$
return $[d]$

Algorithm 4. Homomorphic sum of elements of an encrypted vector (SumVec)

Input: $[m_1], [m_2], \ldots, [m_n]$
Output: $[m_1 + m_2 + \cdots + m_n]$
$[s] \leftarrow [m_1]$
for $i = 2$ **to** n **do**
  $[s] \leftarrow \mathsf{EvalAdd}([\mathsf{s}], [\mathsf{m_i}])$
end for
return $[s]$

Note that 0EncSA requires computation over reals. Although many popular HE schemes do not accept reals by construction, significant work has been done regarding the processing of real numbers over encryption, with [11] containing a nice discussion in this respect.

Note. The absence of negative elements simplifies the problem: if **v** is ordered, comparing against the lowest element suffices. However, in our protocol, this simplification does not apply. For each query, we compute the distance between the encrypted query element and each database element, then search for 0 within this array of distances. As the array changes with each query, the simplification is inapplicable.

5.2 Protocol Description

We generalize the 0-searching algorithm and present a protocol that allows privacy-preserving decentralized searching of an arbitrary value in the settings given in Sect. 4.1. The protocol is based on the threshold version of an FHE scheme [5], as explained in Sect. 3.2. The protocol outputs 1 if there is any database containing the query element and 0 otherwise.

We further assume that each database is a linear array of reals.[3] The protocol involves computing the squared Euclidean distance between two elements, one of which (the queried element) is encrypted. This functionality can be implemented using the homomorphic operations allowed by the scheme as described in Algorithm 3 - EuclDist. Algorithm 4 - SumVec implements another requested functionality: it computes the sum of a linear array over encrypted data.

[3] We leave the translation from a database to a vector out of the scope of this paper.

Figure 2 describes the protocol. The intuition of the protocol is as follows. Given a database in the form of a linear array and a query element, each party first computes the distance between the encryption of the queried element and each element from the array. The outcome of this step is another array with non-negative elements, which encrypts 0 strictly at every position where the corresponding element from the database is equal to the query. The problem is reduced, therefore, to determining if the encryption of 0 belongs to a linear array with non-negative numbers. Our 0EncSA algorithm in Sect. 5.1 solves this problem without using multiplication operations.

1. **Setup and Key Generation.** The parties $\{P_1, \ldots, P_p\}$ in $\mathcal{P}$:
   (a) Run the common setup.
   (b) Run the $\mathsf{TFHE.KeyGen}(setup)$ to obtain a common public key pk, an evaluation key evk and p private keys sk_i, $i = 1, \ldots, p$.
2. **Encrypted query.** The querying party, P_1:
   (a) Runs $\mathsf{TFHE.Enc_{pk}(m)} \to [m]$ to encrypt the query m using the public key pk.
   (b) Sends the ciphertext $[m]$ to each other party
   $$P_1 \to P_j : [m], \forall j = 2, \ldots, p$$
3. **Search.** Each party, $P_j, j = 2, \ldots, p$:
   (a) Uses the Algorithm 3 to compute the squared Euclidean distance between the encrypted query $[m]$ and each plaintext element of the database $\mathbf{D}_j$
   $$[d_j^k] = \mathsf{EuclDist}([m], D_j^k), \forall D_j^k \in \mathbf{D}_j.$$
   (b) Runs the searching $\mathsf{0EncSA}$ over the vector of encrypted squared distances obtained in the previous step
   $$[d_j] = \mathsf{0EncSA}([\mathbf{d}_j]), \text{ where } [\mathbf{d}_j] = ([d_j^k])_k.$$
   (c) Sends the encrypted result $[d_j]$ back to the querying party P_1
   $$P_j \to P_1 : [d_j]$$
4. **Compute final result.** The querying party, P_1:
   (a) Runs $\mathsf{EvalSign}$ on each ciphertext received from the $p-1$ parties, and then homomorphically sums the resulting ciphertexts
   $$[b_j] = \mathsf{EvalSign}\left([d_j]\right),\ 2 \le j \le p$$
   $$[s] = \mathsf{SumVec}\left([b_2], [b_3], \ldots, [b_p]\right)$$
   (b) Involves in the threshold decryption protocol along the other parties $P_2, \ldots, P_p$ and decrypts the ciphertext $[s]$
   $$s = \mathsf{TFHE.Dec}_{sk_1, \ldots, sk_p}([s])$$
   (c) If the result value s equals $p-1$ then output 0; otherwise, output 1
   $$\mathsf{Output}\ 1 - [s == p-1]$$

Fig. 2. Our protocol on decentralized privacy-preserving searching.

Note that at step 4(b), we use the p-out-of-p threshold version of the underlying leveled HE scheme, so the decryption implies the cooperation of all parties, including the querying party P_1.

Theorem 1 (Correctness). *The protocol described in Fig. 2 outputs* 1 *if there is at least one database with an entry equal to the query element and* 0 *otherwise.*

Proof. By computing the EuclDist in Step 3.(a), a database owner P_j, $2 \leq j \leq p$ obtains an array with encrypted non-negative entries. The array has the encryption of 0 in each position where the Euclidian distance is 0 (i.e., the element in the database is equal to the querying element) and the encryption of a positive number elsewhere. Thus, the problem of searching through the database is reduced to the problem of searching for the encryption of 0, which is solvable by 0EncSA. By construction, 0EncSA returns the encryption of a strictly positive number if and only if the encryption of 0 is not within the elements of the encrypted database. Hence, in step 3.(c) each party P_j, $2 \leq j \leq p$ returns to P_1 the encryption of a single element d_j, with $d_j \leq 0$ if and only if $\mathbf{D}_j$ contains the queried element m. After evaluating EvalSign function over all received encrypted results in step 4.(a), the querying party P_1 obtains an encrypted vector $[\mathbf{b}]$ that contains, on each position $j, j = 2, \ldots, p$ the encryption of $b_j = 0$, if m is in $\mathbf{D}_j$ and $b_j = 1$, if m is not in $\mathbf{D}_j$. Thus, $[s]$ in step 4.(b) is the encryption of $s = p-1$ if and only if no database $\mathbf{D}_2, \ldots, \mathbf{D}_p$ contains the querying element m. $[s]$ decrypts to s in step 4.(b). Finally, in step 4.(c), P_1 outputs 0 if no database $\mathbf{D}_2, \ldots, \mathbf{D}_p$ contains the querying element (i.e., s equals $p-1$) and 1 otherwise. □

It is important to note that the protocol accommodates both insertions and deletions for each database $\mathbf{D}_\mathbf{i}, i = 1 \ldots p$. This flexibility ensures that the protocol can handle dynamic data sets without compromising the security of the overall system. This makes the protocol adaptable to various real-world applications where data is frequently changing.

5.3 Security Proof

Adversarial Model. To prove the security of our protocol, we use the Universal Composability (UC) framework that allows the composition of distinct protocols [10]. The framework delineates two types of executions: the *real* execution and the *ideal* execution. In the real execution, the parties interact according to the protocol in the presence of an adversary $\mathcal{A}$ and the environment $\mathcal{Z}$. Conversely, in the ideal execution, the parties interact with an ideal functionality, denoted as $\mathcal{F}_{\text{search}}$, which implements the protocol using a Trusted Third Party (TTP) in the presence of a simulated adversary $\mathcal{S}$ and the environment $\mathcal{Z}$. A protocol is considered secure if, for every adversary $\mathcal{A}$ in the real execution, there exists a simulated adversary $\mathcal{S}$ in the ideal execution such that the environment cannot distinguish between the real and ideal executions. We assume that all the parties are honest-but-curious, meaning they adhere to the protocol specifications but are motivated to glean additional information beyond their prescribed outputs (as explained in Sect. 4.1).

Theorem 2 (Security). *The protocol in Fig. 2 securely realizes $\mathcal{F}_{search}$ in the presence of honest-but-curious adversaries.*

Proof (Sketch). We prove that the environment $\mathcal{Z}$ cannot distinguish between the real and the ideal executions, given the messages exchanged by the parties, until the querying party runs the *threshold decryption algorithm* in step 4.(b).

In the real execution, the environment $\mathcal{Z}$ sees $2p-2$ messages:

1. The querying party P_1 sends a ciphertext encrypting the searched element to each of the $p-1$ database owners. These ciphertexts can be simulated by $\mathcal{S}$ by $p-1$ ciphertexts of random values. Since the encryption scheme is IND-CPA secure, the environment cannot distinguish between the ciphertexts.
2. Each database owner sends the output of the Algorithm 2 - 0EncSA. These output ciphertexts can also be simulated by $p-1$ encryption of random elements because the encryption scheme is IND-CPA secure.

Given the fact that the *threshold decryption algorithm* used in step 4.(b) is secure against honest-but-curious adversaries in the UC framework [5], we conclude that our protocol in Fig. 2 securely realizes $\mathcal{F}_{search}$ in the presence of honest-but-curious adversaries.

□

6 Protocol Evaluation

We compare our encrypted data searching algorithm, 0EncSA, detailed in Algorithm 2, with the most cited privacy-preserving search solutions based on homomorphic encryption (HE). Our comparison focuses on multiplicative depth, communication rounds, and the complexity of the search algorithm. Although our procedure is designed to search for the 0 element in a non-negative array, it can be easily extended to search for any arbitrary value, as shown in Fig. 2. The reason we look into the 0EncSA and not the final proposed protocol is mainly because the other works do not give results in the multi-party settings. Nevertheless, we are aware of the fact that the comparison might not be fair in the sense that 0EncSA allows a particular search and does not accept, by itself, general queries.

Table 1 summarizes the comparison with the protocols introduced in [2,23, 25]. Multiplicative depth affects the running time due to linearly increasing noise, necessitating costly bootstrapping operations. The number of communication rounds impacts the network overhead and decides whether the participants must be online. Finally, the complexity of the search algorithm influences the overall efficiency of the solution. The most efficient protocol in terms of the searching complexity is [2], while our approach demonstrates the highest efficiency in terms of multiplicative depth. From a practical perspective, we conclude that Akavia et al.'s protocol [2] is better suited for static large databases, while our proposal is preferable for scenarios involving relatively small but dynamic databases.

Table 1. Comparison with related work

Ref.	Communication rounds	Multiplicative depth	Overall Complexity
[25]	$O(m)$	$O(m)$	$O(n)$
[23]	$O(1)$	$O(m)$	$O(n)$
[2]	$O(1)$	$O(log(log(m)))$	$O(log(n))$
Our protocol	$O(1)$	$O(1)$	$O(n)$

*n is the number of entries in the database; m is the length of the queried element

7 Conclusions and Future Work

We proposed a new multi-party privacy-preserving searching protocol that maintains a constant multiplicative depth. We proved it correct and secure under the honest-but-curious adversarial model. We compared our proposal with existing works, highlighted its advantages, and concluded that it is appropriate for dynamic databases.

We have also briefly referred to generic approaches to solve the secure search problem. A detailed analysis and comparison to other works is out of the current goal, mostly because of the lack of space, but it is considered for an extension of the paper. We thus postpone the implementation and the numeric performance evaluation of the proposed solution for future work. It is also of interest to look into the performance of the solution in real use cases such as, e.g., the IP address search against multiple blocklists, as exemplified in the introduction.

Besides outputting a boolean result (1 if the element is found in any of the party's databases and 0 otherwise), our protocol can also number the parties that have the queried element in their databases. This is easily reached by changing the protocol's output in the last step. Further investigation of this functionality in different applications could be interesting. Finally, in the current definition, the problem asks that the querying party P_1 be internal to the set of parties. Future work will look into solutions where the queries can also originate from external parties.

Acknowledgements. This work was supported by a grant of the Ministry of Research, Innovation and Digitalization, CNCS/CCCDI - UEFISCDI, project number ERANET-CHISTERA-IV-PATTERN, within PNCDI IV.

References

1. Acar, A., Aksu, H., Uluagac, A.S., Conti, M.: A survey on homomorphic encryption schemes: theory and implementation. ACM Comput. Surv. **51**(4) (2018). https://doi.org/10.1145/3214303
2. Akavia, A., Feldman, D., Shaul, H.: Secure search on encrypted data via multi-ring sketch. In: Proceedings of the 2018 ACM SIGSAC Conference on Computer and Communications Security, pp. 985–1001 (2018)

3. Amorim, I., Costa, I.: Leveraging searchable encryption through homomorphic encryption: a comprehensive analysis. Mathematics **11**(13) (2023). https://doi.org/10.3390/math11132948
4. Andola, N., Gahlot, R., Yadav, V.K., Venkatesan, S., Verma, S.: Searchable encryption on the cloud: a survey. J. Supercomput., 1–33 (2022). https://doi.org/10.1007/s11227-022-04309-6
5. Asharov, G., Jain, A., López-Alt, A., Tromer, E., Vaikuntanathan, V., Wichs, D.: Multiparty computation with low communication, computation and interaction via threshold FHE. In: Pointcheval, D., Johansson, T. (eds.) EUROCRYPT 2012. LNCS, vol. 7237, pp. 483–501. Springer, Heidelberg (2012). https://doi.org/10.1007/978-3-642-29011-4_29
6. Bater, J., Elliott, G., Eggen, C., Goel, S., Kho, A., Rogers, J.: smcql: secure querying for federated databases. Proc. VLDB Endow. **10**(6) (2017)
7. Bösch, C., Hartel, P., Jonker, W., Peter, A.: A survey of provably secure searchable encryption. ACM Comput. Surv. (CSUR) **47**(2), 1–51 (2014)
8. Brakerski, Z.: Fully homomorphic encryption without modulus switching from classical GapSVP. In: Annual Cryptology Conference, pp. 868–886. Springer (2012)
9. Brakerski, Z., Gentry, C., Vaikuntanathan, V.: (Leveled) fully homomorphic encryption without bootstrapping. ACM Trans. Comput. Theor. (TOCT) **6**(3), 1–36 (2014)
10. Canetti, R.: Universally composable security: a new paradigm for cryptographic protocols. In: Proceedings 42nd IEEE Symposium on Foundations of Computer Science, pp. 136–145. IEEE (2001)
11. Cheon, J.H., Kim, A., Kim, M., Song, Y.: Homomorphic encryption for arithmetic of approximate numbers. In: Takagi, T., Peyrin, T. (eds.) ASIACRYPT 2017. LNCS, vol. 10624, pp. 409–437. Springer, Cham (2017). https://doi.org/10.1007/978-3-319-70694-8_15
12. Couteau, G.: New protocols for secure equality test and comparison. In: International Conference on Applied Cryptography and Network Security, pp. 303–320. Springer (2018)
13. Fan, J., Vercauteren, F.: Somewhat practical fully homomorphic encryption. Cryptology ePrint Archive (2012)
14. Han, F., Zhang, L., Feng, H., Liu, W., Li, X.: Scape: scalable collaborative analytics system on private database with malicious security. In: 2022 IEEE 38th International Conference on Data Engineering (ICDE), pp. 1740–1753. IEEE (2022)
15. Handa, R., Krishna, C.R., Aggarwal, N.: Searchable encryption: a survey on privacy-preserving search schemes on encrypted outsourced data. Concurrency Comput. Pract. Exp. **31**(17), e5201 (2019)
16. Iliashenko, I., Zucca, V.: Faster homomorphic comparison operations BGV and BFV. Proc. Priv. Enhancing Technol. **2021**(3), 246–264 (2021)
17. Lee, E., Lee, J.W., Kim, Y.S., No, J.S.: Optimization of homomorphic comparison algorithm on RNS-CKKS scheme. IEEE Access **10**, 26163–26176 (2022)
18. Li, B., Micciancio, D., Schultz, M., Sorrell, J.: Securing approximate homomorphic encryption using differential privacy. In: Annual International Cryptology Conference, pp. 560–589. Springer (2022)
19. Li, B., Micciancio, D.: On the security of homomorphic encryption on approximate numbers. In: Annual International Conference on the Theory and Applications of Cryptographic Techniques, pp. 648–677. Springer (2021)
20. Liagouris, J., Kalavri, V., Faisal, M., Varia, M.: {SECRECY}: secure collaborative analytics in untrusted clouds. In: 20th USENIX Symposium on Networked Systems Design and Implementation (NSDI 23), pp. 1031–1056 (2023)

21. Lyubashevsky, V., Peikert, C., Regev, O.: On ideal lattices and learning with errors over rings. In: Gilbert, H. (ed.) EUROCRYPT 2010. LNCS, vol. 6110, pp. 1–23. Springer, Heidelberg (2010). https://doi.org/10.1007/978-3-642-13190-5_1
22. Poddar, R., Kalra, S., Yanai, A., Deng, R., Popa, R.A., Hellerstein, J.,M.: Senate: a Maliciously-Secure MPC platform for collaborative analytics. In: 30th USENIX Security Symposium (USENIX Security 21), pp. 2129–2146 (2021)
23. Roy, S.S., Vercauteren, F., Vliegen, J., Verbauwhede, I.: Hardware assisted fully homomorphic function evaluation and encrypted search. IEEE Trans. Comput. **66**(9), 1562–1572 (2017)
24. Saha, T.K., Koshiba, T.: Private equality test using ring-LWE somewhat homomorphic encryption. In: 2016 3rd Asia-Pacific World Congress on Computer Science and Engineering (APWC on CSE), pp. 1–9. IEEE (2016)
25. Yamamoto, Y., Oguchi, M.: A decentralized system of genome secret search implemented with fully homomorphic encryption. In: 2017 IEEE International Conference on Smart Computing (SMARTCOMP), pp. 1–6 (2017). https://doi.org/10.1109/SMARTCOMP.2017.7946977

An Evaluation of Post-quantum and Hybrid Noise Protocol Variants on Mobile Devices

Joshua Renckens, Peter B. Rønne(✉), Johann Großschädl, and Peter Y. A. Ryan

SnT and DCS, University of Luxembourg, 6, Avenue de la Fonte, L-4364 Esch-sur-Alzette, Luxembourg
{peter.roenne,johann.groszschaedl,peter.ryan}@uni.lu

Abstract. Noise is a framework for the design and security assessment of Authenticated Key Exchange (AKE) protocols between two parties using Diffie-Hellman (DH) as the only public-key cryptosystem. In this paper, we present an evaluation of the computation and communication cost of Noise and PQNoise, a recently introduced post-quantum version of the Noise protocol framework. Furthermore, we present combinations of the 12 fundamental (interactive) Noise patterns and their PQNoise counterparts, thereby obtaining hybrid handshake patterns, and include them in our evaluation. We integrated PQNoise and the novel hybrid patterns into Noise-C, a reference implementation of the Noise protocol framework written in C. In order to evaluate Noise and its variants, we emulated networks with different latency, throughput, and packet-loss settings using Linux network emulation tools. For all Noise handshakes we chose cryptosystems that provide a comparable (pre-quantum) level of security, namely X25519 and Kyber512. We ran our experiments on two different devices, one is a laptop with an Intel Core i5-10210U CPU and the other an Orange Pi One development board with a 32-bit ARM Cortex-A7 processor. The results we collected show that, under normal network conditions, the Noise patterns and their PQNoise counterparts have nearly identical execution times, except when the latter require an additional handshake message. However, under bad network conditions with high packet-loss rates, PQNoise falls behind Noise, mainly because of the relatively large public-key and ciphertext sizes of Kyber512. The execution times of our hybrid handshakes are almost indistinguishable from the corresponding PQNoise handshakes when the packet-loss rates are low, and at higher loss rates the differences are small.

Keywords: End-to-end security · Post-quantum cryptography · Noise protocol · Key encapsulation mechanism · Hybrid key establishment

1 Introduction

The *Transport Layer Security (TLS)* protocol is one of the most common End-to-End (E2E) security protocols on the Internet and secures billions of HTTPS

L. Morogan et al. (Eds.): SecITC 2024, LNCS 15595, pp. 149–169, 2025.
https://doi.org/10.1007/978-3-031-87760-5_12

transactions daily. It consists of a few sub-protocols, of which the handshake protocol and the record protocol are the most important ones. The former is responsible for authentication and key exchange using public-key cryptographic schemes, while the latter ensures the confidentiality and integrity of application data through symmetric cryptosystems [20,24]. Initially designed in the 1990 s under the name *Secure Sockets Layer (SSL)*, the TLS protocol has since then undergone a number of revisions to extend its functionality and fix weaknesses and flaws [16]. These over 30 years of evolution have made TLS a very complex protocol, which is overloaded with many legacy versions that still need to be supported for backward compatibility and many niche features and extensions with disputable relevance for real-world use cases. The high complexity of TLS has been the root cause for various types of attacks on the protocol itself and on different implementations [22]. In addition, complex protocols like TLS are unattractive for embedded and mobile devices, which are usually constrained in computational power and energy supply compared to conventional PCs.

Noise [19] was introduced by Trevor Perrin in 2014 as a framework for the design of custom E2E security protocols whose AKE component is solely based on Diffie-Hellman (DH) [6] operations. Noise-based protocols aim to reduce the complexity caused by run-time decisions during protocol execution, which are prevalent in TLS and "interwoven" with the handshake, by relegating them to design-time decisions (e.g., one-way or mutual authentication) within a framework and a thin negotiation layer (i.e., an optional prologue) before the actual handshake to agree on a handshake pattern and related cryptosystems. Also, in contrast to TLS, Noise adopts long-term (static) DH keys instead of long-term signature keys to authenticate the ephemeral DH key exchange, thereby minimizing the number of public-key schemes that need to be supported[1]. Once the negotiation phase is completed, the rest of the handshake is a straight sequence of message transfers and DH operations without any conditional statements like branches, which massively simplifies the implementation testing of the protocol and also reduces the attack surface compared to TLS. The concrete handshake pattern determines many of the security properties the resulting protocol will have; for example, if the two parties do not need to be authenticated, then the so-called `NN` pattern will suffice, but if server authentication (with transmission of the server's static key, similar to TLS) is desired, then the `NX` pattern is the best choice [19]. The existence of several handshake patterns with well-studied security properties allows designers to simply choose the Noise variant that fits the security needs of their target application best, and saves them the time and effort of designing a custom protocol from scratch or trying to figure out how to disable and/or remove unnecessary TLS functionalities.

Early versions of TLS (resp., SSL) used "classical" public-key cryptosystems like RSA, DSA, and DH, but over the years they have become largely replaced by elliptic curve schemes (i.e., ECDH for key exchange and ECDSA for authentication). As mentioned above, Noise uses ECDH (based on either Curve25519 or Curve448 [14]) not only for the establishment of shared secrets, but also the

[1] Note that all DH operations/keys of Noise are, in fact, ECDH operations/keys.

authentication of the ephemeral public keys exchanged during a handshake. In 1994, Peter Shor introduced quantum algorithms for efficient (polynomial-time) factorization of large composite numbers and efficient computing of the discrete logarithm problem, thereby enabling quantum computers to break virtually all of the currently prevalent public-key schemes, including DH, RSA, ECDH, and ECDSA [23]. Due to the looming threat of quantum cryptanalysis, it becomes necessary to replace these algorithms by post-quantum alternatives that fulfill the same purpose, but are able to withstand cryptanalytic attacks executed on large-scale quantum computers. A well-known example of such a post-quantum algorithm is *Kyber* [5], a lattice-based KEM selected for standardization by the U.S. National Institute of Standards and Technology (NIST). This transition to *Post-Quantum Cryptography (PQC)* also requires an adaptation and extension of security protocols like TLS and Noise to support the new algorithms. There have been a couple of initiatives for adding post-quantum schemes to TLS; two examples are the crypto provider of the Open Quantum Safe project [25] and KEMTLS [21]. On the other hand, for Noise, the only post-quantum variant we are aware of is *PQNoise* [3], which was published in 2022.

Besides the concrete integration of post-quantum schemes into TLS, a large body of research has been devoted to analyzing how they affect the execution time and the amount of data exchanged in a handshake [2,12,15]. For Noise, on the other hand, the research so far has focussed on proving security properties of different Noise protocols [3,8,13] and automated code generation for various Noise variants [11]. Since PQNoise is still fairly new, relatively little is known about its performance apart from results of a Go implementation for two handshake patterns described in [3]. However, according to [17, Table 4], software developed in the Go language seems to be significantly less efficient, in terms of execution time and energy consumption, than software written in C. A more detailed comparison of pre- and post-quantum Noise, especially a comparison based on efficient C implementations of the handshakes, is still lacking.

In this paper, we study the performance of an optimized C implementation of PQNoise, taking into account the computation and communication cost, respectively, and compare it to Noise as well as TLS. Such kind of performance evaluation is important to assess how the migration to PQC might impact the latency of secure communication of widely-used Internet applications. We are especially interested in measuring and comparing the performance of pre- and post-quantum security protocols on mobile devices that are less powerful than conventional PCs. This means we evaluated these protocols on mobile devices under network conditions (i.e., latency, throughput, packet-loss rate) similar to that of mobile (cellular) networks based on 4G technology. Although Noise has been integrated into a number of applications, e.g., WhatsApp [27] and WireGuard [7], it will most likely not replace TLS on a large scale. However, there is a good chance that Noise will find widespread adoption for use cases where one entity controls all the communication endpoints, e.g., the client app running on smart phones and the back-end servers. In such settings, it often makes sense to use a custom protocol (designed and security-evaluated with help of the Noise framework) that is specifically tailored for the target application.

Apart from an evaluation of the performance of PQNoise, we also describe hybrid variants of Noise handshakes combining X25519 and Kyber512. There has been prior work on creating hybrid versions of Noise [18], which focused on defining Noise patterns that offer *Hybrid Forward Secrecy (HFS)* through the introduction of a "`hfs`'' pattern-modifier and two new tokens. The new tokens represent KEM operations and the transfer of KEM public keys or ciphertexts to the other party. However, the specification of these HFS patterns for Noise was last updated in 2018 (i.e., four years before the publication of the PQNoise paper) and its current status is still unofficial. *Noise-C* [26], which is intended as a reference implementation of Noise, contains a version of the HFS patterns based on NewHope [1] instead of Kyber. In our work, we combine the classical X25519-based Noise patterns with their PQNoise counterparts to obtain novel hybrid Noise handshakes that use Kyber512 as KEM to achieve post-quantum security. We integrated these hybrid patterns to Noise-C and included them in our evaluation of the computation and communication cost of handshakes on mobile devices. Furthermore, we analyze how the combination of classical and post-quantum algorithms, as well as the additional handshake data that have to be transmitted, slows down the hybrid patterns compared to PQNoise.

2 Preliminaries

2.1 Noise Protocol Framework

As mentioned in the previous section, Noise is framework to support the design and security evaluation of custom protocols between two parties, usually called initiator and responder. A concrete instance of a Noise-based security protocol is defined by a protocol name, which includes the handshake pattern, the DH function (either X25519 or X448), an algorithm for Authenticated Encryption with Associated Data (AEAD), and a hash function [19]. A concrete example for a Noise protocol name is `Noise_NX_25519_AESGCM_SHA256`, where `NX` is the handshake pattern. Handshake pattern names usually consist of two uppercase letters, indicating the status of the static DH keys and how they are conveyed to the other party (as will be further discussed below), followed by one or more optional pattern modifiers. The concrete handshake pattern to be used by the protocol, including the underlying cryptosystems, is normally chosen at design time. However, as mentioned in [19, Sect. 6], it is also possible that the parties agree on it interactively; for example, the initiator can send a list of supported Noise protocols to the responder in a so-called preamble. Once this negotiation is completed, the actual handshake is a linear sequence of message (i.e., public-key) transfers and cryptographic operations that does not involve any run-time decisions apart from error handling [19]. Depending on the chosen handshake pattern, a Noise protocol can have different security properties, e.g., unilateral or mutual authentication, weak or strong forward secrecy, identity hiding, and zero round-trip encryption. All patterns have in common that they exchange public

DH keys (static or ephemeral), perform DH operations, and hash all the computed DH results together to derive a shared secret.

Pattern Components. A handshake pattern describes the overall execution of the handshake and consists of a sequence of *message patterns*, which defines the exchange of messages. The message patterns, in turn, are composed of one or more *tokens* that specify the involved DH public keys and DH operations to be executed when sending or receiving the message. Besides such patterns and tokens, the Noise specification also defines a couple of variables, which have to be maintained by each party, irrespective of the used handshake pattern.

- A *handshake hash* value `h` representing a fingerprint of the pre-distributed static DH keys and all exchanged messages. It is initialized by hashing the Noise protocol name. Whenever static public DH keys and/or payloads are AEAD-encrypted, `h` is included in the message as associated data.
- A *chaining key* `ck`, which is also initialized with the hash of the protocol name. The result of every DH operation is "mixed" into `ck` through a hash-based key-derivation function. After completion of the handshake, `ck` serves to generate encryption keys for transport messages.
- An *encryption key* `k` for encryption/decryption of public static DH keys as well as handshake payloads using an AEAD algorithm. This key is derived from the chaining key `ck` and gets updated every time `ck` changes.
- A counter-based *nonce* `n` of 64 bits in length, which is used as input for the AEAD algorithm. The nonce gets reset to zero every time `ck` changes.

There are six different standard tokens that can appear in a Noise message pattern; two represent public keys and the other four DH operations performed on a combination of two DH key-shares, one private and the other public.

- `"e"`: The sender generates a new (ephemeral) DH key pair and then sends the public key to the receiver unencrypted. This public key will be used to update the handshake hash `h` on both sides.
- `"s"`: The sender sends its static public DH key to the receiver. This key is normally encrypted using the encryption key `k` and nonce `n`. However, the DH key is sent in clear when `k` is still empty, which is the case when no DH operation has been carried out yet. Further, the message sent, irrespective of whether it is encrypted or not, is hashed into `h` by both parties.
- `"ee"`, `"es"`, `"se"`, and `"ss"`: These tokens instruct the parties to perform DH computations that involve a key-share of the initiator and a key-share of the responder. The left letter stands for the initiator's key-share and the right letter for the responder's key-share to be used. Each key-share can be ephemeral (`e`) or static (`s`). The result of the DH operation is mixed into the chaining key `ck`, at which point a new `k` is generated and `n` is set to zero.

The tokens can be arranged into a message pattern and several of such message patterns constitute a handshake pattern. How a handshake pattern is executed in detail is best explained using a single example like the `KN` pattern, illustrated in Fig. 1. This handshake pattern contains the delimiter "..." (i.e., an ellipsis or three periods), which separates the so-called *pre-message patterns* from the actual message patterns. A pre-message can be used to pre-distribute a static public DH key, e.g., by means of an out-of-band transmission, before the actual (interactive) part of the handshake starts. In the KN pattern, the pre-message consists of a right arrow and an "s" token, indicating that the initiator's static public key was already shared with the responder at some point prior to the actual handshake. A right arrow represents a message from the initiator to the responder, and a left arrow a message in the other direction. The first message pattern, a right arrow with an "e" token, means that the initiator sends the public share of a freshly-generated ephemeral DH key-pair to the responder. On the other hand, the second message pattern is composed of a left arrow and the tokens "e", "ee", and "se". This means the responder generates an ephemeral DH key-pair and sends its public share to the initiator ("e"). Then, both sides carry out an ephemeral-ephemeral ("ee") DH, followed by a static-ephemeral ("se") DH using the initiator's static public key, which was pre-distributed.

NN:
→ **e**
← **e, ee**

NK:
← **s**
...
→ **e, es**
← **e, ee**

NX:
→ **e**
← **e, ee, s, es**

KN:
→ **s**
...
→ **e**
← **e, ee, se**

KK:
→ **s**
← **s**
...
→ **e, es, ss**
← **e, ee, se**

KX:
→ **s**
...
→ **e**
← **e, ee, se, s, es**

XN:
→ **e**
← **e, ee**
→ **s, se**

XK:
← **s**
...
→ **e, es**
← **e, ee**
→ **s, se**

XX:
→ **e**
← **e, ee, s, es**
→ **s, se**

IN:
→ **e, s**
← **e, ee, se**

IK:
← **s**
...
→ **e, es, s, ss**
← **e, ee, se**

IX:
→ **e, s**
← **e, ee, se, s, es**

Fig. 1. The 12 fundamental interactive Noise patterns

Fundamental Interactive Patterns. The tokes and patterns outlined above provide a flexible toolbox for the design of custom handshake protocols. Alternatively, instead of creating a new handshake from scratch, a designer can also use one of the 12 so-called fundamental interactive patterns that are described in the Noise specification. The security properties of the fundamental patterns are well studied and were even formally proven in [8,13]. As already mentioned earlier, the first letter of a pattern name conveys information on the initiator's static public key, and the second letter on the responder's static public key. In total, there are four possible letters on the initiator's side:

- `N` ("None"): The initiator does not use a static DH key in this pattern and is, therefore, not authenticated during the handshake.
- `K` ("Known"): The initiator's static DH key was pre-distributed, i.e., sent to the responder, before the handshake execution. Hence, the responder knows (and implicitly trusts) the initiator's static key.
- `X` ("Xmitted"): The static DH key of the initiator is sent to the responder in one of the handshake messages, usually encrypted (which can help to hide the initiator's identity).
- `I`: ("Immediate"): The initiator sends its static DH key immediately to the responder (i.e., in the first handshake message), despite the fact that this early transmission reduces or inhibits identity hiding.

The responder's static DH key can have the `N`, `K`, or `X` property, but not `I`. As a consequence, there are 12 possible combinations of initiator/responder static DH keys; the resulting handshake patterns are illustrated in Fig. 1.

2.2 Kyber KEM

CRYSTALS-Kyber (Kyber for short) is a family of post-quantum KEMs whose security is based on the hardness of the Module Learning with Errors (MLWE) problem, which comes with a worst-case to average-case reduction from certain hard problems over module lattices [5]. The NIST is currently working towards standardizing Kyber (under the name "ML-KEM") with three parameter sets providing security levels roughly similar to that of the AES with 128, 192, and 256-bit keys, respectively. The algebraic structure in which Kyber operates is a module[2] of low rank k defined over a polynomial ring $\mathcal{R}_q$. Depending on the security level, k is either 2, 3, or 4. All three instances of Kyber use the same ring, namely $\mathcal{R}_q = \mathbb{Z}_q[X]/(X^n - 1)$ with $n = 2^8$ and $q = 13n + 1 = 3329$. The base field $\mathbb{Z}_q$ contains primitive 256-th roots of unity so that multiplication in $\mathcal{R}_q$ can be implemented very efficiently using the Number-Theoretic Transform (NTT). Besides polynomial arithmetic, other building blocks of Kyber include functions for the sampling of polynomials (i.e., coefficients) from uniform and centered binomial distributions, and SHA3-based functions for pseudo-random number generation from a seed, hashing, and shared-secret derivation.

[2] A module can be seen as a lattice, but is defined over a ring (other than the ring $\mathbb{Z}$).

From a high-level perspective, Kyber (as any other KEM) consists of three functions: key generation (KeyGen), encapsulation (Encaps), and decapsulation (Decaps). By using these functions, two parties can establish a shared secret as follows. First, the initiator generates a key pair consisting of an encapsulation key *ek*, which is public and sent to the responder, and a private decapsulation key *dk*. The responder calls the Encaps function to generate a random 32-byte secret *s* and encapsulate (i.e., encrypt) it using the received *ek*. Encaps outputs *s* both in the clear (for use by the responder) and in encapsulated form, i.e., as ciphertext *ct*, which is sent to the initiator. Finally, the initiator executes the Decaps function with *ct* and *dk* as input to obtain the secret *s*.

2.3 PQNoise: KEM-Based Post-quantum Noise

Key establishment based on a KEM such as Kyber differs from a key exchange system (e.g., DH, ECDH) in some basic aspects. For example, in DH, the two involved parties exchange their public keys, whereas, when using a KEM, one party sends a public key but the other party a ciphertext (i.e., an encapsulated secret). Furthermore, when executing a DH key exchange, each party can send its public key straight away, without having to wait first for the other party's key. When the public keys have been pre-distributed, it is possible for the two parties to agree on a shared secret without any interaction (the other party can even be "off-line"). In a KEM-based key establishment, on the other hand, the secret to be shared can only be encapsulated after receipt of the other party's key, and decapsulation can only be done after encapsulation. Performing Non-Interactive Key Exchange (NIKE) using a lattice KEM is feasible [10], but (in contrast to DH) unattractive in practice due to very large public keys.

Despite these differences between key exchange and key encapsulation, it is possible to design AKE protocols that use a KEM like Kyber instead of DH as underlying public-key cryptosystem. PQNoise [3] is an attempt to leverage the Kyber KEM for making Noise ready for the post-quantum era. However, since Kyber can not serve as a "drop-in" replacement for DH, most Noise handshake patterns require some substantial modifications. Instead of transmitting public DH keys, one party now sends its public (encapsulation) KEM key, which can be either static or ephemeral, and the other party returns a ciphertext (i.e., an encapsulated secret). Accordingly, the DH operations of classical Noise have to be replaced by executions of Encaps or Decaps. To facilitate the transition from DH to Kyber, the PQNoise designers introduced two new tokens:

- `"ekem"`: The sender generates a secret key and encapsulates it using the receiver's ephemeral public KEM key. Thereafter, a message containing the produced ciphertext is sent to the receiver. Both parties hash this message into the handshake hash `h` and the shared secret key into the chaining key `ck`, which triggers the generation of a new encryption key `k`.
- `"skem"`: This token is the static counterpart to `"ekem"`. The only difference is that the message is encrypted should an encryption key `k` be available.

The two Noise tokens "e" and "s" also exist in PQNoise and serve the same purpose, but with public KEM keys instead of public DH keys. Bigger changes were necessary for the tokens "ee", "se", "es", and "ss"; they were dropped and superseded by "ekem" and "skem". An "ee" token can be replaced by an "ekem" token in a straightforward way. The "es" and "se" tokens are replaced by a "skem" token at the side that is supposed to have the other party's public static key, i.e., the initiator for "es" and the responder for "se". However, this does not work for message patterns where an "es" or a "se" token is preceded by a "s" token (i.e., the static key is transmitted to the other party) since, in PQNoise, a "skem" token and the related "s" token can not appear in one and the same message pattern. In these cases, the "skem" token has to be moved to the next message pattern (going in opposite direction), which can increase the overall number of messages. Finally, the "ss" token has to be replaced by two "skem", one in each direction, which may also result in an additional message being necessary for a PQNoise handshake compared to its Noise counterpart.

KN:		**pqKN:**
→ **s**		→ **s**
...	→	...
→ **e**		→ **e**
← **e, ee, se**		← **ekem, skem**

Fig. 2. Transition of Noise (KN pattern) to PQNoise (pqKN pattern)

Figure 2 shows the transition from Noise to PQNoise using the KN pattern as example. There is no change at all in the pre-message pattern ("s") and the first message pattern ("e"). The second message pattern does not contain the second "e" token anymore since PQNoise handshakes generally have only one "e" and one "ekem" token, respectively. In addition, the "ee" token is replaced by "ekem" and "se" by "skem". Here, the "skem" token remains in the same message pattern as "se", which, as mentioned above, is not always the case.

Figure 3 illustrates post-quantum versions of the 12 fundamental handshake patterns as presented in [3, Fig. 2]. pqNX is an example for a handshake pattern requiring an additional message (from the initiator to the responder) since the "es" token of NX was replaced by "skem", and this "skem" can not appear in the same message pattern as "s". This is actually the case for all handshakes containing an X in the handshake name, meaning that at least one static key is transmitted. However, IN and IK show that a "s" token in a message pattern does not always increase the overall number of messages.

3 Hybrid Noise

The security of classical public-key cryptosystems like DH and ECDH has been scrutinized for decades. Lattice-based post-quantum schemes like Kyber have not

pqNN:
→ e
← ekem

pqNK:
← s
...
→ skem, e
← ekem

pqNX:
→ e
← ekem, s
→ skem

pqKN:
→ s
...
→ e
← ekem, skem

pqKK:
→ s
← s
...
→ skem, e
← ekem, skem

pqKX:
→ s
...
→ e
← ekem, skem, s
→ skem

pqXN:
→ e
← ekem
→ s
← skem

pqXK:
← s
...
→ skem, e
← ekem
→ s
← skem

pqXX:
→ e
← ekem, s
→ skem, s
← skem

pqIN:
→ e, s
← ekem, skem

pqIK:
← s
...
→ skem, e, s
← ekem, skem

pqIX:
→ e, s
← ekem, skem, s
→ skem

Fig. 3. The 12 fundamental interactive PQNoise patterns

(yet) undergone similarly rigorous cryptanalytic effort. Therefore, it makes sense to deploy hybrid security protocols that combine pre- and post-quantum cryptography, especially during a transition period until the confidence in post-quantum cryptosystems is sufficiently high to allow them to stand on their own feet. A properly-designed hybrid protocol remains secure even when either the pre-quantum or the post-quantum component gets broken (but not both).

As mentioned in Sect. 1, there was a previous attempt of creating a hybrid version of the Noise protocol framework, which had the goal to achieve Hybrid Forward Secrecy (HFS) [18]. Two new tokens, `"e1"` and `"ekem1"`, were introduced and served the purpose of adding ephemeral KEM keys to the classical (DH-based) Noise handshake patterns. The resulting hybrid handshakes were specified through a `"hfs"` pattern modifier. However, the static keys (used to authenticate the ephemeral keys) were still solely DH keys since post-quantum ephemeral keys are sufficient for post-quantum forward secrecy. Note that, as also mentioned in Sect. 1, the reference C implementation of the HFS patterns uses NewHope instead of the NIST-standardized Kyber KEM.

The main goal of the HFS patterns was to provide protection against the "harvest now decrypt later" threat scenario. Our hybrid Noise handshakes aim for a (slightly) different goal, namely to ensure full post-quantum security, like PQNoise, but with a "safety net" in form of the classical DH-based tokens. The purpose of this safety net is to guarantee pre-quantum attack resistance in the (hopefully unlikely) case that ongoing or future cryptanalysis of Kyber reveals a flaw that could be exploited by a pre-quantum adversary.

Our hybrid handshakes can be seen as a "unification" of the classical (DH-based) Noise handshakes and PQNoise (using the Kyber KEM). In contrast to the HFS patterns, our hybrid handshakes use both static DH keys and static KEM keys. Consequently, each message pattern of our hybrid handshake is the combination of the tokens of the corresponding message patterns of the normal and the post-quantum handshake. The operations associated with each token remain the same, but we have two sets of tokens, representing classical DH and post-quantum KEM operations, respectively. Furthermore, the ephemeral KEM keys are generally encrypted (when possible). The order of the tokens is kept consistent for each token-set to not interfere with the security properties that they provide on their own. In this way, the individual security guarantees of each pattern carry over to the hybrid pattern. An obvious explanation is the fact that adding KEM-keys to a Noise pattern (or, conversely, adding DH-keys to a PQNoise pattern) can be seen as a "mixing" of pseudo-random data into the hash object on both sides at some stage of the handshake execution. This does not imply that the pre- and post-quantum security properties are always the same in each stage of the handshake, but in the end the hybrid handshake inherits the security guarantees that each of them individually provides.

KNhyb:
    → s, sh
    ...
    → e, eh
    ← e, ee, se, ekemh, skemh

Fig. 4. Hybrid `KN` handshake pattern

We created hybrid variants of all 12 fundamental interactive Noise patterns and integrated them to the reference implementation Noise-C [26]. Apart from keeping the tokens of the respective pattern (i.e., Noise, PQNoise) in the same order, we also grouped them into ephemeral and static tokens whenever it was possible. We generally put the ephemeral DH tokens at the very front, followed by the ephemeral KEM tokens, followed by the static tokens (again DH before KEM). Our goal was to enable the encryption of any KEM key prior its transmission, using a symmetric key derived, in part, through the corresponding DH equivalent. Figure 4 depicts a concrete example, namely the hybrid form of the `KN` handshake. The `"h"` tokens here are equivalents of the PQNoise tokens and come from the post-quantum version of the pattern. We just appended `"h"` to distinguish them from the original PQNoise patterns, though they represent, in essence, the same operations. All other tokens are regular Noise tokens.

4 Evaluation

The bulk of past research on the Noise framework has focused on analyzing its security; this includes work on the formal verification of Noise patterns [13] as well as the development of a novel security model to better analyze and prove their security properties. This model enabled full security proofs for individual (classic and post-quantum) patterns in [3,8]. However, our evaluation will focus on the (relative) efficiency of regular Noise, PQNoise, and our hybrid Noise. As already mentioned earlier, we integrated the latter two to the Noise-C reference implementation, which means all three Noise versions use the same set of low-level cryptographic functions. We built the three Noise versions using the same compiler settings to ensure a fair and consistent evaluation. However, since the overall execution time of a security protocol depends on both its computation cost and its communications cost, it makes sense to do the efficiency evaluation under different network conditions. To achieve this, we utilized a Linux feature called *network namespaces* to set up an emulated network for which numerous parameters can be configured, e.g., Round Trip Time (RTT), throughput, and packet-loss rate. This feature was used before for evaluations of post-quantum TLS [12,15,21] and a comparison of Go implementations of the (regular) Noise `KK` and `XX` patterns with their respective PQNoise counterparts [3].

For our experiments, we ran the regular, post-quantum, and hybrid variants of the `NN`, `NK`, `NX`, and `XX` patterns. We chose those as, in our opinion, they have an interesting mix of properties when it comes to differences between the three variants of each pattern. In the case of `NN`, the message flow is the same across all three variants, but the public-key (resp., ciphertext) sizes differ. Hence, this pattern will illustrate how an increased amount of data transferred between the parties (but with the same number of messages) impacts the overall handshake latency. The `NK` pattern is an indicator for how the presence of pre-distributed static key(s) on one side changes the picture. Similar to `NK`, also the `NX` pattern involves static key(s) on one side, but they are transmitted during handshake execution. Therefore, `NX` allows us to assess how static-key transfers impact the three variants. Finally, `XX` is interesting because its post-quantum and hybrid variants require an additional message, i.e., we can expect significant differences between those two and the regular variant.

In addition, we compared the three Noise variants with TLS 1.3, more concretely OpenSSL version 3.0.2 with the provider from the Open Quantum Safe (OQS) project [25]. We configured OpenSSL such that is uses exactly the same public-key algorithms as Noise, namely X25519 for pre-quantum key exchange and Kyber512 for post-quantum key encapsulation. Note that all protocols we compare execute a Kyber512 implementation from the OQS project, which is configured to utilize AVX2 instructions on modern Intel CPUs. However, there are some caveats to consider when comparing Noise and TLS. The static keys used by regular Noise to authenticate the ephemeral DH key exchange are also DH keys, whereas TLS implements a form of "Signed Diffie-Hellman," i.e., the exchanged DH or ECDH keys are signed with static (i.e., long-term) signature keys. Furthermore, in TLS, the static signature keys are authenticated with the help of certificates, whereas, in Noise, it is "up to the application to determine whether the remote party's static public key is acceptable" [19, Sect. 14]. Since post-quantum signatures are outside the scope of this paper, we evaluated the post-quantum and hybrid variants of TLS with ECDSA signatures.

In order to assess the (relative) performance of the protocols, we conducted experiments on a laptop with an Intel Core i5-10210U CPU. Moreover, we ran these experiments also on an Orange Pi One development board housing a 32-bit ARM Cortex-A7 processor, which serves as an example for a less-powerful mobile device and allows us to determine how the computing power impacts the results under the same network conditions. As shown in Table 1, both devices had a recent version of Ubuntu Linux installed on them; for the Orange board we went with a version from Armbian [4] that was optimized for this board. To get results that are as consistent as possible, we set all cores to performance on both devices and disabled hyperthreading and turbo boost on the laptop (the Cortex-A7 on the board lacks these features). We pinned the execution of the server and client to one core each and gave those highest execution priority.

Table 1. Main characteristics of the devices used for our experiments

Device	Processor	Architecture	Frequency	Operating system
Laptop	Intel Core i5-10210U	64 bit	2.1 GHz	Ubuntu 22.04.4
Board	ARM Cortex-A7	32 bit	1.3 GHz	Armbian 24.5.1

To have control over the network conditions (e.g., latency, throughput), we emulated a network using the Linux tools mentioned before. The overall setup is the same for every experiment; we have two network namespaces, *cli_ns* and *srv_ns*, that ran the client-side and server-side of our experiments. These two namespaces were connected using a pair of virtual ethernet interfaces, i.e., one interface in each namespace, named *cli_ve* and *srv_ve*, respectively. This emulated network was set up separately on both the board and the laptop. For the experiments, we varied three major attributes of the network: RTT, packet-loss rate, and throughput. Since we want to compare the protocols under situations that mobile devices can encounter, we oriented ourselves on typical properties of 4G networks, since, on a global scale, they are the most widely-used mobile network infrastructure. For these networks, a throughput of roughly 10 Mbps and latencies of 60–70 ms (i.e., RTTs of 120–140 ms) seem common [9]. We ran our experiments with the following three combinations of network settings:

- RTT 10 ms, throughput 1000 Mbps: This is a special setting, simulating an ideal network scenario that is not supposed to be representative of a real-

Table 2. Average initiator-side computation time in ms

	Laptop				Board			
Variant	NN	NK	NX	XX	NN	NK	NX	XX
Noise	0.19	0.30	0.30	0.41	2.67	4.81	4.82	7.04
PQNoise	0.13	0.18	0.21	0.29	2.05	3.12	3.21	4.55
Hybrid	0.31	0.45	0.50	0.70	4.71	8.11	8.17	11.54

world 4G mobile network. Instead, the purpose of this setting is to serve as a baseline to assess how changing the RTT or throughput affects results.

- RTT 100 ms, throughput 10 Mbps: This setting represents a network close to what an average (or slightly above-average) 4G network might be.
- RTT 200 ms, throughput 10 Mbps: This setting represents long-distance connections with high latency, but with the same average throughput.

For all three sets of network conditions, we varied the packet-loss rate from 0% to 20%. In most network usage scenarios, a packet-loss rate of under 1% is deemed acceptable and in the majority of cases remains below 5%; going up to 20% allowed us to simulate even particularly bad network conditions.

5 Results and Discussion

To collect experimental results, we ran the handshake of the different protocols 1000 times, excluding warm-up runs, and measured the time taken. The overall handshake time includes the overhead introduced by low(er) network layers, in particular TCP, to establish a connection. For every experiment, we collected the handshake times at the median, the 75th, and the 95th percentile to hint on how different network conditions affect 50%, 75%, and 95% of a userbase.

5.1 Computation Costs

We start with analyzing and comparing the computation cost of the Noise protocol variants on the laptop and the board. Table 2 summarizes the execution times of the computational parts (mostly cryptographic operations and various auxiliary functions) of the protocols executed by the initiator. These timings do not include the communication part of the handshake, such as socket functions for initialization of the connection and sending/receving of data. The laptop is between 13 and 18 times faster than the board, which is not very surprising in light of the enormous architectural and micro-architectural differences between a 64-bit Intel CPU and a (much simpler) 32-bit ARM Cortex-A processor. It is important to note that, on the laptop, the computational part of all protocols is less than one hundredth of the RTT of 100 ms, and on the board it is less than one tenth (except for `XXhyb`). When looking at the different patterns, it turns out that the computational cost correlates with the number of tokens (i.e., the number of DH or KEM operations). For example, the computation times of the regular NN and XX patterns differ by a factor of more than two, and the NK and NX pattern are roughly in the middle between them.

When comparing the computation times between the Noise variants, we can see that the PQNoise patterns are less costly than the Noise patterns; this is in line with software benchmarking results reported in the literature, according to which Kyber512 outperforms X25519. The computation times of all our hybrid patterns are almost exactly the sum of the related Noise and PQNoise patterns since the way we put them together does not entail additional computations.

5.2 Comparison of Noise Variants with TLS Variants

Figure 5a shows the median handshake times (including both computation and communication) of the pre-quantum, post-quantum, and hybrid variants of the NX pattern for an RTT of 100 ms, measured on the board. The handshake times of the variants are very similar (for reasonable packet-loss rates) and dominated by the communication cost, i.e., the time spent for message transmission(s). In fact, the pqNX pattern is marginally faster than regular NX, which is due to the lower computation cost, irrespective of the larger key sizes. A Kyber512 public key is $800-32 = 768$ bytes longer than an X25519 public key, but when the throughput is 10 Mbps, the transmission of these additional 768 bytes requires only 0.61 ms and is negligible compared to the RTT. When the packet-loss rate exceeds 10%, the full handshake time of the post-quantum and hybrid variants increases versus the regular NX pattern. The hybrid variant is pretty similar to the post-quantum variant, at both low and high packet-loss rates.

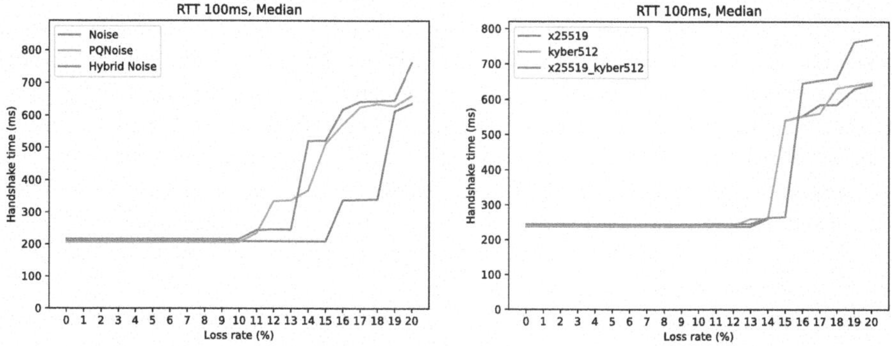

(a) Noise NX results (median)

(b) TLS results (median)

Fig. 5. NX and TLS variants comparison for RTT = 100 ms, measured on the board

Figure 5b illustrates the handshake execution times of pre-quantum, post-quantum, and hybrid TLS (with server authentication) on the board, measured for a 100-ms RTT. For reasonably low packet-loss rates, the handshake times are very similar across the three variants, but about 12% slower than the Noise `NX` variants. However, as explained in the previous section, a direct comparison of Noise and TLS is not easily possible due to certain differences between these protocols. First, the post-quantum and hybrid TLS variants use ECDSA signatures to sign the ephemeral public keys and ciphertexts transmitted during the handshake. They protect against "harvest now decrypt later" threats, but, in contrast to PQNoise and hybrid Noise, are vulnerable to impersonation by an adversary capable to forge an ECDSA handshake signature. Second, the static key used in TLS to authenticate the key agreement is itself authenticated by an (in our case self-signed) ECDSA certificate, which is not the case for Noise.

5.3 Pattern Comparisons

In this subsection, we present results for all four Noise handshake patterns we consider in this paper (i.e., `NN`, `NK`, `NX`, and `XX`) and compare them directly with each other (and with TLS), whereby we focus on the post-quantum and hybrid variants. Under realistic 4G network conditions (i.e., an RTT of 100 ms), the total handshake times are largely dominated by the connection latencies, while the computation times play a minor role. Therefore, we decided to evaluate the Noise patterns also under "idealized" network conditions, i.e., an RTT of 10 ms and a throughput of 1000 Mbps, which will make the computation costs more apparent. Figure 6a depicts the median handshake times of the post-quantum variants of the four patterns under these idealized conditions, measured on the ARM board. For low packet-loss rates, the `pqNN`, `pqNK`, and `pqNX` patterns are nearly identical. The `pqXX` pattern is the by far slowest, which can be explained by the fact that it has the highest computational cost (i.e., one KeyGen, three Encaps, and three Decaps in total) and highest communication cost (i.e., three public keys and three ciphertexts in four messages) of all patterns. When the packet-loss rate increases, the `pqXX` pattern is earlier and more severely affected than the other patterns. Two of the four messages of the `pqXX` pattern contain a Kyber512 public key and a ciphertext, i.e., their length exceeds the Maximum Transmission Unit (MTU) of 4G networks, which is a bit below 1500 bytes. As a consequence, two `pqXX` messages get segmented, thereby making this pattern more susceptible to packet losses, which start to become noticeable at 9% loss rate. The post-quantum TLS protocol performs better than `pqXX` for loss rates above 9%, but worse for lower loss rates.

Figure 6b illustrates the handshake times for the hybrid variants of the protocols, again for an RTT of 10 ms. For low packet-loss rates, the order is the same as for the PQNoise patterns: `NNhyb` is the fastest, followed by `NKhyb` and `NXhyb`, which are almost identical. `XXhyb` is the slowest among the four hybrid patterns, mainly for two reasons: (i) it has the highest computational cost (see Table 2), and (ii) similar to `pqXX`, it requires the transmission of four messages (i.e., one message more than the post-quantum/hybrid `NK` and `NX` patterns). In summary, the "hybridization" of PQNoise causes relatively little overhead, and this little overhead will become even less significant for an RTT of 100 ms.

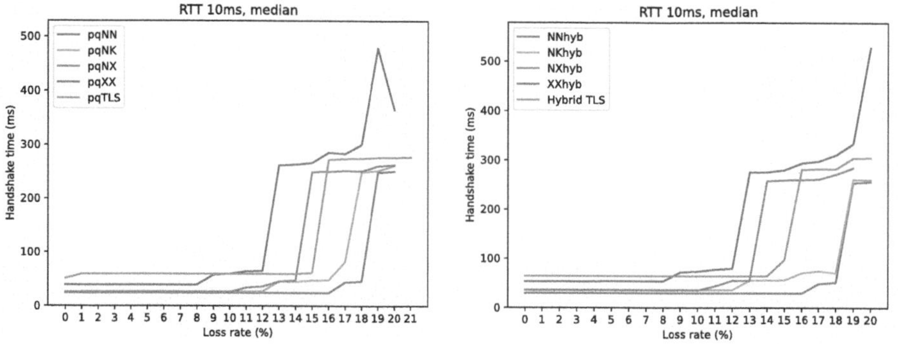

(a) Post-quantum results (median)

(b) Hybrid results (median)

Fig. 6. Direct comparison for the post-quantum and hybrid variants of all protocols in the idealized network scenario (i.e., RTT of 10 ms, throughput of 1000 Mbps)

Figure 7 shows direct comparisons between the different post-quantum protocol variants and their hybrid counterparts for a realistic 4G network scenario (i.e., for an RTT of 100 ms). The graphs represent the handshake times in the average case and for the 75th and the 95th percentile, respectively. Overall, the median results for the post-quantum Noise patterns are very similar to that in the "idealized" network setting. For low packet-loss rates, the `pqNN`, `pqNK`, and `pqNX` patterns have almost the same execution times, while `pqXX` is by far the slowest PQNoise pattern. The high handshake time of `pqXX` is primarily due to high communication cost, originating from the transmission of four messages in total, half of which are segmented into two packets each. We can also observe that Noise `pqXX` and post-quantum TLS swapped their positions compared to the idealized network scenario, i.e., `pqXX` is now slower than TLS. Again, this can be explained by the high communication cost of `pqXX` (Kyber512 keys and ciphertexts are much larger than ECDSA signatures). The median handshake times of the hybrid protocols are, for low loss rates, basically indistinguishable from their post-quantum counterparts.

When the packet-loss rate increases, the relative order of the four PQNoise patterns in the median case remains basically the same. The `pqNN` pattern has the lowest number of messages, and also the lowest number of packets, transmitted between the two parties, followed by `pqNK`, `pqNX`, and finally `pqXX`. We can observe from Fig. 7a that packet losses start to impact the `pqNN` pattern only at a rather high loss rate of above 15%. On the other hand, the `pqNK` and `pqNX` patterns get affected at loss rates above 13% and 10%, respectively. This relatively big difference between the two patterns is caused by the responder's static key, which is pre-shared in `pqNK`, but transmitted during the handshake in `pqNX`, i.e., packet losses affect `pqNX` more severely. `pqXX` is the most sensitive pattern when it comes to packet losses as it's handshake time starts to increase already at a loss rate of above 8%. Overall, these observations hold true for the median, 75th, and 95th percentile, though with each percentile the differences

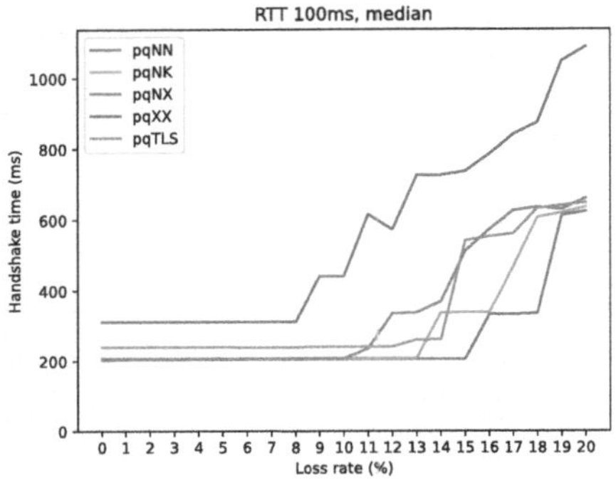

(a) Post-quantum results (median)

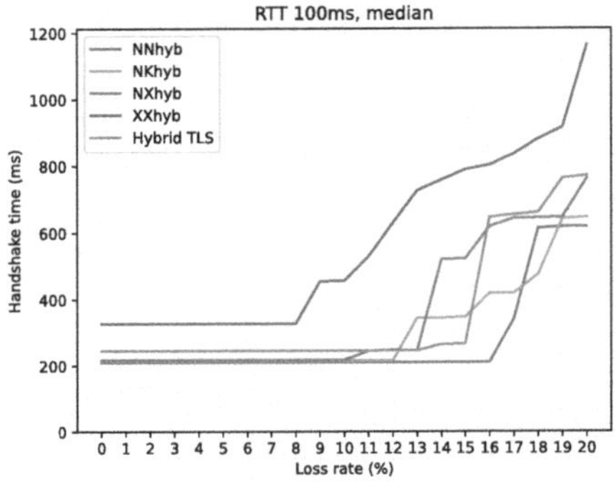

(b) Hybrid results (median)

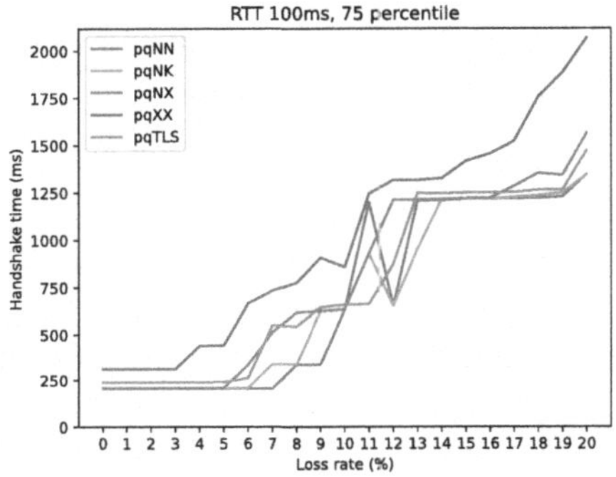

(c) Post-quantum results (75th percentile)

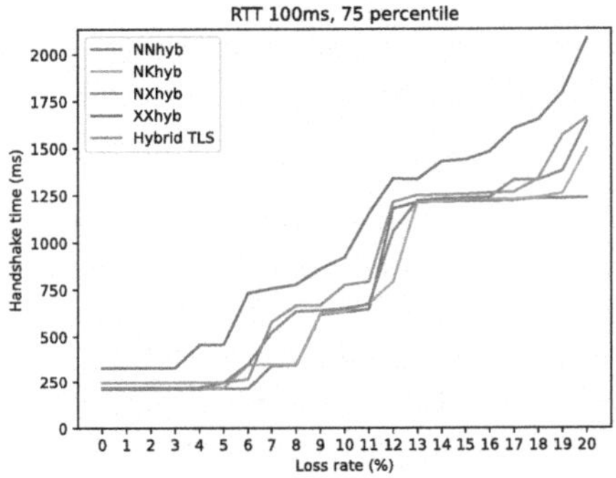

(d) Hybrid results (75th percentile)

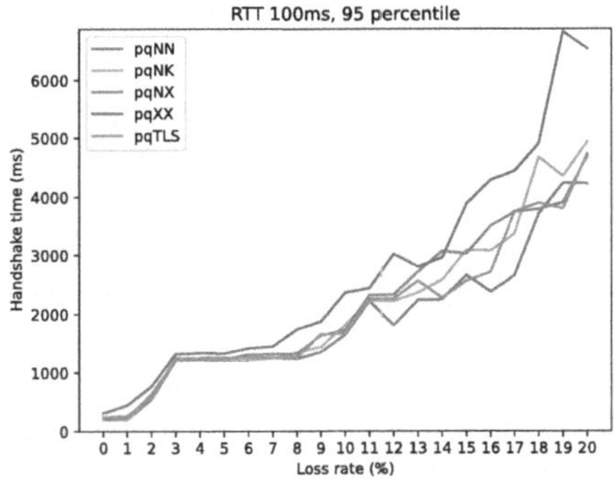

(e) Post-quantum results (95th percentile)

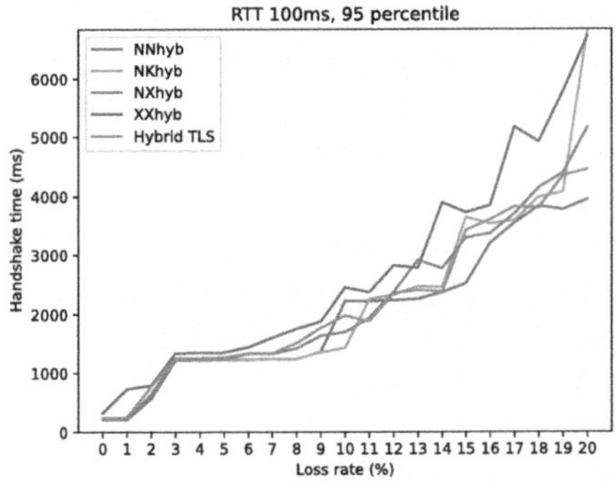

(f) Hybrid results (95th percentile)

Fig. 7. Direct comparison for the post-quantum and hybrid variants of all protocols in the realistic network scenario (i.e., RTT of 100 ms, throughput of 10 Mbps)

between the patterns become smaller. The hybrid handshakes, depicted on the right of Fig. 7, suffer from packet losses in a roughly similar way as PQNoise.

As stated in Sect. 4, the typical packet-loss rate of a 4G network is around 1% and rarely exceeds 5%. Our results indicate that for all post-quantum and hybrid patterns except the XX variants, 95% of the user base in a network with a 1% loss rate would not experience any impact by lost packets. The XX variants start to lose a packet already at a 1% loss rate in the 95th percentile, which is little surprising when considering that they transmit twice as many packets as the pqNN pattern. According to Fig. 7e, the pqNN handshake pattern starts to lose its first packet at a 2% loss rate in the 95th percentile. Even at a high loss rate of 5%, about 75% of network users are unaffected by packet losses, as can be concluded from Figs. 7c and 7d. The only protocols that start to lose packets below a 5% loss rate in the 75th percentile are the XX variants.

6 Conclusions

Using the recently-proposed PQNoise protocol framework as starting point, we developed and implemented hybrid variants of the 12 fundamental interactive Noise patterns. We determined the handshake execution times of regular, post-quantum and hybrid variants of the NN, NK, NX, and XX patterns on two mobile devices, a laptop and an ARM development board. This evaluation was carried out under different network conditions (i.e., RTT, throughput, and packet-loss rate) and took both the computation and communication cost into account.

Overall, the PQNoise and hybrid variants performed very well in comparison to the classical Noise patterns, with only the slightly higher amount of packets becoming an issue at high packet-loss rates. We noticed the biggest differences among the three variants for the XX pattern, partly due to high computational cost (in both the pre- and post-quantum setting) and partly because the post-quantum and hybrid variants entail an additional handshake message. We also found that the overheads of the hybrid patterns versus PQNoise are very small and mainly caused by the additional computing time for X25519, especially on the board. The additional communication cost for transmission of X25519 keys is negligible and does also not cause extra packet fragmentation for any of the patterns. Furthermore, the additional computation cost gets less significant the better the computing power of the mobile device and the worse the RTT of the network becomes. Putting everything together, the experiments and results we presented in this paper encourage the deployment of hybrid Noise handshakes rather than purely post-quantum variants.

Acknowledgments. This research was funded in part by the Luxembourg National Research Fund (FNR), grant reference C21/IS/16221219/ImPAKT. The full source code of Noise-C, including the post-quantum and hybrid patterns, and further results are available at https://github.com/JoshuaRenckens/PQNoise_Master_Thesis.

References

1. Alkim, E., Ducas, L., Pöppelmann, T., Schwabe, P.: Post-quantum key exchange – A new hope. In: Proceedings of the 25th USENIX Security Symposium (USS 2016), pp. 327–343. USENIX Association (2016)
2. Alnahawi, N., Müller, J., Oupický, J., Wiesmaier, A.: A comprehensive survey on post-quantum TLS. IACR Commun. Cryptol. **1**(2) (Jul 2024)
3. Angel, Y., Dowling, B., Hülsing, A., Schwabe, P., Weber, F.: Post quantum Noise. In: Proceedings of the 29th ACM Conference on Computer and Communications Security (CCS 2022), pp. 97–109. ACM (2022)
4. Armbian Operating System Community: Armbian: Linux for ARM development boards. https://www.armbian.com (2024)
5. Avanzi, R., et al.: CRYSTALS-Kyber: Algorithm Specifications and Supporting Documentation (Version 3.02) (2021)
6. Diffie, W., Hellman, M.: New directions in cryptography. IEEE Trans. Inf. Theory **22**(6), 644–654 (1976)
7. Donenfeld, J.A.: Wireguard: Next generation kernel network tunnel. https://www.wireguard.com/papers/wireguard.pdf (2020)
8. Dowling, B., Rösler, P., Schwenk, J.: Flexible authenticated and confidential channel establishment (fACCE): analyzing the Noise protocol framework. In: Public-Key Cryptography — PKC 2020. Lecture Notes in Computer Science, vol. 12110, pp. 341–373. Springer (2020)
9. EE Limited: 4G Speed. https://business.ee.co.uk/help/network-and-coverage/4g-speed-what-you-can-expect/ (2024)
10. Gajland, P., de Kock, B., Quaresma, M., Malavolta, G., Schwabe, P.: SWOOSH: efficient lattice-based non-interactive key exchange. In: Proceedings of the 33rd USENIX Security Symposium (USS 2024), USENIX Association (2024)
11. Ho, S., Protzenko, J., Bichhawat, A., Bhargavan, K.: Noise: A library of verified high-performance secure channel protocol implementations. In: 2022 IEEE Symposium on Security and Privacy (SP), pp. 107–124. IEEE (2022)
12. Kampanakis, P., Childs-Klein, W.: The impact of data-heavy, post-quantum TLS 1.3 on the time-to-last-byte of real-world connections. IACR ePrint Archive (2024)
13. Kobeissi, N., Nicolas, G., Bhargavan, K.: Noise explorer: fully automated modeling and verification for arbitrary noise protocols. In: 2019 IEEE European Symposium on Security and Privacy (EuroS&P), pp. 356–370. IEEE (2019)
14. Langley, A., Hamburg, M., Turner, S.: Elliptic curves for security. Internet Engineering Task Force, Internet Research Task Force, RFC 7748 (Jan 2016)
15. Paquin, C., Stebila, D., Tamvada, G.: Benchmarking post-quantum cryptography in TLS. In: Post-Quantum Cryptography: 11th International Conference, PQCrypto 2020, Paris, France, April 15–17, 2020, Proceedings 11, pp. 72–91. Springer (2020)
16. Paterson, K.G., van der Merwe, T.: Reactive and proactive standardisation of TLS. In: Security Standardisation Research — SSR 2016. Lecture Notes in Computer Science, vol. 10074, pp. 160–186. Springer (2016)
17. Pereira, R., et al.: Ranking programming languages by energy efficiency. Sci. Comput. Program. **205** (2021)
18. Perrin, T.: KEM-based Hybrid Forward Secrecy for Noise. Specification. https://github.com/noiseprotocol/noise_hfs_spec/blob/master/output/noise_hfs.pdf (2018)

19. Perrin, T.: The Noise Protocol Framework, Revision 34. Specification. https://noiseprotocol.org/noise.pdf (2018)
20. Rescorla, E.K.: The Transport Layer Security (TLS) Protocol Version 1.3. Internet Engineering Task Force, Network Working Group, RFC 8446 (Aug 2018)
21. Schwabe, P., Stebila, D., Wiggers, T.: Post-quantum TLS without handshake signatures. In: Proceedings of the 27th ACM Conference on Computer and Communications Security (CCS 2020), pp. 1461–1480. ACM (2020)
22. Sheffer, Y., Holz, R., Saint-Andre, P.: Summarizing Known Attacks on Transport Layer Security (TLS) and Datagram TLS (DTLS). Internet Engineering Task Force, Using TLS in Applications Working Group, RFC 7457 (Feb 2015)
23. Shor, P.W.: Algorithms for quantum computation: discrete logarithms and factoring. In: Proceedings of the 35th Annual Symposium on Foundations of Computer Science (FOCS 1994), pp. 124–134. IEEE (1994)
24. Stallings, W.: Cryptography and Network Security: Principles and Practice. Pearson, 7th edn. (2016)
25. Stebila, D., Mosca, M.: Post-quantum key exchange for the internet and the open quantum safe project. In: International Conference on Selected Areas in Cryptography, pp. 14–37. Springer (2016)
26. Weatherley, R.: Noise-C: A plain C implementation of the Noise protocol. Source code. https://github.com/rweather/noise-c (2023)
27. WhatsApp LLC: WhatsApp encryption overview. Technical white paper. http://www.whatsapp.com/security/WhatsApp-Security-Whitepaper.pdf (2020)

Strengthening Return Address Stack of Rocket Core Against Buffer Overflow Attacks

Lalit Sharma(✉), Satya Jaswanth Badri, and Neeraj Goel

Indian Institute of Technology, Punjab 140001, India
{lalit.19csz0005,neeraj}@iitrpr.ac.in

Abstract. The existing Return Address Stack (RAS) structure in RISC-V-based processor cores, such as the Rocket or Boom, is fixed during the design phase and provides limited performance benefits by predicting the Return Address ('ra') for branch predictor. In literature, RAS is used to avoid Stack-based Buffer Overflow (SBFO) attacks. However, overflow and underflow conditions of existing RAS pose a security risk because it is not always possible to predict and verify the 'ra'. As a result, the current RAS structure cannot be used for 'ra' verification, and SBFO attacks could easily compromise the overall system's Control Flow Integrity (CFI). This paper evaluates and optimizes the current RAS structure to meet specific requirements, resulting in a 0.1% resource overhead and a timing overhead of less than 4% for most embedded applications. This paper proposes a design that modifies the current RAS to provide sufficient storage for embedded applications while holding the RAS hidden from the Instruction Set Architecture (ISA). The proposed design has been evaluated on the Artix 7 FPGA using the Chipyard framework, which is built on the Chisel programming language and offers high-level abstractions, functional programming capabilities, expressive code, and faster development times.

Keywords: RISC-V · Stack-based buffer overflow · Shadow stack · Return address stack · Chisel · Control flow integrity

1 Introduction

An open-source ISA, RISC-V [1,2], is gaining popularity in computing. Unlike proprietary ISAs, RISC-V allows for customization, making it more adaptable and suitable for many systems [3,4]. RISC-V is being incorporated into various domains and applications [5,6], such as in processors used in machine learning applications and energy-efficient micro-controllers in Internet-Of-Things (IoT) devices [7,8]. RISC-V open source also promotes collaboration, as multiple architectures extend and use the RISC-V ISA to meet their unique requirements [9,10], thereby encouraging innovation in the field of processor design.

Introducing a new design at the processor chip level involves many complicated changes at many stages. Firstly, the conceptual design phase, where the

L. Morogan et al. (Eds.): SecITC 2024, LNCS 15595, pp. 170–188, 2025.
https://doi.org/10.1007/978-3-031-87760-5_13

engineers gather up and specify the processor's primary functions. Secondly, the high-level design phase involves developing critical algorithms and creating an architectural diagram. Once the design phase is completed, the design is converted to Register-Transfer Level (RTL) code using Hardware Description Languages (HDLs) like Verilog or VHDL. The next step is to verify the RTL design; simulations can be used to ensure that all design specifications are compiled correctly. Once the verification stage is completed, we must synthesize the RTL code into a gate-level design, considering power and timing constraints.

Secure data handling has become increasingly crucial in RISC-V-based system designs. SBFO attacks are among the most widely and effective methods for manipulating a program's execution flow. The SBFO vulnerability is highly efficient, allowing attackers to modify the stack-stored 'ra'. The SBFO attack involves modifying stack frames from various function calls throughout program execution. Each function call generates a stack frame to store variables, arrays, and other control flow-related information like the 'ra'. Attackers use SBFO to overwrite the 'ra', diverting the execution flow to their malicious code.

Implementing a Shadow Stack (SS), which stores 'ra' in a separate stack alongside the system stack, is a highly effective method of protecting against SBFO attacks. The literature introduces architectures for hardware-assisted SS protection [11–13]. The RISC-V foundation is working on SS-related challenges [14] and new instructions called *Zicfiss* and *Zicfilp* that help maintain CFI during program execution [14]. These solutions require special compilation flags to be enabled to add special instructions that recompile the binary and, as an overhead, increase the code base size. Additional modifications to the compilation tool-chain are needed.

Existing processor architectures use RAS as an SS by storing the 'ra' during a function call. When combined with the Branch History Table (BHT) and Branch Target Buffer (BTB), RAS improves branch prediction accuracy even further [15]. We observed that the configuration of these structures, such as their size, is determined in the first phase, i.e., the conceptual design phase of the chip, and remains constant throughout the processor chip's life cycle because modifying the hardware is difficult once the integrated circuit is fabricated.

The problem with the fixed size of RAS is that it limits the RAS performance and security benefits in cases where the storage requirement exceeds RAS's current size. For example, in the case of deep recursion calls, space becomes limited, and the architect frequently overwrites old 'ra', resulting in incorrect predictions. Due to the nonavailability of 'ra' for such cases, a *correct security check* while returning from a function call is not possible. Furthermore, RAS can be manipulated, allowing an attacker to carry out severe attacks such as SpectreRSB, which compromises the system's CFI [16, 17].

In this paper, we evaluate the current RAS structure of the Rocket core [15], a processor core based on the RISC-V ISA. We optimize RAS size for specific needs, resulting in a 0.1% resource overhead and a timing overhead of less than 4% for the majority of embedded applications. We addressed the challenges of transferring RAS contents from the core to external memory so that RAS doesn't create a security risk to the entire system.

As far as we know, this is the first work to explore the RAS extension framework. We propose a design that modifies the current RAS to provide sufficient capacity to handle all requirements for executing embedded applications. The RAS is kept hidden from the ISA, providing additional security against potential attackers. We also noticed that larger RAS-based designs introduce significant hardware overhead. To overcome the hardware overhead challenge, we propose using a smaller RAS and extending to the main memory or faster SRAM-based memory.

The proposed design's experimental analysis shows a reduced impact on performance while effectively mitigating security risks. We validated the proposed design on the Artix 7 FPGA by prototyping the entire processor. We used the chipyard framework [18] based on the chisel programming language [19]. The primary reason for choosing a chisel over traditional HDLs such as VHDL or Verilog is that it provides significant benefits such as high-level abstractions, functional programming capabilities, the ability to produce more expressive and concise code, and reduced development time, particularly in the design of System-On-Chip (SoC) based boards [20].

Paper organization: Section 2 discusses a variety of related works on RISC-V architectures. Section 3 explains the motivation for the proposed architecture and provides insight into the threat model against the proposed defense. Section 4 explains the existing RAS structure and the challenges to expanding RAS. Section 5 describes the proposed design and changes or additional modules required to add on Rocket core. The experimental setup and results are discussed in Sect. 6. Section 7 concludes this work.

2 Related Works

During our literature review, we investigated numerous architectures proposed to provide security, primarily but not exclusively for RISC-V-based systems, and a few of them are listed in Table 1. This section thoroughly examines various proposed architectures in the literature, concentrating on their protection methods, techniques, co-processing units, setups, overheads, and Hardware/Software (HW/SW) support. All architectures shown in Table 1 primarily target the RISC-V platform, with some entries also addressing OpenRISC and RISC-V/x86 hybrid configurations.

A Lightweight, Secure Processor Prototype (LSPP) utilizes a co-processing unit on a Zedboard to implement key-based protection to prevent Memory Corruption (MC) [21]. LSSP needs additional hardware support but consumes less than 10% of area overhead without any impact on performance. Keystone addresses MC without a co-processor unit using a Trusted Execution Environment (TEE) and memory isolation techniques [22]. Keystone achieves a performance overhead of less than 0.7% and relies solely on software support when deployed on cloud FPGAs.

The Fault Self-Repairing Module (FSRM) design targets Hardware Trojans and Fault Injection (HT/FI) through instruction monitoring, implemented on a Xilinx Virtex-5 with a co-processing unit for additional performance improvement [23]. FSRM results in a 9.85% increase in area and less than 1.92% performance overhead, with no additional HW/SW support other than the co-processor unit. Another approach, BOP, a Buffer Overflow (BFO) detection and defense system, is proposed to mitigate BFO vulnerabilities using ISA extensions on a Xilinx ARTY A7 [24]. BOP leads to a 7% area/code increase but requires both additional hardware and software support.

Shakti-MS [25], a lightweight RISC-V processor, has been proposed to protect against MC and spatial/temporal issues using fat pointers on a Xilinx xcvu095-ffva2104-2-e. Shakti-MS produces 700 LUTs, an 11% area increase, and a 13% performance overhead that necessitates both hardware and software support. Hector-v [26], a secure RISC-V execution environment, is proposed, focusing on CFI via TEE and implemented on a Xilinx Kintex-7. Hector-v has a substantial 23.9% area overhead and a 9.10% performance overhead. Param [27], a microprocessor, is introduced and employs data obfuscation to combat Power-Based Side-Channel Attacks (PBSCA) on the SASEBO-GIII platform, with minimal overhead and HW/SW protection.

Another architecture addresses MC on a Zedboard using Dynamic Information Flow Tracking (DIFT) [28], which results in a 12.50% code overhead and less than 1% area overhead. Domain key efficiency (Donky) has been proposed as a method for providing in-process isolation for MC on a Xilinx Kintex-7 [29]. Donky has a 4% performance overhead and needs hardware and software support. Flow integrity extensions (Fixer) have been proposed for performing CFI checks on the Rocket chipplatform [30]. Fixer has a 2.9% area overhead and a 1.50% performance overhead without hardware support.

Morpheus II [31] proposed encrypting and obfuscating the code pointers to protect against Control Flow Attacks (CFA) on Rocket core Xilinx devices. Morpheus II has taken less than 2% of the area overhead. Raft [32], a hardware-assisted dynamic information flow tracking technique, has been proposed for run-time protection, where the proposed design combines both encryption and obfuscation techniques on Rocket core and Kintex-7 KC 705 devices. Raft has a significant area overhead but has little impact on performance and relies solely on software.

Finally, the various architectures demonstrate diverse techniques for addressing multiple security threats, with different impacts on area and performance overheads. Designs such as Keystone [22] and Param [27] have low-performance overheads, making them ideal for applications where efficiency is critical. On the other side, with higher overheads, solutions such as Hector-v [26] and Shakthi-MS [25] provide reliable safety and are best suited for scenarios where security takes precedence over performance. The comparative study we provided in this section underlines the trade-offs between security robustness and resource utilization (area and performance), which help the designer choose the suitable protection mechanisms for a given application requirements.

Table 1. Comparison of various architectures with protection methods

Design	Architecture	Vector Protection	Techniqure	Setup
LSPP [21]	RISC-V	MC	Key	Zedboard
Keystone [22]	RISC-V	MC	TEE/ Memory Isolation	Cloud FPGAs
FSRM [23]	OpenRISC	HT/FI	Instruction Monitoring	Xilinx Virtex-5
BOP [24]	RISC-V	BFO	ISA Extension	Xilinx ARTY A7
Shakti-MS [25]	RISC-V	MC/ Spatial/ Temporal	Fat Pointers	Xilinx xcvu095-fva2104-2-e
Hector-v [26]	RISC-V	CFI	TEE	Xilinx Kintex-7
Param [27]	RISC-V	PBSCA	Obfuscating Data/Address Lines	SASEBO -GIII
DIFT [28]	RISC-V	MC	DIFT	Zedboard
Donky [29]	RISC-V/x86	MC	In-Process Isolation	Kintex-7
Fixer [30]	RISC-V	CI/CRA	CFI Check	Rocket Chip
Morpheus II [31]	RISC-V	CFA	Encryption/ Obfuscate Code Pointer	Rocket core, Xilinx UltraScale Plus VCU118
Raft [32]	RISC-V	CFA	DIFT	Rocket core, Kintex-7 KC 705
Proposed Design	RISC-V	SBFO	RAS	Rocket core, Artix 7

According to our knowledge, no work has been done on RSA size extension into memory on RISC-V systems; aside from comparing various architectures in Table 1 based on the attack vectors they protect against, we examined [11,12] from a SS perspective. In contrast to our proposed work, these systems employ a fixed-size hardware SS and require software or OS support.

3 Motivation and Threat Model

3.1 Motivation

After exploring relevant architectures and their overhead in terms of hardware or software changes, we experimented with the current bare RISC-V-based system with various attacks and test cases. Table 2 lists some of these test cases. Listing 1 in Table 2 shows a potential SBFO if the input is longer than 9 characters due to the lack of bound checks in the *strcpy* function. Similarly, listing 2 does not check if the input length exceeds the buffer size due to no bound check in the *strlen* function. Listing 3 uses *gets*, which does not check the input length, resulting in a SBFO. Listing 4 shows another case of SBFO caused by incorrect usage of string format. We used the Spike Simulator to test these scenarios and discovered a vulnerability.

We observed that the current RISC-V-based systems are vulnerable to such attacks due to their restricted RAS size and are prone to being attacked. The consequences of inadequate RAS capacity are not limited to basic computational inefficiencies, which also increase the risk of inaccurate predictions and may create opportunities for SBFO attacks. In addition, our investigation proved that the RAS size restriction could also be exploited as a vulnerability in the context of Spectre attacks [16].

Modern computing systems face significant security risks from specter attacks [16], which exploit RAS vulnerabilities. Effective attackers can compromise system security and confidentiality by manipulating speculative execution paths and exploiting RAS constraints. Despite improving branch prediction accuracy, the RAS's fixed size poses challenges for system design and security analysis.

We test our proposed design on an FPGA, and Chisel offered an alternative to the traditional chip design ecosystem. One of Chisel's primary benefits is the capacity to describe complex hardware structures using high-level, parameterized code, which makes it more adaptable and error-free. Chisel enables more expressive hardware design and better component reuse while integrating seamlessly with modern software development practices such as testing and version control, simplifying the hardware development workflow.

3.2 Threat Model

The attacker has no control over the hardware or physical access to the proposed system. We assume that the attacker can only run one application on the system and is not authorized to run any other applications. We also assume that the system application has multiple potential sources of bugs. For example, the application could be written in a language like 'C,' which does not include buffer-bound checks. The attacker uses the previously discussed scenario of overwriting the *'ra'* and overflowing the RAS to execute malicious code.

Furthermore, we assume that the target has no standard hardware defenses. Our threat model does not provide protection against physical side-channel attacks. The attacker could manipulate the 'ra' of other stack frames to change

Table 2. Various SBFO attack scenarios on RISC-V systems

<table>
<tr><th>Listing 1: Overflow with strcpy</th><th>Listign 2: Overflow with unchecked loop</th></tr>
<tr><td>

```
void vulnerableFunction(char *input) {
    char buffer[10];
    strcpy(buffer, input);
    printf("Buffer: %s\n", buffer);
}
int main() {
    char input[20] = "ThisIsTooLong
                     Input";
    vulnerableFunction(input);
    return 0;
}
```

</td><td>

```
void vulnerableFunction(char *input) {
    char buffer[10];
    int i;
    for (i = 0; i < strlen(input); i++) {
    buffer[i] = input[i];
    }
    buffer[i] = '\0';
    printf("Buffer: %s\n", buffer);
}
int main() {
    char input[20] = "ThisIsTooLong
                     Input";
    vulnerableFunction(input);
    return 0;
}
```

</td></tr>
<tr><th>Listing 3: Overflow with gets</th><th>Listing 4: Overflow with snprintf</th></tr>
<tr><td>

```
void vulnerableFunction() {
    char buffer[10];
    gets(buffer);
    printf("Buffer: %s\n", buffer);
}

int main() {
    vulnerableFunction();
    return 0;
}
```

</td><td>

```
void vulnerableFunction(char *input) {
    char buffer[10];
    snprintf(buffer, sizeof(buffer),
        ↪ input);
    printf("Buffer: %s\n", buffer);
}

int main() {
    char input[20] = "ThisIsTooLong
                     Input";
    vulnerableFunction(input);
    return 0;
}
```

</td></tr>
</table>

the control flow from intended to malicious execution. Our threat model only supports single thread-based execution, so context switch issues related to RAS have been excluded. In the future, we plan to handle context switch-based RAS by storing the current context in memory. Furthermore, we assume that the core we are working with is an inorder, not an out-of-order core.

4 Overview of RAS Structure in Rocket Chip Generator

Rocket chip is an open-source SoC generator that combines multiple in-order or out-of-order processors into a single SoC based on specifications and employs the chisel programming language. Rocket chips can generate synthesizable RTL from the configured design. The processor cores are based on the RISC-V ISA, which allows for the use of custom accelerators to improve system performance. Chipyard is an open-source framework that provides configurable options for selecting various processor cores such as Rocket core, BOOM, CVA6 [33], Ibex core, and accelerators such as Hwacha, Gemmini [34], and SHA3 for our SoC design [18].

Our design makes use of the Rocket core, a scalar processor with five stages that are pipelined in order. The Rocket core is a component of the Rocket chip-SoC generator. When combined with L1 caches (data and instruction caches), it forms a Rocket tile, which serves as the replicable unit in the Rocket chip SoC generator.

Chipyard used the tilelink protocol [35] to communicate between different tiles on a target SoC. Single tile is made up of one or more hybrid processor cores, as well as L1 instruction and data caches. The tilelink protocol's communication link interacts with other memory hierarchy levels, such as L2 caches or I/O peripherals, via the system Bus, which communicates using the Axi protocol.

4.1 Existing Rocket Core RAS Structure

The RAS is integrated with the BTB in the Rocket core, which is linked to the front end and used to assemble the Rocket tile, a building block in the design's digital top. Various digital tops are configured to interface with the chiptop, allowing communication with external memory and other I/O interfaces primarily via the Axi Bus protocol.

Figure 1 shows the connection topology from the SoC perspective, starting with the BTB module defined in *BTB.scala* and converting to *BTB.sv* as the output, i.e., RTL form. The *BTBParams* class, located in the *BTB.scala* file, defines all RAS-related parameters. The BTB module connects to the frontend module, which generates a tile module and places it on the digital top, followed by a chip top.

RAS is stack-structured hardware that efficiently stores the address of the instruction to which control needs to return after function calls. RAS is essential for the front end of the Rocket chip generator [15], as it improves the accuracy of branch target address prediction when the application returns from routines during execution. RAS ensures the efficient handling of 'ra' by interacting with the BTB, which is essential for the smooth program execution flow. A notable limitation arises from the fixed size of the RAS, which is established during the design phase and remains unmodifiable after that and is defined in *BTBParams* class for Rocketcore design.

Fixed-size of RAS can be challenging, especially when dealing with scenarios involving deep recursion calls. In such cases, the RAS may run out of space to accommodate all 'ra', compromising the accuracy of branch predictions. The RAS fixed size can accommodate typical program execution scenarios while efficiently using hardware resources. As a result, we must carefully consider the RAS size and management mechanisms to ensure system reliability and security.

4.2 Limitations with Existing RAS

The current RAS size is fixed and cannot be changed after design; in the event of an overflow, the core deletes the previous entries and replaces them with new entries, compromising the accurate prediction of removed 'ra' and potentially helping in SBFO-based control transfer. In such scenarios, the buffer's current values are discarded, and the count is reset to zero while a new 'ra' entry is done at the 0th location of the RAS buffer.

Figure 2 shows Rocket core's hardware structure, which uses a simple MUX to select the next position on the RAS stack (NEXT_POS) for the 'ra' entry. MUX checks if the current position address *(Pos)* is less than *(nras -1))*, where *nras* represents the number of entries in RAS. If the decision is true, the existing design provides an address in the RAS for current 'ra' storage; otherwise, the existing design uses the 0th location as the address and begins overwriting the existing RAS contents. The existing design has a major drawback when dealing with recursive call functions in applications that need deep 'ra' storage for accurate branch prediction. The current RAS's inability to handle such cases is the reason why we can not use Rocket core's existing RAS mechanism for securing systems against SBFO attacks, and we need alternate mechanisms.

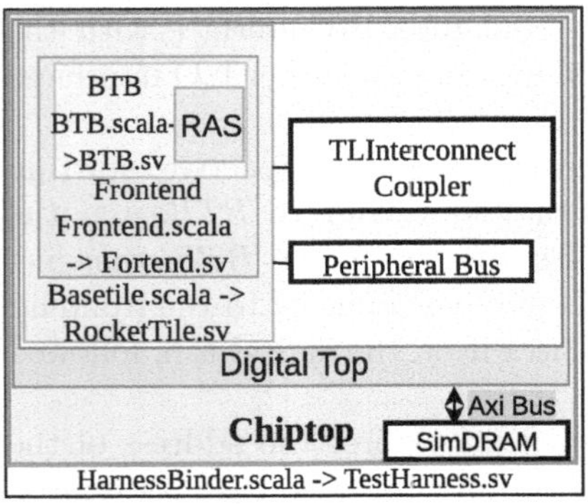

Fig. 1. Existing RAS in Rocket core

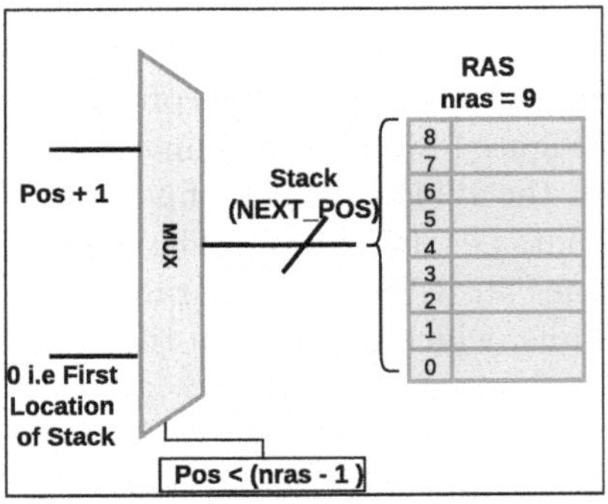

Fig. 2. Mux design of existing RAS

5 Proposed RAS Extension Design

We propose increasing the size of RAS by transferring the entire buffer to memory at a predefined isolated memory location. During each *ras_full* signal, the buffer is copied to the specified memory address, with additional buffer storage based on the offset obtained using the base address, as shown in Fig. 3. A counter *mem_count* monitors memory transfers and updates the counter accordingly. Increasing the RAS size is crucial for mitigating the threat of Spectre attacks, where these scenarios occur due to the RAS overflow or underflow cases [16].

Increasing the RAS capacity enhances the system's defenses against vulnerabilities that arise from speculative execution, thereby decreasing the possibility that attackers exploit speculative execution paths to execute arbitrary code or gain unauthorized access to confidential information. Additionally, the necessity for purposeful RAS pollution techniques is reduced by a larger RAS, which enhances the overall level of security and simplifies system maintenance and design.

Figure 3 shows the flow diagram of the proposed design, which describes the decision-making process for managing the RAS in a branch prediction unit in a Rocket core processor. Figure 1 also shows how the proposed design includes an additional extension *Modified RAS* block to compare to Rocket core's standard RAS flow. The `BTB` class initially determines whether the processor supports RAS in the *Module I* block. Upon confirmation, the proposed design evaluates a variety of parameters to determine the size of the RAS buffer as specified in the `BTBParams` class.

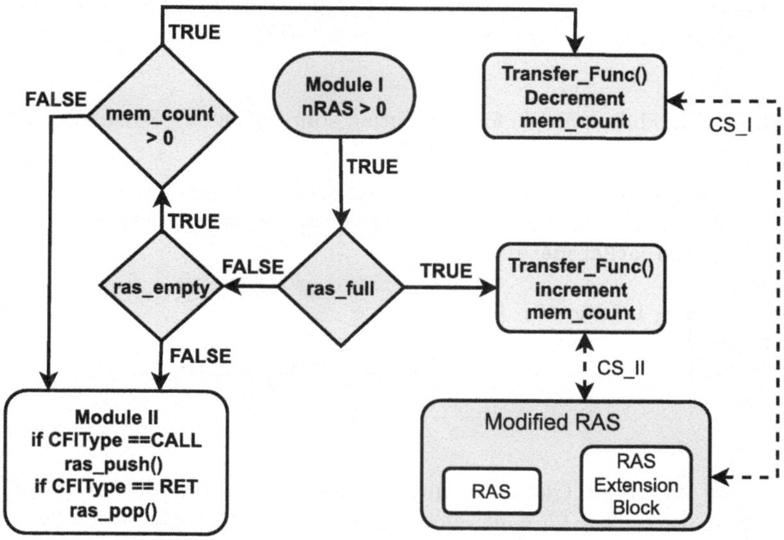

Fig. 3. Proposed RAS design in Rocket core

The proposed design checks whether the buffer size *(nRAS)* is greater than zero or not. If the decision is true, it also checks whether RAS is full or not, i.e., *(ras_full == TRUE)*; otherwise, the proposed design checks whether RAS is empty or not *(ras_empty == TRUE)*. If RAS is full, the proposed design considers the buffer completely occupied, preventing further push operations. In such cases, the system invokes the *Transfer_Func()* module, which moves the buffer to the specified memory location.

The counter *mem_count* is managed by *Transfer_Func()*, which maps the entry in the memory to the number of transfers that have occurred. The count increases (*mem_count + +*) as the buffer is moved into memory. The count decreases when the system detects *ras_empty* and returns TRUE when *mem_count* is greater than zero, as shown in Fig. 3.

If *ras_empty* returns FALSE, the system proceeds to Module II. The system also checks the *CFIType* to determine if it is CALL or RET. The proposed design executes *ras_push()* for CALL modules and *ras_pop()* for RET modules depending on the returned value. The proposed design updates RAS with *ras_update* information. *CS_I* and *CS_II* represent bidirectional control flow signals.

Figure 4 shows the proposed design. We introduced an RAS extension controller to our digital top, which communicates with the front end and features a BTB and RAS. When the configured RAS is full, the front end transmits a signal *(ras_full)* and starts transferring the buffer to the memory location that is specified by the *TLClient* class node.

We are storing overflowed buffers in memory. At the same time, call instructions are executed, and we retrieve buffers from memory and return them to the RAS hardware structure, as shown in Fig. 4. Therefore, the proposed design extends RAS and protects the processor from SBFO.

Table 3. Lazy module example for configuring addresses for reserved RAS memory

```
class MyClient(implicit p: Parameters) extends LazyModule {
  val node = TLClientNode(Seq(TLMasterPortParameters.v1(Seq(
      ↪ TLClientParameters(
    name = "RAS-client",
    sourceId = IdRange(0, 1),
    requestFifo = true,
    visibility = Seq(AddressSet(0xbase, 0xmask)))))))
```

Using the TLClinet Class, we have created a client node configured with parameters name, *sourceId*, *requestFifo*, and *visibility* to define a specific address set. The client node is designed to read and write to these addresses in memory. We communicate with the *FBus* controller, which handles the bus transfer interface and communication with memory.

Listing of Table 3 shows a sample code snippet for TLClinentNode. The base address of memory is *0xbase*, and the other end of memory space is calculated by adding *0xmask* to the base address. By doing so, we provided an address range for the memory transfer.

An approach that directly accesses memory and can transfer register contents between the RAS extension controller and the reserved memory address is employed to mitigate the penalty associated with memory transfer. To achieve our goal, we used several useful functions of the *edge* object, such as *edge.get* and *edge.put*, which read and write data. The process ensures that a unique address is assigned for RAS extension purposes based on the memory.

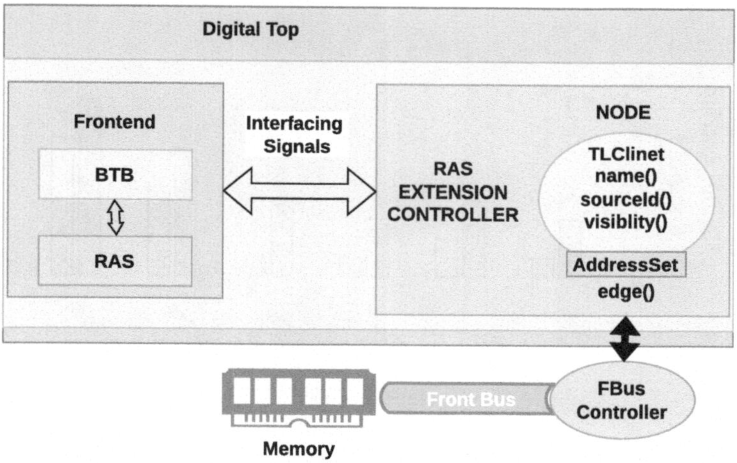

Fig. 4. RAS extension in Rocket core using extension controller

We maintain a hardware counter that indexes the buffer's location in the memory space, as shown in the flow diagram (Fig. 3), with *mem_count*. The proposed design ensures that the first buffer is assigned to the first set of locations corresponding to the buffer size. The hardware counter, *mem_count*, also helps to update the available address locations in memory.

6 Experimental Setup and Results

We used the RISC-V toolchain with the Spike simulator and proxy kernel *pk* to evaluate buffer size for benchmark suites like Beebs and CoreMark. We used the Chipyard framework [18] tool for hardware implementation. Our Chipyard configuration includes a single Rocket core with the default single Axi-4 memory channel interface and serial-tile link interface. We used the Artix 7 xc7a200tsbv484 FPGA board to test RTL on actual hardware. This section discusses various experiments to evaluate the proposed design for overhead and security analysis by varying the RAS buffer sizes.

6.1 Buffer Size Evaluation

We evaluated the current buffer size required for multiple inbuilt benchmarks available in the RISC-V toolchain, as shown in Fig. 5. The benchmarks are analyzed with two RAS buffer sizes of 8 and 12, with the number of memory transfers required in each case specified on the y-axis. The *'mt-wadd'* benchmark requires the most number of transfers (17 times), indicating a much larger RAS buffer requirement than *'median'* benchmark, which requires only two transfers with an RAS buffer of 12 entries. A smaller buffer RAS_8 requires more transfers than a larger buffer RAS_12, which is consistent across all cases. We observed that a larger buffer size can hold a greater number of 'ra', requiring fewer transfers, as shown in Fig. 5.

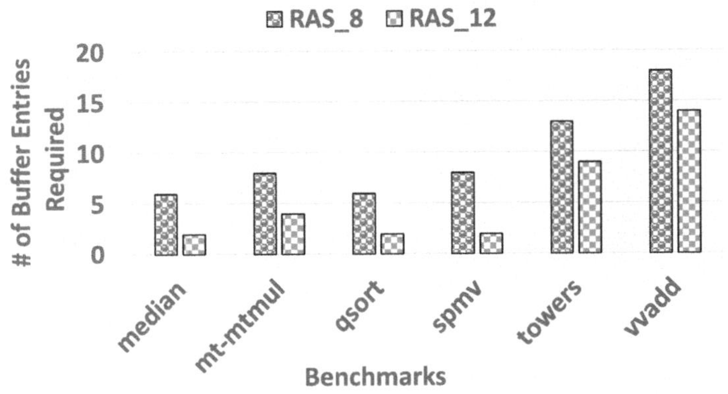

Fig. 5. Size requirement of RAS buffers for various RISC-V inbuilt benchmarks

We also used the CoreMark benchmark on the Rocket core design to detect RAS overflow scenarios when running on a custom SoC design with a single Rocket core as the processor core and the proxy kernel 'pk' to execute RISC-V binary files. Table 4 shows the results based on the number of instructions executed in the proposed setup. We introduced the Overflow Factor (OF) to quantify the RAS overflow rate with the number of execution instructions, where the OF is calculated as determines using Eq. 1. The data from Table 4 indicates that the OF is high when the buffer size is low, as the RASOF count is significantly higher in such scenario.

$$OF = EIC/(RASOF * BS) \tag{1}$$

Figure 6 shows the Beebs benchmark and its OF analysis for various buffer sizes. Figure 6a shows the execution time for various applications on the chipyard setup; the corresponding executed instruction count is shown in Fig. 6b, which is roughly proportional to the execution time for that specific application. Figure 6c shows that as the number of instructions increases, so does the RASOF count. Figure 6d shows the OF. We observed that the OF is lowest when the buffer size is highest, i.e., RAS_128.

6.2 Analysis on Overheads for Fixed RAS Size

Memory Overhead. The amount of memory that must be allocated for RAS extension purposes is dependent upon the designer. Approximately 0.1% of the total typical memory size of 2GB is reserved in our evaluated design, which is 2MB.

Table 4. Overflow factor analysis for CoreMark benchmarks

CoreMark Benchmark			Executed Instruction Count (EIC)	Overflow Factor (OF)
Buffer Size (BS)	Execution Time(s) (ET)	RAS OverFlow Detected (RASOF)		
16	847.8	29714	1510008	3.176129
32	663.6	14223	720779	1.583656
48	696	10830	548574	1.055274
128	702	15458	788679	0.398599
256	493.8	6202	323138	0.2035243
512	774	13279	697122	0.1025353

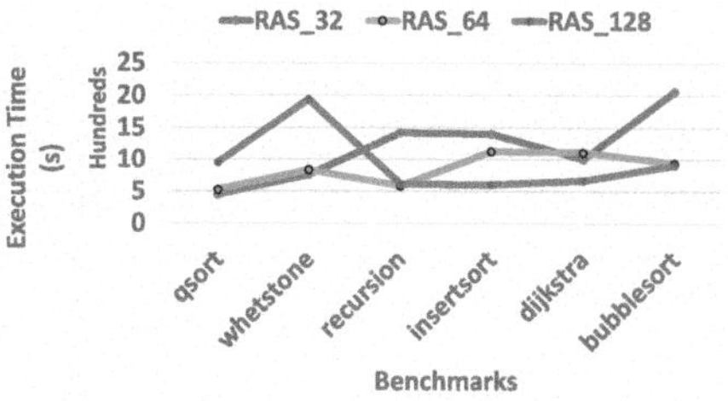

(a) Execution time

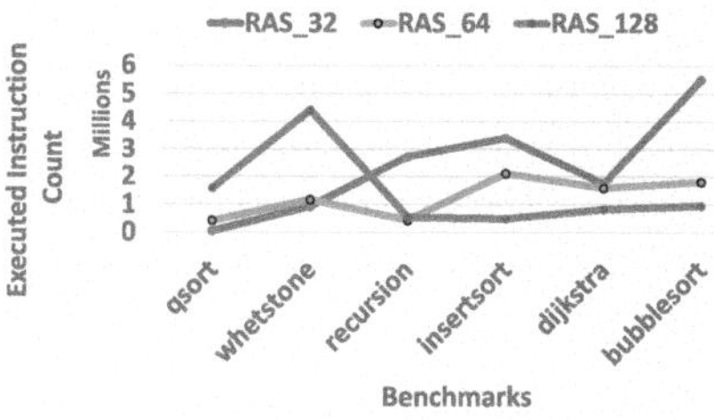

(b) Executed instruction count

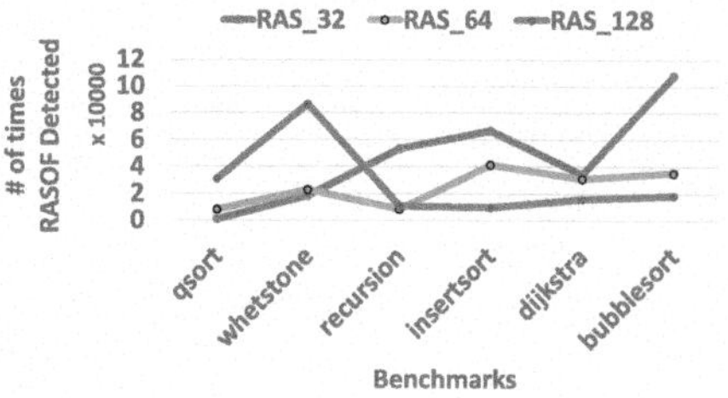

(c) Number of RAS overflows

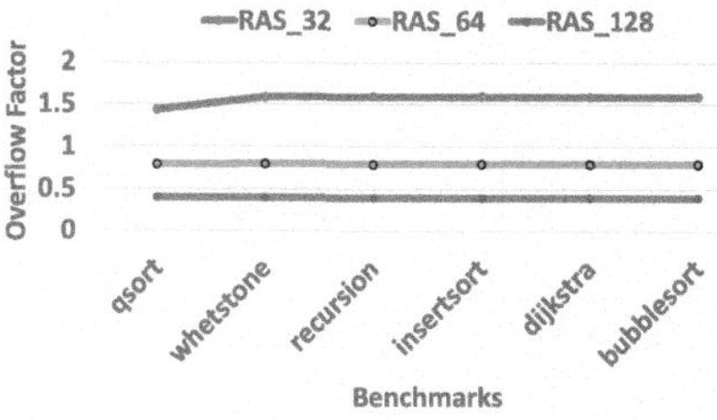

(d) Overflow factor

Fig. 6. RAS and overflow factor analysis for Beebs benchmarks

Performance Overhead. The performance overhead is a result of the transfer that occurs between RAS and memory. The impact of memory transfer depends upon the application's recursive depth and the size of the RAS. We observed that the performance overhead is as low as 2% and, in the worst-case scenario, could increase up to 14% of the total execution time on the chip during the evaluation. If the security benefit of the system is compared, the overhead over base Rocket core is negligible, which is the intended objective of the proposed design.

6.3 Security Analysis

We evaluated our design using the *RIPE* benchmarks [36] and observed no false positives. These benchmarks are used to determine the efficacy and performance of memory error defenses. They provide standardized and representative scenarios to simulate memory errors. These benchmarks use a variety of attack vectors, including *bss-based, heap-based,* and *stack-based* bound checks. We used its stack-based bound checking, which targets 'ra' stored on the stack (Table 5).

Out of various attack vectors, we included vulnerable functions like *memcpy, homebrew, srtrcpy, strcat, spring, sscanf.* We evaluated two techniques: direct BFO and indirect-based overflow, both of which can result in a diversion to heap memory. The direct BFO technique involves overwriting a target pointer that is located in the same memory region as the overflow buffer. In the direct BFO technique, replace the target pointer with an integer value for data-only attacks.

Conversely, the indirect technique initially targets a generic pointer that is situated adjacent to the buffer. Subsequently, the targeted generic pointer is directed to the attack code through a dereference operation. Indirect overflows can occur when data is transferred between memory regions, such as from a

Table 5. Security analysis for Ripe benchmarks

Overflow Technique	Attack Code	Target Code Pointer	Location	Function	Detection
direct	shellcode	ret	stack	memcpy, strcpy	TRUE
indirect	shellcode	ret	stack	memcpy, strcpy	TRUE
direct	returninto libc	ret	stack	memcpy, strcpy	TRUE
indirect	returninto libc	ret	stack	memcpy, strcpy	TRUE
direct	rop	ret	stack	memcpy, strcpy	TRUE

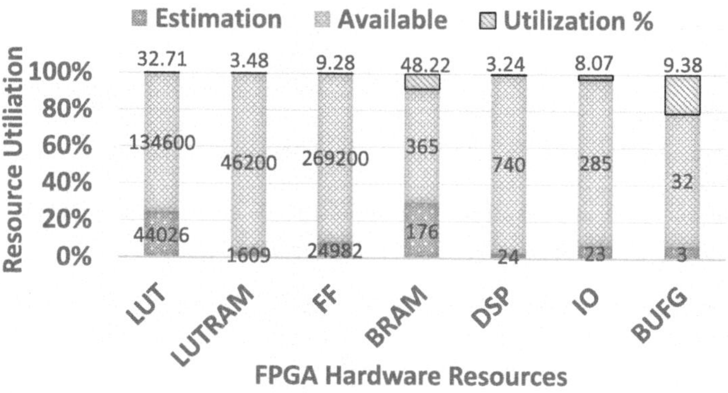

Fig. 7. Resource utilization on Artix 7 FPGA

stack buffer to a heap pointer. In the indirect technique, replace a pointer to the target with a pointer that is located in a different location in memory for data-only attacks. In addition to RIPE benchmarks, we have also evaluated the proposed design with our own test cases, which are by the various listings shown in Table 2.

6.4 Hardware Resourse Cost

When we synthesized the proposed design of the Top Module, *Chiptop*, for the *Artix 7 xc7a200tsbv484* FPGA board as a target, the resource utilization report is shown in Fig. 7. There is negligible hardware cost as compared to the total availability of hardware resources. Our experimental configuration includes a single Rocket core with a default single Axi-4 memory channel interface and serial-tile link interface.

7 Conclusions and Future Scope

We used the existing RAS structure from RISC-V processor cores for 'ra' protection rather than just prediction. In order to achieve this objective, we increased the size of RAS so that it would not pose a problem in 'ra' storage. We proposed a Chisel-based design that employs the Chipyard framework to test its viability, which fast-tracks our understanding of the proposed system at the FPGA level. We could see the entire proposed design on RTL, including the hardware and timing overhead.

We are adding **physical memory protection (pmp)** [1] registers to add an additional layer of security. Before starting the transfer, the system will check for those *csr* registers to see if the transfer is authorized, creating a boundary for the reserved memory. Another approach we're considering is using an onboard SRAM-based design to reduce the timing overhead caused by external DRAM. In most cases, these future designs reduce the performance overhead by $< 1\%$.

References

1. Waterman, A., Asanovic, K.: The RISC-V instruction set manual volume II: privileged ISA
2. Waterman, A., Asanovic, K.: The RISC-V instruction set manual volume I: unprivileged ISA
3. Wessman, N.J., et al.: De-RISC: the first RISC-V space-grade platform for safety-critical systems. In: 2021 IEEE Space Computing Conference (SCC), pp. 17–26. IEEE (2021)
4. Lee, S.-Y., Hung, Y.-W., Chang, Y.-T., Lin, C.-C., Shieh, G.-S.: RISC-V CNN coprocessor for real-time epilepsy detection in wearable application. IEEE Trans. Biomed. Cir. Syst. **15**(4), 679–691 (2021)
5. Mittone, G., et al.: Experimenting with emerging RISC-V systems for decentralised machine learning. In: Proceedings of the 20th ACM International Conference on Computing Frontiers, pp. 73–83 (2023)
6. Kovačević, N., Mišeljić, Đ., Stojković, A.: RISC-V vector processor for acceleration of machine learning algorithms. In: 2022 30th Telecommunications Forum (TELFOR), pp. 1–4. IEEE (2022)
7. Serrano, R., et al.: A low-power low-area soc based in RISC-V processor for IoT applications. In: 2021 18th International SoC Design Conference (ISOCC), pp. 375–376. IEEE (2021)
8. Choi, E., Park, J., Lee, K., Lee, J.-J., Han, K., Lee, W.: Day-night architecture: development of an ultra-low power RISC-V processor for wearable anomaly detection. J. Syst. Architect. **152**, 103161 (2024)
9. Wang, P., Zhi-Bin, Yu.: LLVM RISC-V RV32X graphics extension support and characteristics analysis of graphics programs. IEEE Access **11**, 67285–67297 (2023)
10. Tourres, M., Chavet, C., Le Gal, B., Crenne, J., Coussy, P.: Extended RISC-V hardware architecture for future digital communication systems. In: 2021 IEEE 4th 5G World Forum (5GWF), pp. 224–229. IEEE (2021)
11. De, A., et al.: FIXER: flow integrity extensions for embedded RISC-V. In: Design, Automation & Test in Europe Conference & Exhibition (2019)
12. De, A., et al.: Hardware assisted buffer protection mechanisms for embedded RISC-V. IEEE Trans. Comput.-Aided Des. Integr. Cir. Syst. (2020)
13. Davi, L., et al.: HAFIX: hardware-assisted flow integrity extension. In: Proceedings of the 52nd Annual Design Automation Conference (2015)
14. Waterman, A., Zabrocki, A., et al.: RISCV-CFI (2024). https://github.com/riscv/riscv-cfi/releases
15. Asanovic, K., et al.: The rocket chip generator. EECS Department, University of California, Berkeley, Technical report UCB/EECS-2016-17, vol. 4, pp. 2–6 (2016)
16. Koruyeh, E.M., Khasawneh, K.N., Song, C., Abu-Ghazaleh, N.: Spectre returns! Speculation attacks using the return stack buffer. In: 12th USENIX Workshop on Offensive Technologies (WOOT 18) (2018)
17. Wang, Y., Wu, J., Yue, T., Ning, Z., Zhang, F.: RetTag: hardware-assisted return address integrity on RISC-V. In: Proceedings of the 15th European Workshop on Systems Security, pp. 50–56 (2022)
18. Amid, A., et al.: Chipyard: integrated design, simulation, and implementation framework for custom SoCs. IEEE Micro **40**(4), 10–21 (2020)
19. Bachrach, J., et al.: CHISEL: constructing hardware in a Scala embedded language. In: Proceedings of the 49th Annual Design Automation Conference, pp. 1216–1225 (2012)

20. Amid, A., et al.: Chipyard: integrated design, simulation, and implementation framework for custom socs. IEEE Micro **40**(4), 10–21 (2020)
21. Liu, Y., Cheung, R.C.C., Wong, H.: Lightweight secure processor prototype on FPGA. In: 2018 28th International Conference on Field Programmable Logic and Applications (FPL), pp. 443–4431. IEEE (2018)
22. Lee, D., Kohlbrenner, D., Shinde, S., Asanović, K., Song, D.: Keystone: an open framework for architecting trusted execution environments. In: Proceedings of the Fifteenth European Conference on Computer Systems, pp. 1–16 (2020)
23. Zhang, Z., et al.: Hardware-implemented security processing unit for program execution monitoring and instruction fault self-repairing on embedded systems. Appl. Sci. **12**(7), 3584 (2022)
24. Liu, C., Yan-Jun, W., Jing-Zheng, W., Zhao, C.: A buffer overflow detection and defense method based on RISC-V instruction set extension. Cybersecurity **6**(1), 45 (2023)
25. Das, S., Unnithan, R.H., Menon, A., Rebeiro, C., Veezhinathan, K.: SHAKTI-MS: a RISC-V processor for memory safety in C. In: Proceedings of the 20th ACM SIGPLAN/SIGBED International Conference on Languages, Compilers, and Tools for Embedded Systems, pp. 19–32 (2019)
26. Nasahl, P., Schilling, R., Werner, M., Mangard, S.: HECTOR-V: a heterogeneous CPU architecture for a secure RISC-V execution environment. In: Proceedings of the 2021 ACM Asia Conference on Computer and Communications Security, pp. 187–199 (2021)
27. KF, M.A., Ganesan, V., Bodduna, R., Rebeiro, C.: PARAM: a microprocessor hardened for power side-channel attack resistance. In: 2020 IEEE International Symposium on Hardware Oriented Security and Trust (HOST), pp. 23–34. IEEE (2020)
28. Palmiero, C., Di Guglielmo, G., Lavagno, L., Carloni, L.P.: Design and implementation of a dynamic information flow tracking architecture to secure a RISC-V core for IoT applications. In: 2018 IEEE High Performance extreme Computing Conference (HPEC), pp. 1–7. IEEE (2018)
29. Schrammel, D., et al.:. Donky: domain keys–efficient {In-Process} isolation for {RISC-V} and x86. In: 29th USENIX Security Symposium (USENIX Security 20), pp. 1677–1694 (2020)
30. De, A., Basu, A., Ghosh, S., Jaeger, T.: FIXER: flow integrity extensions for embedded RISC-V. In: 2019 Design, Automation & Test in Europe Conference & Exhibition (DATE), pp. 348–353. IEEE (2019)
31. Harris, A., et al.: Morpheus II: a RISC-V security extension for protecting vulnerable software and hardware. In: 2021 IEEE International Symposium on Hardware Oriented Security and Trust (HOST), pp. 226–238. IEEE (2021)
32. Wang, Y., Wu, J., Zheng, H., Ning, Z., He, B., Zhang, F.: Raft: hardware-assisted dynamic information flow tracking for runtime protection on RISC-V. In: Proceedings of the 26th International Symposium on Research in Attacks, Intrusions and Defenses, pp. 595–608 (2023)
33. Zaruba , F., Benini, L.: The cost of application-class processing: energy and performance analysis of a Linux-ready 1.7-GHz 64-bit RISC-V core in 22-nm FDSOI technology. IEEE Trans. Very Large Scale Integr. VLSI Syst. **27**(11), 2629–2640 (2019)
34. Genc, H., et al.: Gemmini: enabling systematic deep-learning architecture evaluation via full-stack integration. In: Proceedings of the 58th Annual Design Automation Conference (DAC) (2021)

35. Cook, H., Terpstra, W., Lee, Y.: Diplomatic design patterns: a TileLink case study. In: 1st Workshop on Computer Architecture Research with RISC-V, vol. 23 (2017)
36. Wilander, J., Nikiforakis, N., Younan, Y., Kamkar, M., Joosen, W.: RIPE: runtime intrusion prevention evaluator. In: Proceedings of the 27th Annual Computer Security Applications Conference, pp. 41–50 (2011)

Parameterizing Time-Memory Trade-Off for Flexible Implementation of CRYSTALS-Dilithium

Yasushi Takahashi[1(✉)], Naohisa Nishida[1], Yuji Unagami[1], Saburo Toyonaga[1], Naoto Yanai[1], Yasuhiko Ikematsu[2], Koji Nuida[2], and Masaya Yasuda[3]

[1] Panasonic Holdings Corporation, 4-1-62 Minoshima, Hakata-ku, Fukuoka 812-0017, Japan
takahashi.yasushi@jp.panasonic.com

[2] Kyushu University, 744 Motooka, Nishi-ku, Fukuoka 819-0395, Japan

[3] Rikkyo University, 3-34-1 Nishi-Ikebukuro, Toshima-ku, Tokyo 171-8501, Japan

Abstract. CRYSTALS-Dilithium is a digital signature scheme selected by the NIST standardization for post-quantum cryptography. Greconici et al. (at TCHES 2021) proposed several implementation strategies based on the trade-off between computation time and stack size, i.e., time-memory trade-off, of CRYSTALS-Dilithium for IoT devices, but a suitable design for the IoT devices is still unknown due to lack of experiments. In this paper, we provide a detailed analysis and parameterize of the trade-off between computation time and stack size for the signing algorithm of CRYSTALS-Dilithium. We first conduct systematic evaluations of the strategies by Greconici et al. to understand their impact on the trade-off described above. Next, we propose a new implementation method of CRYSTALS-Dilithium, which parameterizes the trade-off by generalizing the systematic evaluation. We also conduct experiments by implementing the proposed method on a hardware board for IoT devices. The most remarkable result is that the trade-off between the computation time and the stack size is non-linear: notably, reducing the stack size also indicates an improvement in the computation time with respect to an implementation for minimizing the stack size.

Keywords: CRYSTALS-Dilithium · digital signatures · post-quantum cryptography · cryptographic implementation

1 Introduction

Background. Digital signatures are an important tool for information security, and regarding the proliferation of IoT devices in recent years, they have also been implemented in IoT devices as well as conventional computers. Nevertheless, the computational resources of IoT devices are constrained compared to conventional computers. It is crucial to design a lightweight scheme for the use of digital signatures in IoT devices.

As another motivation, the current de-facto standard signature schemes, e.g., RSA and ECDSA, will be compromised by quantum computers. Public key cryptography (including digital signatures), whose security is guaranteed even against quantum computers, is known as post-quantum cryptography (PQC) and has been developed in recent

L. Morogan et al. (Eds.): SecITC 2024, LNCS 15595, pp. 189–206, 2025.
https://doi.org/10.1007/978-3-031-87760-5_14

years. In July 2022, National Institute of Standards and Technology (NIST) announced four standardized schemes [20] for public key cryptography in the post-quantum era.

CRYSTALS-Dilithium [3], standardized by NIST, is a lattice-based digital signature scheme that offers superior performance in terms of the computation time of key generation and that of signature generation compared to other standardized post-quantum signature schemes, i.e., Falcon and SPHINCS+. However, since CRYSTALS-Dilithium still needs a large stack size for memory usage compared with RSA or ECDSA, it is sometimes unable to provide reasonable performance on IoT devices whose computational resources are constrained. It may also harm the main process of IoT devices due to a large stack size, e.g., buffer overflows [4, 12] and new side-channel attacks [2] specific to PQC. Consequently, many researchers have improved implementations for CRYSTALS-Dilithium [6, 8, 11, 14, 16, 19, 25].

The most striking effort to reduce the stack size of CRYSTALS-Dilithium is an implementation method by Greconici et al. [10], and we believe that it is the most IoT-friendly. Their main idea is to generate intermediate variables computed dynamically in the signature generation algorithm. By contrast, in a typical implementation of the original signature generation algorithm of CRYSTALS-Dilithium, the intermediate variables are stored in stack memory. Consequently, the implementation method by Greconici et al. can significantly reduce the stack size because the intermediate variables are no longer stored in stack memory. They also provided strategies for the implementation method by considering the trade-off between the computation time and the stack size, i.e., the time-memory trade-off.

Our Research Question. In this paper, we tackle the following research question: *How is the trade-off between the computation time and the stack size for CRYSTALS-Dilithium?*

The motivation for the above question is that the evaluation of the implementation method by Greconici et al. is insufficient. Whereas Greconici et al. provided two strategies[1] regarding the trade-off between the computation time and the stack size as mentioned above, i.e., a time-efficient strategy and a memory-efficient strategy, they evaluated only the time-efficient strategies in detail. In other words, they evaluated just a few cases for the memory-efficient strategy. This means that (dis)advantages of their strategies are still unclear, and simultaneously, it implies that we need to precisely understand the impact of the trade-off on the performance of CRYSTALS-Dilithium.

Contributions. In this paper, regarding the deployment of CRYSTALS-Dilithium into IoT devices, we propose a novel implementation method for the signing algorithm of CRYSTALS-Dilithium, which can parameterize the trade-off between the computation time and the stack size, and then conduct experiments with the proposed method on a hardware board for IoT devices. Specifically, we have three contributions in this paper.

The first contribution is to conduct a systematic evaluation of the implementation method by Greconici et al. [10]. We implement the two strategies by Greconici et al. on a hardware board with an ARM Cortex-M33 CPU and then analyze their performance.

[1] They originally proposed three strategies, but the remaining one is based on flash memory. It is out of the scope of this paper.

We then identify a clear trade-off between the computation time and the stack size for the two strategies, which was not experimentally shown in the original work [10]. It also leads us to a new question for the following contributions. (See Sect. 3 for details.)

The second contribution is to propose a novel implementation method that introduces a new intermediate parameter by generalizing the systematic evaluation in the first contribution. It can parameterize the trade-off between the computation time and the stack size and, therefore, analyze an implementation for any setting by specifying the intermediate parameter. We also show several instantiations of the proposed method. (See Sect. 4 for details.)

The third contribution is to conduct experiments with the above instantiations on a hardware board with an ARM Cortex-M33 CPU and then demonstrate several insights into the trade-off between the computation time and the stack size. In a nutshell, the above trade-off is *non-linear*. Although it might not be a surprising result, we confirm the above fact through the experiments. We demonstrate that possibly reducing the stack size can improve the computation time: the implementation with a minimum stack size is faster than the implementation with a larger stack size. (See Sect. 5 for more details.)

Related Works. Most of the existing works for implementation of CRYSTALS-Dilithium focus on improving either the computation time [6,16,18,22] (known as high throughput) or the stack size [8,11,13,25] (known as compact). They have trade-offs between each other in general, and hence, improving both is non-trivial. Although combinations of the above works with the proposed method are beyond the scope of this study, we believe that hardware acceleration, such as the hint functions [22] and number theoretic transformation (NTT) [19], is possible. We plan to try hardware acceleration of our work based on these works in the future.

The closest works [5,10,16,24,26] to ours focus on the trade-off between computation time and stack size. They can possibly improve both the computation time and the stack size, and are classified into three types, namely, software-based design [10], hardware-based design [5,24], and co-design based on both [16,26]. Only Greconici et al. [10] and Beckwith et al. [5] evaluated the implementations on architectures for IoT devices [15]. While Beckwith et al. proposed a universal design including also for CRYSTALS-Kyber [1], Greconici et al. proposed a specific design for CRYSTALS-Dilithium. We believe that improving the implementation method by Greconici et al. is better for CRYSTALS-Dilithium on IoT devices.

2 Preliminaries

In this section, we describe CRYSTALS-Dilithium [3] and the implementation by Greconici et al. [10].

2.1 CRYSTALS-Dilithium

The algorithms of CRYSTALS-Dilithium consist of key generation, signature generation, and signature verification. Hereafter, we focus on the signature generation algorithm in this paper, and hence we show it in Algorithms 1, where we refer to those by

Algorithm 1. Signature Generation

Require: secret key $sk = (\rho, K, tr, s_1, s_2, t_0)$; message $M \in \{0,1\}^*$
Ensure: signature $\sigma = (z, h, c)$
$\hat{A} \in R_q^{k\times\ell} :=$ ExpandA(ρ), $\mu := H(tr\|M)$; $\kappa := 0$; $(z,h) := \perp$; $\hat{s}_1 :=$ NTT(s_1); $\hat{s}_2 :=$ NTT(s_2); $\hat{t}_0 :=$ NTT(t_0)
$\rho' := H(K\|\mu)$
while $(z,h) = \perp$ **do**
  $y \in S_{\gamma_1-1}^{\ell} :=$ ExpandMask(ρ', κ)
  $w :=$ NTT$^{-1}(\hat{A} \circ$ NTT$(y))$
  $w_1 :=$ HighBits(w)
  $\hat{c} :=$ NTT$(H_B(\mu\|w_1))$
  $z := y +$ NTT$^{-1}(\hat{c} \circ \hat{s}_1)$
  $(r_1, r_0) :=$ Decompose$(w -$ NTT$^{-1}(\hat{c} \circ \hat{s}_2))$
  if $\|z\|_\infty \geq \gamma_1 - \beta$ or $\|r_0\|_\infty \geq \gamma_2 - \beta$ or $r_1 \neq w_1$ **then**
    $(z,h) := \perp$
  else
    $h :=$ MakeHint$(-$NTT$^{-1}(\hat{c} \circ \hat{t}_0), w -$ NTT$^{-1}(\hat{c} \circ \hat{s}_2) +$ NTT$^{-1}(\hat{c} \circ \hat{t}_0))$
    if $\|$NTT$^{-1}(\hat{c} \circ \hat{t}_0)\|_\infty \geq \gamma_2$ or #1's in $h > \omega$ **then**
      $(z,h) := \perp$
    end if
  end if
end while

Greconici et al. [10]. We also show the key generation and the signature verification in Algorithm 3 and Algorithm 4 in Appendix A. CRYSTALS-Dilithium contains security parameters $(k, \ell, d, \gamma_1, \gamma_2, \eta, \beta, \omega)$ and they are defined on the respective NIST security levels. We show these parameters in Table 1 in Appendix. For each level, $n = 256$ and $q = 8380417 (= 2^{23} - 2^{13} + 1)$ are commonly utilized independently of Table 1. We also define several symbols and functions. Let S^ℓ be the set of vectors of degree ℓ, where each element of the vector belongs to the set R_q. Here, R_q is a ring defined by $R_q := \mathbb{Z}_q[X]/(X_n + 1)$. Furthermore, let S_η^ℓ denote the subset of S^ℓ consisting of vectors where all coefficients of the ℓ polynomials are contained within the interval $[-\eta, \eta]$. For any polynomial, vector, and matrix, a variable transformed by NTT is denoted by putting a hat symbol, i.e., $\hat{c} :=$ NTT(c) for any c. ExpandA and Expand-Mask are functions for seed extension. Power2Round, HighBits, and Decompose are rounding functions. MakeHint and UseHint are hint functions. H is a hash function with 384-bit output. H_B is a hash function that outputs a polynomial with 256 coefficients, where a fixed number of coefficients are randomly chosen from $\{-1, +1\}$ and the remaining coefficients are zero. H and H_B are implemented using SHAKE256. We also say intermediate variable to mean any variable generated during the algorithms, e.g., y in Algorithm 1. Here, we specifically mention the sizes of s_1, s_2 and t_0 that will be focused on later. Since $s_1 \in S_\eta^\ell$ and $s_2, t \in S_\eta^k$, s_1 is a vector containing ℓ polynomials, while s_2 and t are vectors containing k polynomials. Given that the size of each polynomial is 1-KiB, s_1 has a size of ℓ-KiB, and s_2 and t have a size of k-KiB. Please refer to the appendix B for the specific values of k and ℓ.

2.2 Implementation Method by Greconici et al.

Greconici et al. [10] proposed an implementation method to reduce the stack size for CRYSTALS-Dilithium. They also proposed two strategies for implementing the signature generation algorithm: reducing the computation time by storing intermediate variables in stack memory, and reducing the stack size by increasing the computation time. We describe the details of each strategy below.

Strategy 1: All the intermediate variables are pre-computed and stored in stack memory. This strategy is identical to a typical implementation of CRYSTALS-Dilithium and is feasible if a device has enough stack memory. Specifically, there are $k \cdot \ell + 4k + 3\ell + 1$ polynomials, and hence 53 KiB of extra stack memory is required.

Strategy 2: The intermediate variables $(\hat{A}, y)$ are computed dynamically. This strategy is suitable for devices whose stack size is limited and with sufficient computation time. It re-generates A and y every time when w is computed at Line 5 in Algorithm 1. It also removes y from stack memory and needs to re-generate it at Line 8.

3 Systematic Evaluations of Implementation by Greconici et al.

In this section, we evaluate the implementation method by Greconici et al. in a systematic way. Specifically, we measure the performance of the two strategies described in the previous section and then describe a new research question through their results. This section corresponds to the first contribution in this paper because Greconici et al. did not evaluate both strategies in detail as described in Sect. 1.

3.1 Evaluation Results

We implemented the strategies described in the previous section with the source code of Greconici et al. [10] and then measured their computation time and stack size on an EFR32MG24 module[2] with ARM Cortex-M33 CPU. This module has up to 1536 KiB of flash memory and 256 KiB of RAM as stack memory, and it runs with 78.0 MHz.

These results are shown in Figs. 1a-1c. According to Fig. 1a, the most frequent computation time of Strategy 1 is about 50 msec with 17% frequency. The computation with about 50% is finished within 70 msec, and the mean of the computation time of Strategy 1 is 118 msec with the variance $\sigma = 76$. On the other hand, according to Fig. 1b, the most frequent computation time of Strategy 2 is about 80 msec with 16% frequency. The mean of the computation time of Strategy 2 is 367 msec. Meanwhile, the stack size of Strategy 1 is about 38.5 KiB while that of Strategy 2 is about 9.2 KiB according to Fig. 1c.

The reason for difference between the above variances is that Starategy 2 needs a longer computation time than Strategy 1 due to computing each variable dynamically. More specifically, to compute w in Strategy 1, we compute y by sampling ℓ polynomials with uniformly random coefficients in $[-(\gamma_1 - 1), \gamma_1 - 1]$. It means to perform ℓn rejection sampling once before computing w. On the other hand, in Strategy 2, we have

[2] https://jp.silabs.com/development-tools/wireless/efr32xg24-pro-kit-20-dbm.

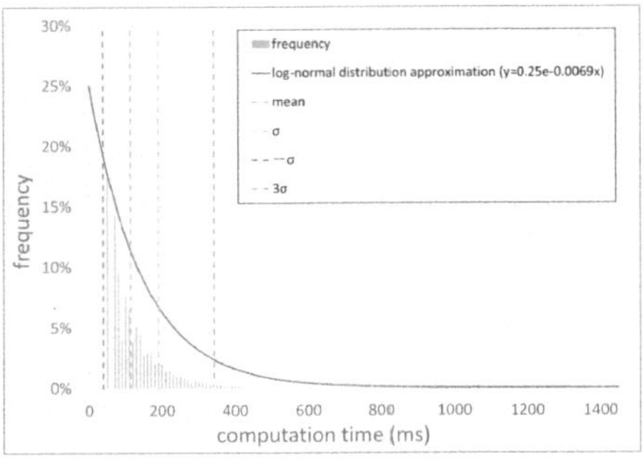

(a) Strategy 1.

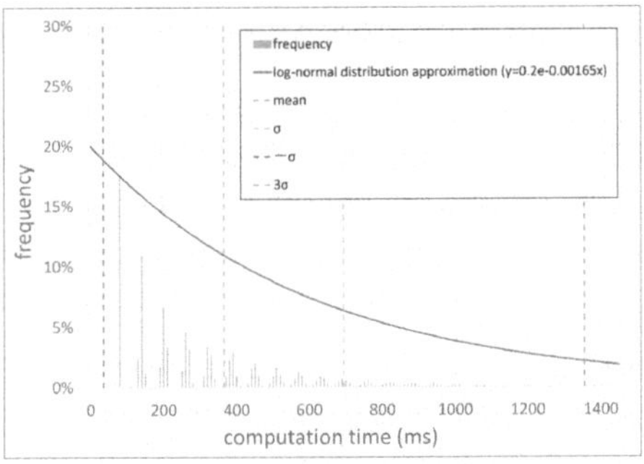

(b) Strategy 2.

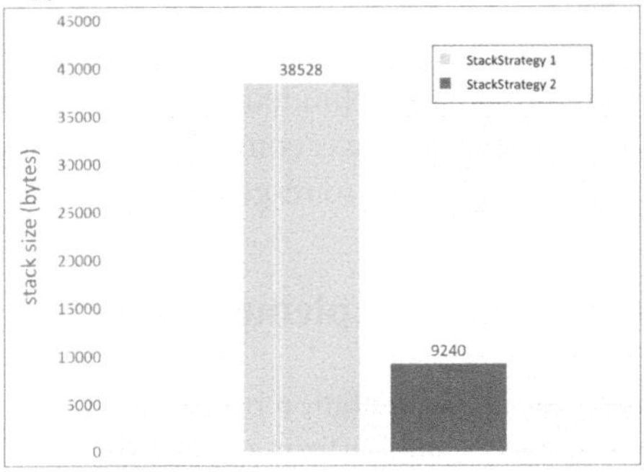

(c) Stack size.

Fig. 1. The evaluation results for the signature generation by each strategy. Figures 1a-1b represent the distribution of the computation time for each strategy, where the red line corresponds to log-normal distribution approximation. In these figures, the horizontal axis represents the computation time, whose range is from 0 msec to 1400 msec, and the vertical axis represents its frequency, whose range is from 0% to 35%. Figure 1c represents the stack size, where the horizontal axis represents bytes.

to compute y for matrix multiplication to obtain w dynamically. It will need to perform ℓnk rejection sampling for computing y.

To summarize the above results, Strategy 1 is three times faster than Strategy 2, whereas Strategy 2 is four times smaller than Strategy 1. In other words, when we compute ratios between Strategy 1 and Strategy 2 with respect to the computation time and the stack size, these are about 3.11 for the computation time of Strategy 1 and about 4.18 for the stack size of Strategy 2. We were able to find a clear trade-off between the computation time and the stack size in comparison between Strategy 1 and Strategy 2.

3.2 New Research Question

The results shown in the previous subsection imply a new research question. The implementation by Greconici et al. sacrifices either computation time or stack size. However, there should be many implementations other than Strategy 1 and Strategy 2, and it is still unclear whether the trade-off between computation time and stack size is consistently linear. In other words, we have another question: *is the trade-off between the computation time and the stack size linear?* Answering this question will enable us to design an implementation for any situation and estimate its computation time and stack size.

4 Proposed Method

In this section, we propose a new implementation method for CRYSTALS-Dilithium as the second contribution. We first describe the overview and the algorithm of the proposed method. We then show its instantiations.

4.1 Overview

As mentioned in the previous section, the next step of this paper is to clarify whether the trade-off between the computation time and the stack size is linear. To this end, we consider that such an implementation will be found if the trade-off is parameterized.

Specifically, the main process of CRYSTALS-Dilithium depends on the computation based on $k \times \ell$ matrix $A \in \mathbb{R}_q^{k \times \ell}$. It means that there are many k-element vectors or ℓ-element vectors within the intermediate variables. We then focus on generalizing the strategies by Greconici et al. for these vectors and then introduce a new intermediate parameter λ, whose range is in $[0, \min(k, \ell)]$, to represent the trade-off for each strategy. This intermediate parameter specifies the number of k-element vectors and ℓ-element vectors stored in stack memory: they specify the amount of the intermediate variables, such as A, stored in stack memory. It can realize an implementation for any situation. We also assume that w and $\hat{c}$ are always stored in stack memory because their computation time is large.

4.2 Algorithm

We present the algorithm of the proposed method in Algorithm 2. We define several new notations below. For any $pr \in S_\eta^\ell \cup S_\eta^k$, we denote by $pr^{\mathrm{tp}(\lambda)}$ the part of pr from the zeroth row to the λ-th row, and by $pr^{\mathrm{bt}(\lambda)}$ the part of pr from the $(\lambda+1)$-th row to the k-th row (resp. the ℓ-th row). We also denote by $\widehat{pr}^{\mathrm{tp}(\lambda)}$ only λ-part of $\widehat{pr}$ transformed by NTT with pr. Concatenation of $\widehat{pr}^{\mathrm{tp}(\lambda)}$ with $\widehat{pr}^{\mathrm{bt}(\lambda)}$ to construct $\widehat{pr}$ is denoted by $\widehat{pr} := \widehat{pr}^{\mathrm{tp}(\lambda)} || \widehat{pr}^{\mathrm{bt}(\lambda)}$. Similarly, $\widehat{pr}^{\mathrm{bt}(\lambda)} := \mathrm{NTT}^{\mathrm{bt}(\lambda)}(pr)$ is defined on $pr^{\mathrm{bt}(\lambda)}$.

The main difference from Algorithm 1 is written in red colors. λ vectors for (s_1, s_2, t_0) are stored in stack memory in accordance with the intermediate parameter λ, and the remaining vectors are dynamically computed to reconstruct (the NTT form of) (s_1, s_2, t_0). This algorithm can potentially improve the computation time compared with the implementation by Greconici et al.: the computation time of $\mathrm{NTT}^{\mathrm{tp}(\lambda)}(pr)$ is estimated as λ/k times of $\mathrm{NTT}(pr)$ because the number of iterations in the loop process is λ/k. We note that theoretical security, i.e., correctness and unforgeability, can be proven because the above differences are not processing any secret data as public. For the details, we refer to the original security proof [3].

Algorithm 2. Proposed Algorithm of Signature Generation

Require: secret key $sk = (\rho, K, tr, s_1, s_2, t_0)$; message $M \in \{0,1\}^*$
Ensure: signature $\sigma = (z, h, c)$
1: Set λ $(0 <= \lambda <= min(k, \ell))$
2: $\hat{A} \in R_q^{k\times\ell}$:= ExpandA(ρ); $\mu := H(tr\|M)$; $\kappa := 0$; $(z,h) := \perp$; $\rho' := H(K\|\mu)$; $\hat{s}_1^{\mathrm{tp}(\lambda)} := \mathrm{NTT}^{\mathrm{tp}(\lambda)}(s_1)$; $\hat{s}_2^{\mathrm{tp}(\lambda)} := \mathrm{NTT}^{\mathrm{tp}(\lambda)}(s_2)$; $\hat{t}_0^{\mathrm{tp}(\lambda)} := \mathrm{NTT}^{\mathrm{tp}(\lambda)}(t_0)$
3: **while** $(z,h) = \perp$ **do**
4: $\quad y \in S_{\gamma_1-1}^{\ell}$:= ExpandMask(ρ', κ)
5: $\quad w := \mathrm{NTT}^{-1}(\hat{A} \circ \mathrm{NTT}(y))$
6: $\quad w_1 :=$ HighBits(w)
7: $\quad \hat{c} := \mathrm{NTT}(H_B(\mu\|w_1))$
8: $\quad \hat{s}_1^{\mathrm{bt}(\lambda)} := \mathrm{NTT}^{\mathrm{bt}(\lambda)}(s_1)$
9: $\quad \hat{s}_1 := \hat{s}_1^{\mathrm{tp}(\lambda)}\|\hat{s}_1^{\mathrm{bt}(\lambda)}$
10: $\quad z := y + \mathrm{NTT}^{-1}(\hat{c} \circ \hat{s}_1)$
11: $\quad \hat{s}_2^{\mathrm{bt}(\lambda)} := \mathrm{NTT}^{\mathrm{bt}(\lambda)}(s_2)$
12: $\quad \hat{s}_2 := \hat{s}_2^{\mathrm{tp}(\lambda)}\|\hat{s}_2^{\mathrm{bt}(\lambda)}$
13: $\quad (r_1, r_0) :=$ Decompose$(w - \mathrm{NTT}^{-1}(\hat{c} \circ \hat{s}_2))$
14: $\quad$ **if** $\|z\|_\infty \geq \gamma_1 - \beta$ or $\|r_0\|_\infty \geq \gamma_2 - \beta$ or $r_1 \neq w_1$ **then**
15: $\quad\quad (z,h) := \perp$
16: $\quad$ **else**
17: $\quad\quad \hat{t}_0^{\mathrm{bt}(\lambda)} := \mathrm{NTT}^{\mathrm{bt}(\lambda)}(t_0)$; $\hat{s}_2^{\mathrm{bt}(\lambda)} := \mathrm{NTT}^{\mathrm{bt}(\lambda)}(s_2)$;
18: $\quad\quad \hat{t}_0 := \hat{t}_0^{\mathrm{tp}(\lambda)}\|\hat{t}_0^{\mathrm{bt}(\lambda)}$; $\hat{s}_2 := \hat{s}_2^{\mathrm{tp}(\lambda)}\|\hat{s}_2^{\mathrm{bt}(\lambda)}$;
19: $\quad\quad h :=$ MakeHint$(-\mathrm{NTT}^{-1}(\hat{c} \circ \hat{t}_0), w - \mathrm{NTT}^{-1}(\hat{c} \circ \hat{s}_2) + \mathrm{NTT}^{-1}(\hat{c} \circ \hat{t}_0))$
20: $\quad\quad \hat{t}_0^{\mathrm{bt}(\lambda)} := \mathrm{NTT}^{\mathrm{bt}(\lambda)}(t_0)$
21: $\quad\quad \hat{t}_0 := \hat{t}_0^{\mathrm{tp}(\lambda)}\|\hat{t}_0^{\mathrm{bt}(\lambda)}$
22: $\quad\quad$ **if** $\|\mathrm{NTT}^{-1}(\hat{c} \circ \hat{t}_0)\|_\infty \geq \gamma_2$ or #1's in $h > \omega$ **then**
23: $\quad\quad\quad (z,h) := \perp$
24: $\quad\quad$ **end if**
25: $\quad$ **end if**
26: **end while**

4.3 Instantiations

The algorithm presented in the previous subsection can provide an instantiation for any motivation by specifying λ. Specifically, the proposed method enables us to store either k-element vectors, ℓ-element vectors, or both in stack memory. The following instantiations inherit the trade-off of Greconiti et al. through specifying λ.

Instantiation 1: $\ell 2k1$-method This instantiation computes ℓ-element vectors dynamically and stores all of the k-element vectors in stack memory. In other words, the ℓ-element vectors are computed based on strategy 2, and the k-element vectors are computed based on strategy 1. Therefore, we will refer to this instantiation as the $\ell 2k1$-method. In this method, to compute (r_1, r_0) and h at Line 13 and Line 19 in Algorithm 2, respectively, $\hat{s}_2$ is stored at Line 1 and loaded from stack memory at Lines 11–12 and Lines 17–18 in Algorithm 2 instead of computing them. On the other hand, $\hat{s}_1$ is always computed for z, i.e., at Lines 8–9 in Algorithm 2. The detail of the algorithm is shown in Algorithm 5 in Appendix.

Instantiation 2: $k2\ell1$-method This instantiation computes k-element vectors dynamically and stores all of the ℓ-element vectors in stack memory. In other words, the k-element vectors are computed based on strategy 2, and the ℓ-element vectors are computed based on strategy 1. Therefore, we will refer to this instantiation as the $k2\ell1$-method. In contrast to the previous instantiation, to compute z at Line 10 in Algorithm 2, $\hat{s}_1$ is stored at Line 1 and loaded from stack memory at Lines 8–9 instead of computing it. On the other hand, $\hat{s}_2$ is always computed for (r_1, r_0) and h, i.e., at Line 13 and Line 19 in Algorithm 2. The detail of the algorithm is shown in Algorithm 6 in Appendix.

Instantiation 3: λ-method This instantiation deals with k-element vectors and ℓ-element vectors in a common fashion. It means a straightforward usage of Algorithm 2. Based on the intermediate parameter λ $(0 \leq \lambda \leq \min(k, \ell))$, this instantiation stores vectors from zeroth to λ-th in stack memory and computes the remaining $(k - \lambda)$ vectors and $(\ell - \lambda)$ vectors dynamically.

5 Experiment and Discussion

In this section, we evaluate the computation time and the stack size of the proposed method through experiments with the instantiations in Sect. 4.3. We then discuss several standpoints, including the trade-off between the computation time and the stack size, of the proposed method. This section corresponds to the third contribution.

5.1 Experimental Purpose and Environment

Our primary purpose for this experiment is to shed light on the trade-off through the proposed method. Namely, we aim to identify whether the trade-off between the computation time and the stack size is consistently linear rather than outperforming the implementation by Greconici et al. in comparison with the proposed method itself.

We built the source code of the proposed method on an EFR32MG24 module with ARM Cortex-M33 CPU, i.e., the same environment in Sect. 3. (See Appendix D for the implementation.) We recall that the EFR32MG24 module used in this paper has up to 1536kB of flash memory and 256kB of RAM, and is run with 78.0 MHz. The compilation options are `-g3 -gdwarf-2 -mcpu=cortex-m33 -mthumb -std=c99 -O2 -Wall -mcmse -c -fmessage-length=0`. We utilize $\lambda = 1$ and $\lambda = 2$ for Instantiation 3 as typical numbers. Hereafter, we denote the instantiations by $\ell2k1$-method, $k2\ell1$-method, λ-method ($\lambda = 1$), and λ-method ($\lambda = 2$) for the sake of convenience.

5.2 Experimental Results

The results for the computation time and the stack size are shown in Figs. 2b- 2e, respectively. We also compare these results with the strategies by Greconici et al. [10].

$\ell2k1$-Method. According to Fig. 2a, the most frequent computation time is about 50 msec with 17% frequency, and these results are close to Strategy 1 shown in Fig. 1a.

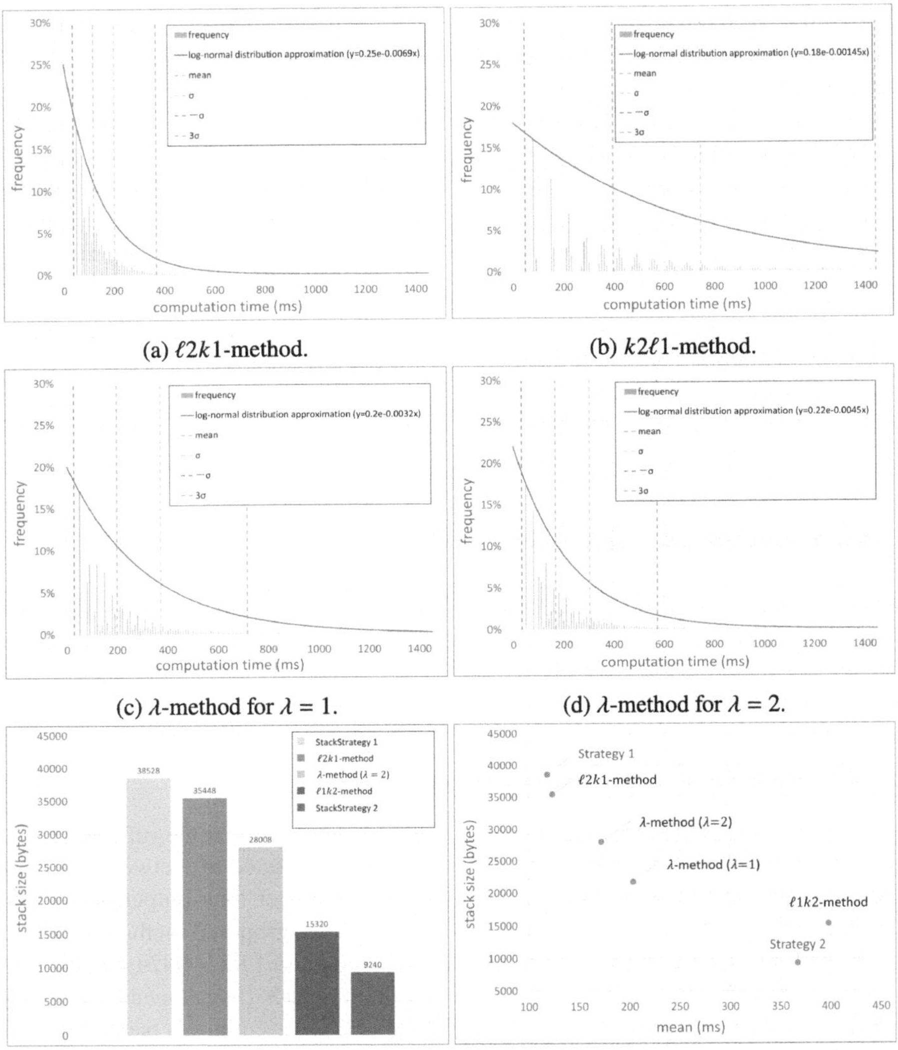

(a) $\ell 2k1$-method.

(b) $k2\ell 1$-method.

(c) λ-method for $\lambda = 1$.

(d) λ-method for $\lambda = 2$.

(e) Stack size.

(f) Trade-off.

Fig. 2. The results for each instantiation. Figures 2b-2d represent the distribution of the computation time by each instantiation presented in Sect. 4.3, where the setting is common with Fig. 1. Figure 2e represents the stack size, where the setting is common with Fig. 1c. Figure 2f represents the trade-off, i.e., the horizontal axis represents the mean of the computation time, and the vertical axis represents the stack size.

The mean of the computation time for $\ell 2k1$-method is 123 msec with variance $\sigma = 82$ while that for Strategy 1 is 118 msec with variance $\sigma = 76$. Meanwhile, according to Fig. 2e, the stack size of $\ell 2k1$-method is 3KiB-smaller than Strategy 1. The ratio of the computation time is about 3.2 while that of the stack size is about 4.18. We recall that the ratios between Strategy 1 and Strategy 2 are 3.11 for the computation time and 4.18 for the stack size as shown in Sect. 3.1. It means that the trade-off between the computation time and the stack size is monotonic but slightly different from a typical linear form.

$k2\ell1$-Method According to Fig. 2b, the most frequent computation time is about 80 msec with 16% frequency, and these results are close to Strategy 2 shown in Fig. 1b. The mean of the computation time for $k2\ell1$-method is 397 msec with variance $\sigma = 350$, while that for Strategy 2 is 367 msec with variance $\sigma = 320$. According to Fig. 2e, the stack size of $k2\ell1$-method is 3KiB larger than Strategy 2. Unexpectedly, the computation time and the stack size deteriorate compared with Strategy 2, which means non-linear for the trade-off. It is considered that a small stack size by Strategy 2 improves the computation time because of reducing the memory access.

λ-Method We suppose $\lambda = 1$ and $\lambda = 2$ in this instantiation as described above. According to Figs. 2c-2d, the most frequent computation time is about 50 msec with 17% frequency for both $\lambda = 1$ and $\lambda = 2$. The mean of the computation time for $\lambda = 1$ is 203 msec with variance $\sigma = 171$ while that for $\lambda = 2$ is 172 msec with variance $\sigma = 135$. According to Fig. 2e, the stack size is 21.7 KiB for $\lambda = 1$ and 28.0 KiB for $\lambda = 2$.

Impact of λ The results described above mean that the stack size is improved while the computation time deteriorates in proportion to the value of λ. Interestingly, the trade-off for $\lambda = 1$ to $k2\ell1$ is better than that for $\lambda = 2$ to $\lambda = 1$: reducing 6.3 KiB for the stack size from $\lambda = 2$ to $\lambda = 1$ increases only 32 msec for the computation time, while reducing 6.4 KiB from $\lambda = 1$ to $k2\ell1$ increases 194 msec. It also means that increasing λ is potentially effective for improving the trade-off if the value of λ is small.

5.3 Discussion

We discuss the proposed method in terms of the analysis of the trade-off, the possibility of side-channel attacks, and the compatibility of the proposed method with the existing implementation techniques.

Analysis of Trade-Off. Based on the results in the previous subsection, we discuss the trade-off between computation time and stack size. We summarize the results of the trade-off in Fig. 2f and then confirm that the trade-off is non-linear. More specifically, we identify two key insights described below.

First, we believe that reducing the stack size potentially contributes to the computation time as long as the computation time is small. The trade-off is different for each instantiation according to Fig. 2f. Remarkably, $k2\ell1$-method deteriorates worse than Strategy 2 with respect to both computation time and stack size. It is considered that this phenomenon is caused by memory access, and consequently, minimizing the stack size is beneficial for resource-constrained devices such as IoT.

Second, it is considered that storing k-element vectors is better than ℓ-element vectors in order to improve the entire performance. The value of (k, ℓ) for Dilithium2 is $(4, 4)$ according to the current NIST security level (as shown in Appendix), and hence,

$\ell 2k1$-method and $k2\ell 1$-method store four vectors in stack memory, respectively. However, the computation time of $\ell 2k1$-method is quite shorter than $k2\ell 1$-method. Although the stack size of $k2\ell 1$-method is smaller than $\ell 2k1$-method, an improvement of the stack size is rather limited compared with the increase of the computation time in spite of storing the same number of vectors.

According to Fig. 2f, there is a difference in the trade-off behavior between $\ell 2k1$-method and $k2\ell 1$-method. It is considered that this arises due to the difference in stack usage between the intermediate parameters of the k-element vectors and the ℓ-element vectors. As shown in Fig. 2f, the trade-off for $\ell 2k1$-method is similar to that of Strategy 1. The difference between Strategy 1 and $\ell 2k1$-method lies in the handling of the intermediate parameters of the ℓ-element vectors, which are processed as Strategy 2. Therefore, $\ell 2k1$-method uses slightly less stack than Strategy 1, and this difference can be attributed to the fact that the ℓ-element vectors are not stored in the stack. On the other hand, the trade-off for $k2\ell 1$-method is similar to that of Strategy 2. The difference between the algorithms of Strategy 2 and $k2\ell 1$-method also lies in how the ℓ-element vectors are handled; they are processed as Strategy 1, meaning they are computed once and then stored in the stack. Consequently, $k2\ell 1$-method uses slightly more stack than Strategy 2, and this difference can be attributed to the fact that the ℓ-element vectors are stored in the stack. From above discussion and the difference in stack usage between Strategy 1 and Strategy 2, it can be concluded that the stack usage of the k-element vectors is larger than that of ℓ-element vectors.

Compatibility with Existing Techniques. The proposed method is a generalization of CRYSTALS-Dilithium with respect to the trade-off between the computation time and the stack size, and hence, it has compatibility with the existing implementation techniques [8,25]. For instance, Bos et al. [8] and Zheng et al. [25] proposed implementation with a small stack size. Their techniques are similar: compressing the size of polynomials for optimization and designing their multiplication, including a new NTT.

The proposed method assumes multiplication and NTT as a black box, and therefore, the above techniques are applicable to the proposed method. In particular, w, $\hat{c} \circ \hat{t}_0$, and $c \circ \hat{s}_2$ are compressed. According to Bos et al., their technique can make the stack size one-order of magnitude smaller compared with the implementation by Greconici et al. Thus, we will obtain a superior performance for both computation time and stack size than our current result. Evaluating the performance by combining the proposed method with the above existing works is an future research topic.

6 Conclusion

In this paper, we investigated the trade-off between the computation time and the stack size for an implementation of the signing algorithm of CRYSTALS-Dilithium on IoT devices. Our contributions are threefold. We first conducted systematic evaluations of the two strategies by Greconici et al. [10] and then identified a clear trade-off, which implies a new question. Second, we proposed an implementation method that parameterizes the trade-off between computation time and stack size for CRYSTALS-Dilithium. Finally, we demonstrated that the trade-off is non-linear through experiments with the proposed method on a hardware board with ARM Cortex-M33 CPU: possibly reducing the stack size is potentially able to improve the computation time. Further studies, which take a combination of the proposed method with the existing techniques for a small stack size [8,25] into account, will need to be undertaken. We are also in the process of investigating side-channel attacks based on intermediate variables [7,17,21] and hardware acceleration [19,22].

A Algorithms of CRYSTALS-Dilithium

The key generation algorithm and the verification algorithm of CRYSTALS-Dilithium are described in Algorithm 3 and Algorithm 4, respectively.

Algorithm 3. Key Generation

Ensure: secret key $sk = (\rho, K, tr, s_1, s_2, t_0)$; public key $pk = (\rho, t_1)$

$\rho \leftarrow \{0,1\}^{256}$; $K \leftarrow \{0,1\}^{256}$, $(s_1, s_2) \leftarrow S_\eta^\ell \times S_\eta^k$

$\hat{A} \in R_q^{k\times\ell} := \text{ExpandA}(\rho)$

$t := \text{NTT}^{-1}(\hat{A} \circ \text{NTT}(s_1)) + s_2$

$(t_1, t_0) := \text{Power2Round}(t)$

$tr \in \{0,1\}^{384} := H(\rho || t_1)$

Algorithm 4. Verification

Require: public key $pk = (\rho, t_1)$; message $M \in \{0,1\}^*$; signature $\sigma = (z, h, c)$

Ensure: Valid or Invalid

$\hat{A} \in \mathbb{R}_q^{k\times\ell} := \text{ExpandA}(\rho)$; $\mu \in \{0,1\}^{384} := H(H(\rho||t_1)||M)$

$w_1' := \text{UseHint}(h, \text{NTT}^{-1}(\hat{A} \circ \text{NTT}(z) - \text{NTT}(c) \circ \text{NTT}(2^d \cdot t_1)))$

if $c = H_B(\mu || w_1')$ and $||z||_\infty < \gamma_1 - \beta$ and $\#1$'s in $h \leq \omega$ **then**

    return Valid

else

    return Invalid

end if

B Parameters of CRYSTALS-Dilithium

The security parameters of CRYSTALS-Dilithium for each NIST security level are shown in Table 1. To align with the experiments in [10], we use the parameters on the second round submission [9] because the original work of Greconici et al. [10] have utilized them. We note that our method is also applicable to the parameters for Round 3 [3] and FIPS-204 [23].

Table 1. Parameters

	Level 2	Level 3	Level 4
(k, ℓ)	$(4, 3)$	$(5, 4)$	$(6, 5)$
d	14	14	14
$\gamma_1 = (q-1)/16$	523776	523776	523776
$\gamma_2 = \gamma_1/2$	261888	261888	261888
η	6	5	3
β	325	275	175
ω	80	96	120

C Algorithm Details of Other Instantiations

The details of the instantiations proposed in Sect. 4.3 are shown in Algorithm 5 and Algorithm 6.

Algorithm 5. Signature Generation by $\ell 2k1$-method

Require: Secret Key: $sk = (\rho, K, tr, s_1, s_2, t_0)$
Require: Message: $M \in \{0,1\}^*$
Ensure: Signature: $\sigma = (z, h, c)$
$\hat{A} \in R_q^{k \times \ell} :=$ ExpandA(ρ)
$\mu \in \{0,1\}^{384} := H(tr \| M)$
$\kappa := 0; (z, h) := \perp$
$\rho' \in \{0,1\}^{384} := H(K \| \mu)$
$\hat{s}_2 :=$ NTT(s_2); $\hat{t}_0 :=$ NTT(t_0)
while $(z, h) = \perp$ **do**
  $y \in S_{\gamma_1 - 1}^{\ell} :=$ ExpandMask(ρ', κ)
  $w := \mathrm{NTT}^{-1}(\hat{A} \circ \mathrm{NTT}(y))$
  $w_1 :=$ HighBits(w)
  $\hat{c} := \mathrm{NTT}(H_B(\mu \| w_1))$
  $(r_1, r_0) :=$ Decompose$(w - \mathrm{NTT}^{-1}(\hat{c} \circ \hat{s}_2))$
  $\hat{s}_1 := \mathrm{NTT}(s_1)$
  $z := y + \mathrm{NTT}^{-1}(\hat{c} \circ \hat{s}_1)$
  if $\|z\|_\infty \geq \gamma_1 - \beta$ or $|r_0\|_\infty \geq \gamma_2 - \beta$ or $r_1 \neq w_1$ **then**
    $(z, h) := \perp$
  else
    $h :=$ MakeHint$(-\mathrm{NTT}^{-1}(\hat{c} \circ \hat{t}_0), w - \mathrm{NTT}^{-1}(\hat{c} \circ \hat{s}_2) + \mathrm{NTT}^{-1}(\hat{c} \circ \hat{t}_0))$
    if $\|\mathrm{NTT}^{-1}(\hat{c} \circ \hat{t}_0)\|_\infty \geq \gamma_2$ or #1's in $h > \omega$ **then**
      $(z, h) := \perp$
    end if
  end if
end while

D Implementation

In this section, we describe implementations for the instantiations of the proposed methods. The implementations are based on the public source code by Greconici et al.: github.com/dilithium-cortexm/dilithium-cortexm. We briefly describe the change from the public source code for each instantiation below.

Instantiation 1: $\ell 2k1$-method The computation for s_1 is based on Strategy 2, and the computation for s_2 and t_0 is based on Strategy 1, respectively. Then, `unpack_sk()` is performed for only s_2 and t_0. For the computation related to s_1, its operations are performed within the `for` loop process following the comment "`Compute z`": `unpack_sk_s1()` and `poly_ntt()`. For the computation related to s_2, within the `for` loop process following the comment "`Check that subtracting cs2`", the operation `poly_pointwise_montgomery (&tmp, &c, &s2.vec[i])` is performed. Also, the same process is performed within the `for` loop process following the comment "`Compute hints for w1`" for t_0.

Instantiation 2: $k2\ell 1$-method The computation for s_1 is based on Strategy 1, and the computation for s_2 and t_0 is based on Strategy 2. Then, `unpack_sk()`

Algorithm 6. Signature Generation by $k2\ell 1$-method

Require: Secret Key: $sk = (\rho, K, tr, s_1, s_2, t_0)$
Require: Message: $M \in \{0,1\}^*$
Ensure: Signature: $\sigma = (z, h, c)$
$\hat{A} \in R_q^{k \times \ell} :=$ ExpandA(ρ)
$\mu \in \{0,1\}^{384} := H(tr \| M)$
$\kappa := 0; (z, h) := \perp$
$\rho' \in \{0,1\}^{384} := H(K \| \mu)$
$\hat{s}_1 := \mathrm{NTT}(s_1)$
while $(z, h) = \perp$ **do**
  $y \in S_{\gamma_1 - 1}^{\ell} :=$ ExpandMask(ρ', κ)
  $w := \mathrm{NTT}^{-1}(\hat{A} \circ \mathrm{NTT}(y))$
  $w_1 :=$ HighBits(w)
  $\hat{c} := \mathrm{NTT}(H_B(\mu \| w_1))$
  $z := y + \mathrm{NTT}^{-1}(\hat{c} \circ \hat{s}_1)$
  $\hat{s}_2 := \mathrm{NTT}(s_2)$
  $(r_1, r_0) :=$ Decompose$(w - \mathrm{NTT}^{-1}(\hat{c} \circ \hat{s}_2))$
  if $\|z\|_\infty \geq \gamma_1 - \beta$ or $\|r_0\|_\infty \geq \gamma_2 - \beta$ or $r_1 \neq w_1$ **then**
    $(z, h) := \perp$
  else
    $\hat{t}_0 := \mathrm{NTT}(t_0); \hat{s}_2 := \mathrm{NTT}(s_2)$
    $h :=$ MakeHint$(-\mathrm{NTT}^{-1}(\hat{c} \circ \hat{t}_0), w - \mathrm{NTT}^{-1}(\hat{c} \circ \hat{s}_2) + \mathrm{NTT}^{-1}(\hat{c} \circ \hat{t}_0))$
    $\hat{t}_0 := \mathrm{NTT}(t_0)$
    if $\|\mathrm{NTT}^{-1}(\hat{c} \circ \hat{t}_0)\|_\infty \geq \gamma_2$ or #1's in $h > \omega$ **then**
      $(z, h) := \perp$
    end if
  end if
end while

is only performed for s_1. As s_1 is stored in stack memory, the operations `poly_pointwise_montgomery (&z_elem, &c, &s1.vec[i])` and `poly_invntt_tomont(&z_elem);` are performed for the computation of z. For the computation related to s_2 and t_0, within the `for` loop following the comment "`Check that subtracting cs2`," the operations `unpack_sk_ s2()` and `poly_ntt()` are performed. Also, the same process is performed within the `for` loop following the comment "`Compute hints for w1`" for t_0.

Instantiation 3: λ-method First, `w1[K]` is changed to `w1[lmd]`, and new types `polyvect_lmd` and `polyvect_lmd_2` are defined. The type `polyvect_lmd` is a variable whose number of operations for Strategy 1 is determined by λ, and s_1 is defined with this type. Similarly `polyvect_lmd_2` is a variable whose number of operations for Strategy 2 is determined by λ, and w is defined with this type. Then, `expand_lmd_mat` and `polyvect_lmd_ntt` are newly created to replace the loop process in the function within `unpack_sk` with λ iterations.

References

1. Avanzi, R., et al.: Crystals-Kyber, NIST, Technical report (2017). https://csrc.nist.rip/CSRC/media/Presentations/crystals-kyber-round-2-presentation/images-media/crystals-kyber-schwabe.pdf
2. Aydin, F., et al.: Horizontal side-channel vulnerabilities of post-quantum key exchange and encapsulation protocols. ACM Trans. Embed. Comput. Syst. **20**(6), 110:1-110:22 (2021). https://doi.org/10.1145/3476799
3. Bai, S., et al.: CRYSTALS-Dilithium algorithm specifications and supporting documentation (Version 3.1) (2021). https://pq-crystals.org/dilithium/data/dilithium-specification-round3-20210208.pdf
4. Baseri, Y., Chouhan, V., Ghorbani, A.A.: Cybersecurity in the quantum era: assessing the impact of quantum computing on infrastructure. arXiv preprint arXiv:2404.10659 (2024)
5. Beckwith, L., Abdulgadir, A., Azarderakhsh, R.: A flexible shared hardware accelerator for NIST-recommended algorithms CRYSTALS-Kyber and CRYSTALS-Dilithium with SCA protection. In: Rosulek, M. (ed.) Topics in Cryptology – CT-RSA 2023: Cryptographers' Track at the RSA Conference 2023, San Francisco, CA, USA, April 24–27, 2023, Proceedings, pp. 469–490. Springer, Cham (2023). https://doi.org/10.1007/978-3-031-30872-7_18
6. Beckwith, L., Nguyen, D.T., Gaj, K.: High-performance hardware implementation of CRYSTALS-Dilithium. In: International Conference on Field-Programmable Technology, (IC)FPT 2021, Auckland, New Zealand, December 6-10, 2021, pp. 1–10. IEEE (2021). https://doi.org/10.1109/ICFPT52863.2021.9609917
7. Berzati, A., et al.: Exploiting intermediate value leakage in Dilithium: a template-based approach. IACR Trans. Cryptogr. Hardw. Embed. Syst. **4**, 188–210 (2023). https://doi.org/10.46586/TCHES.V2023.I4.188-210
8. Bos, J.W., Renes, J., Sprenkels, A.: Dilithium for memory constrained devices. In: Batina, L., Daemen, J. (eds) Progress in Cryptology - AFRICACRYPT 2022. AFRICACRYPT 2022. LNCS, vol 13503. Springer, Cham (2022). https://doi.org/10.1007/978-3-031-17433-9_10
9. Ducas, L., et al.: CRYSTALS-Dilithium algorithm specifications and supporting documentation (part of the round 2 submission package) (2019). https://pq-crystals.org/dilithium/data/dilithium-specification-round2.pdf

10. Greconici, D.O.C., Kannwischer, M.J., Sprenkels, A.: Compact Dilithium implementations on Cortex-M3 and Cortex-M4. In: IACR Transactions on Cryptographic Hardware and Embedded Systems, pp. 1–24 (2021). https://doi.org/10.46586/TCHES.V2021.I1.1-24
11. Gupta, N., et al.: Lightweight hardware accelerator for post-quantum digital signature CRYSTALS-Dilithium. IEEE Trans. Cir. Syst. I Regul. Pap. **70**(8), 3234–3243 (2023). https://doi.org/10.1109/TCSI.2023.3274599
12. Kannwischer, M.J., et al.: Improving software quality in cryptography standardization projects. In: 2022 IEEE European Symposium on Security and Privacy Workshops (EuroS&PW), pp. 19–30 (2022). https://doi.org/10.1109/EuroSPW55150.2022.00010
13. Land, G., Sasdrich, P., Güneysu, T.A.: Hard crystal - implementing Dilithium on reconfigurable hardware. In: Grosso, V., Pöppelmann, T. (eds.) Smart Card Research and Advanced Applications. CARDIS 2021. LNCS, vol 13173. Springer, Cham (2021). https://doi.org/10.1007/978-3-030-97348-3_12
14. Li, L., et al.: Compact instruction set extensions for Dilithium. ACM Trans. Embed. Comput. Syst. **23**(2), 23:1–23:21 (2024). https://doi.org/10.1145/3643826
15. Lorenser, T.: The DSP capabilities of ARM Cortex-M4 and Cortex-M7 processors. ARM White Pap. **29**, 1–19 (2016)
16. Mao, G., et al.: High-performance and configurable SW/HW Co-design of post-quantum signature CRYSTALS-Dilithium. ACM Trans. Reconfigurable Technol. Syst. **16**(3) (2023). https://doi.org/10.1145/3569456
17. Marzougui, S., et al.: Profiling side-channel attacks on Dilithium: a small bit-fiddling leak breaks it all. Cryptology ePrint Archive, Paper 2022/106 (2022). https://eprint.iacr.org/2022/106
18. Nguyen, T.-H., et al.: High-speed NTT accelerator for CRYSTAL-Kyber and CRYSTAL-Dilithium. IEEE Access **12**, 34918–34930 (2024). https://doi.org/10.1109/ACCESS.2024.3371581
19. Pham, T.X., Duong-Ngoc, P., Lee, H.: An efficient unified polynomial arithmetic unit for CRYSTALS-Dilithium. IEEE Trans. Cir. Syst. I Regular Pap. **70**(12), 4854–4864 (2023). https://doi.org/10.1109/TCSI.2023.3316393
20. PQC Standardization Process: Announcing four candidates to be standardized, plus fourth round candidates (2022). https://csrc.nist.gov/News/2022/pqccandidates-to-be-standardized-and-round-4
21. Qiao, Z., et al.: Practical public template attack attacks on CRYSTALS Dilithium with randomness leakages. IEEE Trans. Inf. Forensics Secur. **18**, 1–14 (2023). https://doi.org/10.1109/TIFS.2022.3215913
22. Ricci, S., et al.: Implementing CRYSTALS-Dilithium signature scheme on FPGAs. In: Reinhardt, D., Müller, T. (eds.) ARES 2021: The 16th International Conference on Availability, Reliability and Security, Vienna, Austria, August 17-20, 021, pp. 1:1–1:11. ACM (2021). https://doi.org/10.1145/3465481.3465756
23. National Institute of Standards and Technology: Module-lattice-based digital signature standard, Technical report, Federal Information Processing Standards Publications (FIPS PUBS) 204. Washington, D.C., U.S. Department of Commerce (2024). https://doi.org/10.6028/NIST.FIPS.204
24. Zhao, C., et al.: A compact and high-performance hardware architecture for CRYSTALS-Dilithium. IACR Trans. Cryptogr. Hardw. Embed. Syst. **2022**(1), 270–295 (2022). https://doi.org/10.46586/TCHES.V2022.I1.270-295 https://doi.org/10.46586/TCHES.V2022.I1.270-295
25. Zheng, J., et al.: Parallel small polynomial multiplication for Dilithium: a faster design and implementation. In: Annual Computer Security Applications Conference, ACSAC 2022, Austin, TX, USA, December 5-9, 2022, pp. 304–317. ACM (2022). https://doi.org/10.1145/3564625.3564629

26. Zhou, Z., et al.: A software/hardware co-design of Crystals-Dilithium signature scheme. ACM Trans. Reconfigurable Technol. Syst. **14**(2), 11:1–11:21 (2021). https://doi.org/10.1145/3447812

QUICPot. A HTTP/3 Protocol Honeypot

Maria Teodor[1], Bogdan-Costel Mocanu[1(✉)], Cătălin Negru[1], and Florin Pop[1,2,3]

[1] National University of Science and Technology Politehnica, Bucharest, Romania
maria.teodor@stud.acs.upb.ro,
{bogdan_costel.mocanu,catalin.negru,florin.pop}@upb.ro
[2] National Institute for Research and Development in Informatics - ICI Bucharest, Bucharest, Romania
florin.pop@ici.ro
[3] Academy of Romanian Scientists, Bucharest, Romania

Abstract. A valuable resource in the field of cybersecurity, honeypots could be described as reverse phishing tools, referring to servers that are used as decoys, seemingly vulnerable, with the hope that, in the event of their discovery by an attacker, their exploitation can yield important information concerning the methods employed by the hacker and their identity. Seeing as they are built with this purpose, they can be hardened against several attacks to ensure that no valuable data falls into the wrong hands. Their value can also be in finding unknown vulnerabilities for new technologies by analyzing the attacker's patterns. Developed by Google, QUIC is a novel protocol that lays on top of UDP, employing TLS to encrypt data, and is the base for HTTP/3, a new, improved version of one of the most widely used protocols on the internet. Therefore, in this paper, we propose QUICPot, a novel Honeypot solution for QUIC protocol. We design and implement a honeypot server that implements QUIC protocol for vulnerability identification and evaluate the performance of the proposed solution using Pytest.

Keywords: Honeypot · QUIC · Cybersecurity · HTTP3 · Security

1 Introduction

Honeypots, in the context of cybersecurity, are tools that serve to lure attackers in order to analyze their behavior. They are helpful in gaining an insight into their objectives and tactics, and provide them with false opportunities to monitor their behavior through detailed logging. They can even be systems put in place to alert system administrators of possible security breaches. In a world that relies progressively more on the internet and digital technologies, the field of cybersecurity is forced to evolve as fast, hopefully even faster, as the threats attackers pose, to protect sensitive data and ensure access to the systems the world has become dependent on. This type of tools demand constant innovation and improvements in the current technologies used. By analysing real-world

L. Morogan et al. (Eds.): SecITC 2024, LNCS 15595, pp. 207–222, 2025.
https://doi.org/10.1007/978-3-031-87760-5_15

cyber-attack data, honeypots are beneficial for the development and improvement of defensive mechanisms, and validation of complex intrusion detection systems.

Even though, honeypots seems to be on the best deceptive solution, the face numerous limitations. They are passive by nature and rely on attackers' initiative to engage. Therefore, If they are not properly configured, they can become a liability, and can be exploited for launching further attacks.

QUIC [6] (Quick UDP Internet Connections) was developed, as the name suggests, over UDP [13], making possible the innovation of HTTP/3 [2], a protocol already in use throughout the Internet. It combines the benefits of UDP with TCP features, such as connection-oriented communication and congestion control. The main advantage of this protocol is the fact that it incorporating TLS for encryption making it a secure protocol. Other benefits of this protocol are: (i) reduced latency, resulting in faster connection establishment; (ii) high performances over unreliable networks. As a improvement over the HTTP/2 [18] protocol over TCP [12], QUIC use a multiplexing approach that prevents head-of-line blocking. A potential downside of this protocol refers to its encrypted headers that might lead to difficulties for traditional traffic analysis tools and intrusion detection systems.

To understand an HTTP/3 honeypot server, further knowledge pertaining QUIC is required. It is described as the next-generation multiplexed transport over UDP.

To better grasp the benefits of UDP over TCP, a short comparison of the two is necessary. TCP is a reliable connection-oriented protocol that ensures all packets are delivered in the same order as they were sent and requires retransmission in case of packet loss. Its main advantage is that it ensures data is sent in its entirety, but this feature comes at a cost, with its overhead and latency being very high due to the need to establish a connection. Meanwhile, UDP is connection-less, and it offers no guarantees as to packet reception or order, being more suitable for applications where a few undelivered packets are acceptable, such as video calls. However, the overhead is brought to a minimum, and latency is reduced due to no connection setup being needed. Therefore, both protocols have their benefits, the choice between the two being based on the application's requirements.

As websites progressed to have less static content, the need for a faster HTTP arose. The second version of the protocol, based on the experimental SPDY [16] [10], was already a significant step forward, introducing the concept of multiplexing, the possibility of multiple requests and responses being sent over a single TCP connection simultaneously, as well as the concept of server pushes, which refers to the server now being able to send resources to the client proactively, before the client requests them. It also switched to a binary protocol, which proved to be more efficient than the text-based HTTP/1.x, and it allowed persistent connections, reusing the same connection for multiple requests or responses, in addition to the concept of stream prioritization, where clients can assign a higher importance level to the resources that must be loaded first. All of these led to the success of the second version of the protocol, its adoption reducing latency considerably. However, there were still several causes for latency that could not have been resolved as long as the protocol was on top of TCP. The main issue among these is head-of-line blocking, referring to the fact that, although HTTP/2 multiplexes its streams over one connection, if any TCP packet gets lost, then all subsequent packets must wait for it to be retransmitted, which causes considerable delays. Because usually only one connection is used, if this connection were to experience congestion or packet loss, all streams that use it would experience considerable latency. Another disadvantage is that network changes can cause reduced performance, requiring establishing a new connection and involving a handshake process once again.

Considering the above limitations, designing a honeypot solution for tailored for the QUIC protocol is an unique challenge [11] that involves considerable research and innovation. Such a tools must emulate QUIC's behavior convincingly, including its connection establishment, multiplexing, and encryption to attract and engage potential attackers of modern HTTP/3 [2] applications.

However, implementing such a honeypot involves overcoming technical hurdles, including handling encrypted headers and accurately simulating protocol behavior. Furthermore, ethical considerations must be addressed when capturing and analyzing encrypted traffic. Despite these challenges, a QUIC-focused honeypot could significantly advance research on securing next-generation internet protocols.

Due to its low latency, encryption, and connection efficiency, QUIC protocol is a an attractive solution for IoT systems [8]. Unfortunately, the same features that make QUIC a desired approach makes it make vulnerable to in botnet operations, where attackers exploit IoT devices to establish resilient and covert command-and-control (C2) channels [1]. This type of attacks can be mitigated using honeypots.

Therefore, the objective of this paper is to propose and validate a novel custom honeypot for QUIC protocol, that lures attackers and captures their behavior in order to provide actionable intelligence and enhance cybersecurity defenses. The proposed solution targets HTTP/3 protocol

The rest of this paper is structured as follows. In Sect. 2, we present a critical analysis of other similar solutions and showcase the novelty of our approach. In Sect. 3 we present the QUICPot solution, its design and implementation. In Sect. 4 we show the experimental evaluation and the obtained results. Finally in Sect. 5 we conclude the paper and present future research directions.

2 Related Work

Based on the way they interact with the attackers, honeypots are usually classified into three categories: low, medium, and high interaction [9]. The first refers to those that emulate certain functionalities in a very primitive way. They serve to alert against unauthorized access and their nature allows them to be designed in a way that they can withstand attacks against their emulated vulnerability.

The second one refers to those that emulate a real service more credibly, while the latter often involves real systems, being able to mimic the functionalities of a real operating system. High-interaction honeypots offer system administrators a lot more information compared to low-interaction ones, being capable of flagging previously unknown vulnerabilities, but they are harder to develop and maintain, needing to be customized specifically for the system they are in charge of emulating. They also present a potential risk of the attacker gaining control over them, possibly compromising the system.

With this classification in mind, the next step is delving into a couple of existing solutions.

Pandora [15] is a project meant to serve the purpose of an IoT-based Intrusion Detection honeypot with real-time monitoring, being classified as a low interaction honeypot, which supports attacks varying from login attempts to port scan attacks. The proposed solution is is designed for home and gadget networks, making it a viable solution of IoT systems but it does not support HTTP/3 protocols.

A closed-source project that proposes an approach to designing and implementing a scalable and flexible HTTP honeypot platform, capable of emulating a vast range of IoT devices, as well as web applications and cloud services. They proposed a distributed architecture managed by one of the components and detailed logging and ran a four-month experiment to validate their system [14]. Their approach uses both server-side and client-based approaches for data collection and proved to be an optimal solution for detection of potential threat. Despite this feature, the proposed solution is limited to the HTTP protocol.

A system that handles horizontal requests on all TCP and UDP ports, HoneyPort [4] proposes an architecture that deploys a set of honeypots behind an aggregator, which redirects all incoming traffic through a socket port, and a classifier, which acts as a proxy and extracts the protocol to forward the traffic to the appropriate honeypot. One of those is Cowrie, an open-source program that emulates the shell interaction that takes place when connecting over SSH and Telnet. Another is a simple HTTP server, which uses web scraping to extract data from existing websites to store and use as possible answers to the HTTP requests that it's forwarded. The third is Socat [3], which establishes a low-level connection in case the protocol doesn't match any of the patterns of the other two honeypots. It was described as a "*Swiss army knife*".

Despite the valuable existing solution, to the best of our knowledge we did not find a complete HTTP/3 QUIC honeypot that can be use in low latency network designed for IoT systems.

The first choice to be made was the QUIC implementation to be used by the third version of the HTTP protocol. Aioquic is an asynchronous I/O implementation designed to work with the *asyncio* Python framework. It provides the support for using keywords such as "*async*" and "await", making it possible to write concurrent code that proves to be more scalable and efficient than synchronous programming models. Among the features it implements are co-routines: functions that can be defined as *async* that can use *await* to pause execution until the asynchronous operation completes, as well as co-routine objects, that can be scheduled to run in parallel. Its *Event Loop* can manage and distribute tasks in case of multi-tasking, ensuring efficiency. As for concurrency primitives, *Futures* offer a way of representing the result of an asynchronous operation, while *Tasks* can wrap around co-routines, allowing them to be scheduled by an event loop. The module also implements a thread-safe, asynchronous queue implementation that can be used for communication and synchronization between tasks that use the *put()* and *get()* operations. These operations are, by default, non-blocking, but they can force a blocking behavior with the "await" keyword. The main advantage to using this module is the ability to handle thousands of concurrent connections without the overhead brought about by threads, and the simplicity compared to thread-based applications, due to the seamless integration with the Python ecosystem.

Just like other protocols implementations that make use of the *asyncio* package, such as *aiohttp*, *aioftp*, *aioimaplib* and *aiosmtpd*, *aioquic* employs asynchronous I/O features to handle efficient communication while ensuring secure and low latency connections. When implementing the protocol, it considers the specifications provided by RFC 9000 [6] and related drafts, including support for QUIC versions 1 and 1.3. To secure the QUIC connections, it integrates minimal version 1.3 of TLS for encryption and authentication. The module provides APIs to be used for creating QUIC servers and clients, managing connections, handling streams, and even implementing custom protocols over QUIC. However, there is no need to implement HTTP-over-QUIC, since the package already has support for this functionality, conforming with the official RFC for HTTP/3 [2]. *Aioquic* is frequently tested for interoperability against other QUIC implementations, such as *quiche*, a Rust implementation, *quic-go*, implementation in Go. The module's approach in both QUIC and HTTP/3 is one following the pattern of "bring your own I/O", referring to the decoupling of protocol logic from the actual input and output operations, leaving the details pertaining the sending and receiving data on the network to the user of the APIs. The main advantage of this approach is the testability of the solution, allowing the tests to focus on the core functions of the protocol rather than on network operations. Additionally, this pattern offers flexibility in the I/O implementation, allowing users to adapt the I/O handling to their application. Among the functionalities of the QUIC *aioquic* stack can be counted support for IPv4, as well as IPv6, the feature of connection migration and NAT rebinding in case of network changes, logging of TLS traffic secrets, as well as detailed logs for QUIC event in QLOG format. The HTTP/3 stack includes server push support, helpful for pushing CSS, JavaScript, or other resources needed for rendering a web page. Furthermore, it provides support for WebSocket over HTTP/3 [5], meaning full-duplex communication channels over a single connection, as well as datagram support [17] for applications that can tolerate some packet loss.

Considering the fact that Twisted does not, as of yet, offer any implementation for versions of HTTP higher than 1.1, this project takes another approach when designing a honeypot for the third version of the protocol. The implementation combines *aioquic* with an ASGI, Asynchronous Server Gateway Interface, application, an object that can receive HTTP or WebSocket requests and generate responses. For this, Starlette is an excellent choice, being a lightweight ASGI designed for simplicity and offering vast support for essential HTTP operations. It is fully asynchronous, being compatible with the *asyncio* library, and thus facilitates the efficient handling of concurrent requests. Its design is minimal, providing essential components needed for web development without complicated dependencies. Among those components is routing, which defines routes and maps them to request handling functions in an intuitive manner. Another advantage is the support for middleware components for authentication, sessions, cookies, logging and CORS, Cross-Origin Resource Sharing. It is not coupled to a particular templating engine, but Jinja2 can be integrated seamlessly for this purpose. Most importantly, Starlette can be integrated into a HTTP/3 handler, and thus, can be the base of a HTTP/3 honeypot, because it includes support for server push, making it possible to push resources to the client in order to reduce page load latency.

3 Proposed Solution

The proposed solution aims to tackle the issue of a lack of HTTP/3 or QUIC honeypots by developing one to be integrated into the Python *honeypots* module. This will require a good understanding of the existing implementation of the module, as well as of the QUIC implementation chosen, *aioquic*, which will involve a close analysis of the code that comprises the two projects. A main overview of the module's architecture, including the relevant components, can be observed in Fig. 1.

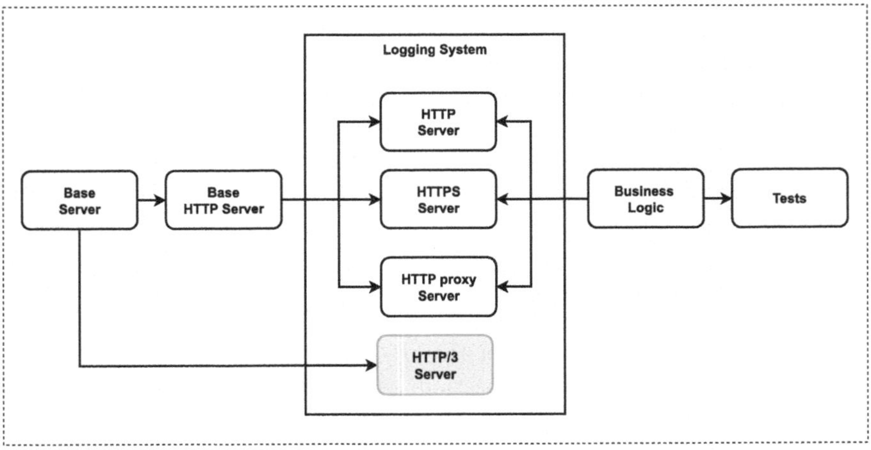

Fig. 1. Honeypots Architecture.

QUICPot architecture is presented in Fig. 1, underlining the three main components of the project, the aggregator, the classifier, and the responder.

The honeypots that offer HTTP functionalities all inherit the *BaseHttpServer*, another abstract class. They comprise of a simple HTTP server, one that implements HTTPS, and one handles requests as a HTTP proxy. The *BaseHttpServer* uses the Python package Twisted to create the web server, integrating the logs into its *MainResource*. Twisted is a versatile networking engine, designed to handle network programming tasks, while abstracting the complexities involved by asynchronous I/O. It supports a variety of protocols, which makes it particularly useful in the honeypots package, being used for handling DNS, FTP, IMAP, POP3, Telnet, SIP, IRC, PJL, and IPP requests in their respective servers throughout the project. However, it only offers built-in support for HTTP/1.1, requiring integration with a HTTP/2 capable library, such as *h2* to support this improved version of the protocol. Although this is possible, the HTTP honeypots already present in the package only support HTTP/1.1, a version of the protocol that, while still in use, is a lot less efficient than the second version, and significantly behind the third. Therefore, to implement a HTTP/3 server in the project, the use of Twisted would only complicate matters, with other Python libraries presenting more advantageous support.

3.1 HTTP/3 Server

Making use of the technologies, a HTTP/3 server can be integrated into the *honeypots* project, adding another easily deployable server with configurable functionalities, to the existing module components.

Unlike honeypots with more complex interactions with attackers, the HTTP/3 server offers limited use cases, as noticed in Fig. 2. The server is designed with simplicity and adaptability in mind, allowing the system administrator to run it with a certain configuration to detect unauthorized access. The generated logs can be analyzed to provide valuable insight into security breaches. On the other hand, an attacker can send requests and receive simulated responses, and even attempt to log in, possibly trying to brute force the user and password. The vigorous logging is useful for identifying the behavior of attackers in a controlled environment. The simplicity of the server offers the possibility of it being deployed in a variety of setups, making it easy to manage and ensuring that the minimal interactions are thoroughly recorded and analyzed.

3.2 Server Component

To efficiently log QUIC events, a good command of the *aioquic* classes was necessary. The *QHTTP3Server* is the honeypot server, matching the pattern defined by the rest of the package's honeypots. It used the serve function from *aioquic.asyncio.server* to start accepting HTTP/3 requests. The function required a *QuicConfiguration* object, which was previously created in the same class, as well as a reference to a subclass of *QuicProtocol*, which is the *Http3ServerProtocol*. This class contains multiple handlers for HTTP/3 requests, for each stream

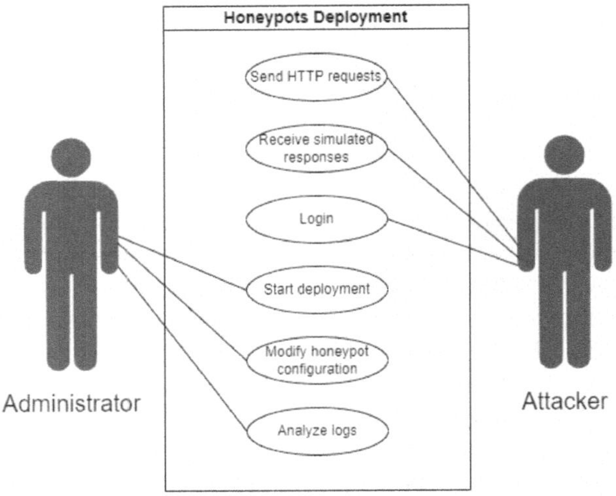

Fig. 2. QUICPot honeypot use case diagram.

being handled, as well as an instance of the *Http3StarletteApp*, which is to be passed as an argument to the handler's *run_ asgi()* function in order to process the request. Since the actual logging logic will happen in *Http3ServerProtocol* and *Http3StarletteApp*, an instance of the honeypot server has to be available in order to log events. The logs pertinent to a honeypot server are the following:

- **New connections**, regardless of the protocol requested. For this, in the *quic_ event_ received()* function of the *Http3ServerProtocol*, it was necessary to access its *QuicConnection* instance in order to get the *NetworkPath* at the head of the list of *_ network_ paths* and log its address.
- **TLS secrets**, in the same function of the *Http3ServerProtocol* class. In order to retrieve them, it was necessary to access the *QuicConnection*'s *QuicConfiguration*, to get the *secrets_ log_ file* field and get its value.
- **Method and path of request**, this time in *Http3ServerProtocol*'s *http_ event_ received()*, by getting the handler responsible for the stream and using its QUIC connection to get the IP address and port in a similar manner as to the one employed for new connections.
- **QUIC logs**, in the same function, logs which store valuable information concerning the QUIC events received, found by accessing the QUIC connection's configuration to get the *QUICLogger*.
- **Login attempts**, in *Http3StarletteApp*'s login handler, using the *request.client.host* and *request.client.port* to obtain the attacker's address.

The following diagram, presented in Fig. 3, may be helpful in untangling the multitude of classes and their interaction with one another. Further details are offered in the Implementation Details chapter.

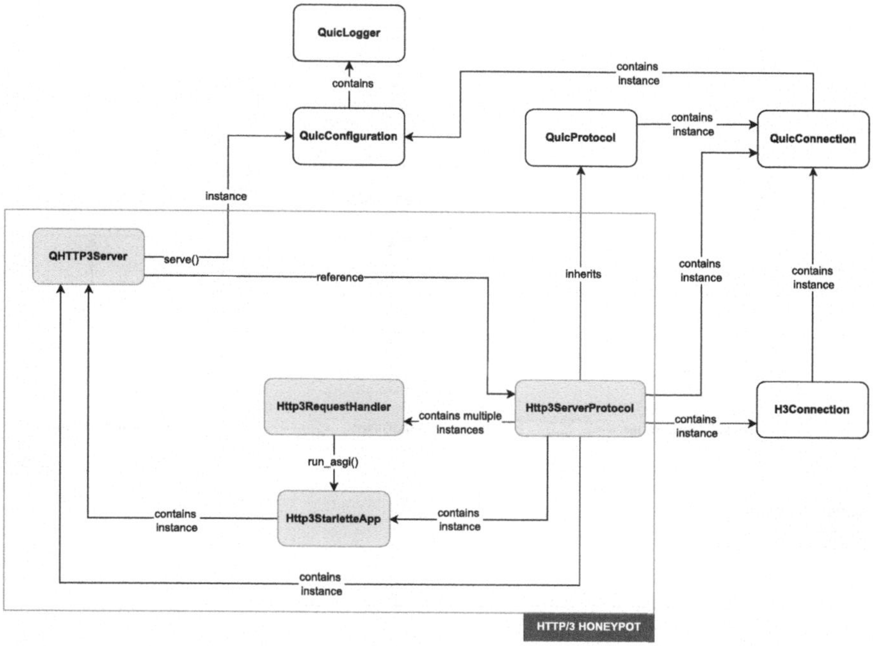

Fig. 3. Aioquic and HTTP/3 server classes.

3.3 Client Component

For the solution to be complete, it was also necessary to develop an HTTP/3 client, to ensure that the server can correctly handle and log requests. Thus, there was a need for an additional 2 classes, one that inherits *QuicConnectionProtocol*, *Http3Client*, and implements the I/O operations as well as the GET and POST logic, and a *Http3ClientHandler* that will be used to perform the actual requests (Fig. 4).

3.4 Logging Component

Based on its configuration, the server logs can be captured in several ways. The default option is the terminal, this option being helpful during developing the server's deployment, but not so much once the honeypot is deployed, since it does not facilitate log collection. There is also the possibility of log files, whose maximum size and location can be configured, with the events being stored in JSON format.

However, these options are not preferable in the case of a long-term deployment, so having a database to push the logs into would be a more advantageous alternative. The server supports logging through PostgreSQL, as well as through a SQLite db file. The database structure contains an ID, the date, and a data field that stores the log being pushed into the database. Thus, the logs need not have a standard format, and a variety of different events can be logged.

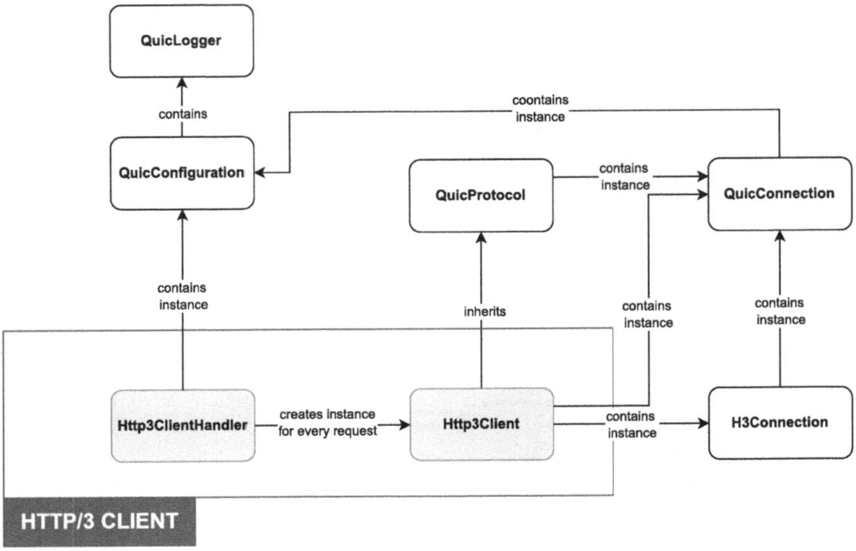

Fig. 4. Aioquic and HTTP/3 client classes.

The project also supports system logs, syslogs for short. These are a the fundamental means of logging data in Unix-based systems, and could be helpful in the case of deploying one or more honeypots on an embedded system which has such an operating system. Syslogs are designed to be lightweight and efficient, and therefore ensure minimal impact on system performance when logging a high volume of events. An example of syslogs can be noted in Fig. 5.

By implementing various logging methods, the most suitable to the user's needs can be chosen based on the deployment methods. Our solution can extract valuable security insights and help on understanding the attackers behavior. For example, logs can reveal efforts to exploit QUIC's multiplexing to create denial-of-service conditions or uncover attempts to bypass firewalls through obfuscated UDP traffic.

The main events logged are the creation of a new process for the server, new TLS connections, TLS secrets, storing QUIC build-in logs, GET an POST requests and login attempts. The basic log format is the following:

- **server** - the type of server that the log belongs to,
- **action** - the action that the log refers to, in case of the HTTP/3 server can be process, connection, quic_logs, POST, GET, login, or secrets_log,
- **src_ip** - the attacker's IP address,
- **src_port** - the attacker's port,
- **dest_ip** - the server's IP address,
- **dest_port** - the port the server is running on,
- *timestamp* - time of logging.

Fig. 5. Syslogs example.

The logs can also contain retain additional information depending on the log type:

- **quic_logs**, the logs captured by default by a *QuicLogger*,
- **secrets_log**, the TLS secrets, useful for decrypting traffic,
- **method**, *path* and *headers* for GET and POST requests,
- **username** and **password** for login attempts.

However, since logging is supported on syslogs and also on PostgreSQL and SQLite, all of which have an upper limit on the size of logs accepted (or row size for the databases), it was necessary to add a special option to the server, in which TLS secrets and QUIC default logs are not inserted into the database or tracked through syslogs. Seeing as the other honeypot server do not log such information, this was a way of satisfying multiple use cases, by offering the option to enable the logging of this auxiliary data in case it is needed.

4 Experimental Evaluation and Results

4.1 Environment

The application was tested on an ASUS VivoBook laptop, model 14 X403FA, with an Intel i7-8565U CPU, 8 total threads, 8GB RAM, which runs Windows 10, Education edition. All development took place in the Windows Subsystem for Linux 2, inside of a Ubuntu 22.04 distribution of Linux. The Python version used was v3.10.12.

4.2 Integration into Honeypots Tests

A lot like most Python modules, *honeypots* has a directory for tests. The setup uses Pytest, Python's most popular testing framework, due to its versatility and variety of features. It implements fixtures as a way of promoting code reuse, allowing for different scopes varying from function to session, and it allows parameterized testing, further eliminating boilerplate code and allowing the testing of multiple different scenarios with just one test function.

Each honeypot server has a corresponding test to check its functionality, in particular its ability to log pertinent information about its interaction with possible attackers. To that, a good choice for the HTTP/3 server test would be to send a login request and check the logs generated, which is the same scenario that is tested for the other HTTP servers. Using a custom test configuration, the server is set up, and its logs are read from a log file. The events that should be registered by the server are the following:

- new connection;
- secrets log, where the handshake traffic secret and the traffic secret 0 for both client and server should be stored;
- QUIC logs for the connection;
- POST request for "/" path;
- QUIC logs for the POST request;
- login credentials.

What the *test_server()* function does is create a client which generates a GET request for the home page, and later a POST request with a login attempt, both establishing a new QUIC connection which has its connection ID.

4.3 Performance Testing

To prove the efficiency of the solution, two main conditions must be met. Taking into account that a honeypot is likely going to be in an idle state for most of its lifetime and that, to be discovered by attackers, it must be running permanently, it would be ideal that it does not consume a lot of system resources while in this state. Additionally, it must be able to withstand several simultaneous requests, in case the attacker discovers it and attempts a Denial of Service attack, or even attempts to crack the password through brute force or other means.

To establish the CPU and memory usage of the HTTP/3 server, the Unix */proc* file system was used, parsing the data necessary to calculate the memory and CPU consumption percentage. Since the values are relative to the last time they were read, checking them every 5 s is a good way of obtaining accurate results. In order to handle the process monitoring, the *ProcStats* class was helpful.

The next step was defining the scenarios to be tested by the process monitor, varying the number of new connections created. Testing the performance when in the idle state for a long time is necessary, and beyond that, having an increasing number of threads that create new connections and send requests both for the home page and for logging in would help determine how well the application scales upward. Therefore, tests were run with 0, 1, 10, 100, and 1000 threads that loop to establish two connections, send two requests and wait a random interval between 0 and 0.5 s for each iteration. The duration of the tests was 20 min for each scenario, checking the resource usage every 5 s. The resulted results were mapped and are pictured in Figs. 6, 7a, 7b, 7c, and 7d.

The general conclusions of the resulting plots are the following: calculating the CPU usage for smaller intervals is significantly less reliant than calculating

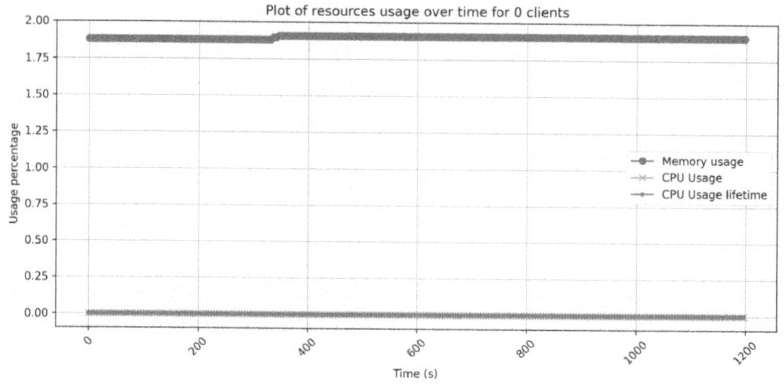

Fig. 6. Resources usage when server is idle.

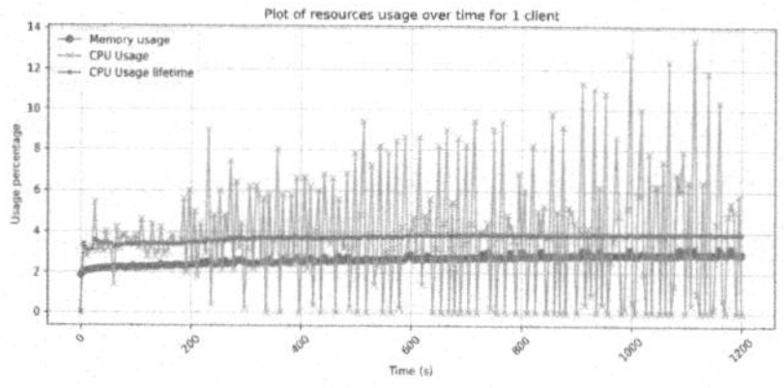

(a) 1 client.

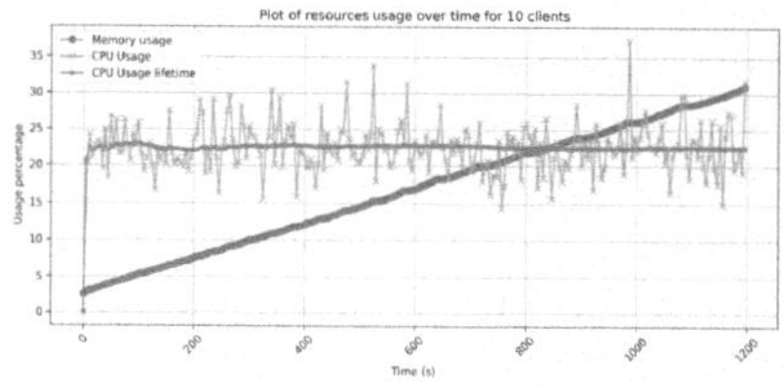

(b) 10 clients.

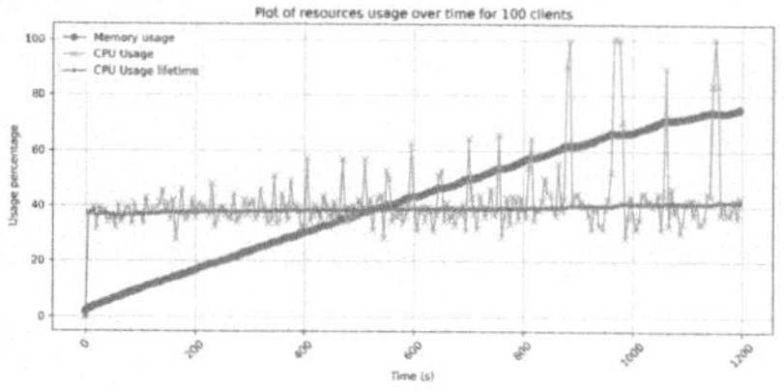

(c) Resources usage for 100 clients.

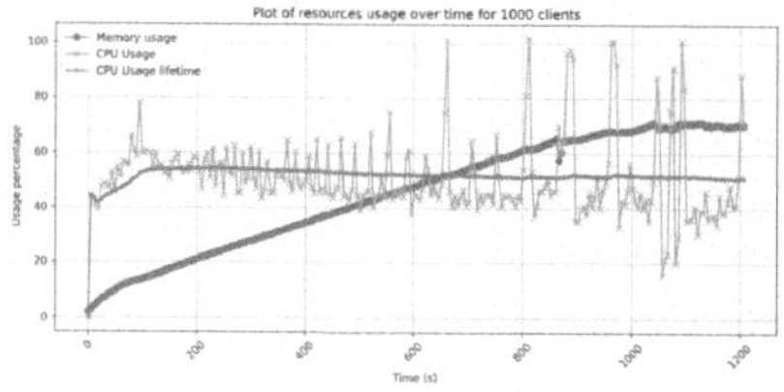

(d) Resources usage for 1000 clients.

Fig. 7. Comparison of resource usage when server is idle and for different numbers of clients sending requests.

the percentage of time spent running during its entire lifetime. The calculated CPU usage percentage over the server's lifetime seems to be almost constant in time, increasing only with the increase in the number of requests. The memory percentage is growing along with the new connections created, which is to be expected considering more TLS secrets must be stored, as well as more QUIC logs, meaning an increase is inevitable under the circumstances.

Examining Fig. 6, it is evident that the requirement of the server consuming minimal resources in its idle state was met. Without any requests, the server spends no time on the processor and only consumes around 1.90% of memory.

Looking at Fig. 7a, one can notice that the memory is very slowly increasing from lower than 2% to around 3%, which is an acceptable rate for one client constantly generating new connections that are to be stored. The CPU usage percentage over the process's lifetime is constant at around 4%, which owes to new connections constantly being negotiated.

By examining the other Figs. 7b, 7c, and 7d, one would think, at first, that the memory usage growth is linear, but the last two charts seem to suggest more of a logarithmic growth, which would place a threshold below 80%. The CPU usage over the lifetime appears to be constant, if anything it seems to decrease slightly over time. However, the testing conditions also influence the results a lot, the queries being sent from only 8 cores, rather than a device better equipped for stress testing programs, like a Threadripper Workstation, which possesses up to 86 cores.

Another observation noted during the testing process is the inefficiency of logging TLS client secrets and default QUIC logs, as their size can increase significantly along with the number of connections established. Seeing as the other honeypots that implement protocols using TLS already present in the *honeypots* package do not log this data, probably due to this exact reason, adding the server option for opting out of these logs was necessary. An added reason was the limitation of some logging methods, syslogs having an upper size limit for logged information, and PostgreSQL and SQLite having upper size limits for row size.

The results of the performance tests were altogether positive, indicating how the server would perform under stress, being able to maintain a relatively constant CPU percentage for a constant number of new connections. Seeing as the application is implemented in Python, an interpreted programming language, a bottleneck was to be expected when compared to applications implemented in lower-level languages such as Rust.

5 Conclusions and Future Works

Having noticed the lack of implementations for HTTP/3 honeypots throughout the field of network decoys, the proposed solution enriches a prolific honeypot package with another server, which integrates seamlessly among the other servers, implementing the same functionalities the others offered for a new, recently standardized protocol. Thus, the mentioned objectives and requirements were met and compatibility of features, functionality testing, and performance were achieved. The result is an HTTP/3 module that can be adapted and deployed in a variety of manners, ensuring that honeypot detection is unlikely. Deployment of the solution in an isolated environment that offers a centralized logging platform, such as Grafana, is bound to be efficient in imitating a network of IoT devices, for example, with uses in private companies' networks and even in personal use networks.

Continuous progress in cybersecurity will always be crucial in order to safeguard sensitive data and detect new threats. Seeing as HTTP is not the only protocol that can be wrapped around QUIC, the *honeypots* package could benefit from other additional servers, such as one for DoQ. DNS-over-QUIC brings significant improvements to the name-resolving protocol, despite the original version also being over UDP. The QUIC built-in TLS support ensures that the connection is secure, while under normal circumstances DNS packets are not encrypted by any means, which leaves it vulnerable to several security risks, such as spoofing, which is also referred to, in this case, as DNS poisoning, or Man-in-the-Middle attacks. Additionally, DoQ has the advantage of sending multiple requests over one connection, offering improved efficiency. Considering that DoQ outperforms other secure versions of the DNS protocol [7], DNS-over-HTTPS and DNS-over-TLS, it is likely become widely spread throughout the internet in the following years, which means that a DoQ honeypot could possibly help expose this new protocol's vulnerabilities. The *aioquic* Python module already has an implementation for this protocol, which would facilitate the development of such a honeypot server.

As well as DoQ, a QUIC server can currently be developped in order to accept WebSockets, or even their improved version, the WebTransport protocol. Both of these protocols have the purpose of facilitating real-time, bidirectional communication between servers and clients, WebSockets laying on top of TCP and WebTransfer on top of QUIC. While WebSockets are widely used, their implementation over QUIC is yet to be standardized by the IETF. Therefore, the development of honeypots for these protocols would be an important step towards finding their possible vulnerabilities and a valuable addition to the *honeypots* package.

These proposals would integrate into the existing implementation described in this paper, opening the door for further improvements and providing a unified honeypot solution that can mitigate DoQ attacks, in complex IoT systems such as smart cities.

Acknowledgment. The research presented in this paper was supported by the Research Grant no. 94/11.10.2023 *Modern Distributed Platform for Educational Applications in Cloud Edge Continuum Environments* GNAC-ARUT 2023. Also, this paper is partially by the following grants of the Ministry of Research, Innovation and Digitization, CCCDI - UEFISCDI, project number PN-IV-P6-6.3-SOL-2024-2-0207 (*INFRAINIS*), PN-IV-P6-6.3-SOL-2024-2-0248 (*COLGS-RO*) and PN-IV-P6-6.3-SOL-2024-0068 (*CORAL*), within PNCDI IV.

The authors would like to thank the editors and the anonymous reviewers for providing insightful suggestions and comments to improve the quality of the research paper.

References

1. Al-Bakhat, L., Almuhammadi, S.: Intrusion detection on quic traffic: A machine learning approach. In: 2022 7th International Conference on Data Science and Machine Learning Applications (CDMA), pp. 194–199. IEEE (2022)
2. Bishop, M.: HTTP/3. RFC 9114 (Jun 2022)

3. Bruneo, D., Distefano, S., Longo, F., Merlino, G., Puliafito, A.: A cloud-based overlay networking for the internet of things: quantitative. systems modeling: methodologies and tools, p. 237 (2018)
4. Filippi, E.: HoneyPort-a scalable meta-honeypot system for security applications. Ph.D. thesis, Politecnico di Torino (2019)
5. Hamilton, R.: Bootstrapping WebSockets with HTTP/3. RFC 9220 (Jun 2022)
6. Iyengar, J., Thomson, M.: QUIC: A UDP-Based Multiplexed and Secure Transport. RFC 9000 (May 2021)
7. Kosek, M., Doan, T.V., Granderath, M., Bajpai, V.: One to rule them all? a first look at DNS over QUIC. In: Hohlfeld, O., Moura, G., Pelsser, C. (eds.) Passive and Active Measurement, pp. 537–551. Springer International Publishing, Cham (2022)
8. Kumar, P., Dezfouli, B.: Implementation and analysis of QUIC for MQTT. Comput. Netw. **150**, 28–45 (2019)
9. LaBar, J., Chowdhury, M., Jochen, M., Kambhampaty, K.: Honeypots: security by deceiving threats. In: The Midwest Instruction and Computing Symposium 2019 (2018)
10. Megyesi, P., Krämer, Z., Molnár, S.: How quick is quic? In: 2016 IEEE International Conference on Communications (ICC), pp. 1–6 (2016). https://doi.org/10.1109/ICC.2016.7510788
11. Nawrocki, M., Hiesgen, R., Schmidt, T.C., Wählisch, M.: Quicsand: quantifying quic reconnaissance scans and dos flooding events. In: Proceedings of the 21st ACM Internet Measurement Conference, pp. 283–291 (2021)
12. Postel, J.: Transmission control protocol. RFC793 (1981)
13. Protocol, U.D.: Rfc 768 j. postel isi 28 august 1980. Isi **7** (1980)
14. Rabzelj, M., Juznic, L.S., Volk, M., Kos, A., Kren, M., Sedlar, U.: Designing and evaluating a flexible and scalable http honeypot platform: architecture, implementation, and applications. Electronics **12**(16) (2023)
15. Ramakrishnan, K., Gokul, P., Nigam, R.: Pandora: An Iot based intrusion detection honeypot with real-time monitoring. In: 2021 International Conference on Forensics, Analytics, Big Data, Security (FABS), vol. 1, pp. 1–7 (2021)
16. Salam, A.A., Luglio, M., Roseti, C., Zampognaro, F.: Spdy multiplexing approach on long-latency links. In: 2014 IEEE Wireless Communications and Networking Conference (WCNC), pp. 3450–3455 (2014)
17. Schinazi, D., Pardue, L.: HTTP Datagrams and the Capsule Protocol. RFC 9297 (Aug 2022)
18. Thomson, M., Benfield, C.: HTTP/2. RFC 9113 (Jun 2022)

Another Lattice Attack Against an RSA-Like Cryptosystem

George Teşeleanu[1,2(✉)]

[1] Advanced Technologies Institute, 10 Dinu Vintilă, Bucharest, Romania
tgeorge@dcti.ro

[2] Simion Stoilow Institute of Mathematics of the Romanian Academy, 21 Calea Grivitei, Bucharest, Romania

Abstract. Let $N = pq$ be the product of two balanced prime numbers p and q. In 2015, Roman'kov introduced an interesting RSA-like cryptosystem that, unlike the classical RSA key equation $ed - k(p-1)(q-1) = 1$, uses the key equation $ed - kr = 1$, where $r|p-1$ and is a large prime number. In this paper, we study if small private key attacks based on lattices can be applied to Roman'kov's cryptosystem. More precisely, we argue that such attacks do not appear to be applicable to this scheme without substantial adaptations.

Keywords: lattice attack · small private key attack · RSA

1 Introduction

RSA is one of the most widely adopted cryptosystems and was designed by Rivest, Shamir and Adleman [16] in 1978. The standard version of RSA has as an underlying group $\mathbb{Z}_N^*$, where N is the product of two large prime numbers p and q. To encrypt a message m such that $m < N$, the process involves computing $c \equiv m^e \bmod N$, where e satisfies $\gcd(e, \varphi(N)) = 1$ and $\varphi(N) = (p-1)(q-1)$ is Euler's totient function. The inverse operation requires computing $m \equiv c^d \bmod N$, where $d \equiv e^{-1} \bmod \varphi(N)$. Note that (N, e) are public, while (p, q, d) are kept secret. The standard RSA, termed balanced RSA, employs primes p and q that have the same bit-size (*i.e.* $q < p < 2q$). This paper exclusively focuses on balanced RSA and its variations.

In parallel with the development of modulus factoring methods, several specific attacks have been developed in order to extract as much information as possible from the public key (N, e). Therefore, Wiener showed in [19] that if $d < N^{0.25}/3$, then one can retrieve d from the continued fraction expansion of e/N, and thus factor N. This bound was improved by Boneh and Durfee [3] to $N^{0.292}$. The main tools that they used are Coppersmith's method [5] and lattice reduction techniques [12]. Later on, Herrmann and May [8] obtain the same bound, but using simpler techniques. For more details about RSA attacks we refer the reader to [2,14,18].

L. Morogan et al. (Eds.): SecITC 2024, LNCS 15595, pp. 223–231, 2025.
https://doi.org/10.1007/978-3-031-87760-5_16

A variant of RSA was proposed by Roman'kov [17] in 2015. Compared to the classical RSA, this new proposal is randomized, and factoring N does not lead to recovering encrypted messages. To achieve these properties, Roman'kov considers two distinct subgroups of $\mathbb{M}, \mathbb{H} \subset \mathbb{Z}_n$, one of order r and the other of order t, where r and t are prime numbers. In this scheme, the encryption exponent is chosen such that $\gcd(e, r) = 1$, and the corresponding decryption exponent is computed as $d = td_1$, where $d_1 \equiv (te)^{-1} \bmod r$. The encryption and decryption processes are similar to RSA. More precisely, to encrypt a message $m \in \mathbb{M}$, we compute $c \equiv (hm)^e \bmod N$, where h is a random element from $\mathbb{H}$. To decrypt, we simply compute $m \equiv c^d \bmod N$.

In this paper, we provide the first security analysis of Roman'kov's scheme. We argue that lattice based attacks do not seem to work against this cryptosystem. To substantiate our claims, we show that the results provided in [1,11] cannot be applied. Given that the result presented in [11] is optimal under certain reasonable assumptions, we conclude that this class of attacks do not seem to work against the Roman'kov cryptosystem without substantial adaptations.

Structure of the Paper. Preliminary notions are provided in Sect. 2. In Sect. 3 we describe our impossibility results. We conclude our paper in Sect. 4.

2 Preliminaries

Notations. Throughout the paper, λ and τ denote security parameters. Also, the notation $|S|$ denotes the cardinality of a set S. By $|n|$ we denote the size of n in bits. We use $\simeq$ to indicate that two values are approximately equal. The action of selecting a random element x from a sample space X is denoted by $x \xleftarrow{\$} X$.

2.1 RSA-Like Cryptosystem

Instead of choosing the message space as the entire $\mathbb{Z}_N^*$ group, Roman'kov [17] selects two subgroups $\mathbb{M}, \mathbb{H} \subset \mathbb{Z}_N^*$ and encrypts only messages from $\mathbb{M}$. This approach allows the sender to use random elements from $\mathbb{H}$ to mask the message. We further present the cryptosystem as described in [17].

Setup(λ, τ): Randomly generate two distinct large prime numbers r and t such that $|r| = |t| = \lambda$. Choose randomly two integers α and β such that $|\alpha| = |\beta| = \tau$ until $p = 2\alpha r + 1$ and $q = 2\beta t + 1$ are both prime. Compute the product $N = pq$. Choose generators u and v such that their order are r and t, respectively. Choose an integer e such that $\gcd(e, r) = 1$ and compute d_1 such that $ted_1 \equiv 1 \bmod r$. Output the public key $pk = (N, e, u, v, \mathbb{M}, \mathbb{H})$, where $\mathbb{M} = \langle u \rangle$ and $\mathbb{H} = \langle v \rangle$. The corresponding secret key is $sk = (p, q, r, t, d)$, where $d = td_1$.

Encrypt(pk, m): To encrypt a message $m \in \mathbb{M}$ we choose a random element $h \xleftarrow{\$} \mathbb{H}$ and then we compute $c \equiv (hm)^e \bmod N$. Output the ciphertext c.

Decrypt(sk, c): To recover the message, simply compute $m \equiv c^d \bmod N$.

Remark 1. When choosing the public key, we have to select two generators. An effective way to accomplish this is to first randomly choose the value $u_1 \xleftarrow{\$} \mathbb{Z}_p^*$ until the order of u_1 is r. Using the Chinese Remainder Theorem, we compute the desired value $u \in \mathbb{Z}_n^*$ such that $u \equiv u_1 \bmod p$ and $u \equiv 1 \bmod q$. A similar process applies for v.

2.2 Useful Lemmas

The results provided in this section will be used in Sect. 3 to bound the solutions of equations $xy + 1 \equiv 0 \bmod e$ and $xH(y) - 4\alpha\beta t \equiv 0 \bmod e$, which are derived from the key equation[1] $ed - kr = 1$. We start by providing lower and upper bounds for p and q (see [15, Lemma 1]).

Lemma 1. *Let $N = pq$ be the product of two unknown primes with $q < p < 2q$. Then the following property holds*

$$\frac{\sqrt{2}}{2}\sqrt{N} < q < \sqrt{N} < p < \sqrt{2}\sqrt{N}.$$

The bounds for $\varphi(N)$ are provided in [7, Corollary 1]. This result implies that $\varphi(N)$ can be approximated by N.

Corollary 1. *Let $N = pq$ be the product of two unknown primes with $q < p < 2q$. Then the following property holds*

$$\left(\sqrt{N} - 1\right)^2 > \varphi(N) > N\left(1 - \frac{3}{\sqrt{2N}}\right) + 1.$$

2.3 Finding Small Roots

In this section, we outline some tools used for solving the problem of finding small roots, both in the modular and integer cases.

Coppersmith [4–6] provided rigorous techniques for computing small integer roots of single-variable polynomials modulo an integer, as well as bivariate polynomials over the integers. In the case of modular roots, Coppersmith's ideas were reinterpreted by Howgrave-Graham [9]. We further provide Howgrave-Graham result.

Theorem 1. *Let $f(x_1, \ldots, x_n) = \sum a_{i_1 \ldots i_n} x_1^{i_1} \ldots x_n^{i_n} \in \mathbb{Z}[x_1, \ldots, x_n]$ be a polynomial with at most ω monomials, α be an integer and let*

$$||f(x_1, \ldots, x_n)|| = \sqrt{\sum |a_{i_1 \ldots i_n}|^2}$$

be its norm. Suppose that

- *$f(y_1, \ldots, y_n) \equiv 0 \bmod \alpha$ for some $|y_1| < X_1, \ldots, |y_n| < X_n$,*

[1] equivalently written as $ed - k\varphi(N)/4\alpha\beta t = 1$, since $r = \varphi(N)/4\alpha\beta t$.

- $||f(y_1X_1,\dots,y_nX_n)|| < \alpha/\sqrt{\omega}$,

then $f(y_1,\dots,y_n) = 0$ *holds over integers.*

Lenstra, Lenstra and Lovász [12] proposed a lattice reduction algorithm (LLL) that is widely used in cryptanalysis and is typically combined with Howgrave-Graham's lemma. We further provide the version presented in [10,13].

Theorem 2. *Let* L *be a lattice of dimension* ω*. In polynomial time, the LLL algorithm outputs a reduced basis* $(b_1,\dots,b_\omega)$ *that satisfies*

$$||b_1|| \le \dots \le ||b_i|| \le 2^{\frac{\omega(\omega-1)}{4(\omega+1-i)}} det(L)^{\frac{1}{\omega+1-i}},$$

where $det(L)$ *is the determinant of lattice* L*.*

Note that the condition

$$2^{\frac{\omega(\omega-1)}{4(\omega+1-i)}} det(L)^{\frac{1}{\omega+1-i}} < \alpha/\sqrt{\omega}$$

implies that the polynomials corresponding to b_i match Howgrave-Graham's bound. This leads to

$$det(L) \le \varepsilon\alpha^{\omega+1-i},$$

where ε is an error term that is usually ignored.

In order to find a solution $(y_1,\dots,y_n)$ we need the following assumption to be true.

Assumption 3 *The LLL reduced basis polynomials are algebraically independent*[2]*, and the resultant computations for* b_i *yields the common roots of these polynomials.*

In [11], a lattice based method for finding small solutions of the equation $xH(y) + c \equiv 0 \bmod \beta$ is provided. This result extensions the Boneh and Durfee method [3] and uses the LLL algorithm [12] and Howgrave-Graham's lemma [9] to derive the solutions. The author shows that the bounds provided in [11] are optimal under reasonable assumptions. Note that, using a different lattice construction the authors of [1] prove a similar result.

Theorem 4. *Let* $H(y) \in \mathbb{Z}[y]$ *be a monic polynomial with degree* $r \ge 1$ *and* β *be an integer. Suppose that*

- $x_0H(y_0) + c \equiv 0 \bmod \beta$ *for some* $|x_0| < X = \beta^\delta, |y_0| < Y = \beta^\gamma$,
- $|c| < XY^r$,

then one can solve the equation $xH(y) + c \equiv 0 \bmod \beta$ *if*

$$\begin{cases} \delta \le \frac{r+2}{2(r+1)} - \frac{r+1}{2}\gamma & \text{when } 0 < \gamma < r/(r+1)^2, \\ \delta \le 1 - \sqrt{r\gamma}, & \text{when } r/(r+1)^2 \le \gamma \le 1/r. \end{cases}$$

[2] they do not share a non-trivial gcd.

3 Application of Lattices

We further provide two negative results. Namely, that we cannot devise a lattice based attack to factor N or recover r in polynomial time using the results presented in [1,11].

Theorem 5. *Let $N = pq$ be the product of two unknown primes with $q < p < 2q$. Also, let $e = N^\delta$, $2^{\tau+2} = N^\varepsilon$ and $d < N^\gamma$. We cannot factor N in polynomial time using the method presented in Theorem 4.*

Proof. Note that

$$\varphi(N) = N - (p+q) + 1$$

and thus, finding $p+q$ is equivalent to solving the equation

$$h(y) = -y + N + 1,$$

or analogously the monic polynomial $H(y) = -h(y)$.

By rewriting the key equation $ed - k\varphi(N)/4\alpha\beta t = 1$, we obtain the congruence $k\varphi(N) + 4\alpha\beta t \equiv 0 \bmod e$, that is equivalent to $k(-\varphi_n(N)) - 4\alpha\beta t \equiv 0 \bmod e$. Consequently, we deduce the equation $xH(y) - 4\alpha\beta t \equiv 0 \bmod e$, which has k and $p+q$ as solutions.

In order to be able to apply Theorem 4 we first need to bound k and $p+q$. Since we have

- $k\varphi(N) = 4\alpha\beta t(ed-1) < 4\alpha\beta ted$,
- $\alpha < 2^{\tau+1} = N^\varepsilon/2$,
- $2\beta t = q - 1 < \sqrt{N}$ (see Lemma 1),
- $N \simeq \varphi(N)$ (see Corollary 1),

we obtain that

$$k < \frac{4\alpha\beta ted}{\varphi(N)} < N^{\delta+\gamma+\varepsilon-0.5}.$$

Using Lemma 1 we have that $p+q < 3\sqrt{N}$. Therefore, we have that $k < X = e^{(\delta+\gamma+\varepsilon-0.5)/\delta}$ and $p+q < Y \simeq e^{0.5/\delta}$.

Note that, we also need

$$|-4\alpha\beta t| < XY = N^{\delta+\gamma+\varepsilon-0.5}N^{0.5} = N^{\delta+\gamma+\varepsilon}. \tag{1}$$

We assume at this point of the proof that $\delta \geq 1/2$. We will later see that this assumption always holds and it is derived from the remaining solvability conditions of Theorem 4. Therefore, since $4\alpha\beta t < N^{\varepsilon+0.5}$, using our assumption $0.5 \leq \delta < \delta+\gamma$ we obtain that Equation (1) holds.

According to Theorem 4, we can find the solutions $x_0 = k$ and $y_0 = p+q$ to equation $xH(y) - 4\alpha\beta t \equiv 0 \bmod e$ if certain conditions are met.

Let consider the first case of Theorem 4. We have

$$0 \leq \frac{1}{2\delta} < \frac{1}{4} \Leftrightarrow 2 < \delta,$$

and

$$\begin{aligned}\frac{\delta + \gamma + \varepsilon - 0.5}{\delta} \leq \frac{3}{4} - \frac{0.5}{\delta} &\Leftrightarrow \delta + \gamma + \varepsilon \leq \frac{3\delta}{4}\\ &\Leftrightarrow \gamma \leq -\frac{\delta}{4} - \varepsilon.\end{aligned}$$

Since we also want $\gamma > 0$, we obtain that in this case is not possible to solve the equation.

In the second case of Theorem 4 we have

$$\frac{1}{4} \leq \frac{1}{2\delta} \leq 1 \Leftrightarrow \frac{1}{2} \leq \delta \leq 2$$

and

$$\begin{aligned}\frac{\delta + \gamma + \varepsilon - 0.5}{\delta} \leq 1 - \frac{1}{\sqrt{2\delta}} &\Leftrightarrow \delta + \gamma + \varepsilon - 0.5 \leq \delta - \sqrt{0.5\delta}\\ &\Leftrightarrow \gamma \leq 0.5 - \varepsilon - \sqrt{0.5\delta}.\end{aligned}$$

Since we also want $\gamma > 0$ we must have

$$0 < 0.5 - \varepsilon - \sqrt{0.5\delta} \Leftrightarrow \delta < \frac{(1 - 2\varepsilon)^2}{2}.$$

But we obtain a contradiction with

$$\frac{1}{2} \leq \delta < \frac{(1 - 2\varepsilon)^2}{2}.$$

Therefore, it is not possible to solve the equation. □

Remark 2. In a similar way, we can prove that we cannot factor N when $p < q < 2p$. Note that the only change in Theorem 5's proof is that we need to use the approximation $p - 1 \simeq \sqrt{N}$, instead of $q - 1 < \sqrt{N}$.

Theorem 6. *Let $N = pq$ be the product of two unknown primes with $q < p < 2q$. Also, let $e = N^{\delta}$, $2^{\lambda} = N^{\eta}$ and $d < N^{\gamma}$. We cannot recover the secret key r in polynomial time using the method presented in Theorem 4.*

Proof. By rewriting the key equation $ed - kr = 1$, we obtain the congruence $kr + 1 \equiv 0 \bmod e$. Consequently, we deduce the equation $xy + 1 \equiv 0 \bmod e$, which has k and r as solutions.

In order to be able to apply Theorem 4 we first need to bound k. Since $kr = ed - 1 < ed$ and $N^{\eta} < r$, we obtain that

$$k < \frac{ed}{r} < N^{\delta+\gamma-\eta}.$$

We also have that $r < 2N^{\eta}$. Therefore, we have that $k < X = e^{(\delta+\gamma-\eta)/\delta}$ and $r < Y \simeq e^{\eta/\delta}$.

According to Theorem 4, we can find the solutions $x_0 = k$ and $y_0 = r$ to equation $xy + 1 \equiv 0 \bmod e$ if certain conditions are met.

Let consider the first case of Theorem 4. We have

$$0 \le \frac{\eta}{\delta} < \frac{1}{4} \Leftrightarrow 4\eta < \delta$$

and

$$\begin{aligned} \frac{\delta+\gamma-\eta}{\delta} \le \frac{3}{4} - \frac{\eta}{\delta} &\Leftrightarrow \delta + \gamma \le \frac{3\delta}{4} \\ &\Leftrightarrow \gamma \le -\frac{1}{4}\delta. \end{aligned}$$

Since we also want $\gamma > 0$, we obtain that in this case is not possible to solve the equation.

In the second case of Theorem 4 we have

$$\frac{1}{4} \le \frac{\eta}{\delta} \le 1 \Leftrightarrow \eta \le \delta \le 4\eta$$

and

$$\begin{aligned} \frac{\delta+\gamma-\eta}{\delta} \le 1 - \frac{\sqrt{\eta}}{\sqrt{\delta}} &\Leftrightarrow \delta + \gamma - \eta \le \delta - \sqrt{\eta\delta} \\ &\Leftrightarrow \gamma \le \eta - \sqrt{\eta\delta}. \end{aligned}$$

Since we also want $\gamma > 0$ we must have

$$0 \le \eta - \sqrt{\eta\delta} \Leftrightarrow \delta \le \eta.$$

But we obtain the following contradiction

$$\eta \le \delta < \eta.$$

Therefore, it is not possible to solve the equation. □

4 Conclusions

In this paper, we presented two impossibility results for the Roman'kov scheme [17]. First, we showed that lattice attacks based on the results presented in [1,11] cannot be used to factor N. Then, in a similar manner, we showed that r also cannot be recovered. Since the bounds provided in Theorem 4 are optimal under reasonable assumptions, our results show that this class of lattice attacks do not seem work in the case of Roman'kov's scheme without substantial adaptations.

References

1. Abderrahmane Nitaj, N.N.H.A., Ariffin, M.R.B.K.: Cryptanalysis of a New Variant of the RSA Cryptosystem. In: AFRICACRYPT 2024. Springer (2024)
2. Boneh, D.: Twenty years of attacks on the RSA cryptosystem. Notices AMS **46**(2), 203–213 (1999)
3. Boneh, D., Durfee, G.: Cryptanalysis of RSA with Private Key d Less than $N^{0.292}$. In: EUROCRYPT 1999. Lecture Notes in Computer Science, vol. 1592, pp. 1–11. Springer (1999)
4. Coppersmith, D.: Finding a small root of a bivariate integer equation; factoring with high bits known. In: Maurer, U. (ed.) EUROCRYPT 1996. LNCS, vol. 1070, pp. 178–189. Springer, Heidelberg (1996). https://doi.org/10.1007/3-540-68339-9_16
5. Coppersmith, D.: Finding a small root of a univariate modular equation. In: Maurer, U. (ed.) EUROCRYPT 1996. LNCS, vol. 1070, pp. 155–165. Springer, Heidelberg (1996). https://doi.org/10.1007/3-540-68339-9_14
6. Coppersmith, D.: Small solutions to polynomial equations, and low exponent RSA vulnerabilities. J. Cryptol. **10**(4), 233–260 (1997). https://doi.org/10.1007/s001459900030
7. Cotan, P., Teşeleanu, G.: Small private key attack against a family of RSA-like cryptosystems. In: NordSEC 2023. Lecture Notes in Computer Science, vol. 14324, pp. 57–72. Springer (2023)
8. Herrmann, M., May, A.: Maximizing small root bounds by linearization and applications to small secret exponent RSA. In: Nguyen, P.Q., Pointcheval, D. (eds.) PKC 2010. LNCS, vol. 6056, pp. 53–69. Springer, Heidelberg (2010). https://doi.org/10.1007/978-3-642-13013-7_4
9. Howgrave-Graham, N.: Finding small roots of univariate modular equations revisited. In: IMA 1997. Lecture Notes in Computer Science, vol. 1355, pp. 131–142. Springer (1997)
10. Jochemsz, E., May, A.: A strategy for finding roots of multivariate polynomials with new applications in attacking RSA variants. In: Lai, X., Chen, K. (eds.) ASIACRYPT 2006. LNCS, vol. 4284, pp. 267–282. Springer, Heidelberg (2006). https://doi.org/10.1007/11935230_18
11. Kunihiro, N.: On optimal bounds of small inverse problems and approximate GCD problems with higher degree. In: Gollmann, D., Freiling, F.C. (eds.) ISC 2012. LNCS, vol. 7483, pp. 55–69. Springer, Heidelberg (2012). https://doi.org/10.1007/978-3-642-33383-5_4
12. Lenstra, A.K., Lenstra, H.W., Lovász, L.: Factoring polynomials with rational coefficients. Math. Ann. **261**, 515–534 (1982)
13. May, A.: New RSA Vulnerabilities Using Lattice Reduction Methods. Ph.D. thesis, University of Paderborn (2003)
14. May, A.: Using LLL-Reduction for solving RSA and factorization problems. In: The LLL Algorithm: Survey and Applications, pp. 315–348. Information Security and Cryptography, Springer (2010)
15. Nitaj, A.: Another generalization of Wiener's attack on RSA. In: AFRICACRYPT 2008. Lecture Notes in Computer Science, vol. 5023, pp. 174–190. Springer (2008)
16. Rivest, R.L., Shamir, A., Adleman, L.: A method for obtaining digital signatures and public-key cryptosystems. Commun. ACM **21**(2), 120–126 (1978)
17. Roman'kov, V.A.: New probabilistic public-key encryption based on the RSA cryptosystem. Groups Complex. Cryptol. **7**(2), 153–156 (2015)

18. Shi, G., Wang, G., Gu, D.: Further cryptanalysis of a type of RSA variants. In: ISC 2022. Lecture Notes in Computer Science, vol. 13640, pp. 133–152. Springer (2022)
19. Wiener, M.J.: Cryptanalysis of short RSA secret exponents. IEEE Trans. Inf. Theory **36**(3), 553–558 (1990)

Hybrid Solutions for 2PC: How Much do they Cost?

Antonio Toppi(✉) and Paolo D'Arco

Università degli Studi di Salerno, Fisciano, Italy
a.toppi@studenti.unisa.it, pdarco@unisa.it

Abstract. Secure multiparty computation is becoming a concrete option in protocol design. Indeed, due to the astonishing improvement in computing power and refined optimization techniques, developed during the past years, the general solutions for secure multiparty computation are almost practical in several applications. The circuit-based solutions can be executed in reasonable times, and homomorphic-encryption-based solutions, for certain input sizes and suitable choices of methods and parameters, are doable too. In this paper our goal is to understand more the *current costs of implementing* such solutions, by using *off-the-shelf tools* for secure multiparty computation. Precisely, we focus on the well-known *private set-intersection* problem, and on private computation of *statistics on the set-intersection*. Our contribution is the following:

- we implement *circuit-based* solutions and *homomorphic-encryption based* solutions, and evaluate the corresponding performances and limits
- we implement *hybrid* solutions, with a garbled-circuit part built on top of an homomorphic encryption-based part, estimate the cost of each part and evaluate the overall performance
- we compare several *optimized versions*, in order to figure out the current ranges of concrete applicability, pointing out efficiency gains and bottlenecks

We conclude the paper discussing open issues and providing some hints for future researches.

Keywords: secure two-party computation · private set-intersection · homomorphic encryption · statistics · circuit-based solutions

1 Introduction

Looking for Efficient Solutions. The growing demand for privacy-preserving technologies has driven significant advancements in *secure multiparty computation* (MPC). MPC enables multiple parties to jointly compute a function over their inputs, while keeping those inputs private as much as possible. This capability is crucial in settings where sensitive data, from different sources, needs to be analyzed collectively, without compromising individual privacy. One fundamental problem in this domain is *private set intersection* (PSI), where, in the

L. Morogan et al. (Eds.): SecITC 2024, LNCS 15595, pp. 232–251, 2025.
https://doi.org/10.1007/978-3-031-87760-5_17

simplest form, two parties, A and B, wish to compute the intersection of their datasets, X and Y, respectively, without revealing any additional information about the elements outside the intersection. Various cryptographic techniques ensure the private computation of $X \cap Y$ and the private computation of statistics on $X \cap Y$ (PSI-stat).

2 Some Methods for PSI: A Quick Overview

Cryptographic hashing offers an efficient but limited solution. Roughly speaking, let H be a collision-resistant hash function. B computes the hash values $b_j = H(y_j)$'s, for all his y_j's, and sends them to A. Then, A computes the hash values $a_i = H(x_i)$'s, for all her x_i. Let H_A and H_B be the two sets of hash values. A computes $H_A \cap H_B$ and sets $X \cap Y = \{x \,|\, H(x) \in H_A \cap H_B\}$. Unfortunately, this method is not secure when the ground set of X and Y is small or the sets X and Y are sampled according to low-entropy distributions.

Protocols based on the Diffie-Hellman key-exchange, starting from [15], enhance the security by leveraging a cyclic group and a mapping function. More precisely, let G be a cyclic group of order q with generator g, and let H be a mapping of the set elements to G. A chooses $a \in Z_q$, computes the element $H(x_i)^a$, for all her x_i's and sends them to B. Then, B chooses $b \in Z_q$ and computes the element $H(y_j)^b$, for all his y_j's; moreover, he computes the elements $(H(x_i)^a)^b$, preserving the order in which the $H(x_i)^a$'s are received. He sends all of them to A. Finally, A, computes the elements $(H(y_j)^b)^a$ and sets $X \cap Y = \{x \,|\, (H(x)^a)^b = (H(y_j)^b)^a \text{ for some } j\}$. This method requires a suitable choice of the group to ensure security. It is communication-efficient.

The method based on Oblivious Polynomial Evaluation (OPE) [10] employs additively homomorphic encryption. It represents one party's set as the roots of a polynomial. The other party evaluates an encrypted version of the polynomial on her elements. More precisely, the elements in A's set are represented as

$$P(x) = \prod_{i=1}^{v} (x - x_i) = \sum_{i=0}^{v} c_i x^i$$

and the encrypted coefficients $E(c_i)$ are sent to B. Then, using the additive homomorphic property of the encryption scheme, the polynomial is evaluated by B on each element of his set. Precisely, B computes

$$u_j = E(r_j P(y_j) + y_j)$$

where the r_j's are chosen uniformly at random, for each element y_j of his set. Finally, the u_j's are sent to A. Upon decryption of the ciphertext u_j, if $y_j \in X \cap Y$, then A gets exactly y_j (because $r_j P(y_j)$ equals zero); otherwise, A gets a random value. Hence, denoting with $\overline{Y}$ the set of decrypted u_j ciphertexts, A computes $X \cap Y = X \cap \overline{Y}$. The method does not leak information on non-intersecting elements. It benefits from the properties of homomorphic encryption but can be computationally intensive.

Oblivious Pseudorandom Function (OPRF) [9,12] protocols allow secure two-party function evaluation: precisely, one party learns the function output on his input without learning the function key, and the other party, who holds the key, learns nothing about the input. An OPFR can be used to efficiently compute the intersection while maintaining privacy, and it gives rise to efficient solutions when combined with advanced data structures like hashing tables and the cucko hashing technique. To get the picture, let f be a PRF, let k be a key held by B, and let x be an input held by A. An OPRF is a two-party protocol for computing f in such a way that A gets $f_k(x)$ but does not get anything about k, while B does not get anything about x and $f_k(x)$. A PSI protocol is constructed as follows: given k, B compute the values $f_k(y_j)$, for all y_j's and sends $V_B = \{f_k(y_j)\}$ to A. Later on, A and B engage in $|X|$ executions of the OPRF protocol, where A, in each execution, has private input x_i and B has private input k. As a result, A learns $V_A = \{f_k(x_i)\}$ and computes $X \cap Y = \{x \mid f_k(x) \in V_A \cap V_B\}$.

Fully Homomorphic Encryption (FHE) represents a powerful yet computationally demanding approach, enabling operations on encrypted data without decryption. In the contest of PSI, it allows one party to send encrypted elements to the other, who then performs computations on these ciphertexts and returns a result. The first party can decrypt the result to find the intersection. The method offers strong privacy guarantees at the cost of significant computational resources [4,13].

Traditionally, for secure two-party computation (2PC), the predominant approach has been the use of garbled circuits [22]. This method represents the function of interest as a circuit. Then, roughly speaking, one party generates an encrypted version of the circuit, the garbled circuit, and the other party evaluates it, in such a way that neither party learns more than necessary. While garbled circuits provide a robust foundation for secure computation, they often face challenges related to computational complexity and efficiency, particularly when dealing with large datasets. We will provide more details later on on fully homomorphic encryption and garbled circuits.

Recent advancements have introduced hybrid protocols that combine the strengths of garbled circuits with homomorphic encryption techniques. They aim to optimize the trade-off between computational cost and communication overhead, making secure computations more practical for real-world applications. By preprocessing the data with homomorphic encryption, these protocols reduce the complexity of the garbled circuit construction and evaluation, thereby enhancing the overall performance. An example of such an approach, focused on protocols for PSI-stat, can be found in [6].

Our Contribution. This paper presents a comprehensive evaluation of several protocols for PSI and for PSI-stat. More precisely, it focuses on some of the protocols described in [6], and provides:

- implementations of garbled circuit-based solutions
- implementations of hybrid protocols that integrate homomorphic encryption and garbled circuits

- a comparative analysis and evaluation of different optimized versions of the latter, to identify the most efficient and practical solutions

The paper aims at assessing the current costs and performance, *using off-the-shelf tools and technologies.* It seeks to provide valuable insights in the potential of MPC protocols for the future. The findings are expected to guide further research in the field, contributing to the broader adoption of privacy-preserving technologies in applications.

Organization. Section 3 describes the private computation model used in this study. Then, Sect. 4 outlines the primitives and the platforms employed for the implementation and evaluation of the protocols. Section 5 details the specific protocols investigated. Section 6 presents the implementation details and the findings of our testing. Finally, Sect. 7 provides the conclusions and discusses a few future research directions.

3 Private Computation: The Model

PSI and PSI-stat are special cases of secure two-party computation. Hence, we consider the standard security definitions for secure two-party computation. We focus mostly on the semi-honest model, i.e., the parties follows the protocol but try to get as much information as they can from the protocol run. The model guarantees that the protocol *does not inadvertently leak information.*

Let F be a two-party functionality[1] defined by $f(X,Y) = (f_A(X,Y), f_B(X,Y))$, where X and Y are the inputs held by Alice and Bob, and $f_A(X,Y)$ and $f_B(X,Y)$ are the corresponding outputs. In an ideal world, Alice and Bob privately send X and Y to F (which can be thought of figuratively as an ideal trusted party that evaluates the functionality and sends the results), and privately get back $f_A(X,Y)$ and $f_B(X,Y)$, respectively. Let Π be, in the real world, a two-party protocol, run by Alice and Bob, which emulates F. Alice and Bob are probabilistic polynomial time (*ppt*) algorithms (all the algorithms in the paper are assumed to be *ppt*), which run on input X and Y, respectively. Let $view_A^{\Pi}(X,Y)$ and $view_B^{\Pi}(X,Y)$ be the views that Alice and Bob get during the run of the protocol Π. A view consists of the input, the random choices and of all the messages a party receives from the other party. Let also $out^{\Pi}(X,Y) = (out_A^{\Pi}(X,Y), out_B^{\Pi}(X,Y))$ be the protocol output. Loosely speaking, Π is a secure emulation of F, if the view *and* the output distribution of each party can be *efficiently simulated* by an algorithm, which, without interaction, only uses the input and the output of the party. Intuitively, if a party can generate by herself a transcript that cannot be distinguished from a real transcript, then the protocol does not leak any secret information. More formally:

[1] A functionality is a randomized generalization of the concept of a function (which corresponds to the deterministic case).

Semi-honest Security. Protocol Π is a semi-honest secure realization of the functionality F if there exists two *ppt* simulators S_A and S_B such that, for all inputs X and Y,

$$(view_A^{\Pi}(X,Y), out^{\Pi}(X,Y)) \overset{c}{\approx} (S_A(X, f_A(X,Y)), f(X,Y))$$

$$(view_B^{\Pi}(X,Y), out^{\Pi}(X,Y)) \overset{c}{\approx} (S_B(Y, f_B(X,Y)), f(X,Y))$$

where $\overset{c}{\approx}$ denotes computational indistinguishability.

Notice that we have specified the model to clearly state the problem and the properties we want to achieve. However, due to the spirit and goals of this work, we will not provide formal proofs. They can be found in the papers that introduced the protocols.

The *ideal* functionalities we would like to emulate are defined in Figs. 1 and 2. We assume that only one party gets the result of the computation. Moreover, in Fig. 2, we assume that the ground set $\mathcal{U}$ from which X and Y are drawn is ordered, and A and B need to compute a statistic on $X \cap Y$.

- Inputs to F_{PSI}: Alice inputs a set of elements $X = \{x_1, \ldots, x_v\}$ and Bob inputs a set of elements $Y = \{y_1, \ldots, y_w\}$
- Outputs from F_{PSI}: Alice receives $I = X \cap Y$, Bob receives $\perp$ (nothing)

Fig. 1. F_{PSI} : ideal functionality for PSI.

- Inputs to $F_{PSIstat}$: Alice inputs a set of elements $X = \{x_1, \ldots, x_v\}$ and Bob inputs a set of elements $Y = \{y_1, \ldots, y_w\}$
- Outputs from $F_{PSIstat}$: Alice receives the statistic on $X \cap Y$ (if $X \cap Y \neq \emptyset$), Bob receives $\perp$ (nothing).

Fig. 2. $F_{PSIstat}$: ideal functionality for a given statistic.

4 Primitives and Platforms

In this section we briefly mention the primitives and the platforms we have used in our implementations of the protocols.

4.1 Yao's Garbled Circuit

Yao's construction [22] enables two parties, Alice and Bob, to privately evaluate a functionality $f(\cdot,\cdot)$ on their inputs, x and y, in such a way that each party gets the result and, at the same time, *preserves* the privacy of its own input, apart from what can be inferred about it by the other party from its input and the function value $f(x, y)$. For example, if the functionality $f(\cdot,\cdot)$ is the `xor` function, given x `xor y` and one of the input, it is impossible to preserve the other input.

In a nutshell, the construction works as follows: the functionality $f(\cdot,\cdot)$ is represented through a boolean circuit $C(\cdot,\cdot)$ for which, for each x, y, it holds that $C(x, y) = f(x, y)$. Yao's idea is to use the circuit as a *conceptual guide* for the computation which, instead of a sequence of `and`, `or` and `not` operations on strings of bits x and y, becomes a *sequence of decryptions* of ciphertexts. More precisely, one of the party, say Alice, given $C(\cdot,\cdot)$, computes a new object $\tilde{C}$, which is usually referred to as the *garbled circuit* where:

- to each wire w of $C(\cdot,\cdot)$ are associated in $\tilde{C}$ two random keys, k_w^0 and k_w^1, which (secretly, the correspondence is not public) represent 0 and 1, and
- to each gate $G(\cdot,\cdot)$ of $C(\cdot,\cdot)$ corresponds in $\tilde{C}$ a *gate table* $\tilde{G}$ with four rows, each of which is a *double encryption*, obtained by using two different keys $k_{w_1}^a$ and $k_{w_2}^b$, for $a, b \in \{0, 1\}$, of a message which is itself a random key $k_{w_3}^c$, for $c \in \{0, 1\}$. In detail, each double encryption $Enc_{ab}{=}Enc_{k_{w_2}^b}(Enc_{k_{w_1}^a}(k_{w_3}^c))$ uses *one of the four* possible pairs of keys $(k_{w_1}^a, k_{w_2}^b)$, associated to the input wires (w_1, w_2) of gate $G(\cdot,\cdot)$, and the message which is encrypted is the random key $k_{w_3}^c$, associated to the wire w_3 of the output of the gate $G(\cdot,\cdot)$ *if and only if* $G(a, b) = c$. The four double encryptions $Enc_{00}, Enc_{01}, Enc_{10}$ and Enc_{11} are stored in the gate table rows in a *random* order.

Once $\tilde{C}$ has been computed, Alice sends to Bob all the gate tables $\tilde{G}$ associated to the circuit gates $G(\cdot,\cdot)$, and *reveals* the random keys k_w^0 and k_w^1, associated to all the circuit *output* wires w, and their correspondences with the values 0 and 1. Moreover, for the input wires of the circuit, she sends to Bob the random keys $k_{w_1}^{x_1}, k_{w_2}^{x_2}, \ldots, k_{w_n}^{x_n}$ corresponding to the bit-values of her own input $x = x_1 x_2 \ldots x_n$. To perform the computation represented by $\tilde{C}$, then Bob needs only the keys associated to the input wires corresponding to *his own* input, and he needs to get them without revealing his input bits to Alice. This issue is solved by means of *executions* of a 1-out-of-2 *oblivious transfer* protocol [7], through which Bob receives the random keys $k_{w_{n+1}}^{y_1}, k_{w_{n+2}}^{y_2}, \ldots, k_{w_{2n}}^{y_{2n}}$ corresponding to the bit-values of his own input $y = y_1 y_2 \ldots y_n$ while Alice does not get any information from the transfer, that is, Alice is not able to tell which specific keys Bob has recovered.

Finally Bob, according to the topology of the original circuit $C(\cdot,\cdot)$, level after level, decrypts *one and only one* entry from each gate table $\tilde{G}$ in $\tilde{C}$, until he computes *one and only one* random key associated to each output wire. Indeed, the encryption is such that only one decryption in each table is correct. The binary string which corresponds to the sequence of computed random keys, associated to the output wires, is the value $C(x, y)$. Bob sends the result of the computation to Alice.

Efficiency. Notice that *branching* with Yao's garbled circuit method is costly, due to the inherent need to garble and evaluate *multiple* potential execution paths, regardless of which path is actually taken. For example, if the functionality is expressed with a program in a certain code or pseudocode, typically it presents several conditional branches. Then, the garbler must create separate garbled circuits for each branch of the condition to ensure that the evaluator can proceed without knowing which branch will be taken. This results in a significant increase in the size of the garbled circuit, as all possible branches must be garbled and transmitted to the evaluator. Furthermore, the evaluator must process each garbled branch to some extent, increasing the computational overhead. The complexity of garbling grows with the number of conditional branches. This redundancy ensures security and obliviousness but at the cost of efficiency.

4.2 Homomorphic Encryption

Homomorphic encryption is a powerful cryptographic primitive that enables computations to be performed directly on encrypted data without requiring any decryption. Such a property allows secure processing of sensitive information in untrusted environments. More precisely, in homomorphic encryption, the data are first encrypted using a public key. The encryption process ensures that specific operations, such as addition and/or multiplication, can be performed on the ciphertexts with effect on the underlying plaintexts.

Homomorphic encryption schemes can be categorized depending on the types of operations they support on encrypted data.

- *Partially Homomorphic Encryption* (PHE) supports only a single type of operation on ciphertexts, either addition or multiplication, but not both.
- *Somewhat Homomorphic Encryption* (SHE) supports both addition and multiplication operations but only for a limited number of times.
- *Fully Homomorphic Encryption* (FHE) extends the capabilities of SHE by supporting an arbitrary number of both addition and multiplication operations on ciphertexts. This allows for the computation of any function on encrypted data without decrypting it.

4.3 Encryption Schemes

Paillier Cryptosystem. The Paillier cryptosystem [18] is a partially homomorphic encryption scheme. It has been chosen because it implements an additive homomorphism, allowing for the *addition of the values* underlying the encryptions, and *multiplication by a constant*. This unique feature makes the Paillier cryptosystem particularly useful in several applications requiring secure computation. The cryptosystem security relies on the hardness of the decisional composite residuosity assumption.

BFV Scheme. The Brakerski-Fan-Vercauteren (BFV) scheme [3,8], is a widely recognized fully homomorphic encryption scheme that supports *both addition and multiplication* on encrypted data. Its security is based on the Learning With Errors (LWE) problem [19] and its ring variant, Ring Learning With Errors (RLWE) problem [17], both of which are fundamental problems in lattice-based cryptography. The LWE problem requires solving a system of linear equations that are perturbed by small random errors, a task believed to be computationally infeasible even for quantum computers. The RLWE problem extends to polynomial rings. Solutions based on RLWE enhance efficiency and scalability while maintaining strong security assumptions. This scheme has been chosen because optimizations in the key generation, the encryption, and the decryption processes improve its practical performance, making it feasible for real-world use.

4.4 A Platform: MP-SPDZ

MP-SPDZ is a software platform *to benchmark* various secure multi-party computation protocols in different security models, with support for both semi-honest and malicious behaviours. The underlying technologies span secret sharing, homomorphic encryption, and garbled circuits [16].

4.5 Libraries

Microsoft **SEAL** (Simple Encrypted Arithmetic Library) [20] is an open-source homomorphic encryption library developed by the Cryptography and Privacy Research Group at Microsoft. It implements the BFV [8] scheme, and also other two homomorphic encryption schemes: the BGV [2] and CKKS [5] schemes.

An efficient pure-Rust library for Paillier's encryption scheme is **kzen-paillier**, offering also packed encoding for encrypting several values together, as well as several zero-knowledge proofs for typical use-cases.

Rayon is a high-performance library for the Rust programming language, designed to simplify the parallelization of computations over collections. The library leverages Rust's ownership model and type system to provide safe and efficient concurrency, without the typical pitfalls of parallel programming, such as race conditions and data corruption.

5 Protocols

In this section we describe the protocols we have implemented and tested.

5.1 Circuit-Based Protocols

A basic approach to implementing a practical PSI protocol consists in constructing a circuit to perform set intersection, which is then encrypted using Yao's protocol. For example, the circuit could simply compare each element of X with all the elements of Y.

However, a drawback of this method lies in its computational complexity: it requires $O(|X| \cdot |Y|)$ operations to be executed. Furthermore, this approach fails to leverage the orderliness of the sets, which could otherwise enable a more efficient intersection implementation. A more efficient protocol has been presented in [14]. In particular, the circuit is called *Sort-Compare-Shuffle* (SCS). In this circuit, the two sorted sets are merged into a single sorted list, and neighboring elements are compared to determine the intersection. The resulting intersection is then shuffled to prevent leakage of additional information. Compared to the original proposal [14], we implement this approach utilizing the sorting method described in [11], and employing a Waksman network [21] for the shuffling process, since on the platform we used to conduct the tests the method in [11] outperforms bitonic sorting.

5.2 Hybrid Protocols for Statistics

A statistic could be computed, as before, by designing an ad-hoc circuit and using Yao's protocol. However, another implementation strategy involves using homomorphic encryption to preprocess the sets and create an *intermediate representation* that can be evaluated with a simpler circuit. Examples of this method are shown in Figs. 3 and 4, which use additive homomorphic encryption (AHE) and fully homomorphic encryption (FHE) schemes, respectively. The intermediate representation offers several advantages, such as ensuring both encoded sets have the same size and lack any direct link to the original sets [6]. This allows for simpler circuits like the ones shown in pseudocode in Appendix A for computing statistics over the intersection in a private way. Although these methods retain a complexity of $O(|X| \cdot |Y|)$, they avoid the need for garbling, transmitting, and evaluating a quadratic number of gates, potentially enhancing performance.

Computing the Intersection with AHE and FHE. Notice that, the protocol in Fig. 4 can be simplified. Computing the intersection *does not require* the representation with intermediate values. More precisely, B does not need to use the random t_i's values: he can use the real values y_j's. In such a simpler form, when A receives $d_1, \ldots, d_w$, then she decrypts and gets, from each d_j, either a random value or a real value from B's set, which belongs to the intersection. Hence, A can compute the intersection by computing a plain intersection between X and the set of decrypted values. Similarly, if A is only interested in computing the *cardinality* of the intersection, then B does not need to use the t_i's values at all. Indeed, when A receives $d_1, \ldots, d_w$, then she decrypts and gets 0 each time one of B's element belongs to the intersection. In this form the protocol is exactly the protocol proposed in [4]. The same argument applies to the protocol in Fig. 3 that coincides with the protocol proposed in [10]. Still, the representation with intermediate values is *fundamental* for computing other statistics on the intersection, while preserving the privacy of the intersection.

A hybrid AHE-based protocol

- B chooses the parameters of an additive homomorphic encryption scheme (E, D), chooses the public and the private keys, and sends to A the parameters and the public key. Then, he represents his private set as roots of a polynomial, i.e., $P(x) = \prod_{i=1}^{w}(x - x_i) = \sum_{i=0}^{w} c_i x^i$ and sends to A the encrypted coefficients $E(c_0), \ldots, E(c_w)$.
- A, for each $j = 1, \ldots, v$,
  1. chooses two random values, r_j and r_{x_j}, and
  2. computes homomorphically $u_j = E(r_j \cdot P(x_j) + r_{x_j})$

  Finally, A sends $u_1, \ldots, u_v$ to B.
- B, for $j = 1, \ldots, v$, computes $z_j = D(u_j)$
- B, with input $z_1, \ldots, z_v$, and A, with input $r_{x_1}, \ldots, r_{x_v}$, in this order, securely evaluates a circuit which gives in output the desired statistic on the intersection.

Fig. 3. An AHE-based protocol for computing a statistic on the intersection.

A hybrid FHE-based protocol

Let $FHE.Enc$ and $FHE.Dec$ be the encryption and decryption algorithms.

- A for $i = 1, \ldots, v$, using the public key P_A, computes $c_i = FHE.Enc(x_i)$ and sends the v ciphertexts $c_1, \ldots, c_v$ and P_A to B
- B, for each c_i,
  1. samples two random non-zero values, r_i and t_i
  2. homomorphically computes $d_i = r_i \prod_{j=1}^{w}(c_i - y_j) + t_i$,

  and sends $(d_1, \ldots, d_v)$ to A.
- A decrypts the ciphertexts $(d_1, \ldots, d_v)$ obtaining for $j = 1, \ldots, v$, the values $z_j = FHE.Dec(d_j)$
- A, with input $z_1, \ldots, z_v$, and B, with input $t_1, \ldots, t_v$, in this order, securely evaluates a circuit which gives in output the desired statistic on the intersection.

Fig. 4. A FHE-based protocol for computing a statistic on the intersection.

5.3 Improving Efficiency

The protocols outlined in Figs. 3 and 4 can be optimized through various techniques (see Figs. 5 and 6). The optimizations trade-offs efficiency vs security.

Decreasing the Output Lengths. Using a collision-resistant hash function to truncate input sizes reduces the number of gates required, improving the overall efficiency.

Partitioning the Ground Set. The most computationally intensive step is polynomial evaluation. Partitioning the ground set $\mathcal{U}$ into n parts simplifies this process by generating n polynomials with lower degree, each containing roots from a single part.

Information Leakage. Partitioning the ground set and transmitting the partitioned initial set to the other participant can reveal the distribution of the elements, potentially leaking additional information. To mitigate this issue, the initial set can be randomly transformed using mapping functions such as pairwise hashing functions. Another approach to reduce information leakage involves adding extra invalid values to the initial set, as described below:

- *AHE-based protocol*: Party A can send not only the encrypted coefficients but also encryptions of zero at arbitrary positions within the polynomial since zero is an invalid value. This modification increases the degree of the polynomial without affecting its roots. Consequently, when party B receives the polynomials, he cannot discern the number of zeroes versus the number of genuine coefficients.
- *FHE-based protocol*: Party A can send additional pairs containing the encryption of zero in any position and labelling them with an arbitrary part. This approach ensures that party B cannot determine whether a given evaluation involves a zero or a valid value.

Both methods enable party A to hide the real size of the parts sent to B, making it impossible for party B to ascertain the exact number of elements in each partition. Only an upper bound on the number of elements can be determined. Additionally, the extra values sent to party B allow party A to conceal the exact size of her set.

However, this approach has the downside of increasing the protocol execution time, since party B has to evaluate a larger number of elements.

6 Implementation and Evaluation

The protocols described were implemented on the following computing system:

- *Hardware specification*: CPU AMD Ryzen 9 5900HX, RAM 16GB, Network type: LAN
- *Software specification*: OS Kubuntu 22.04, Rust compiled using version 1.78.0 of *rustc*, Microsoft SEAL version: 6.0.2, MP-SPDZ built from source, kzen-paillier version: 0.4.3, rayon version: 0.4.3
- *Protocol security specification*: Pairwise hashing from arbitrary size items using a linear equation modulus a random 128-bit prime, $\mathcal{H}$ instantiated using SHA-256., Paillier using a 2048-bit key, BFV instantiated with a security level of 128-bit according to [1], MP-SPDZ setting the security parameter to 40.

Optimized hybrid AHE-based protocol Let $P = \{S_1, \dots, S_n\}$ be a partition of $\mathcal{U}$, let $\mathcal{H}$ be a collision resistant hash function, and let $P_i := \prod_{t \in Y \cap S_i}(x - t)$.

- B chooses the parameters of an AHE scheme (E, D), chooses the public key and the secret key, and sends to A the parameters and the public key. Then, he represents his private set as a set of polynomial $\mathcal{P} = \{P_i\}_{i=1}^{n}$ and sends to A the encrypted coefficients of each polynomial
- A, for $j = 1, \dots, v$,
  1. chooses two random values, r_j and r_{x_j}, and
  2. computes homomorphically $u_j = E(r_j \cdot P_{i:x_j \in S_i}(x_j) + r_{x_j})$

  Finally, A sends $u_1, \dots, u_w$ to B.
- B, for $j = 1, \dots, w$, computes $z_j = D(u_j)$
- B, with input $\mathcal{H}(z_1), \dots, \mathcal{H}(z_w)$, and A, with input $\mathcal{H}(r_{x_1}), \dots, \mathcal{H}(r_{x_w})$, in this order, securely evaluates a circuit which gives in output the desired statistic on the intersection.

Fig. 5. Optimized hybrid AHE-based protocol for computing a statistic on the intersection without additional zero encryptions.

6.1 Implementation Details

For our implementation we used arbitrary long numbers as elements of the set. The pairwise hashing function converts the values into 128-bit strings.

6.2 Implementation of Specific Optimizations

The protocol in Fig. 5 has been implemented using the Paillier cryptosystem, while the protocol in Fig. 6 has been implemented using the BFV cryptosystem. Once the cryptosystems had been chosen it was possible to apply specific optimizations. In particular:

Paillier Cryptosystem Optimization. Paillier cryptosystem uses modular exponentiation, which is faster for numbers which can be represented using fewer bits. Since the ground set can be several orders of magnitude larger than the effective sets of the parties, then the input item size can be reduced using a simple pairwise independent hashing function.

BFV Cryptosystem Optimization. By selecting specific values for the plaintext modulus, a technique known as batching can be employed. This technique allows the plaintext to be represented as a matrix containing multiple elements, enabling a *single* plaintext to encapsulate multiple elements. Consequently, any operation performed on a ciphertext generated using this method will be applied simultaneously to every element within the matrix.

Optimized hybrid FHE-based protocol

Let $\mathcal{H}$ be a collision resistant hash function, let $FHE.Enc$ and $FHE.Dec$ be the encryption and decryption algorithms, let $P = \{S_1, \ldots, S_n\}$ be a partition of $\mathcal{U}$

- A, for $i = 1, \ldots, v$, using the public key P_A, computes $c_i = FHE.Enc(x_i)$ and sends $(c_1, [x_1]), \ldots, (c_v, [x_v])$ and P_A to B. The values $[x_1], \ldots, [x_v]$ denote a representation of the classes of the partition, where the elements belong to.
- B, for each $(c_i, [x_i])$,
  1. samples two random non-zero value, r_i and t_i
  2. homomorphically computes $u_i = r_i \prod_{y:y \in [x_i] \cap Y}(c_i - y) + t_i$,

  and sends $(u_1, \ldots, u_v)$ to A.
- A decrypts the ciphertexts $(u_1, \ldots, u_v)$ obtaining for $j = 1, \ldots, v$, the values $z_j = FHE.Dec(u_j)$
- A, with input $\mathcal{H}(z_1), \ldots, \mathcal{H}(z_v)$, and B, with input $\mathcal{H}(t_1), \ldots, \mathcal{H}(t_v)$, in this order, securely evaluates a circuit which gives in output the desired statistic on the intersection.

Fig. 6. Optimized FHE-based protocol for computing a statistic on the intersection without additional zero encryptions.

6.3 Results

To estimate the best performance of the protocols, a series of tests were conducted. The sets for both parties were randomly generated using the cryptographically secure pseudorandom number generator provided by the Linux kernel, one-sixteenth of the elements of the sets were duplicated in both sets to make the intersection non-empty. The detailed results of these tests are reported in Tables 1 and 2 and in Fig. 7.

Table 1. Paillier protocol execution time in seconds with different partition sizes.

Set	Partition size												
Size	1	2	4	8	16	32	64	128	256	512	1024	2048	4096
256	2.00	1.25	0.84	0.68	0.59	**0.56**	**0.56**	0.62					
512	7.06	3.93	2.45	1.72	1.36	1.17	**1.14**	1.17	1.24				
1024	27.76	14.77	8.03	5.00	3.73	2.76	2.42	**2.29**	2.34	2.53			
2048	105.16	53.01	28.90	16.15	10.06	7.06	5.53	4.90	**4.65**	**4.65**	5.11		
4096	406.01	204.57	105.66	54.90	31.15	19.38	13.65	10.77	9.50	**8.96**	9.02	9.88	
8192	$\perp$	$\perp$	407.07	211.97	115.24	65.14	41.30	28.80	22.32	19.52	**18.52**	18.76	20.55

Table 2. BFV protocol execution time in seconds with different partition sizes.

Set	Partition size												
Size	1	2	4	8	16	32	64	128	256	512	1024	2048	4096
256	3.24	3.42	3.39	3.47	0.69	0.70	0.83	**0.42**					
512	5.88	5.73	6.02	6.05	5.96	1.23	1.36	1.39	**0.76**				
1024	11.55	11.42	11.16	11.48	10.94	11.34	2.30	2.51	3.12	**1.58**			
2048	21.35	22.70	22.10	22.34	21.57	22.71	24.25	4.66	5.45	5.66	**3.25**		
4096	432.05	43.93	45.11	44.68	45.07	44.22	45.24	46.53	10.11	10.94	12.16	**7.29**	
8192	⊥	⊥	97.91	97.66	95.69	95.42	95.23	97.28	95.15	23.62	24.89	27.67	**17.38**

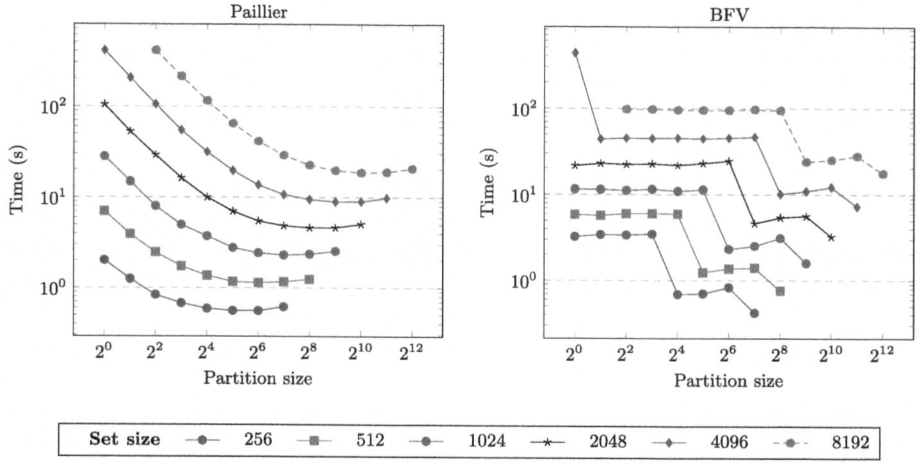

Fig. 7. Execution times with a specific set size for different partition sizes.

The best performance for the Paillier protocol is achieved with a partition size of *approximately one-eighth* of the set size. Conversely, the BFV protocol shows a significant reduction in execution time when using less computationally intensive parameters, attributable to a decreased multiplicative depth. Consequently, the execution time for the BFV protocol remains nearly constant when the same parameters are used due to batching. Later on, the best partition, for each set size, was used to compute the execution time for the entire protocol.

The results for the entire protocols using the *intersection* as the function to compute (see Fig A.5 in Appendix A), are reported in Tables 3 and 4, with a visual representation in Fig. 8. These tables show the performance outcomes of several protocols, namely the naive PSI protocol, the Sort-Compare-Shuffle circuit presented in Sect. 5.1, the protocols in Figs. 3, 4, and the protocols in Figs. 6 and 5, with the optimizations described in Subsects. 5.3 and 6.2 using partitioning, across different set sizes, in both the symmetric and the asymmetric settings. The columns in the tables follow the same order as the protocols listed here.

The results of the computation of the circuital component of the hybrid protocols are presented in Tables 5 and 6, with a visual representation in Fig. 9. Each circuit takes the intermediate representation of both parties sets as input. Notably, the intersection operation is the fastest, which perfectly fits the intuition that the intersection reveals more information than the other functions of the intersection.

To estimate the most efficient performance obtainable, the tests were conducted without additional zero encryptions. The protocols listed in Figs. 3 and 4 were included in the comparative analysis to assess their performance compared to the naive PSI protocol, which lacks any optimization and partitioning features. Each test was constrained by a time limit of 600 seconds to reflect real-world performance expectations; instances where this limit was exceeded are denoted by ⊥.

The results show that the protocol in Fig. 5 achieved a better performance in terms of both bandwidth usage and execution time for symmetric sets. In some asymmetric scenarios, the protocol in Fig. 6 proved to be the fastest in a local context; however, its high bandwidth usage significantly impacts performance over non-local connections. The optimizations described in Sect. 5.2 notably reduced the bandwidth requirements for executing the protocol, particularly for the Paillier scheme. Conversely, approaches relying solely on garbled circuits exhibited excessive complexity in bandwidth, making them impractical for non-local implementations. Meanwhile, in terms of execution time, the *Sort-Compare-Shuffle* method demonstrated competitiveness compared to the hybrid protocols.

Table 3. Time in seconds needed to execute the protocols

SIZE ALICE	SIZE BOB	YAO NAIVE	YAO SCS	PAILLIER NO PARTITION	BFV NO PARTITION	PAILLIER PARTITION	BFV PARTITION	PAILLIER ONLY	BFV ONLY
256	256	15.624	1.853	3.063	3.266	0.631	0.693	0.606	0.669
512	512	63.228	4.425	8.137	5.931	1.233	1.297	1.184	1.249
1024	1024	267.791	10.682	27.962	11.643	2.468	2.589	2.376	2.493
2048	2048	⊥	25.002	102.024	21.546	4.928	5.086	4.750	4.885
4096	4096	⊥	60.623	403.558	432.361	9.959	10.966	9.585	10.659
8192	8192	⊥	133.294	⊥	⊥	21.170	25.710	19.193	25.035
256	8192	508.048	58.168	57.281	⊥	13.523	4.759	11.546	4.736
8192	256	518.181	57.651	129.937	12.052	9.096	12.099	9.072	11.424
512	4096	507.705	26.055	53.125	427.542	6.307	9.102	5.933	9.054
4096	512	515.136	25.298	69.190	11.423	5.041	4.236	4.992	3.929

Table 4. Data to be transferred to execute the protocols

SIZE ALICE	SIZE BOB	YAO NAIVE	YAO SCS	PAILLIER NO PARTITION	BFV NO PARTITION	PAILLIER PARTITION	BFV PARTITION	PAILLIER ONLY	BFV ONLY
256	256	2.70 GB	305.96 MB	264.75 KB	23.21 MB	1.34 MB	31.43 MB	297.31 KB	30.39 MB
512	512	10.80 GB	739.54 MB	528.25 KB	24.25 MB	2.68 MB	60.15 MB	593.95 KB	58.07 MB
1024	1024	43.18 GB	1.75 GB	1.06 MB	26.34 MB	5.29 MB	117.59 MB	1.12 MB	113.42 MB
2048	2048	⊥	4.12 GB	2.11 MB	30.51 MB	10.58 MB	232.48 MB	2.24 MB	224.14 MB
4096	4096	⊥	9.58 GB	4.22 MB	157.91 MB	21.16 MB	462.25 MB	4.48 MB	445.57 MB
8192	8192	⊥	22.01 GB	⊥	⊥	42.34 MB	921.79 MB	8.97 MB	888.43 MB
256	8192	86.37 GB	9.58 GB	4.35 MB	⊥	37.85 MB	225.19 MB	4.48 MB	224.15 MB
8192	256	86.37 GB	9.58 GB	4.35 MB	66.5 MB	5.52 MB	921.79 MB	4.48 MB	888.43 MB
512	4096	86.37 GB	4.14 GB	2.37 MB	143.3 MB	19.12 MB	447.65 MB	2.44 MB	445.56 MB
4096	512	86.37 GB	4.14 GB	2.37 MB	42.51 MB	4.73 MB	462.25 MB	2.64 MB	445.57 MB

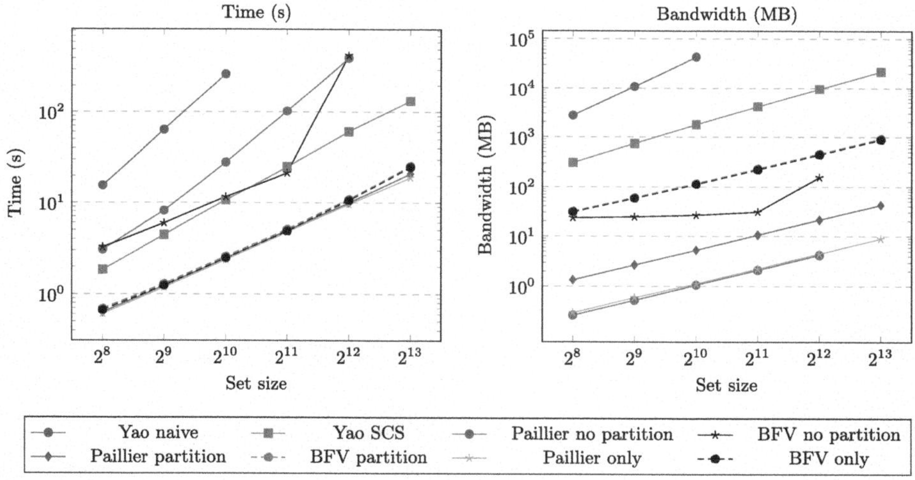

Fig. 8. Resources used by the protocols in the symmetric cases.

Table 5. Time in milliseconds needed to execute the circuital part for every statistic

Protocol		Parties input size					
		256	512	1024	2048	4096	8192
Max	[A.1]	41.874	117.581	144.480	291.181	792.840	3220.33
Min	[A.2]	38.935	85.147	193.771	440.488	659.663	2669.09
Size	[A.3]	69.280	128.995	252.143	623.986	1194.57	2219.94
Median	[A.4]	103.806	227.958	354.166	704.952	1490.83	2568.43
Intersection	[A.5]	24.673	48.847	92.043	178.611	373.717	1976.83

Table 6. Data to be transferred in MB for the circuital part for every statistic

Protocol		Parties input size					
		256	512	1024	2048	4096	8192
Max	[A.1]	2.089	4.178	8.356	16.712	33.424	66.847
Min	[A.2]	3.138	6.275	12.550	25.101	50.201	100.402
Size	[A.3]	4.268	8.536	17.072	34.145	68.289	136.578
Median	[A.4]	10.633	21.267	42.533	85.066	170.132	340.264
Intersection	[A.5]	1.043	2.085	4.171	8.342	16.683	33.366

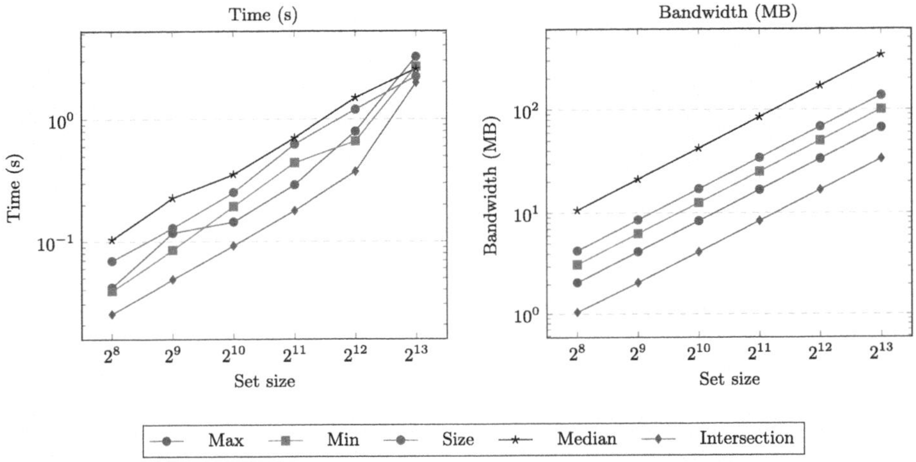

Fig. 9. Protocol's resources used by the circuital part.

7 Conclusions and Open Problems

We have presented an implementation with off-the-shelf tools and an evaluation of several cryptographic protocols for privacy-preserving operations on set intersection. Using standard optimization techniques, improvements in efficiency and scalability of these protocols were obtained. More precisely, leveraging specific optimizations tailored to the Paillier and the BFV cryptosystems, alongside parallelization using the Rust programming language, non-trivial performance enhancements were achieved across various protocol configurations.

Results underscore the efficacy of these optimizations in enhancing both execution time and bandwidth utilization. The optimized hybrid protocol, utilizing the Paillier cryptosystem (Fig 5), emerged as the top performer in terms of both bandwidth efficiency and execution time for *symmetric sets*. Conversely, for certain *asymmetric sets*, the optimized BFV protocol (Fig 6) showed a better execution time but at a higher bandwidth and computation resources used. Such findings confirm previous studies in the field (e.g., [4]).

Notably, the evaluation highlighted the cost of the protocols relying solely on garbled circuits for *large datasets*, given the high bandwidth demands, rendering them unsuitable for most implementations.

Overall, the findings offer valuable insights into the practical implementation and optimization of privacy-preserving cryptographic protocols, shedding light on strategies to enhance efficiency and scalability in real-world applications.

Still, several open problems need to be addressed. In particular, while the study provides an idea of the performance of the protocols in a controlled environments, their real-world deployability and practical usability remain open questions. Further investigations considering additional factors, e.g., the communication between two separate devices over a Wide Area Network (WAN), are needed.

Addressing these open issues could lead to advancements in the field, and contribute to the development of more efficient, scalable, and practical solutions for secure computation.

Acknowledgment. This work was partially supported by project *SERICS* (*PE*00000014) under the NRRP MUR program funded by the EU - NGEU.

Appendix

A Circuit Descriptions

A.1 Max circuit for intermediate set representation

- A and B input their respective sets X and Y
- Let $max = \perp$
- For $i = 1, \ldots, |X|$:
  - if $X_i = Y_i$ then $max := i$
- A receives max, B receives $\perp$

A.2 Min circuit for intermediate set representation

- A and B input their respective sets X and Y
- Let $min = \perp$
- For $i = 1, \ldots, |X|$:
  - if $min = \perp$ and $X_i = Y_i$ then $min := i$
- A receives min, B receives $\perp$

A.3 Size circuit for intermediate set representation

- A and B input their respective sets X and Y
- Let $size := 0$
- For $i = 1, \ldots, |X|$:
  - if $X_i = Y_i$ then increment $size$
- A receives $size$, B receives $\perp$

A.4 Median circuit for intermediate set representation

- A and B input their respective sets X and Y
- Let $size$ be the result of the execution of the protocol described in A.3
- Let $median := \perp$ and let $acc := 0$
- For $i = 1, \ldots, |X|$:
  - if $X_i = Y_i$ then increment acc
  - if $acc = \lceil size/2 \rceil$ and $X_i = Y_i$ then $median := X_i$
- A receives $median$, B receives $\perp$

A.5 Intersection circuit for intermediate set representation

- A and B input their respective sets X and Y
- Let I be a boolean array of size $|X|$
- For $i = 1, \ldots, |X|$:
  - $I_i := X_i = Y_i$
- A receives the I array, B receives $\perp$

References

1. Albrecht, M., et al.: Homomorphic encryption security standard. Tech. rep., HomomorphicEncryption.org, Toronto, Canada (November 2018)
2. Brakerski, Z., Gentry, C., Vaikuntanathan, V.: (leveled) fully homomorphic encryption without bootstrapping. ACM Trans. Comput. Theor. **6**(3) (Jul 2014). https://doi.org/10.1145/2633600
3. Brakerski, Z., Vaikuntanathan, V.: Efficient fully homomorphic encryption from (standard) lwe. SIAM J. Comput. **43**(2), 831–871 (2014). https://doi.org/10.1137/120868669
4. Chen, H., Laine, K., Rindal, P.: Fast private set intersection from homomorphic encryption. In: Proceedings of the 2017 ACM SIGSAC Conference on Computer and Communications Security, pp. 1243–1255. CCS '17, Association for Computing Machinery, New York, NY, USA (2017). https://doi.org/10.1145/3133956.3134061
5. Cheon, J.H., Kim, A., Kim, M., Song, Y.: Homomorphic encryption for arithmetic of approximate numbers. In: Takagi, T., Peyrin, T. (eds.) ASIACRYPT 2017. LNCS, vol. 10624, pp. 409–437. Springer, Cham (2017). https://doi.org/10.1007/978-3-319-70694-8_15
6. D'Arco, P., De Santis, A.: Private computations on set intersection. In: Colbourn, C.J., Dinitz, J.H. (eds.) New Advances in Designs, Codes and Cryptography, pp. 77–95. Springer Nature Switzerland, Cham (2024)

7. Even, S., Goldreich, O., Lempel, A.: A randomized protocol for signing contracts. Commun. ACM **28**(6), 637–647 (1985)
8. Fan, J., Vercauteren, F.: Somewhat practical fully homomorphic encryption. Cryptology ePrint Archive, Paper 2012/144 (2012). https://eprint.iacr.org/2012/144
9. Freedman, M.J., Ishai, Y., Pinkas, B., Reingold, O.: Keyword search and oblivious pseudorandom functions. In: Kilian, J. (ed.) Theory of Cryptography, pp. 303–324. Springer, Berlin Heidelberg, Berlin, Heidelberg (2005)
10. Freedman, M.J., Nissim, K., Pinkas, B.: Efficient private matching and set intersection. In: Cachin, C., Camenisch, J.L. (eds.) EUROCRYPT 2004. LNCS, vol. 3027, pp. 1–19. Springer, Heidelberg (2004). https://doi.org/10.1007/978-3-540-24676-3_1
11. Hamada, K., Ikarashi, D., Chida, K., Takahashi, K.: Oblivious radix sort: an efficient sorting algorithm for practical secure multi-party computation. Cryptology ePrint Archive, Paper 2014/121 (2014). https://eprint.iacr.org/2014/121
12. Hazay, C., Lindell, Y.: Efficient protocols for set intersection and pattern matching with security against malicious and covert adversaries. In: Canetti, R. (ed.) Theory of Cryptography, pp. 155–175. Springer, Berlin Heidelberg, Berlin, Heidelberg (2008)
13. Hemenway Falk, B., Noble, D., Ostrovsky, R.: Private set intersection with linear communication from general assumptions. In: Proceedings of the 18th ACM Workshop on Privacy in the Electronic Society, pp. 14–25. WPES'19, Association for Computing Machinery, New York, NY, USA (2019). https://doi.org/10.1145/3338498.3358645
14. Huang, Y., Evans, D., Katz, J.: Private set intersection: are garbled circuits better than custom protocols? In: Network and Distributed System Security Symposium (2012)
15. Huberman, B.A., Franklin, M., Hogg, T.: Enhancing privacy and trust in electronic communities. In: Proceedings of the 1st ACM Conference on Electronic Commerce, pp. 78–86. EC '99, Association for Computing Machinery, New York, NY, USA (1999). https://doi.org/10.1145/336992.337012
16. Keller, M.: MP-SPDZ: A versatile framework for multi-party computation. In: Proceedings of the 2020 ACM SIGSAC Conference on Computer and Communications Security (2020). https://doi.org/10.1145/3372297.3417872
17. Lyubashevsky, V., Peikert, C., Regev, O.: On ideal lattices and learning with errors over rings. Cryptology ePrint Archive, Paper 2012/230 (2012). https://eprint.iacr.org/2012/230
18. Paillier, P.: Public-key cryptosystems based on composite degree residuosity classes. In: Stern, J. (ed.) Advances in Cryptology – EUROCRYPT '99, pp. 223–238. Springer, Berlin Heidelberg, Berlin, Heidelberg (1999)
19. Regev, O.: On lattices, learning with errors, random linear codes, and cryptography. J. ACM **56**(6) (Sep 2009). https://doi.org/10.1145/1568318.1568324
20. Microsoft SEAL (release 4.1). https://github.com/Microsoft/SEAL (Jan 2023). microsoft Research, Redmond, WA
21. Waksman, A.: A permutation network. J. ACM **15**(1), 159–163 (Jan 1968). https://doi.org/10.1145/321439.321449
22. Yao, A.C.C.: How to generate and exchange secrets. In: 27th Annual Symposium on Foundations of Computer Science (sfcs 1986), pp. 162–167 (1986). https://doi.org/10.1109/SFCS.1986.25

32-bit and 64-bit CDC-7-XPUF Implementations on a Zynq-7020 SoC

Oğuz Yayla[1] and Yunus Emre Yılmaz[1,2](✉)

[1] Institute of Applied Mathematics, Middle East Technical University, 06800 Ankara, Turkey
oguz@metu.edu.tr, yeylmz@gmail.com
[2] Aselsan Inc., Ankara, Turkey

Abstract. Physically (or Physical) Unclonable Functions (PUFs) are basic and useful primitives in designing cryptographic systems. PUFs are designed to facilitate device authentication, secure boot, firmware integrity, and secure communications. To achieve these objectives, PUFs must exhibit both consistent repeatability and instance-specific randomness. The Arbiter PUF (APUF), recognized as the first silicon PUF, is capable of generating a substantial number of secret keys instantaneously based on the input, all while maintaining a lightweight design. This advantageous characteristic makes it particularly well-suited for device authentication in applications with constrained resources, especially for Internet-of-Things (IoT) devices. Despite these advantages, APUFs are vulnerable to machine learning (ML) attacks. Hence, those APUF designs were improved to achieve increased resistance against such attacks while maintaining usefulness and efficiency for IoT applications, and Component-Differentially Challenged XOR Arbiters (CDC-XPUFs) were proposed. In this work, ML-resistant 32-bit and 64-bit implementations of the Component-Differentially Challenged XOR Arbiter PUF with 7-stream (CDC-7-XPUF) are carried out. These CDC-7-XPUFs are evaluated using PUF metrics from the literature, and the resource utilization ratios of both implementations are also presented. The implementation setup contains the ZC702 Rev1.1 Evaluation Board, featuring the Xilinx Zynq-7020 SoC, and utilizes a configuration involving three boards for experimental validation.

Keywords: PUF · Arbiter PUF · CDC-XPUF · SoC FPGA

1 Introduction

A Physically (or Physical) Unclonable Function (PUF) is a mechanism that creates a unique relationship between a set of inputs (challenges) and outputs (responses) based on the complex physical properties of a system. This relationship is static and unique to each physical instance. PUFs can only be evaluated through their specific physical systems, and even identical circuits will have different responses due to manufacturing variations, as explained in [1]. In this

L. Morogan et al. (Eds.): SecITC 2024, LNCS 15595, pp. 252–266, 2025.
https://doi.org/10.1007/978-3-031-87760-5_18

research, the focus is on silicon PUFs, which leverage timing and delay variations in integrated circuits. These variations arise from inconsistencies in the production process, even when circuits are made with the same design layout.

PUFs enhance security by generating secrets from the complex properties of physical systems, eliminating the need for storing them in memory. Another advantage is that PUFs do not require any specialized manufacturing processes or additional programming and testing steps. PUFs are typically compact and durable, making them ideal for use in devices like radio frequency identification (RFID) tags, smart cards, and other low-cost Internet-of-Things (IoT) devices, as described in [2]. More detailed information about PUFs can be found in [5].

For hardware implementation, PUFs can be integrated into application-specific integrated circuits (ASICs) or Field-Programmable Gate Arrays (FPGAs). While ASICs may offer better performance, they are difficult to modify once designed. In contrast, FPGAs allow for flexible reconfiguration, which is particularly useful in hardware development. Modern System-on-Chip (SoC) FPGAs combine programmable logic with processor cores, offering benefits like higher integration, lower power consumption, smaller sizes, and faster communication between the processor and FPGA. Furthermore, improvements or modifications in PUF algorithms can be implemented in SoCs or FPGAs more easily than in ASICs, primarily because such changes are not affordable in ASICs. Therefore, an SoC is chosen for the PUF implementation in this work due to these reasons.

The Arbiter PUF (APUF), the first silicon-based PUF, generates numerous secret keys efficiently from input data while maintaining a lightweight design. This makes it well-suited for device authentication in environments with limited resources, such as IoT applications. However, its vulnerability to machine learning attacks highlights the need for enhanced design solutions to improve security.

Consequently, in order to improve resistance to machine learning (ML) attacks, arbiter PUF designs have been enhanced. In this study, an ML attack-resistant component-differentially challenged XOR arbiter PUF (CDC-XPUF) is implemented, following the reference designs from [3,4]. The implementation utilizes the ZC702 Rev1.1 Evaluation Board [6], equipped with the Xilinx Zynq-7020 SoC, and a configuration of three such boards for experimental validation. Research in [4] demonstrates that designs with 64-bit or longer challenges and at least 7-stream PUFs are resistant to the most advanced ML attack techniques. Consequently, this work implements a referenced 32-bit CDC-7-XPUF, followed by an improved 64-bit version for enhanced ML attack resilience. The performance results for both the 32-bit and 64-bit CDC-7-XPUFs are presented and compared to the reference design. Additionally, the utilization rates of these designs are evaluated, showing that they are well-suited for IoT systems by providing sufficient space for other software or firmware.

Contribution of this Work

Our work presents two primary contributions:

- We implement the referenced 32-bit CDC-7-XPUF detailed in [3,4], and also the machine learning attack-resistant 64-bit version of CDC-7-XPUF. Then, we evaluate them by using the evaluation metrics of steadiness, correctness, diffuseness, uniformity, and uniqueness. It is shown that both PUF designs have good scores to use in IoT systems, see our summary in Table 1.
- It is also demonstrated that 32-bit and 64-bit CDC-7-XPUF designs can be implemented efficiently in terms of space on an SoC FPGA. Our implementation for designs consumes low amount of resourse in the FPGA, so they leave enough space for other software or firmware. The utilization ratio of these designs in our implementation given in Table 2 shows that these designs are suitable to use in any IoT systems.

Outline

The paper is organized as follows. Section 2 provides the basic background information to explain how both 32-bit and 64-bit CDC-7-XPUF works. In Sect. 3, the implementation details of both CDC-7-XPUFs are explained. In Sect. 4, the test results of PUF implementations are presented and compared with the referenced design. In the end, Sect. 5 concludes the paper and states our future works.

2 Background Information About 32-bit and 64-bit CDC-7-XPUF

2.1 Basics of PUFs

PUF extracts entropy from the physical characteristics of an integrated circuit (IC). Each chip exhibits variations due to the inherent unpredictability in the manufacturing process. PUFs harness static entropy from the fluctuations in the manufacturing process. Once the chip is fabricated, the disparities in the manufacturing process become consolidated and undergo minimal changes throughout the chip's lifespan. Consequently, this form of entropy is termed static entropy, as described in [7].

Basically, a PUF generates a sequence (response) of the unique signature by input initial states (challenge), so-called challenge-response pairs (CRPs). Each PUF can be represented as a black box, $R = f(C)$, as illustrated in Fig. 1, where the $f()$ is secret, as stated in [7].

Fig. 1. Generic PUF model [7].

In the literature, there are various types of PUFs, and they can be classified with respect to their entropy sources and their CRPs, as explained in [8]. In this research, an intrinsic and delay-based strong PUF, named Arbiter PUF (APUF), is implemented. It is important to note that the APUF is a strong PUF. A strong PUF can generate a vast number of CRPs, making it impractical to read all possible CRPs within a reasonable timeframe. This property makes them suitable for applications requiring high security due to their extensive challenge-response space.

2.2 Types of Arbiter PUFs

2.2.1 Basic Arbiter PUF (APUF)

An APUF, which was first defined in [9], is a robust PUF relying on delay, featuring a race condition between two symmetrical digital paths. In each delay stage, two multiplexers (MUXes) are incorporated, and their operation is governed by challenges (C_0 C_{n-1}).

Upon activation, the APUF initiates its operation with a trigger signal. This signal traverses two paths determined by a pre-input challenge, ultimately reaching an arbiter. The arbiter then determines which of the two paths is faster in generating the binary response that aligns with the black-box model ($R = f(C)$), as it is illustrated in Fig. 1, where C is the challenge and R is the response.

2.2.2 XOR Arbiter PUF (XOR-PUF)

Due to the limited resistance of APUFs against machine learning modeling attacks, a new PUF design was introduced in [1]. This new design incorporates a non-linear XOR gate into multiple APUFs to generate the final response and is referred to as the XOR arbiter PUF. An n-XOR-PUF consists of n-component APUFs (also known as streams or sub-challenges), wherein the responses from all n-component arbiter PUFs are XORed together at the XOR gate to produce a single-bit response. It is important to note that all component APUFs in an XOR-PUF are supplied with the same challenge bits, as stated in [4].

2.2.3 Component-Differentially Challenged XOR-PUF (CDC-XPUF)

Component-differentially challenged XOR-PUF (CDC-XPUF) and XOR-PUF share a similar architecture, comprising multiple APUF components and XOR gates. The key distinction between CDC-XPUF and XOR-PUF lies in the challenge inputs: each component APUF in a CDC-XPUF receives different challenge inputs, whereas all component APUFs in an XOR-PUF receive the same challenges, as expressed in [4]. Figure 2 illustrates the structure of CDC-XPUF with 2 sub-streams and n-bit of each stream, which is named n-bit CDC-2-XPUF.

Studies [10–13] indicate that applying different challenges to the components of an XOR-PUF can mitigate its vulnerability to ML modeling attacks. Existing

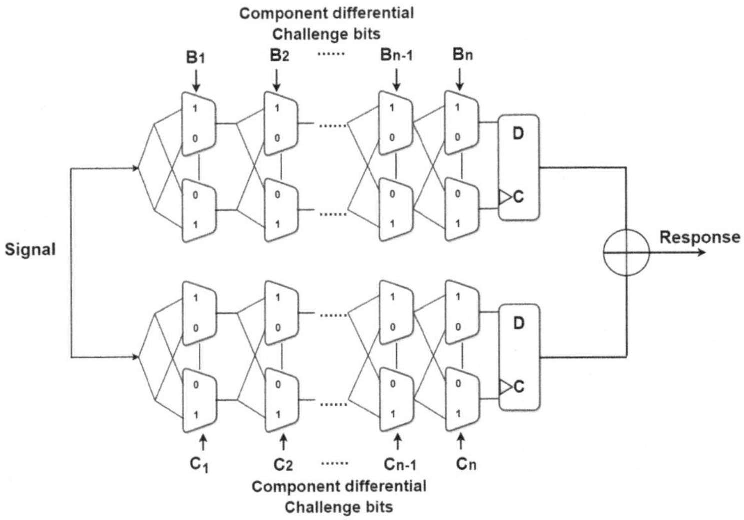

Fig. 2. An n-bit CDC-2-XPUF [4].

ML attack methods on 64-bit CDC-XPUFs with four components achieve a success rate of less than 90% even when utilizing over one million challenge-response pairs (CRPs). Experimental results consistently demonstrate that CDC-XPUFs with four or more components are either unbreakable or prohibitively expensive to breach with current attack methods. Consequently, CDC-XPUFs are considered strong candidates in terms of security performance, as stated in [4].

In order to generate different challenge bits, a pseudorandom number generator (PRNG) structure is proposed in [4] as follows:

$$C_{n+1} = (a * C_n + g) \ \ mod\, m, \tag{1}$$

where C is the sequence of the generated random number, a is a multiplier, g is a given constant, and m is 2^K, where K is the number of stages.

2.3 Evaluation Metrics of PUFs

This section outlines a set of PUF characteristics to evaluate the suitability of a PUF design for security applications. Certain statistical properties, such as stability, correctness, diffuseness, uniformity, and uniqueness, can be empirically demonstrated through silicon-based experimentation. Other attributes, including the security vulnerability of PUFs, require computational analysis for thorough assessment.

The first following section explains how implemented PUFs are not vulnerable to ML attacks. In the subsequent subsections after the initial one, the evaluation criteria developed by either Hori et al. [14] or Maiti et al. [15] are explained. The responses are categorized based on three distinct properties: the reliability and entropy of the responses generated by the same PUFs, as well as the fingerprint characteristic. The metrics in the first and the second groups evaluate the responses of the same PUFs, although the metrics in the third group evaluate how the responses vary between different devices.

The quality of random numbers is pivotal in cryptography, necessitating a thorough evaluation of their properties. While Hori et al. [14] defines the randomness metric, Maiti et al. [15] defines the uniformity metric. In this work, we think that the uniformity metric is more suitable to use. Because, although randomness in Hori et al. [14] indicates that randomness is evaluated, only some kind of uniformity is evaluated as in [15]. This choice can be understood better by the explanation in Sect. 2.3.4.

2.3.1 Resistance to Machine Learning (ML) Attacks

PUFs are considered secure due to their inherently unclonable architecture. However, several successful studies have demonstrated that PUFs can be mathematically cloned using the additive delay model, as explained in [17]. Additionally, if adversaries gain access to a sufficient number of silicon CRPs, PUFs may become susceptible to machine learning attacks, as explained in [18–21]. Therefore, it is imperative for users to ensure that PUFs are resistant to all forms of attacks before deploying them in practical applications.

The study in [4], a comprehensive evaluation of the security of CDC-XPUFs against advanced ML attack methods, utilizing problem-specific parameter values, was conducted to assess the robustness of CDC-XPUFs. Compared to previously reported findings, their study uncovered vulnerabilities in the CDC-XPUF with PUF circuit parameter configurations that were previously not considered insecure. Specifically, they successfully compromised 64-bit CDC-6-XPUFs using approximately 100 million simulated CRPs, and 64-bit CDC-5-XPUFs with 4.5 million simulated CRPs or 2.5 million silicon CRPs. Additionally, they managed to break 128-bit CDC-5-XPUFs with 40 million simulated CRPs, instances that had previously been considered resistant to any existing ML attack methods. Notably, the method in [4] was able to break 64-bit CDC-4-XPUFs using only around 80,000 CRPs, significantly fewer than those used in earlier studies. On the other hand, it also demonstrates that the security of CDC-XPUFs improves substantially as the number of component PUFs increases, with 64-bit CDC-XPUFs featuring seven components proving entirely resilient to the two ML attack methods employed. This finding is particularly encouraging for the IoT security community, as many CDC-XPUFs remain secure, especially those with 64-bit or longer challenges and seven or more component PUFs, which are resistant to the most advanced ML attack methods developed to date. Consequently, the experimental attack study in [4] redefines the boundary between secure and insecure regions within the PUF circuit parameter space, offering valuable insights to PUF manufacturers and IoT security developers for refining the protocols of CDC-XPUF-based applications and mitigating potential risks.

As a result, due to the reasons explained in this section, the 64-bit CDC-7-XPUF, whose resistance to ML attacks has been demonstrated in the study by Li et al. [4], has been implemented in this work.

2.3.2 Reliability of Responses from the Same PUFs

PUF responses must be reliable and trusted in real-world applications. A PUF is considered reliable if it consistently generates the same response when the same challenge is applied to the same device. Several factors can affect the reliability of these responses, particularly changes in the operating environment. These factors include, but are not limited to, ambient temperature, humidity, the junction temperature of the circuit, power supply voltage, and circuit aging. In this work, the environmental variances listed above have not been changed. We have worked at an ambient room temperature of approximately 27 °C, stable humidity, and stable core voltage of Zynq SoC.

In terms of the reliability of responses from the same PUFs, steadiness, and correctness are examined in this section.

Steadiness
Steadiness is a reliability metric that is defined by Hori et al. [14]. When generating the same responses multiple times on the same device, it is expected that all responses must be identical. Steadiness indicates how stably a PUF outputs the same responses to the same challenge sets. The steadiness result is 1 if there are no changes in the responses that were recorded during the experiment. Steadiness can be calculated as follows:

$$S = 1 + \frac{1}{N_c}\sum_{k=1}^{N_c} \log_2 max\{\frac{\sum_{j=1}^{N_a} b_{k,j}}{N_a}, 1 - \frac{\sum_{j=1}^{N_a} b_{k,j}}{N_a}\},$$

where N_c denotes the number of different challenges used, N_a denotes the number of times each challenge is applied, and $b_{k,j}$ denotes the j-th response among all N_a responses to the k-th challenge in the set of all N_c challenges. The stable CRPs that pass the steadiness test are known as *Correct ID*, as defined in [3].

Correctness
This metric is defined by Hori et al. [14] and is almost the same metric as reliability, which is defined by Maiti et al. [15]. The only difference between their equations is the normalization factor. Correctness is normalized by the maximum value of the fractional Hamming distance of the responses, while reliability is normalized by the average. Hence, we only computed the correctness value and ignored the reliability. The ideal value of the correctness is 1, which can be calculated as follows:

$$C = 1 - \frac{2}{N_c \times N_a}\sum_{k=1}^{N_c}\sum_{j=1}^{N_a}(b_k \oplus b_{k,j}),$$

where b_k is the *Correct ID*. This *Correct ID* is determined by the majority voting of all of the giving responses for the input challenge. N_c is the number of challenges in the dataset. $b_{k,j}$ is the response of the j-th response in the set of all N_a responses to the k-th challenge.

2.3.3 Entropy of Responses From the Same PUFs

A PUF is considered uniform if it generates an equal distribution of zeros and ones in response to a set of challenges. This characteristic is particularly desirable in block and stream cipher processes, as repeated patterns in secret keys are deemed detrimental. In terms of entropy, Hori et al. [14] introduced the diffuseness metric, while Maiti et al. [15] proposed the uniformity metric. Given the close resemblance between Hori's [14] randomness metric and Maiti's [15] uniformity metric, only the uniformity metric is assessed in this context.

Diffuseness
The diffuseness metric, introduced by Hori et al. [14], is an intra-chip metric that assesses the variability of a PUF's responses to different challenges. A PUF is considered to exhibit diffuseness if it produces distinct responses for distinct challenges; for instance, the response to a specific challenge C_i should differ from the responses generated by other challenges. Diffuseness is quantified by calculating the fractional Hamming distance between the responses produced by the same device in response to a set of challenges. The diffuseness can be computed using the following formula:

$$D = \frac{4}{K^2 \times L} \sum_{l=1}^{L} \sum_{i=1}^{K-1} \sum_{j=i+1}^{K} (b_{i,l} \oplus b_{j,l}),$$

where L is the responses' length, counted in bits, and K is the number of such multi-bit responses used in the experimental study.

Uniformity
The uniformity, which was introduced by Maiti et al. [15], of a PUF measures the degree of zeros and ones in the produced responses. Its ideal value is 0.5. The uniformity can be calculated as follows:

$$U = \frac{1}{N_r} \sum_{i=1}^{N_r} b_i, \tag{2}$$

where N_r is the response length in a set, and b_i is the i-th response bit.

The randomness metric, defined by Hori et al. [14], is not used for the evaluation since it is very similar to the uniformity. In order to make this statement more clear, the equations to calculate the randomness by Hori et al. [14] are provided below:

$$H = -\log_2 max(p, 1-p), \tag{3}$$

where p is the frequency of '1' in the response set given by:

$$p = \frac{1}{N_r} \sum_{i=1}^{N_r} b_i, \tag{4}$$

where N_r is the response length in a set, and b_i is the i-th response bit.

It is obvious that the Eqs. (2) and (4) are nearly the same. These two equations define the same thing actually, and it is the uniformity of the responses. Hori et al. [14] claim that taking this uniformity and using them in (3) calculates the randomness. The approach presented by Hori et al. [14] is not suitable for accurately calculating randomness. Equation (3) can only provide information regarding the percentage distribution of 0 s and 1 s, which is already captured in the uniformity metric proposed by Maiti et al. [15] in Eq. (2). Thus, using this equation does not contribute to a deeper understanding of randomness beyond what uniformity already indicates. As stated in [16], how to determine the exact entropy of the PUF responses is another very important open research problem. Hence, in order to evaluate entropy, we use the uniformity metric introduced by Maiti et al. [15].

2.3.4 Fingerprint Property

Uniqueness

The uniqueness was introduced by Maiti et al. [15], and it can be calculated using the Hamming distance between two devices' responses. The calculation is as follows:

$$U_k = \frac{2}{N(N-1)} \sum_{i=1}^{N-1} \sum_{j=i+1}^{N} \frac{HD(ID_i, ID_j)}{L},$$

where ID_i and ID_j are two L-bit responses of a PUF installed on two different chips (the i-th and j-th chip) to the k-th challenge repeatedly applied L times. The ideal value of the Maiti's uniqueness [15] is 0.5.

Besides these metrics, the resource utilization rate serves as an important indicator for evaluating the suitability of PUFs for IoT systems. If a PUF demands substantial resources within an SoC or FPGA, it is considered unsuitable for integration into IoT environments.

3 32-bit and 64-bit CDC-7-XPUF Implementation Details

In this study, our aim is to implement an ML-resistant PUF with good cryptographic properties explained in Sects. 2.3.1, 2.3.2, 2.3.3 and 2.3.4. Based on the explanations provided in Sect. 2.3.1, the 64-bit CDC-7-XPUF is considered resistant to ML attacks and is utilized accordingly. The five evaluation metrics named *steadiness*, *correctness*, *diffuseness*, *uniformity*, and *uniqueness* are explained between Sects. 2.3.2, 2.3.3, 2.3.4. These are examined in [3], but only for a maximum of 32-bit CDC-7-XPUF. Hence, we decided that firstly, we implemented 32-bit CDC-7-XPUF and showed that the design satisfies good cryptographic properties, as the referenced PUF design does. After that, we implemented the 64-bit, in other words, ML-resistant version of CDC-7-XPUF. Obviously, we also calculated the metrics for this version of the PUF.

In this work, the MUX-based CDC-XPUF arbiter structures are implemented using Vivado 2019.1 [22] in VHDL [25].

Since the CDC-XPUF is a delay-based PUF, relying on the calculation of delays incurred by the internal gates and interconnections, the correct placement of its components is crucial. To ensure equal delay lines, the top and bottom of each stage in the CDC XPUF must be precisely aligned in the placement phase of SoC design in Vivado 2019.1. Hence, we placed the stages carefully by considering this equal delay line approach.

For generating different challenges for different stages, a PRNG is proposed in Equation (1). Obviously, two PRNGs with two different parameter sets are used for the 32-bit and 64-bit designs.

The implementation setup illustrated in Fig. 3 is used. The software developed in Python [24] using Visual Studio 2022 [23] is utilized to calculate the scores for the five evaluation metrics from the generated bitstreams.

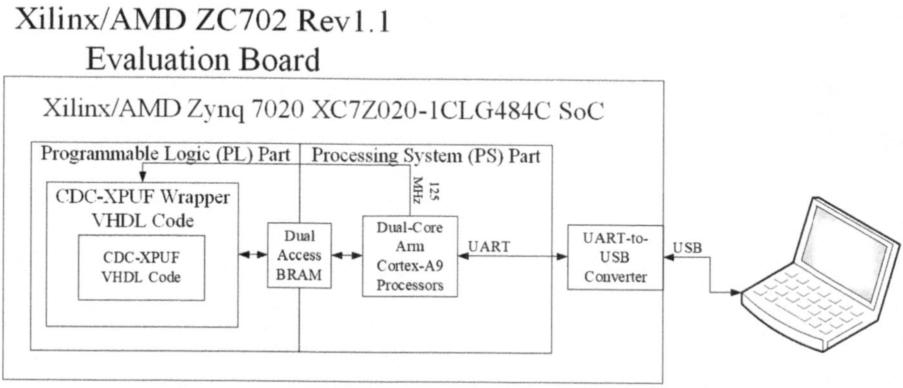

Fig. 3. Block Diagram of Implementation Setup of CDC-7-XPUFes.

Using the setup in Fig. 3, for the statistical characteristics CRPs, we generated up to 16,000 (challenges) ×32 (iterations) ×128 (response length) ×3 (Zynq-7020 SoCs) CRPs out of each design. The repetition of the CRPs is needed to study the statistical characteristics and investigate related metrics such as correctness and steadiness. The CRPs were captured at an ambient temperature of approximately 27°C, and the core voltage was set to 1.0V. The ambient temperature does not reflect the temperature of the chip, which has changed as long as the experiments continue. Through a dual-access Block Random Access Memory (BRAM), CRPs are sent to the processing system (PS) part from the programmable logic (PL) part. From the PS part via Universal Asynchronous Receiver-Transmitter (UART), the CRPs are sent to the personal computer (PC) with a baud rate of 230,400 bits/second between the PuTTY [26] terminal and the SoCs.

4 32-bit and 64-bit CDC-7-XPUF Experimental Results and Comparisons

As explained between Sects. 2.3.2, 2.3.3, 2.3.4, the implementation result of *steadiness*, *correctness*, *diffuseness*, *uniformity*, and *uniqueness* are presented in Table 1 for both 32-bit and 64-bit CDC-7-XPUF implementations. Also, in this table, the results of the referenced design in [3] are presented. Furthermore, in the following sections, these comparative results in Table 1 are analyzed.

Table 1. Results of CDC-XPUFs with Respect to Evaluation Metrics

Evaluation Metric	**Score of Referenced Work 32-bit CDC-7-XPUF** [3]	**Score of 32-bit CDC-7-XPUF Implementation**	**Score of 64-bit CDC-7-XPUF Implementation**
Steadiness	98.18%	97.09%	96.70%
Correctness	97.63%	96.64%	96.19%
Diffuseness	99.90%	99.96%	99.99%
Uniformity	50.40%	50.94%	49.89%
Uniqueness	17.90%	18.06%	18.96%

4.1 Steadiness and Correctness

The steadiness and correctness metrics, which measure stability and error rate, respectively, are both calculated on a scale from 0 to 1. The results for the 32-bit implementation are slightly worse than those of the reference design but remain within acceptable limits. Furthermore, the performance of the 64-bit implementation is marginally lower compared to the 32-bit version. As discussed by Mursi [3], increasing the number of stages negatively impacts both steadiness and correctness.

4.2 Diffuseness

The diffuseness metric, which assesses the spread of the generated responses, showed a slight improvement over the reference design for the 32-bit version and further improved with the 64-bit version. This is consistent with [3], which indicate that increasing the stage number generally enhances diffuseness.

4.3 Uniformity

Uniformity, which ideally has an expected value of 0.5, was also calculated and normalized as percentages. The results indicate that the 64-bit implementation exhibits slightly better uniformity compared to both our 32-bit design and the reference design, despite Mursi's observation [3] that increasing the number of stages often has a negative effect on uniformity. In this case, however, the increase in the number of stages appears to have led to an improvement in uniformity.

4.4 Uniqueness

The uniqueness metric, which evaluates the ability of the PUF to generate distinct responses, also demonstrated improvement with an increase in bit length. The 32-bit results were slightly better than those of the reference design, and the 64-bit results further enhanced the uniqueness, in alignment with Mursi's findings [3], which suggest that increasing the number of stages positively influences uniqueness.

4.5 Utilization Results of CDC-7-XPUFs in Zynq-7020 SoC FPGA

For the implementation, we use state machines in the PL part so that we can take the challenges from the PS part, and we can send responses derived from these challenges through the Dual Access BRAM. Although the PL part consists of not only CDC-7-XPUFs but also state machines which are necessary for the implementation, the utilization rate is relatively low, as it can be seen in Table 2 for both 32-bit and 64-bit CDC-7-XPUF implementations.

As expected, the 64-bit design has a higher utilization rate, especially in digital signal processor (DSP) resources. In order to generate different challenges for each of the streams, we use PRNGs, which multiply 64-bit numbers requiring more DSP than 32-bit design. That relatively low utilization result makes 64-bit CDC-7-XPUF a promising candidate for applications that require a PUF.

Table 2. Utilization Table Generated Using Vivado 2019.1 [22] for 32-bit and 64-bit CDC-7-XPUF Implementations

Resource Type	Available Resource Quantity	Utilization Quantity (Utilization Rate as %) of 32-bit CDC-7-XPUF	Utilization Quantity (Utilization Rate as %) of 64-bit CDC-7-XPUF
LUT	53200	1500 (2.82%)	1740 (3.27%)
LUTRAM	17400	72 (0.41%)	72 (0.41%)
FF	106400	1781 (1.67%)	1933 (1.82%)
BRAM	140	2 (1.43%)	(1.43%)
DSP	220	12 (5.45%)	68 (30.91%)
IO	200	8 (4.00%)	8 (4.00%)

5 Conclusion and Future Works

In this study, we implemented and evaluated machine learning-resistant 32-bit and 64-bit designs of the Component-Differentially Challenged XOR Arbiter PUF with 7 streams (CDC-7-XPUF), drawing from established designs in the literature. We evaluated these CDC-7-XPUFs using standard PUF metrics and provided an analysis of the resource utilization ratios for both implementations. We have thoroughly examined the resilience against ML attacks in Sect. 2.3.1. As discussed in this section and demonstrated in [3], the 64-bit CDC-XPUF designs with 7 streams are resistant to ML attacks. In the sections that follow the discussion on ML resilience, five evaluation criteria are detailed. The PL portion of the Zynq-7020 exhibits an architecture closely resembling that of the Artix-7, which was employed to implement the reference design of the CDC-XPUF in [3]. Consequently, we anticipated similar results to those reported in [3], and, as expected, observed comparable outcomes, as presented in Table 1 in Sect. 4. In addition to these examinations, lastly, the utilization rate of both 32-bit and 64-bit designs are examined, and it is shown that both designs are suitable for an IoT application since they provide a lot of space in the PL part for future applications.

As the future works, the following two items would be considered.

- CDC-7-XPUF designs are also applicable to other FPGA and SoC platforms. Hence, this design would be tested over other platforms.
- CDC-7-XPUF designs would be tested in various environmental conditions such as varying temperature and varying voltage.

Acknowledgements. The authors acknowledge the support of Aselsan Inc. in the preparation of this work, as well as their provision of three Xilinx ZC702 Evaluation Boards used for the implementation of the 32-bit and 64-bit CDC-7-XPUF algorithms presented in the paper.

References

1. Suh, G.E., Devadas, S.: Physical unclonable functions for device authentication and secret key generation. In: 2007 44th ACM/IEEE Design Automation Conference, pp. 9–14 (2007). https://doi.org/10.1145/1278480.1278484
2. Ebrahimabadi, M., Younis, M., Lalouani, W., Karimi, N.: A novel modeling- attack resilient arbiter-PUF design. In: 2021 34th International Conference on VLSI Design and 2021 20th International Conference on Embedded Systems (VLSID), pp. 123–128 (2021). https://doi.org/10.1109/VLSID51830.2021.00026
3. Mursi K.T.: From XOR PUF to CDC XOR PUF: Cost-Effectiveness, Statistical Characteristics, and Security Assessment, Ph.D. Thesis, Texas Tech University (2021). https://ttu-ir.tdl.org/bitstreams/d26a326c-9494-47e4-a9e2-9af57d949e88/download

4. Li, G., T. Mursi, K., O. Aseeri, A., S. Alkatheiri, M., Zhuang, Yu.: A new security boundary of component differentially challenged XOR Pufs against machine learning modeling attacks. Int. J. Comput. Netw. Commun. **14**(3), 1–15 (2022). https://doi.org/10.5121/ijcnc.2022.14301
5. Böhm, C., Hofer, M.: Physical Unclonable Functions in Theory and Practice. Springer New York, New York, NY (2013). https://doi.org/10.1007/978-1-4614-5040-5
6. Xilinx Zynq-7000 SoC ZC702 Evaluation Kit. https://www.xilinx.com/products/boards-and-kits/ek-z7-zc702-g.html. Accessed 01 Sept 2023
7. Cao Y., et al.: Entropy sources based on silicon chips: true random number generator and physical unclonable function. In: Entropy, 24(11), ISSN 1099-4300 (2022). https://doi.org/10.3390/e24111566
8. Srinivas, M., Elango, K.: Era of sentinel tech: charting hardware security landscapes through post-silicon innovation, threat mitigation and future trajectories. IEEE Access **12**, 68061–68108 (2024). https://doi.org/10.1109/ACCESS.2024.3400624
9. Gassend, B., Clarke, D., Dijk, M. van, Devadas, S.: Silicon physical random functions. In: Proceedings of the 9th ACM Conference on Computer and Communications Security, CCS '02, pp. 148–160, Association for Computing Machinery, New York, NY, USA, ISBN 1581136129 (2002). https://doi.org/10.1145/586110.586132
10. Mursi, K.T., Zhuang, Yu.: Experimental examination of component-differentially-challenged XOR PUF circuits. J. Phys.: Conf. Series **1729**(1), 012006 (2021). https://doi.org/10.1088/1742-6596/1729/1/012006
11. Mursi, K.T., Thapaliya, B., Zhuang, Y., Aseeri, A.O., Alkatheiri, M.S.: A fast deep learning method for security vulnerability study of XOR PUFs. Electronics **9**(10), ISSN 2079-9292 (2020). https://www.mdpi.com/2079-9292/9/10/1715
12. Wisiol, N., Becker, G.T., Margraf, M., Soroceanu, T., Tobisch, J., Zengin, B.: Breaking the lightweight secure PUF: understanding the relation of input transformations and machine learning resistance. In: Belaïd, S., Güneysu, T. (eds.) Smart Card Research and Advanced Applications: 18th International Conference, CARDIS 2019, Prague, Czech Republic, November 11–13, 2019, Revised Selected Papers, pp. 40–54. Springer International Publishing, Cham (2020). https://doi.org/10.1007/978-3-030-42068-0_3
13. Yu, M.-D., Hiller, M., Delvaux, J., Sowell, R., Devadas, S., Verbauwhede, I.M.R.: A Lockdown Technique to Prevent Machine Learning on PUFs for Lightweight Authentication. In: IEEE Transactions on Multi-Scale Computing Systems, 2, pp. 146–159 (2016). https://api.semanticscholar.org/CorpusID:1355676
14. Hori, Y., Yoshida, T., Katashita, T., Satoh, A.: Quantitative and statistical performance evaluation of arbiter physical unclonable functions on FPGAs. In: 2010 International Conference on Reconfigurable Computing and FPGAs, Cancun, Mexico, pp. 298–303 (2010). https://doi.org/10.1109/ReConFig.2010.24
15. Maiti, A., Gunreddy, V., Schaumont, P.: A systematic method to evaluate and compare the performance of physical unclonable functions. In: Athanas, P., Pnevmatikatos, D., Sklavos, N. (eds) Embedded Systems Design with FPGAs. Springer, New York, NY. (2013). https://doi.org/10.1007/978-1-4614-1362-2_11
16. Anandakumar, N.N., Hashmi, M.S., Tehranipoor, M.: FPGA-based physical unclonable functions: a comprehensive overview of theory and architectures. Integration **81**, 175–194 (2021). https://doi.org/10.1016/j.vlsi.2021.06.001
17. Lim, D., Lee, J.W., Gassend, B., Suh, G.E., van Dijk, M., Devadas, S.: Extracting secret keys from integrated circuits. IEEE Trans. Very Large Scale Integr. (VLSI) Syst. **13**(10), 1200–1205 (2005). https://doi.org/10.1109/TVLSI.2005.859470

18. Alamro, M.A., Mursi, K.T., Zhuang, Yu., Aseeri, A.O., Alkatheiri, M.S.: Robustness and unpredictability for double arbiter PUFs on silicon data: performance evaluation and modeling accuracy. Electronics **9**(5), 870 (2020). https://doi.org/10.3390/electronics9050870
19. Alkatheiri, M.S., Zhuang, Y.: Towards fast and accurate machine learning attacks of feed-forward arbiter PUFs. In: 2017 IEEE Conference on Dependable and Secure Computing, Taipei, Taiwan, pp. 181–187 (2017). https://doi.org/10.1109/DESEC.2017.8073845
20. Aseeri, A.O., Zhuang, Y., Alkatheiri, M.S.: A machine learning-based security vulnerability study on xor pufs for resource-constraint internet of things. In: 2018 IEEE International Congress on Internet of Things (ICIOT), San Francisco, CA, USA, pp. 49–56 (2018). https://doi.org/10.1109/ICIOT.2018.00014
21. Mursi, K.T., Zhuang, Y., Alkatheiri, M.S., Aseeri, A.O.: Extensive examination of xor arbiter pufs as security primitives for resource-constrained IoT devices. In: 2019 17th International Conference on Privacy, Security and Trust (PST), Fredericton, NB, Canada, pp. 1–9 (2019). https://doi.org/10.1109/PST47121.2019.8949070
22. Xilinx (AMD) Vivado and SDK 2019.1 Design Software for Xilinx (AMD) Adaptive SoCs and FPGAs. https://www.xilinx.com/support/download/index.html/content/xilinx/en/downloadNav/vivado-design-tools/archive.html Accessed 01 Sept 2023
23. Microsoft Corporation, Visual Studio 2022 (2022). https://visualstudio.microsoft.com/. Accessed 01 Nov 2023
24. Python Software Foundation, Python Language Reference, version 3.x. https://www.python.org/. Accessed 01 Nov 2023
25. IEEE Computer Society, IEEE Standard VHDL Language Reference Manual, IEEE Std 1076-2008 (2008)
26. PuTTY - a free and open-source terminal emulator, serial console, and network file transfer application. https://www.putty.org/. Accessed 01 Sept 2023

Author Index

L. Morogan et al. (Eds.): SecITC 2024, LNCS 15595, pp. 267–268, 2025.
https://doi.org/10.1007/978-3-031-87760-5

The manufacturer's authorised representative in the EU is Springer Nature Customer Service Centre GmbH, Europaplatz 3, 69115 Heidelberg, Germany. If you have any concerns regarding our products, please contact ProductSafety@springernature.com

Printed and bound by CPI Group (UK) Ltd, Croydon, CR0 4YY

30/09/2026

02225560-0007